NASA SP-2000-4520

Black Magic and Gremlins: Analog Flight Simulations at NASA's Flight Research Center

by
Gene L. Waltman

NASA History Division
Office of Policy and Plans
NASA Headquarters
Washington, DC 20546

Monographs in
Aerospace History
Number 20
2000

Library of Congress Cataloging-in-Publication Data

Waltman, Gene L., 1935-
   Black magic and gremlins : analog flight simulations at NASA's Flight Research Center /by Gene L. Waltman.
     p. cm. — (Monographs in aerospace history ; no. 20)
   Includes bibliographical references and index.
   1. Flight simulators—History. 2. Flight Research Center (U.S.)—History. I.Title. II. Series

TL712.5.W35 2000
629.132'52'078—dc21

00-064321

For sale by the Superintendent of Documents, U.S. Government Printing Office
Internet: bookstore.gpo.gov Phone: (202)512-1800 Fax: (202)512-2250
Mail: Stop SSOP, Washington, DC 20402-0001

978-1-78039-322-3
978-1-78039-342-1

Table of Contents

List of Photos v

Foreword vi

Preface viii

Analog Simulations 1

Four-Stage Boost-Vehicle Simulation 34

X-15 Simulator 46

General Purpose Airborne Simulation 59

Hybrid Simulations 65

Lifting-Body Simulation Systems 91

Short Take-Off and Landing Simulations 94

Personal Accounts of FRC Simulation Laboratory Personnel 98
    Edward N. Videan 98
    Richard O. Musick 101
    John P. Smith 106
    Gene L. Waltman 108
    John J. Perry 109
    Donald C. Bacon 114
    Lawrence Caw 124
    Art Suppona 129
    Charles A. Wagner 132

Personal Accounts of FSL Users 136
    Richard D. Banner 136
    Richard E. Day 137
    Donald Reisert 140
    Robert W. Kempel 145
    Dwain A. Deets 148
    Stanley P. Butchart 153
    William H. Dana 157
    Thomas C. McMurtry 159

Finale 162

Appendices
    1. Memorandum for Engineering Division Chief, Richard D. Banner and
       Albert E. Kuhl, "The determination of the directional stability parameter
       C_{n_β} from flight data," 11 March 1955. 164

    2. Richard E. Day, "Training Considerations during the X-15 Development," paper
       presented to the Training Advisory Committee of the National Security Industrial
       Association, Los Angeles, California, 17 November 1959. 171

    3. Milton O. Thompson, "General Review of Piloting Problems Encountered
       during Simulation and Flights of the X-15" [1964]. 189

4. Robert E. Andrews, "The Analog Simulator Programming," originally published as an appendix to Windsor L. Sherman, Stanley Faber, and James B. Whitten, *Study of Exit Phase of Flight of a Very High Altitude Hypersonic Airplane by Means of a Pilot-Controlled Analog Computer* (Washington, DC: NACA Research Memorandum L57K21, 1958), pp. 19-25, 30, 40, 47-53. 199

Glossary 215

Index 219

Bibliography 223

About the Author 231

Monographs in Aerospace History 231

List of Photos

E-1841	Dick Day at GEDA Inertia Coupling Simulation	6
E-2145	Dick Musick with Film Reader	102
E-2581	Iron Cross with Stan Butchart	153
E-2626	GEDA Analog Computers	7
E-2906	Iron Cross 3-axes Side-arm Controller	154
E-2950	Reaction Control Stick	103
E-3395A	Holleman in Reaction Control Cockpit (Black Box)	10
E-4287	Crowded Analog Simulation Laboratory	2
E-4396	F-104 Reaction Control Simulation—Black Box Cockpit	14
E-4548	Boost Simulation Couch, Panel, Controls (in FSL)	35
E-4550	Boost Simulation Instrument Panel	15
E-4661	Centrifuge Seat, Gondola	36
E-4662	Centrifuge Seat, Gondola	36
E-4725	Boost Simulation Side Arm Controller	35
E-4870	Boost Program photos	37
E-4967	EAI-31R and EAI-131R and Black Box (F-104) Cockpit	9
E-4969	Black Box (F-104) Cockpit	49
E-4990	Boost Program Centrifuge Seat	37
E-5035	Orbital Rendezvous program photos	107
E-5037	Orbital Rendezvous program photos	108
E-5040	Boost Program Restraint Straps	38
E-5636	Fixed Based Simulator Diagram	1
E-5808	X-15 Simulator Analog Computers	23
E-5809	X-15 Simulator Analog Computers	23
E-5810	X-15 Simulator Analog Computers	34
E-8100	Paresev Simulation Cockpit	25
E-10278	M2-F1 Simulator Cockpit	15
E-10591	Early M2 Simulator Cockpit (Norden Display and TR-48)	91
E-10840	LLRV Simulator Cockpit	125
E-11778	X-15-3 Instrument Panel	16
E-12942	Simulation Cockpit	25
E-14648	Servo to Synchro Units (LLRV Sim Cockpit)	105
E-15530	X-15 Simulator (Iron Bird) with Bill Dana	50
E-16219	X-15 Simulator (Iron Bird) with Bill Dana	50
E-16464	Lifting Body Simulator Cockpit	92
E-18728	GP Transport Simulator Cockpit	16
E-18902	HL-10 Simulator and Display with J. Manke	17
E-22438	STOL Simulation Cockpit (ARC Moving Base Simulator)	96
E-22756	STOL Wind-Tunnel Mode	94
E-23281	STOL Simulation Cockpit, Displays and Controls	95
E-23594	DFBW Simulation (Early—pre Iron-Bird—in Lean-to)	80
E-26099	RPRV Simulator Cockpit	18
E-27824	JetStar (GPAS) Simulator	60
E-27825	JetStar (GPAS) Computers with H. Rediess and D. Musick	61
ECN-637	LLRV with Joe Walker and Don Mallick	126
ECN-1346	Ken Szalai and GPAS Computers	59
ECN-1456	Larry Caw with X-15 Simulation Analog Computer and Plotter	53
ECN-2399	General Purpose Airborne Simulator	60
ECN-6375	CYBER 73-28	68
ECN-7074	F-8 DFBW Iron Bird Cockpit	79
ECN-7075	F-8 DFBW Iron Bird Cockpit	80
EC91-661-005	Research Aircraft Integration Facility	3
ED97-44197-1	Ed Videan and Dick Musick at EAI 31-R Analog Computer	101
ED00-0091-1	Applied Dynamic AD-4 Computer System	67
EC00-0088-1	Drawing templates used for analog wiring diagrams	19

Foreword

This history of the Flight Research Center (FRC) Simulation Laboratory (FSL) describes the development of experimental flight-test simulators and the rapid evolution of the computers that made them run. (The FRC was a predecessor of NASA's Dryden Flight Research Center, Edwards, California.) Gene Waltman has provided a smooth blend of anecdotal narrative and technical jargon that maintains reader interest whether or not the reader is computer literate.

Less than a year after the end of World War II (WWII), the National Advisory Committee for Aeronautics (NACA) moved a small group of flight test personnel from the Langley Memorial Aeronautical Laboratory (later, NASA's Langley Research Center, Hampton, Virginia) to the large dry lake at Muroc, California, in the Mojave Desert to perform flight testing and aeronautical research on the XS-1 high-speed experimental aircraft. (The XS stood for eXperimental Sonic, later shortened to X-1.) Among the first personnel to arrive and set up shop was a group of "computers" under the direction of Roxanah Yancey. These "computers" were young women who read flight-test data recorded on film, typed these data into their mechanical calculators, and laboriously plotted the results. This was the burdensome forerunner of today's instantaneous telemetered data displaying plotted information on ground-based multi-channel recorders, X-Y plotters, or cathode ray tubes. For many years Roxy and her complement of "computers" performed these computations with slide rule, planimeter, and calculators. High-speed, large-memory computers were still a decade or two in the future; nerds, geeks and hackers were still in gestation, and college degrees in Computer Science did not exist.

Prior to the establishment of the FSL, in the mid-fifties, the Air Force Flight Test Center (AFFTC) purchased an analog computer on the advice of the NACA. The first use of this computer was by NACA engineers Richard Banner and Al Kuhl who helped assemble the computer and then mechanized (programmed) the three degrees of lateral freedom to analyze directional stability from flight data. This analog, the Goodyear Electronic Differential Analyzer (GEDA), was used by the NACA for a series of flight research programs such as X-2 flight planning and pilot training, the newly encountered inertial roll coupling, reaction control, and other studies. Walt Williams, the director of the NACA High-Speed Flight Station (HSFS, as the FRC was then named), seeing the results of such a powerful research tool, purchased the Station's first analog computer in 1957.

This was the start of the FSL series of simulators that ran the gamut of aircraft and spacecraft of this period. This was when the high key and steep approach for orbital entries and landings were developed. This was when Neil Armstrong polished his talents on simulations of orbital launch, as well as simulations *and* flight tests of the Lunar Landing Research Vehicle (LLRV) and the X-15 rocket-powered aircraft. The LLRV simulator simulated the LLRV "flying bedstead," which in turn simulated the actual Lunar Module; hence, the LLRV simulation was unique in that it was a simulation of a simulator.

The history of calculation and computing is one of discovery, development, and obsolescence with new technology replacing the old, much like the end of a geological period with some species dying and new species evolving. As the author has indicated, even in the brief time span of this history, the shelf life of various computers has been brief with most of them now residing in landfills. As an example, computers went from analog to hybrid (combined analog and digital), to all-digital using paper tape, punch cards, and various types of magnetic devices with short half-life operating spans.

Also during this period, as is true today, the rapid demise of particular programming formats hastened the turnover cycle.

In this evolutionary period, digital computer speed increased to the point where digital technology replaced analog for real-time computation and piloted simulation. In addition to accuracy, the Boolean-logic capabilities of the digital vastly increased the realism and selectivity of simulators. Although the analog was subject to noise and some inaccuracies, it would render a truer answer to a rapid, continuous action and is still being used for high-frequency phenomena. Another favorable aspect of the analog for those working prior to the year 2000 was that analog computers were not Y2K-prone (i.e., subject to errors because digital programmers had used two digits to indicate calendar years, and digital computers could not tell the difference between, e.g., 1900 and 2000).

When digital computers started to perform administrative as well as technical functions and bottlenecks began to form, priority number one was never disputed by administrative or technical personnel. Payroll always came first.

Richard E. Day
NASA engineer, retired

Preface

This publication describes the development of the Flight Research Center Simulation Laboratory during the period from 1955 to 1975. These are the years in which analog computers were used as a major component of every flight simulation that was mechanized in support of the many different flight research projects at the High-Speed Flight Station (HSFS–redesignated the Flight Research Center [FRC] in 1959 and the Dryden Flight Research Center [DFRC] in 1976). Initially, analog computers were used along with a ground-based cockpit for these simulators. This started in 1955. In 1964 a small scientific digital computer was bought and added to the X-15 simulator. This was the start of the hybrid (combined analog and digital) computer period of flight simulators. Both of these periods are covered in this document.

The simulation laboratory has had a number of different names over the years. I have chosen to use a single designation—FRC Simulation Laboratory (FSL)—to avoid confusing the reader with different names throughout this document.

This publication discusses *how* we developed the many different analog simulations. However, it is also important to mention the reasons *why* we did so. For this purpose I have included in the appendices a copy of a paper by Dick Day, "Training Considerations During the X-15 Development," which was presented to the Training Advisory Committee of the National Security Industrial Association in November 1959. In this paper, Dick talks about the early use of analog computers to study instabilities that were occurring with the X-1, X-2, X-3, and some of the century series aircraft. Dick Day was an active participant in the early use of analog computers at the NACA HSFS to study the problems that were being encountered by the pilots during the testing of these vehicles. His paper explains the reasons that analog computers were originally bought and used for real-time flight simulators and why flight simulators are still being developed and used at the Dryden Flight Research Center. This paper by Dick Day plus the comments from Dick Banner (in the section on analog simulations and in his personal account) provide a good introduction to the events that began it all, and why it all happened.

This narrative has been written with the help of many of the simulation programmers and technicians, research engineers, and pilots who developed, used, and flew the many different analog simulators. A number of these people have contributed much in the way of information and anecdotes about what we did and how we went about developing and using those simulators. I am extremely grateful to each and every one who contributed in any way. For most of these people, their stories are included as personal accounts and are at the end of the narrative. These personal accounts (or PAs as they are referred to throughout this publication) are brief biographical discussions of their experiences with the analog simulators. Without these inputs, this would be a short and dull accounting of the history of analog computers. We all see and experience events and happenings in different ways. We also have our own styles and when asked to talk about our experiences, do so in our own ways. The PAs are a very important part of this history. They are as unique and individual as we all are and offer many personal perspectives.

I worked for what is today the DFRC from 1957 until 1993. For the first 17 years I was a part of the FRC Simulation Laboratory and have first-hand knowledge of a lot that went on during those days. I also got stuck with buying many of the computer systems that we used during that period. And as you will read, many of the events that occurred were a direct result of the ever-changing computer systems that we bought and used for our simulations. I also was involved with implementing several major flight simulators during that period. I feel fortunate to have had such a part in the ongoing evolution of the FRC Simulation Laboratory. This publication is something I started thinking about doing after I retired from the DFRC in 1993. I have had a lot of fun collecting the information and talking to (and doing a lot of coaxing—even begging—of) the many people who contributed. In several cases, this was the first time I had talked with several of them since they left or retired. It has taken several years to get this all together and to write this account, and I have enjoyed every minute of it.

I am also grateful to the NASA DFRC for providing me the opportunity to publish this history. NASA is doing a lot to record and archive its history. I am happy to contribute towards that goal.

This particular monograph is the first of several anticipated histories of the FRC Simulation Laboratory. The second publication will cover the history of the FSL from about 1975 to 1991. This period covers the first era of the all-digital simulations, during a time when the FSL was still in the same general area as the analog systems used to be. In 1991 the FSL moved into a new building know then as the Integrated Test Facility (ITF). There is some overlap in simulations during the transitions between these three periods (1957-75, 1975-91, 1991 to the present). Consequently there will be some repetition of events and simulator history that will be included in the different studies. That is unavoidable, but necessary. The same can be said about many of the people who were key participants during these transitions. I will try to point these people and their contributions out appropriately.

For those who may be using the present document for information-gathering purposes, I have included an extensive bibliography listing almost every publication during the period 1955-1975 that was written about a project at the HSFS/FRC in which analog or analog-and-hybrid simulations were used. Most of the bibliography is taken from Dave Fisher's publication: *Fifty Years of Flight Research: An Annotated Bibliography of Technical Publications of NASA Dryden Flight Research Center, 1946-1996* (NASA TP-1999-206568). I have also included many photographs. All of these photos are in the DFRC Photo Archive, and someday they may be available on the DFRC Web site.

I wish to acknowledge and thank everyone who has helped in getting this bit of the NASA Flight Research Center's history into publication. They include: Dill Hunley of the DFRC History Office for his encouragement and help in getting this publication into print; Rob Binkley and Mike Najera of the Dryden Research Aircraft Integration Facility (RAIF, which includes the present-day simulation facilities) for providing the funds for this task and their support; Larry Schilling and Lee Duke for their support at the upper management level: Dick Day, "the father of simulation," (as research pilot Bill Dana likes to call him) for his efforts in getting the pilots—in those early days—to actually use the simulators for flight planning and training purposes as well as for his contributions to this publication, including the Foreword; and every one else who contributed to this publication. The list includes Ed Videan, John P. Smith, and Dick Musick of the very first Simulation Group. Also: John Perry, Don Bacon, and Larry Caw, simulation programmers; Al Myers, simulation engineer; Art Suppona and Billy Davis, simulation technicians; Charlie Wagner, simulation hardware engineer; Stan Butchart, Bill Dana, and Tom McMurtry, DFRC pilots; and many research engineers, including Dick Banner, Don Reisert, Ed Holleman, Dwain Deets, Bob Kempel, Neil Matheny, Bruce Powers, Roy Bryant, Dave Hedgley, Tom Wolf, Wilt Lock, Bob James, Jack Ehernberger, and Don Gatlin; Judy Duffield in the pilot's office; Dennis Ragsdale and Erin Gerena in the Dryden library; Jim Young from the AFFTC History Office (and anyone else I may have talked with but have forgotten to mention). Larry Schilling, Bruce Powers, Rob Binkey, and Bob Kempel were kind enough to read an early draft and provide technical comments that have improved the book immensely. I've also been able to go through the history files of Chester Wolowicz, FRC research engineer, and found some important information about his analog computer usage. There are others whom I have talked with while writing this monograph (including several who had important roles) but who unfortunately chose not to be involved. That was their choice, and I am sorry that I wasn't able to get their inputs. Several active participants have died and their inputs have been collected from friends, co-workers, publications, and archives. A few have left the area and their whereabouts are unknown. I also want to thank Carla Thomas and Tony Landis as well as the rest of the staff of the Dryden Photo Lab for their help in collecting and scanning the photos in the volume; Steve Lighthill, NASA visual information specialist, for his creative work in laying out the book; Darlene Lister for her skill at copy editing; and Camilla McArthur for seeing the book through the publication process.

Although I have written this publication, I feel that it is "our" story, and not just mine. I wanted to get everyone's input, but that was just not possible. I feel that those who are included do provide a very good cross section of the programmers, technicians, engineers, and pilots who developed and used the analog simulators. This story is about us and our experiences with the analog flight simulations at the NASA Flight Research Center.

Gene Waltman, simulation engineer

Analog Simulations
Introduction

This is a history of the many aircraft simulations that were implemented during the early days at what later became Dryden Flight Research Center using the early generations of analog and hybrid computers. The period to be reviewed is from 1955 to about 1975. This is when analog computer systems were being used at the Flight Research Center (and its predecessor, the NACA HSFS) as major components of all the aircraft simulations that were mechanized and used in support of the various flight research programs.

In August of 1960, Euclid Holleman and Melvin Sadoff presented their report *Simulation Requirements For The Development Of Advanced Manned Military Aircraft* (Citation #269)[1] at the Institute of Aeronautical Sciences, Inc. National Meeting. The following is from the beginning of that paper:

> Paralleling the large increase in performance capability of present airplanes has been the increase in the problems connected with the design and operation of these vehicles. Indications are that the designer of advanced military aircraft will be faced with the present "crop" of problems as well as additional problems as yet unborn.

Many methods have been devised to study these problems, but perhaps no single method of analysis has achieved the success and universal acceptance accorded the flight simulator as a design and research tool. This was made possible by the tremendous advances in development of the analog computer which has been used to solve any problem that can be represented by a differential equation.

Some of the most useful simulations have involved the pilot in the control loop. A drawing illustrates a pilot-operated simulator in the control loop. [See photo E-5636.] Illustrated is the flow of information from the computer to the pilot and back to the computer. The pilot is the key link closing the control loop.

FIXED-BASE SIMULATOR

Fixed-Based Simulator Diagram (July 1960). (NASA photo E-5636)

---

[1] The Citation Number is a reference number assigned to all publications; see the Bibliography.

NASA has had considerable experience with a wide variety of piloted flight simulators, from relatively simple, inexpensive, fixed-chair types to complex and expensive human centrifuges and variable-stability and control airplanes . . . .

The report went on to discuss the different forms of piloted simulators that had been used by the research engineers at the FRC up to that point in time. The FRC Simulation Laboratory (FSL) and its capabilities play a very important part of the simulator history of this Center.

In 1989, J. P. Smith, L. J. Schilling, and C. A. Wagner wrote the paper: *Simulation at Dryden Flight Research Facility from 1957 to 1982,* NASA TM 101695 (Citation No. 1689.). That particular paper reviews the history of the FRC Simulation Laboratory, with emphasis on the philosophy behind the development and use of the simulation laboratory (i.e., why we did simulations). This publication will talk about how we went about the process of mechanizing analog and hybrid simulations. The era of all-digital simulations will be covered in yet another publication.

The following paragraph is from the Introduction to the paper by Smith, Schilling and Wagner:

> Simulation at Dryden has developed over the past 25 years into an integral and essential part of the flight research program. Today, pilots as well as engineers demand that simulation be included in the flight program. When the manager of one joint NASA/DOD program first learned the cost of a simulator, he asked, 'What did you do before simulators?' The project pilot replied. 'We named a lot of streets after pilots!' [Meaning that they died in aircraft accidents.] This statement reflects the most important value of simulation as it is practiced at Dryden: flight safety.

It did not start out that way, but the role of simulation has certainly changed during the years. Today's simulators are much more sophisticated and complex and play a very important role in the job that the NASA Dryden Flight Research Center does. The simulation facility has grown from a single analog computer in one office in the main building into an impressive facility of its own known as the

Crowded Analog Simulation Laboratory (October 1958). (NASA photo E-4287)

Walter C. Williams Research Aircraft Integration Facility (RAIF). (See photos E-4287 and EC91-661-005[2] of the first lab and the current RAIF.)

One of the Best

The FRC Simulation Laboratory was (and still is) one of the premier facilities of its type in the United States. At least that is how we felt about it. The FSL got started about the same time that analog computers were really beginning to be appreciated as worthy tools for implementing real-time aircraft simulations. Not only were airplane manufacturers beginning to use analog simulation to help design and study the airplanes they built, but colleges and universities were beginning to teach classes in this technology. Analog computers had been around for several years. Both the Ames and Langley Research Centers had analog computer facilities before the HSFS simulation laboratory bought its first analog computer. The U.S. Navy used analog computers during the World War II. However, the analog computers of those days never really caught on until the early '50s, when the development had reached a point where the operational amplifiers had both the accuracy and stability that the users were asking for. These qualities were necessary for aircraft simulation due to the long periods of time used by some of the simulation runs.

Analog Computer Courses

I graduated from Michigan Technological University in 1957 with a BS in Mathematics. Michigan Tech taught its first course in analog computation in my senior year, which was 1956/7. This course was taught by one of the Mathematics Department professors (he was a U.S. Navy Reserve officer and had just returned from temporary duty at one of the Navy's facilities that had analog computers). He and one of the professors from the Physics Department had spent most of the 1956 summer break building two Heath Kit[3] analog computers. These were used for the classes on analog computation.

Research Aircraft Integration Facility (1991). (NASA photo EC91-611-005)

---

[2] The photo of the first sim lab was taken in late 1958 and does (more or less) represent the actual lab as it was in those days. Bill Dana is the pilot sitting in the cockpit, and he started work the day that NASA was officially founded (1 October 1958). Normally, only two or three people were needed in the lab to run a simulation. This particular photo was staged to give the impression of a very crowded facility. The peripheral equipment shown in this photo was jammed together, with extra people as a ploy to finagle a larger room for the FSL analog computers.

[3] The Heath Company once manufactured electronic products in kit form that anybody could successfully build, if he or she followed the instructions. The company no longer sells such kits.

Unfortunately, I did not take the class on analog computation. At the time it did not seem like something I would ever use. Little did I know then that I would spend the next 17 years programming analog and hybrid computer simulations.

While I was interviewing for jobs, during my senior year, I talked to an engineer from the NACA facility at Cleveland. This is now the NASA Glenn Research Center. I really did not feel like working in Ohio, and when he told me that the NACA had a flight research facility at Edwards Air Force Base in California, I asked him to send my interview papers and college transcript out there. After all, I had been living in Southern California since 1943 and I really preferred to work in California. The NACA High-Speed Flight Station at Edwards Air Force Base offered me a job. This wasn't the best offer I got, but it was one of the best from any company in California. Most of my other offers came from companies in New York and Michigan. I had had enough of the snow and cold weather while attending Michigan Tech (which is way up in the Keweenaw Peninsula of Michigan and averages over 200 inches of snow each winter). So I accepted the offer from the NACA HSFS, and I went to work on 22 July 1957. Just over a year later, NASA was created, and the NACA HSFS became the NASA Flight Research Center.

Day 1—NACA HSFS

I had been living in Fontana, California, while enrolled at Michigan Tech. The Saturday before I actually started work for the NACA, I drove to Edwards Air Force Base and spent the day scouting the area, and locating the NACA facilities and housing. The following Monday morning I drove to Edwards, early in the morning, hoping to get there at 7:30, when work began. I was driving one of my granddad's cars (I did not own one, then), and the fuel gauge did not work. I ran out of gas near the community now called Pinon Hills, on highway 138. It was about 6:30 a.m. Luckily I was able to coast right into the only gas station in that area. But it didn't open until 8:00 a.m. So, I sat and waited till it opened, got gas, and was late to work. What a great way to start a job! Looking back on that day and what happened to me on the way to work, I can see that it was just the first of many strange events that were to happen to me while I was a part of the FSL.

I actually thought that I was being hired to program the digital computer that had recently been installed at the NACA HSFS. It was an IBM CPC (Card Programmed Calculator). My boss, Ed Videan, upon looking at my college transcript and noting that I had taken quite a few courses in analytical mechanics and differential equations, thought that I might want to work in the brand-new simulation facility. There really wasn't an opening in the digital programming group, but there was one in the simulation group. So I agreed to try it out. I have always wondered just what I would be doing now if circumstances had been different and I had actually become a digital computer programmer at that time. I never regretted being an analog programmer. This job was a lot of fun, and besides, several years later, when we bought digital computers to add to our all-analog simulations, I did get to program digital computers.

As one of the original simulation programmers (and the only one who is still working at Dryden), I feel that writing down just what we did and how we went about doing our jobs in those days is an important step in documenting a part of the history of this simulation facility. A lot of aviation history has occurred in the Mojave Desert, and simulators have contributed to this in a big way. Looking back on all this, I am quite proud of what we did. It was fun and it was exciting. We were working with great people, challenging equipment, fantastic aircraft, and we really looked forward to coming to work every day—and a lot of nights and weekends, too. Unfortunately, we never really took the time to write things down then. We were too busy growing and doing the fun stuff, and as typical programmers, we hated to document. So, now, let me take this time to reminisce, and at the same time document an important part of the NACA HSFS/NASA FRC history.

The Beginnings of Simulations at the FRC

A lot of what is covered in this study comes from the people who worked at the HSFS and in the FSL during this period, including some of the engineers and pilots whom we worked with while implementing the various simulations. The entire process of constructing a simulation has undergone many, many changes over the years. This is due to the ever-changing technology in the computers, aircraft, and other hardware that is being used. The difficult part of collecting the information for this paper comes about because we (in the FSL) were not expected to write technical papers on what and how we did our jobs. Reports were not required to get promotions, so we didn't write. I have been able to get inputs from many of the people who were involved with the FSL during those first years.

This history is not intended to be a re-hash of all the research studies that used the different analog/hybrid computer mechanizations (or their results). There were many reports and papers written covering that subject matter. A selected few of these papers may be briefly mentioned, when appropriate, throughout this monograph. Following the appendices is a bibliography of publications of many different studies that used some form of simulation during the time span of this publication.

This history is intended to describe just how we went about this job of programming the analog and hybrid computers, the various tasks involved in getting the cockpits set up and running, and a lot of related tales that hopefully will illustrate the myriad problems encountered along the way. Looking back on these times, I can say that programming analog computers was interesting in spite of all the inherent problems that analog computers and analog simulators exhibited.

There were times when each of us felt that a part of what we did bordered on "black magic." The larger simulators, such as the X-15 simulator, seemed to have personalities of their own. These personalities were frequently described as cantankerous, malicious, mulish, or other less friendly terms. It seemed like each of these simulations had its own "master," which was usually the original programmer. Generally they behaved themselves when that programmer was operating the simulation, but if anyone else had to fill-in when the "master" was out, then the 'Jekyll and Hyde' nature of the simulation showed up and changed its persona to the evil side.

I'm sure that many a pilot or engineer using one of our simulators felt that we kept a couple of gremlins hidden away in the back room and let them loose in the analog computer labs when no one was around. There were too many unexplainable incidents that happened during those years. A few of these incidents can seemingly be considered serendipitous, but there were many more that can only be attributed to gremlinity.[4]

For anyone familiar with the aviation history around Edwards, many of the aircraft that were flown are well known. But there were others, some of which were only ideas or concepts and were never built or flown but often simulated.

---

[4] Gremlinity, as used here, is the opposite of serendipity. *Webster's New World Dictionary of the American Language*, College Edition, defines serendipity [a noun coined by Horace Walpole (c. 1754) after his tale *The Three Princes of Serendip* (Ceylon), who made such discoveries] as an apparent aptitude for making fortunate discoveries accidentally. The opposite of such an aptitude is creating unfortunate happenings on purpose. This is what gremlins do. So the word gremlinity, as used here, is an antonym for the word serendipity.

We programmed many types of real-time simulations. It was a constant learning experience for us. Not only were the equations different, from simulation to simulation, but so too was the equipment we were using. We were always buying and using the newest stuff. And not just the newest of computers. We were also involved in developing the interfaces and hardware being used in the cockpits of those simulations. It really helped to be a jack-of-all-trades in those days in order to get a new simulation up and running. It was very much a group effort, with research engineers, simulation programmers, and simulation technicians working together to implement each new simulation.

The Very First Analog Simulations

The use of analog computers for flight simulation had already begun when I started work in 1957. The first such simulations had been implemented using GEDA (Goodyear Electronic Differential Analyzer) computers that had been bought by the Air Force. This was in 1955. The first NACA HSFS simulation, on the AFFTC analogs, was a study by Dick Banner and Al Kuhl, and is discussed in an in-house memo entitled "The determination of the directional stability parameter C_{n_β} from flight data," dated 11 March 1955. This was an analog computer investigation of the F-100, and was implemented in early 1955. A copy of this memo is included in the appendices. This study was also reported in NACA RM H55E17B, *Flight Experience of Inertia Coupling in Rolling Maneuvers.* (Citation No. 130), by J. Weil, O. B. Gates, R. D. Banner, and A. E. Kuhl in July 1955.

The following paragraphs from Dick Banner briefly describe this first-ever analog simulation by anyone at the HSFS:

Dick Day at GEDA Inertia Coupling Simulation (July 1955). (NASA photo E-1841)

I don't remember the dates, but it was not long after we moved from the main base to the new facility [a move that occurred in 1954]. De Beeler, then Director of Research, asked Al Kuhl and me to look at the subject of Vertical Tail Loads in Rolling Pullout maneuvers. He apparently had been in contact with someone at the Air Force Flight Test Center and had arranged for Al and me to look at its new analog equipment in hopes of using it to simulate flight conditions. When Al and I saw the equipment it was just being uncrated, and the Air Force lieutenant who was assigned to work with us didn't seem to know much about it. It was manufactured by Goodyear and called GEDA (Goodyear Electronic Differential Analyzer). [See photos of this equipment (E-1841 and E-2626).]

The Douglas X-3 airplane, before being turned over to us at NACA, had undergone the usual Air Force acceptance testing, which included rolling pullout maneuvers. I went to Douglas and got the time history data and the flight derivatives that were available. Al and I "programmed" the GEDA analog computer to simulate the flight conditions and were struggling with the high angle-of-attack simulation when an F-100 crashed somewhere between Lancaster and Rosamond.

We were asked if we could simulate the F-100 on the GEDA. We did, and as we did, we discovered that the lateral-directional period simulated with the derivatives given us did not match the flight data. Al took a look at the way that the in-flight directional stability parameter was obtained and decided it was not correct. He went on to derive a new set of equations, which gave us a better method of obtaining the in-flight directional stability parameter, allowing us to simulate the F-100 flight conditions.

To the best of my knowledge, we were the first at NACA, Edwards, to simulate aircraft motions on a computer.

Prior to these analog investigations, Hubert Drake and Joseph Weil went to the Langley Research Center to witness a 5

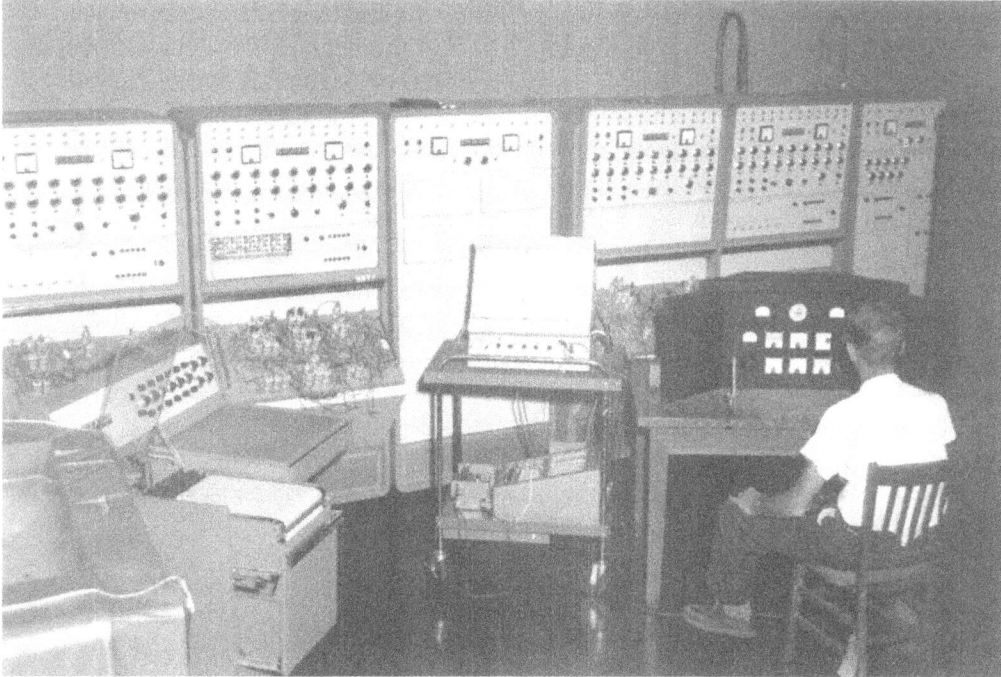

Dick Day with the GEDA analog computers (October 1956). (NASA photo E-2626)

DOF[5] analog simulation for studying roll coupling. This simulation did not have a cockpit, but instead used controlled inputs. Subsequently, the NACA urged the AFFTC to buy the GEDA computers.

The Banner/Kuhl simulation was followed shortly by several studies by Dick Day, Joe Weil, and Don Reisert. Day and Weil were investigating roll coupling and implemented a comprehensive analog simulation for that study. These results are reported in two different publications written by them: NACA RM H56A06, *An Analog Study of the Relative Importance of Various Factors Affecting Roll Coupling,* and NACA RM H56F08, *Correlation of Flight and Analog Investigations of Roll Coupling.* The GEDA analog computers were also used for additional studies, including X-2 studies, analysis, pilot training, and X-1B reaction-control-systems studies. It was some time before the Air Force had its own engineers programming its GEDA computers. The cockpits used for these simulations were very simple set-ups, using spring-loaded control sticks, voltmeters for instruments, and a CRT (cathode ray tube) for an out-the-window display. (See photos E-1841 and E-2626.) The small control stick shown in some of these photos is a formation stick (as it was called) used in some of the later U. S. bombers during World War II. Dick Day was a B-17 pilot in the 386th Bomb Group, England, during the war and states that he was the first pilot to ever use one of those "formation sticks." (See the second PA section for the personal accounts of Don Reisert and Dick Day.)[6]

The following paragraph, also from Dick Banner, further describes the events of those days.

The usefulness of aircraft motion simulation was becoming obvious to many of us at the time Al [Kuhl] and I were working on the GEDA, but I had no sense of what it would become. Langley had much more capability at the time, and Joe Weil went there to work with Ordway Gates on problems of other aircraft similar to those of the F-100. Al and I continued to support their simulation studies, sending them our GEDA results for the F-100. The results were published in a paper given at a conference at Langley, with all four of us as authors (Citation 158). After that, Al and I were re-assigned to other work, and Dick Day was assigned to the GEDA. I worked a little with Ed Videan (some kind of a committee) to choose the first type of simulation equipment we were to use at our facility (REAC or something like that, using ±100 volts DC). I even attended classes at Ames with Ed Videan, Dick Musick, and Dick Day on programming the equipment. My first simulation (not documented) on the new equipment was a simple heat transfer problem. I did no more documented aircraft motion simulations after the GEDA experience, but I remember that Chet Wolowicz worked on aircraft motions simulations on the REAC in those early days, and we consulted occasionally. My recollection is that Dick Day was working mostly on getting the pilot into the simulation at that time. I had at first thought that the REAC equipment would be useful in the coming heat transfer and aerodynamic heating studies that I

---

[5] A DOF (Degree Of Freedom) is a movement up or down, sideways, front or back, or around the pitch, roll, or yaw axis. Five degrees of freedom are movements in five of these directions but not all six.

[6] Sections at the end of the narrative contain PAs of a number of the people who worked with the early analog computers. These accounts provide individual experiences about what these people did with the computers and are very much a part of this history. I will identify, at the appropriate places throughout this paper, the personal accounts of interest to the subject being discussed. I recommend that you take the time to read those accounts at that time.

had been assigned to, but as it turned out, I worked mostly with Ray Jackson on the IBM digital computers, setting up methods to predict aircraft skin temperatures in flight, and backing out heat transfer data from the measured skin temperatures.

The X-2 simulation was the first HSFS implementation that was used for both research and pilot training. Early-day simulations were not completely accepted by the pilots of those days as useful tools. Since analog simulations were so new, the concept of practicing the actual maneuvers on the ground before they actually flew the real flight had not been accepted by many of the pilots. It was several years before most of the NACA/NASA pilots really accepted this idea. The older pilots were slowest at appreciating the value of ground-based simulators. The new pilots not only accepted the idea but in some cases insisted on the development of such simulators. The X-15 simulator was the first complete ground-based simulation built by the FSL for pilot training, mission planning, and research purposes.

The First HSFS Analog Computer

In January of 1957, the FSL installed its first analog, an EAI 16-31R analog computer. It had 48 amplifiers, 20 of which could be used for integration. It also had a number of multipliers, resolvers, potentiometers, and function generators. This computer was state-of-the-art and included a removable patch panel for connecting the many components. Many of the first generation of analog computers (such as the GEDA and Heath Kits) did not have removable patch panels. Patch panels allowed for quick changeover of the analog computers from one simulation to another. The HSFS bought a second analog computer and installed it in late 1957. It was an EAI 131R and had about the same complement of equipment as the earlier EAI 31R. (See photo E-4967.)

The FSL was located in the area now occupied by the Center Director for his office and conference room on the second floor in the northeast corner of building 4800. At that time the hallway along the front row of offices on the second floor ended at the door to the room shared by the FSL and the woman computers.[7] The hallway on the second floor was in the shape of the letter T, with one hall parallel to the front of the building and one central hall extending towards the back of the

Electronic Associates, Inc EAI 31R (on the left) and EAI 131R and Black Box (F-104) Cockpit (October 1959). (NASA photo E-4967)

---

[7] See Sheryll Goecke Powers' *Women in Flight Research at NASA Dryden Flight Research Center from 1946 to 1995* (Washington, DC: NASA Monographs in Aerospace History #6, 1997) for what is meant by the term "women computers." Dick Day also explains this term in the Foreword of the present study.

building. The Center Director's offices were in the middle of the front hallway. The pilots and other flight operations personnel occupied the offices at the back of the building on this floor.

The office I shared (with John P. Smith) was a small inner office in this larger room at the east end of the front hall. My desk faced the wall and the only window. This window is currently hidden by a bookcase in the Director's Conference Room, and can still be seen from the outside, right next to the front wall of the Calibration Hangar (Building 4801). I could look out this window and see the Borax plant in Boron, and I could swivel around in my chair and look down the front hall to the other end, which happened to be the door into the Research Library. Out the window, I could see planes take off and land on the north base runway, and I could watch airplanes, such as the X-1B, coming in to land on the dry lakebed. Nowadays, the Data Analysis Facility (DAF), the Research Aircraft Integration Facility (RAIF), and the Shuttle Facility block this view.

The simulation group consisted of Ed Videan, John P. Smith, Dick Musick, and myself. Ed was head of this group. John, an Army Signal Corps lieutenant detailee, was a simulation programmer, and Dick was the electronics technician for the group. Many of the other offices along the front hall and the central hall were where the research engineers were located. It was a very convenient arrangement. Everyone we worked with was only a few steps away.

(For further details, see the personal accounts of Ed Videan, Richard Musick, and John Smith.)

The First Cockpit

The FSL had one "black-box" cockpit. This was truly a "black box" since that is the color the wooden cockpit had been painted. (See photo E-3395A.) It was constructed of plywood, with a movable seat, removable instrument panel, a hydraulic-powered control stick, and bungee-loaded rudder pedals. This first cockpit was built in-house in the model shop and originally did not have the hydraulics. Richard Musick talks about this cockpit in his PA. The hydraulics unit was also built in-house and installed later and can be seen in the photos. The pump was quite loud and was moved to the other side of the wall. This just happened to be inside the calibration hangar. Because the pump was so loud when in

Holleman in Reaction Control Cockpit (Black Box—April 1957). (NASA photo E-3395A)

operation, it tended to annoy the technicians who were working there. A couple of times, after several hours of use, they would trudge upstairs as a group, and ask us to please turn the d--- thing off.

If you were sitting in the cockpit, it was important not to slouch down in the seat when the hydraulics were on. On several occasions, an electrical power fluctuation caused the pilot's control stick to slam forward or back very quickly. This would also happen if the computer operator turned the computer mode switch into Pot-Set[8] by mistake. There were physical stops to prevent the control stick from coming back too far, but if you were slouched down too far, you could get a very unpleasant kick in a very tender part of the anatomy. I'm surprised that no one ever broke a thumb when the hydraulics hiccuped. Simulation was not as dangerous as flying, but it did have its perils.

There were several simulators during the early years that used hydraulic pumps to provide power for the pilots' controls. One essential member of those simulator support crews was the building facilities technician responsible for operating the hydraulics stand. The simulation technicians were not allowed to operate the hydraulic equipment. We had to call and get someone "qualified" in this equipment to come handle this chore for us. Nowadays the simulations use an FSL-developed DC-torque-motor-powered control stick and rudder pedals. It is much better and quieter (and not so insidious!). The DC-torque-motor-powered controls were one of the FSL developments that greatly advanced simulator technology. They are described later in this paper.

Analog Computer Programming

Programming an analog computer was akin to building something out of Tinkertoys. Except that the pieces we used were electrical components, which were built using direct current vacuum tube circuitry with a ±100 volt range. These components were quite accurate and linear throughout their voltage range. The primary component in an analog computer was the operational amplifier. Amplifiers could be used to add, subtract, change sign, and to integrate or differentiate with respect to time, and many other things. Analog computers also had many potentiometers (usually just called "pots") to scale variables or provide constants, multipliers to multiply or divide two variables, and function generators to generate nonlinear functions. With these components it was possible to build an analog computer modal of a set of nonlinear differential equations, where time was the independent variable.

The equations of an aircraft in flight constitute such a set of equations. It consists of the six-degree-of-freedom (6 DOF) equations describing a typical aircraft's attitudes, accelerations, and velocities that we programmed in implementing a simulation. In the beginning before we had sufficient equipment to implement full 6 DOF simulations, we simplified the equations to 3 or 5 DOF. The outputs of the amplifiers (summers or integrators) were the calculated accelerations, velocities, angles or other parameters or variables required in solving the very complex nonlinear 6DOF equations of an aircraft. These variables could be recorded on a strip-chart recorder, plotted on an X-Y plotter, or displayed in the cockpit for the pilot to see. The cockpit's pilot controls were built to provide the required inputs into the equations. Instruments were designed and built to display the calculated variables in a manner similar (and usually identical) to what the pilot would see in the real airplane. Visual display units provided an out-the-window view to add even more realism to the simulators.

This was the state-of-the-art in analog simulations at that time. Analog comput-

---

[8] Pot-Set is one of the modes of the analog computer. When in Pot-Set, the operator could adjust the potentiometers used in the simulation.

ers were quite linear throughout their voltage range (± 100 volts) and had an accuracy of about 1 part in 10,000. This accuracy is certainly lower than what we get from today's digital computers and was one of the drawbacks in using analog computers. However, the digital computers being built in those days were not fast enough for us to use in real time. Everyone doing real-time simulations of airplanes, submarines, nuclear reactors, or whatever, used analog computers. There were several vendors that marketed analog computers. The FSL eventually bought analogs from three of these vendors (Electronic Associates Inc., Applied Dynamics, Inc., and Comcor Computer Company).

Parallel Computing

One of the advantages of an analog computer was that all variables were being calculated in parallel and in real time. You could see immediately, when you went into the operate mode (as it was called), exactly what was happening. It was also possible to either speed the time frame up or slow it down, depending on just what you were simulating. I don't remember any simulations in which we actually slowed the time frame for something that happened so fast it couldn't be observed or studied in real time. But we did on several occasions speed the time frame up and run simulations faster. For a number of derivative-matching simulations, where either there was no pilot or the pilot's inputs had been recorded and could also be speeded up, we ran the simulation at up to 100 times faster than normal. In fact, a number of the analog computers that were being marketed had this capability built right into the mode control. This feature was called "repetitive operation" and allowed the outputs to be displayed on a multi-channel oscilloscope rather than a standard strip-chart recorder. More on this faster-than-real-time mode of simulation in the following sections.

Generation of nonlinear functions was difficult, but possible. Generating a nonlinear function of one variable was usually quite easy to do. Nonlinear functions of two variables were a little more difficult but still possible. Functions of three (or more) variables took a lot of equipment and were usually not implemented. Many of the aerodynamic coefficients in the equations of motion of an aircraft were functions of at least two variables. The X-15 simulation had over 100 function generators, which was an order of magnitude greater than the typical simulation of those days.

The 48-amplifier analog computer that was there (when I started in 1957) had enough components for a fairly complete three-degrees-of-freedom simulation with some nonlinear coefficients or a five-degrees-of-freedom with few, if any, nonlinear functions. (In photo E-4967, the EAI 31-R is the computer on the left.) Consequently, most of my early simulations were limited to studies using either the lateral-directional equations or the longitudinal equations. A second analog computer was installed shortly after I arrived. With this new computer we were able to implement two separate simulations, or we could combine the two computers and implement a fairly complete 5 DOF simulation with nonlinear coefficients and a constant velocity, or a limited 6 DOF simulator with only a few nonlinear coefficients. (In photo E-4967 the EAI 131R is the computer on the right.) It wasn't until we bought a third analog computer (an EAI 231R), which had about 100 amplifiers and a corresponding number of pots, multipliers, and function generators, that we were able to implement a complete 6 DOF simulation with many nonlinear functions.

Cockpit Mechanizations

You have to remember that the aircraft being built and flown then were not as complex as current airplanes, especially with regard to the number and type of control surfaces. Rudders, ailerons, and elevators were the norm. Also, the highly complex digital control systems in today's planes hadn't been built. The analog computer mechanization for simulating control surfaces was not a difficult task, although at times it could be frustrating because of their unusual nonlinear characteristics. Deadbands, hysteresis,[9] limits, and other discontinuities were quite common in this circuitry on an analog computer simulation. To make matters worse, the various pieces of hardware in the simulator cockpits had their own characteristics, and we had to occasionally compensate for those characteristics in trying to create the characteristics for the airplane being simulated. This is where the art of analog programming bordered on "black magic." This type of analog computer programming was not taught in the classroom. One learned it on one's own—by trial and error, usually, or by sharing circuits with the other analog programmers.

Most of the difficulties in building a new simulator in those days came about in designing and building the hardware and instruments used in the simulator cockpits. The technology of analog simulation was so new that it was not possible to buy off-the-shelf cockpit hardware. We had to build or modify everything we used. The cockpit instruments used in aircraft were not designed to accept the ±100-volt DC analog computer signals as inputs. The simulation technicians spent a lot of time developing the instrumentation we used in our cockpits. The same thing was true for the control stick (or yoke), rudders and throttles, and other controls in the cockpit. Everything we used had to be built in the machine and instrument shops downstairs. Fortunately, we had the best in the industry. These were the same shops building most of the special-purpose instrumentation that went into the planes we were flying. The equipment they turned out for us was always first rate and had a lot to do with why our simulation facility was one of the best in the country. The simulation technicians spent almost as much time working with the people in the machine and instrumentation shops as they did working in the simulation laboratory. (See the PAs of Richard Musick, Art Suppona, and Charlie Wagner for more on the efforts that went into designing and building the cockpits.)

X-1B Simulations

My first two simulations were of the X-1B, which was still flying in 1957. I also did several X-1E simulations. The X-1E is now mounted on a pedestal in front of Building 4800 at Dryden. During this first couple of years I also did simulations of some of the Century-series airplanes, including the F-100, F-101, F-102, and F-104. I can recall implementing at least four different F-104 simulators for various research studies. The F-104 airplanes that the FRC had were used for both chase and research flights for many years.

I had the task of implementing the first complete 6 DOF simulation in the FSL. The other two engineers who had been programming analog simulations, when I started, had both been promoted to management and were no longer programming simulations. So, I was the last one of the very first official simulation group and got to do many new things first. For a number of years, I was the only one who got to program simulations that used moving-base cockpits. Moving-base simulators were never implemented in the FSL. The few that I did were implemented at the Ames Research Center, and the one big one that we did used the Navy's centrifuge at Johnsville, Pennsylvania (see below). There were a couple of simulations at Ames for which I took our own patch panels. They had the same analog computers as we did, and by wiring up the panels and taking them with me, I was able to save a day or two of temporary duty (TDY) at another location. I also did several simulations of skin temperature studies using partial differential equations.

---

[9] Deadbands and hysteresis were both types of delays or lags.

Each simulation was assigned to a single simulation programmer and that person usually "lived" with that simulation from beginning to end. In the beginning, when we only had one analog computer, we took turns. These simulations usually lasted for weeks. During that time other programmers could get their simulations programmed and ready to run. Simulations were usually assigned on a who's-next basis.

Simulator Cockpits

Since we only had one cockpit, getting the cockpit changed over to the next airplane configuration was frequently the real "hurry-up" task in this on-going parade of simulations. Fortunately the pilots and engineers were willing (in the beginning) to get by with a generic black-box cockpit. The airplanes that were being flown had similar instrument panels in the cockpits. This meant that only minor changes were necessary to change our black-box cockpit to the next simulation. This, of course, did not last.

As the airplanes got more sophisticated, so too did their cockpit instrumentation. The FSL kept up with this by expanding the number of simulator cockpits being used and by buying more analog computers. This allowed us to have several simulations operational at one time. More technicians were hired to help keep up with the task of developing the cockpit hardware. The "black-box" wooden cockpits gave way to blue wooden boxes with metal instrument panels. These were designed to be even more flexible and to reduce the time needed to change between simulations. The instrument panels were also designed to be even more quickly and easily changed. (See photos E-4396, E-4550, E-10278, E-11778, E-18728, E-18902, and E-26099 for several cockpits with different instrument panels as they evolved over the years.)

F-104 Reaction Control Simulation—Black-Box Cockpit (January 1959). (NASA photo E-4396)

Boost Simulation Instrument Panel (January 1959). (NASA photo E-4550)

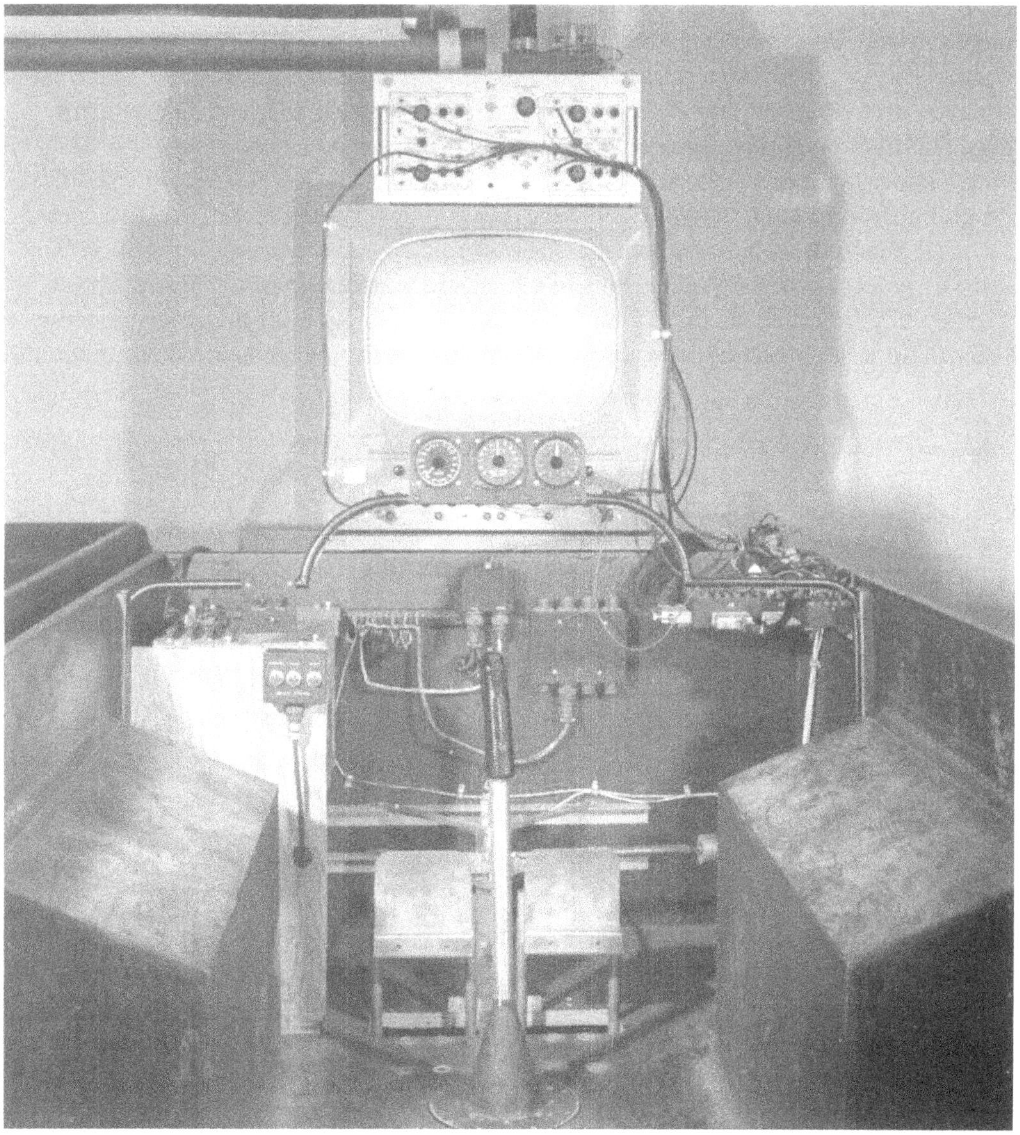

M2-F1 Simulator Cockpit (August 1963). (NASA photo E-10278)

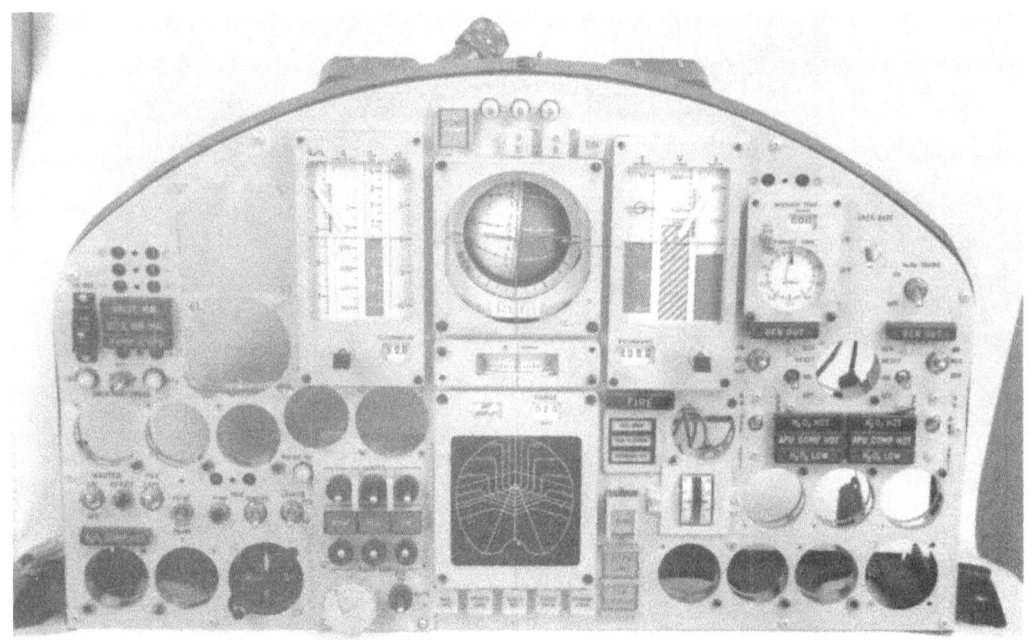

X-15-3 Instrument Panel (August 1964). (NASA photo E-11778)

In addition, the analog computer manufacturers were designing and selling computers that could be more easily changed over from simulation to simulation. Servo set potentiometers coupled with a paper-tape reader allowed a programmer to have all the pots (and there could be hundreds of these) automatically set. The process of setting all the pots in a simulation was one of the more time-consuming tasks in getting an analog computer changed over to another simulation.

Patch-Panel Wiring Diagrams

During the first several years of simulation programming at the FRC, we drew our patch-panel wiring diagrams on large 22-inch drafting paper. These diagrams showed just how the many analog components were to be connected. The diagrams

General Purpose Transport Simulator Cockpit (March 1967). (NASA photo E-18728)

HL-10 Simulator and Display with J. Manke (June 1968). (NASA photo E-18902)

also had the component numbers and other information used in wiring the patch panel. We typically used several different colored pencils to indicate different attributes of the computer components. As the simulations got bigger and bigger, the single large wiring diagrams soon became too cumbersome to use. At that point, we changed to 11x17-inch drafting paper and put these diagrams into binders. Each page usually contained a diagram of one of the main equations of the simulation. These simulation binders also included many other pages of data, such as the settings for the potentiometers, function generators, initial conditions, and test cases.

Sample Wiring Diagram

There is a wiring diagram of a typical analog mechanization in the appendices to this monograph (Appendix 4 by Robert E. Andrews). This set of diagrams is itself from an appendix to a Langley Aeronautical Laboratory report[10] (and is discussed in more detail in Don Reisert's PA). I have not been able to find a good example of such patch-panel wiring diagrams prepared by anyone who programmed the FSL analogs. The Langley mechanization is very similar to the ones we in the FSL prepared and is included as an example for this reason. It is unfortunate that none of the early wiring diagrams that we did were ever archived. In addition, the many reports that were written about the simulation studies and their results never included any descriptions of the analog mechanizations.

Ozalid Copy Process

These wiring diagrams were made using black ink on standard drafting paper that was translucent for copying purposes. The only copier available in those days was the ozalid (blue print) machine in the reproduction shop. These diagrams always smelled of the ammonia that was used in the copy process. We had to make the originals without any of the component numbers, since we used several

---

[10] This facility is currently called the Langley Research Center (LaRC).

RPRV Simulator Cockpit (May 1973). (NASA photo E-26099)

different colored pencils to indicate different types of information on the diagrams about the various components (amplifiers, multipliers, etc.). The various numbers and IDs were written on the copies afterwards. In addition, the forms we used to write down the pot settings were usually typed, on translucent copy paper using a special orange copy paper that was turned so that the orange coating was facing the back of the original. This forced the orange coating to be deposited on the back of the page being typed. This page, with black type on the front and the orange type on the back, would then be copied with the ozalid machines. The orange coating was a waxy crayon-like substance and wore off after a number of copies, but this process made for a very good copy. That is the way things were back then.

A couple of whiffs of a binder full of new ozalid copies was better (as a quick wake-up) than a cup of coffee, but too much exposure caused headaches. That ammonia smell would linger for many weeks. In addition, the ozalid copies faded with age. Just another couple of nuisances of those early days of simulation.

Diagramming Templates

For our wiring diagrams, we all used plastic templates that were usually provided free by the analog computer manufacturers. The accompanying photo (EC00-0088-1) shows several templates. These templates evolved over the years as the computers themselves changed. The analog computer sales representatives seemed to have an endless supply of these templates. We all had our own favorite template(s), and later on when hybrid/digital components were added to the computers, we usually had to have several—one for the analog components, one for the hybrid components, and frequently another for the special-purpose basic electrical components (i.e., resistors, capacitors, etc.). These templates were always disappearing from our desks, for they were also fancied by others around the Center. We had to lock them up along with our slide rules.

In those early days of analog simulation, all the research engineers and all the analog programmers were still using slide rules. The FSL even bought several of the 20-inch slide rules for use in the computer

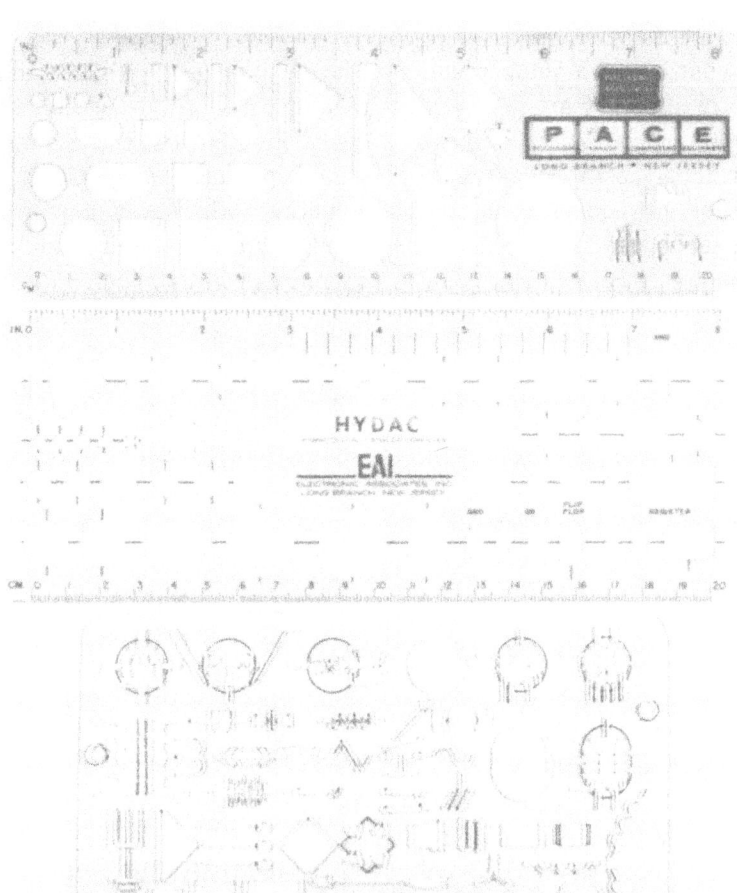

Drawing templates used for analog wiring diagrams. (NASA photo EC00-0088-1)

labs. Fortunately the typical engineer would never buy one of these long slide rules for personal use, so we never had the problem of their disappearing from the labs. They were too obvious and well known. The calculations needed for the pots (i.e., four-digit accuracy) were possible with the longer slide rules, although most of us usually just went with what we got from our standard 10-inch slide rules.

Patch Panels and Patch Cords

All of the larger analog computers we worked with used patch cords to interconnect the many electronic components. A typical simulation took hundreds of patch cords to connect all the pieces. Fortunately, the analog computers (and especially the 100-volt systems) used a patch board system for this process. All of the component inputs and outputs were connected to the patch board in an ordered array. An amplifier used as a summer or integrator had from four to eight input holes (on the patch board) and a corresponding number of output holes. Each piece of equipment (for example, amplifier, pot, multiplier, function generator) had an adequate number of input and output holes. Each piece of equipment had its own area on the patch panel. These areas were silk-screened using different colors to designate the types of component and the input and output holes. Programming an analog computer included the task of wiring the patch panel.

The patch cords came in an assortment of lengths. These varied from as short as 6 inches (including the plug at each end) to as long as 30 inches. The lengths were color-coded. There were jumper plugs of several styles to connect two adjacent holes in either the vertical or horizontal direction. The spacings between holes in these two directions were not the same and required different plugs. The amplifiers that could be used as a summer or an integrator also had a special jumper plug that would make the necessary selection of feedback components. When used as a summer, the feedback component was a precision resistor, and when used as an integrator, the feedback component was a precision capacitor. Special jumper plugs were used to select the appropriate components.

The patch cables and jumper plugs were quite expensive and used gold plating on the contacts and shielded ends of the plugs. This reduced the introduction or propagation of noise. Signal noise was not tolerated and analog computers were designed to reduce signal noise as much as possible. Extensive shielding was required on all signals. Patch cords were all shielded. The patch panel and patch-panel bay were also designed to help eliminate noise and the propagation of noise. Shielding also reduced crosstalk of signals from adjacent cables. The computers were also designed to separate the DC and AC signals. The few AC wires were kept in separate bundles and kept away from the DC parameter signals to help reduce any cross-talk pick-up.

For those simulations that required two or more analog computers, the patch panels had many (hundreds of) holes for the purpose of interconnecting analog computer components together. Cables of these interconnections (called trunks) linked the analog computers together. It was also possible to slave the operational control of one or more analog computers to a master computer. This allowed an operator to run a simulation from a single master analog computer. There were separate cables between the analog computers just for this purpose of slaving operational control. A separate and remote control box was usually mounted in each cockpit so that the pilots could start and stop the simulations. There were other trunks connecting the computer and the cockpits and running to the various output recorders (strip-chart recorders and X-Y plotters).

The technicians spent many an hour making cables for us, and on a few occasions some of the programmers would chip in and help. Generally our soldering skills were not quite good enough, but we could certainly measure and cut the wires. Much of the wire and many of the connectors had to be bought, at least in the beginning, because the warehouse did not stock the sort of stuff we needed for the analog computers. This was also true for all the precision resistors, capacitors, and other such supplies that we were using to interface the instruments and control sticks in the cockpits to our simulations.

Bob Kempel, one of the FRC research engineers (who also learned to program analog computers while working for the Air Force at Edwards) recalls the following from his experiences:

The Midnight Patcher

Analog computer mechanizations were very precarious, in that the computer mechanization consisted of a myriad of various length wires on a front patch panel, which linked the various analog components. To the uninitiated, this panel looked like multicolored spaghetti. A complex simulation patch panel was typically a real mess. Once a simulation was mechanized and thoroughly checked, the wires in the patch panel were not to be touched by anyone but the simulation engineer. Analog mechanizations were required to be statically and dynamically checked quite frequently (like daily) due to the problem of occasional component failure. If a component failed, the simulation could be mildly or grossly invalid depending on the criticality of that particular component.

It was always suspected that we

had a "midnight patcher" due to some of the problems with patch panels found by some simulation engineers on their next shift. The "midnight patcher" being a real or mythical person who would either pull or rearrange a wire on a patch-panel. These problems were typically unusual and unexplained, ones that could only be attributed to the "midnight patcher." [See Bob Kempel's PA.]

One might also attribute these "midnight patcher" attacks to our gremlins!

Along the same line, there was one research engineer (whose name is best left unmentioned) who had the annoying habit of changing the position of one of the many switches on one of the analog computers in the FSL. He usually switched it back before he left the lab. But not always. I guess he thought he was never seen doing this, but he was. So, in an attempt to discourage this practice, one of the unused switches (on the X-15 analogs) was wired up with a big battery, a resistor, and a fan. When the switch was thrown, the resistor was connected to the battery and burnt up. The fan came on and blew the smoke out though the front of the analog, where this engineer was standing. Everyone in the FSL knew about the switch, but no one else. It was several days before the engineer actually threw this particular switch. The smoke must have really shaken him up, because it was a long time before he ever did this again. Someone must have squealed, because he eventually returned to his old habit of randomly switching switches. We tried never to leave him alone in the FSL lab. Fortunately he left the FRC to work at one of the other NASA centers. This was before smoke detectors or sprinklers were installed throughout the building.

Patch panels allowed the patch cords to extend behind the panel in order to make contact with the connector pins located in the panel bay. This made it possible for these patch cords to be dislodged if the panel was accidentally set down on some small item on a table, such as a pencil. It was also possible to dislodge a cord just by moving one or more of them aside when looking through the mass of wires on a patch board. We eventually had special panel holders built to hold the panels when they were not mounted in the patch bay of the analog computer. This helped to eliminate (for the most part) any problems caused by the "midnight patcher." However, a thorough check of the backside of a patch panel was a prudent thing to do before inserting the panel in the patch panel bay of an analog computer. For simulations such as the X-15, where the panels were only removed for maintenance and trouble-shooting, patch cords became dislodged by pawing through the large number of cords on a panel. There was always a shortage of the longer cords, and many times the shorter cords were stretched so tight that they almost came loose by themselves. When we were checking the backside of a wired panel, it helped to keep a pair of needle-nose pliers handy to pull the loose patch cords back into place.

Room Temperature

Room temperature was also an important factor for the analog computers. The 100-volt vacuum-tube analog computers generated a lot of heat and required special air-conditioning (A/C). The computers were mounted on top of A/C plenums with cold air blown into the bottom of the computer racks and the warm air collected out the top and returned to the A/C unit. Photo E-4967 shows the early A/C ducting, before we had raised floors. Initially the A/C unit was hung from the ceiling. When the X-15 analogs were installed, the A/C unit was mounted on the roof above the lab, with large air ducts between the compressors and the air plenums. The sim lab was always quite cold, especially on Monday mornings. Monday morning was not a good time to schedule any important simulation runs. The computer racks took several hours to reach a good, stable temperature after having been turned off over the weekend. For the larger simulations (such as the X-15 with over 400 amplifiers), it usually took all Monday morning before the equipment rack temperatures stabilized and the simulation was ready for use. The integrators tended to drift before they were "warmed up" and had to be continually adjusted. Each amplifier/integrator had a pot and meter on the front of the unit just for this purpose.

Fuses

The simulator facilities were quite sensitive to power outages. Thunderstorms in the area caused occasional power outages. There were only a few high-power lines coming into the lab, and they was no filtering for power fluctuations. The X-15 simulator was very fragile in this respect. The X-15 simulation had over 100 function generators, 80 of which were specially built diode-function generators (DFGs). This particular type of function generator was used with a special type of servo multiplier called a "pot-padder" to generate functions of two variables. Each of these pot-padders had five multiplier "pots," each pot having 15 equally spaced taps (or junctions). Each tap also had a fuse to protect the servo pot. The 80 DFGs were connected to taps on the pot-padders. Each DFG also had 15 fuses. There were several occasions, after a particular hard hit (usually lightning) on the incoming power lines, when hundreds of these fuses would blow. Replacing the blown fuses was a time-consuming job. There were several occasions when the simulation pilot would join in and help. In his PA, Bill Dana talks about doing this. It wasn't always obvious when looking at a fuse if it was blown or not. Each fuse had to be removed and checked with an ohmmeter. 80 DFGs times 15 fuses each equalled 1,200 total fuses to be checked! In addition, each of the 1,200 pots had to be set using a jeweler's screwdriver. The pots were that small. This was state-of-the-art analog computer equipment. Makes you wonder!

Amplifiers and Integrators

The different operations of an amplifier were determined by the relationship of input and feedback components (normally, resistors or capacitors). For addition and subtraction, both the input and feedback components were resistors. When we needed an integrator, the components used were input resistors and feedback capacitors. These resistors and capacitors were quite expensive because of their construction to assure their accuracy. They were kept in a temperature-controlled oven inside the computer to help maintain their specifications. Differentiation (input capacitor and feedback resistor) was a no-no on an analog computer due to the tendency of the amplifiers to magnify any low-level noise in the amplifier, which tended to mask the input signals. Integration had the effect of reducing such noise.

The gain of an amplifier was determined by the ratio of the feedback component to the input component. If both were resistors of equal value, the gain was one. If the two components were of different values, the gain of the amplifier was determined by the ratio: R_f/R_i, where R_f is the value of the feedback resistor and R_i is the value of the input resistor. Most of the amplifiers of that era had input and feedback resistors that provided 1 and 10 gains, respectively. Some of the analog computers had 5-gain inputs. It was also possible to wire other components for different gains. We did this so often that the sim lab technicians were always making special patchable components that we could use when we needed some unusual gains for a particular simulation. These patchable components were just high-quality resistors or capacitors with patch cord connectors soldered and shielded such that we could patch them in series with the standard analog computer components.

Black Boxes

In addition to the patchable resistors and capacitors, the technicians were frequently called upon to build us a black box. These black boxes were standard electronic

Consoles E and F of the X-15 Simulator Analog Computer (September 1960). (NASA photo E-5808)

Console D of the X-15 Simulator Analog Computer (September 1960). (NASA photo E-5809)

equipment boxes, of various sizes, containing some special circuit or component that was not standard equipment on the analog's patch panel. The multi-wafer stepping switches that were used for the boost (four-stage rocket) simulation that we did with the Johnsville centrifuge (see below) is an example of one type of black box that was built. These black boxes used very high-quality resistors, capacitors, diodes, and other components so as to maintain the accuracy and precision of the analog simulation. Most of these components were ordered especially for this purpose, since the warehouse did not normally stock those high-quality components. The Sim Lab, over the years, always had a well-stocked supply of those special high-quality components. They were essential to the operation of the FSL.

The early-generation analogs did not have many components to use in generating nonlinearities such as limits or dead-bands. We were frequently called upon to mechanize these nonlinearities using some unusual circuitry built into a black box. The box would then be patched into the patch panel using standard analog computer patch cords. Shielding and grounding were always important considerations, and the black-box circuits were always built with these factors in mind. Many hours were spent designing and building these black boxes. There were several simulations that would not have been completely implemented if we hadn't been able to use one or more of our special black boxes. The photos of the X-15 analog computers (E-5808 and E-5809) show several black boxes patched into the patch panels.

Because of the way we took turns implementing simulations, there was often an idle analog computer that could be used to develop and test these special black-box circuits. I spent many an hour doing just this. This is when we tuned and perfected these unusual circuits. Most of these circuits were used to simulate portions of the mechanical and hydraulic controls and surfaces in the airplanes of those days. We also implemented a number of transfer functions, which involved the use of the S-plane technology.[11] The downside of all this is that many analog computer components were devoted to the cockpits, and consequently not available to be used in the mechanization of the model. This did have an impact on the size of the model. We were constantly taking analog components from the equations-of-motion mechanization and using them in getting the cockpits on-line. Many simulations grew to almost twice the number of analog components to order to get all parts of the cockpits and visual displays ready to use. Nowadays, the approach is to simply add another digital computer. Much better, in many ways.

Cockpit Instrumentation

Not only did we have to simulate unusual aircraft controls, but we also frequently had to simulate unusual cockpit instrumentation and displays. Airplane cockpits were really beginning to evolve in those days. We also had to develop special circuitry to simulate this cockpit instrumentation and these displays. For several years we did not have the luxury of being able to use the actual instruments. We had to develop "look-a-likes" that simulated the actual instruments. Many of the instruments were driven directly from the analog computer's amplifiers. This was before the days of the special interface computers that were later developed in-house, which conditioned the signals going to the cockpit instruments. The black-box circuits were really the beginning of this in-house development of cockpit-instrumentation signal-conditioning computers. The Sim Lab technicians and engineers were quite ingenious in developing the many special components and interfaces we needed to implement our simulations. The PAs of Richard Musick and Charlie Wagner describe some of these efforts.

Visual Displays

Almost every cockpit had some type of visual display, in addition to the normal instruments. During the early days, this display was a large CRT with one or more lines drawn that represented the horizon or the airplane or a visual representation of one or more of the calculated parameters—such as angle of attack, sideslip angle, or roll angle. Since we did not have an actual 8-ball,[12] we many times tried to represent the parameters (normally displayed on an 8-ball) with lines on the scope. These lines moved as the parameters changed. On many occasions the display tried to represent a target or the horizon, depending on the particular study that was mechanized. We spent many hours working the equations to provide a display that the research engineer wanted. (See photos E-1841, E-10591, E-12942, and E-8100 for several cockpits that have CRT display units.) The out-the-window displays were an attempt to provide something more than just a set of instruments for the pilots to look at. Dick Day is the one who initially came up with this idea and helped to develop the first CRT display.

In some simulations the visual display was an important part of the study. Dwain Deets, in his PA, talks about a CRT display of a

---

[11] This term refers to the use of Fourier transforms to convert differential equations to algebraic expressions that are more easily calculated.

[12] An 8-ball is the colloquial term for the attitude indicators used in the airplanes of those days. They provide the pilot an indication of the airplane's pitch angle, roll angle, heading angle, and maybe even angles of attack and sideslip.

Paul Loschke in a Simulation Cockpit (April 1965). (NASA photo E-12942)

Milt Thompson in the Paresev Simulation Cockpit (May 1962). (NASA photo E-8100)

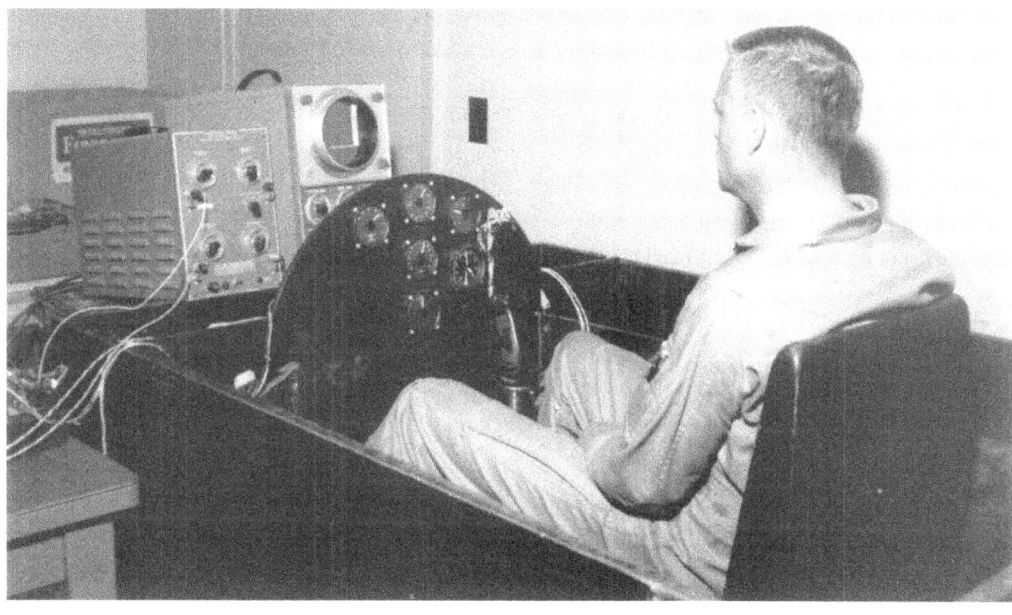

side-view of an airplane that showed a canard control surface and its location as determined by the simulation that was mechanized using one of the FSL portable analog computers.

For the X-15 simulator, one of the various displays that were provided over the years was an energy-management display. This display provided a heart-shaped view on a CRT that outlined the area where the X-15 could glide to at all times during the flight. For the X-15-3, this display was a small scope mounted in the instrument panel (see photo E-11778) rather than using a large oscilloscope above the instrument panel. A small special-purpose computer was developed under contract to generate the display. During the development of the database used by this special-purpose computer, the larger CRT was used for the display.

In his PA, Charlie Wagner talks about several of the display units that he was personally involved with. I recommend you take the time to read his PA now, for he describes many of the problems we had with the different visual display units that were used with the analog simulators. Charlie spent many hours fussing with this hardware, and his recollections are a good accounting of the troubles we had with this display hardware.

These visual displays got more sophisticated (and expensive) as the FSL grew. However, there were many times when they were not enough. Many of the pilots always complained about inadequate visual displays. The out-the-window cues are particularly important during the landing phase of a flight. However, every visual display we had did not have sufficient resolution to allow us to adequately simulate this part of a flight simulator, especially for those simulations that were mechanized for the entire flight regime of an aircraft. Only those few special landing simulations that we did (in which the altitude range was limited to the very last portions of an approach and landing) had the resolution necessary to provide a reasonable visual presentation. Until digital computers came along, the analog systems we built or bought were just not good enough. The approach taken at the FRC was to use an airplane that had similar landing characteristics and have the pilot fly that vehicle to practice landings. The F-104 was often used for landing practice for the X-15 and several of the lifting bodies, for example.

In 1964, Milt Thompson made a presentation to the Society of Experimental Test Pilots Symposium. This paper was entitled "General Review of Piloting Problems Encountered During Simulation and Flights of the X-15" (Citation 412). Since so much of this paper is directly related, it is included in its entirety in the appendices. It provides a very good presentation of some of the problems the X-15 pilots had because of the deficiencies of the X-15 simulator—and not just the lack of good visual cues, but in other areas of the simulation. I recommend that you take the time, now, to read that paper.

Repetitive Operation Simulations

Repetitive operation (or Rep Op, as it was usually called) was one of the features available on the analog computers in the FSL. It was quite useful for a certain class of problems, especially those that did not have a human in the loop. The analog solution was speeded up by a factor of 100. This was accomplished by using a 0.01 Microfarad feedback capacitor in the integrators instead of the usual 1.0 Microfarad capacitor. The output results were displayed (usually) on an oscilloscope. The computer was cycled between OPERATE and RESET modes 100 times faster than normal. If a solution normally took ten seconds in real time, in Rep Op it would take 0.1 seconds. There was special circuitry in the analog computers that caused the computer to repetitively switch back and forth from RESET to OPERATE modes. The repetitive recalculation of the solution allowed the user to see immediately (on the oscilloscope) the effects of parameter changes. A solution could be attained very quickly. The strip-chart recorders of those days could not be used during the fast Rep Op runs, as they could not keep up with the data. However, once a solution had been reached, the time constant would be returned to one and the data plotted on strip-chart recorders in real time. The different capacitors used in the feedback circuitry of the integrators were built into the analog computer's integrators. We did not have to use external capacitors for this purpose.

Rep Op was used in the FSL for derivative matching—a way of analyzing post-flight data of specific in-flight maneuvers to determine the aircraft's derivatives. Neil Matheny, a research engineer, suggested the use of Rep Op for derivative matching at the FRC in 1966. He received an award for this suggestion. Neil was an active user of the portable analog computers for a number of small simulations that he programmed in his office. He was involved with the early derivative-matching activities at the FRC and recommended using the analog computer Rep Op capability to help in the determination of aircraft derivatives. Larry Caw was the FSL programmer who was assigned to work with Matheny to implement his first Rep-Op derivative-matching programs. Initially this was implemented using one of the TR-48 portable analog computers. Later on, derivative matching was done using one of the EAI 231-RV analog computers. Theron Manning, John Perry, Larry Caw, and other FSL analog programmers also got involved in these Rep-Op derivative-matching simulations.

Neil Matheny had been involved with a similar real-time analog simulation in which a tape recording was used to provide the pilot's inputs. This short time history, recorded from an actual flight, was originally copied onto the (magnetic) tape many times. The tape was read and used as input to an analog implementation of the airplane's equations of motion, over and over, but in real time. The derivatives used in the simulation were changed between runs until the output of the simulation matched those recorded in real time during flights. The magnetic tape was subsequently changed to a continuous loop, with only one time-history set of inputs. This process eliminated having to rewind the original tape and speeded up the process of trying to match the derivatives. The use of Rep Op was an outgrowth of the original process that Neil was using. Since there were no pilots in the loop, the transition to Rep Op was fairly easy. Derivative matching was a perfect example of the type of simulations that Rep Op was designed for.

For derivative matching, the equations of motion—frequently only 5 DOF—were implemented. The pilot's inputs were simulated with pulses or time-varying inputs using function generators. These were input after the program was put into OPERATE mode and the equations were solved, but with time being 100 times faster than normal. The coefficients, for a particular flight condition, could be varied until the high-speed solution matched actual flight recordings of the same variables using the same inputs. In this way the actual vehicle derivatives could be determined. The desired solution was plotted on a transparent overlay that was attached to the front of the oscilloscope. The appropriate parameters being calculated were then displayed with the proper scaling, and the two solutions were compared (by looking at the two traces). Differences between the desired solution and the calculated solution were easy to see and correct. Many of the derivatives used in the airplane simulations were obtained from wind-tunnel studies. The wind-tunnel data had its limitations, due to the inherent inaccuracies of such research facilities. Rep Op was a way of fine-tuning the wind-tunnel data to get it to agree with the real aircraft's data. These derivative matching simulations were eventually phased out when parameter estimation algorithms were developed for a digital computer.[13]

Rep Op simulations did not require a cockpit and could be run by one person. Chester Wolowicz and Roxanne Yancey were two more of the FRC folk who spent

---

[13] The following two paragraphs about parameter estimation (also known as parameter identification) are from Lane E. Wallace, *Flights of Discovery: 50 Years at the NASA Dryden Flight Research Center* (Washington, DC: NASA SP-4309, 1996), pp. 56-57:

Once the X-15 flew, researchers at Dryden used the data collected during flight to understand better the relationship of theory, wind-tunnel data, and the realities of actual flight. During the early years of the X-15 program, comparisons of flight data with those from wind tunnels had to be done by traditional methods that were time-consuming and not fully consistent.

Moreover, the methods in use at that time were unable to provide values for many dynamic aircraft responses in flight. In 1966 Dryden researchers Lawrence W. Taylor, Jr., and Kenneth W. Iliff began developing a more automated technique for obtaining numerical values for aircraft behavior. This involved theoretical contributions resulting in computer programs (later improved by Richard E. Maine) for manipulating multiple differential equations to obtain the unknown values of the parameters that define aircraft behavior. Called **parameter identification**, this technique allowed researchers to determine precisely the differences between values predicted from wind tunnel data and those actually encountered in flight. Such precision is essential for understanding and fixing undesirable or dangerous flight characteristics. This significant flight test and flight research technique has been used on over 50 other aircraft at Dryden, including all of the lifting bodies, the XB-70, the SR-71, the Space Shuttles, and the X-29. This technique has spread to virtually all flight test organizations throughout the world and has been used to enhance the safety, flight procedures, and control system designs of most current supersonic aircraft as well as to improve flight simulators, submarines, economic models, and even biomedical models.

many an hour sitting in front of one of the FSL EAI 231R analog computers and running derivative-matching cases. This type of simulation was used for many different airplanes over the years. The notes I have (copies of some of the files of Chester Wolowicz) contain Rep Op simulation mechanizations for the X-15 and XB-70. These were just two of the many vehicles for which Rep Op was used. The report NASA TN D-4578 (*Preliminary Flight Evaluation of the Stability and Control Derivatives and Dynamic Characteristics of the Unaugmented XB-70-1 Airplane Including Comparisons with Predictions* by Chester H. Wolowicz, Larry W. Struts, Glenn B. Gilyard, and Neil W. Matheny, May 1968, [Citation No. 528]) describes the results of the use of Rep Op for derivative matching purposes for the XB-70. This report references another report by John M. Rampy and Donald T. Berry of the AFFTC: FTC-TDR-64-8 (*Determination of Stability Derivatives From Flight Test Data By Means Of High Speed Repetitive Operation Analog Matching,* 1964). This AFFTC report provides an excellent overview of the Rep Op process involved.

The portable analog computers that were loaned out for the engineers to use in their own offices had Rep Op capability. The TR-48s were used for such studies, with the outputs being displayed on a small CRT. These were fairly simple simulations with few or no nonlinear functions. It sometimes took longer to get the simulation programmed than it took to run through all the cases under study.

Not all the research engineers were willing to do their own programming. For those engineers, the FSL would do whatever was needed to get their simulations operational, including programming and helping to run the various cases. However, the nature of the analog computers provided an interactive awareness with the problem being solved that was not available with the digital computers of that time. A number of the research engineers appreciated the interactive and analogous relation between the electronic analog model and the real-world system, and they preferred to implement and run their own simulation studies. To see the results being calculated in parallel and in real time was something most of them had never experienced before. They could see the effects of any changes they made and could do so immediately. They could also determine if the equations they had programmed were in fact correct and accurately represented the real physical system.

Testing

Each analog implementation had to be tested before it was turned over to the engineers for their studies. We used both static and dynamic tests to check out the simulation. Thereafter we usually used the dynamic test(s) for daily checkouts.

Static testing consisted of calculating the results of the equations, at one point in time, with known input values. This was done using just a pencil, paper, and a calculator (or slide rule). These test cases were then used with the analog computer set-up. Each integrator on the analog computers had the capability of having a known initial value applied (known as an Initial Condition or IC). This value allowed for establishment of preset conditions at the start of each run. These were usually needed for variables such as altitude, velocity, X/Y coordinates, and other parameters that were not zero at the start of a run. We could also use the IC pots to provide known inputs for many of the parameters as a part of the static test cases. For those parameters that were usually provided by the pilots' controls, etc., we just used pots to provide an equivalent input. With these known inputs, we would then calculate the expected accelerations (i.e., roll, pitch, and yaw accelerations, alpha and beta accelerations,[14] etc.). We would then read out the corresponding values as calculated by the implemented equations. If we were getting the correct results, we probably had the patch board patched correctly and the pots set right. Sometimes it took several different static test cases to really verify the correctness of the implementation. Since the test cases were not actually run, we could use parameter values of any magnitude. The values selected were really to check out the circuits and did not have to be realistic flight values. It was common to set most of the parameters to the maximum, which usually resulted in a better test of the components and the circuits. Analog computer components seemed to have the most problems when calculated values were near either zero or the maximums. These conditions tended to show up any scaling deficiencies.

Scaling

The process of converting the actual calculated parameters' units of measurements to the analog computers ±100 voltage range was called scaling. The maximum expected values of each of the variables used in an analog simulation had to be estimated and then converted to the ±100 voltage range. This was just one of the steps in getting a simulation set up. Some variables were frequently scaled at a maximum (or minimum) value that was much greater (or much less) than would actually be calculated. These types of parameters could easily overload the amplifiers used for calculation. Dynamic pressure was one such parameter that we always had trouble with since the maximum dynamic pressure (usually) calculated was often 50 to 100 times less than possible. To get a voltage reading that was usable and could be displayed on recorders or some other display, the analog circuit calculating dynamic pressure usually had a gain of 100 or more. High gains like this were avoided if possible, as they tended to increase the noise level correspondingly. They were usually the first ones to overload when any analog component malfunctioned.

Each of the amplifiers in an analog computer had an alarm that went off when the component was overloaded (i.e., loaded over 100 volts). These alarms were annoying and really got your attention. They were there to warn of equipment failure but could also be triggered when maximum values (and corresponding voltages) were exceeded. The use of maximum values during static testing was a good way to ferret out such possible problems in scaling.

Dynamic testing was used to further test the correctness of the implementation. It was frequently used to determine the condition of the analog computer. Because of the structure of the analog computer, there were no diagnostics (as there were with a digital computer) to determine if all the components were working correctly. It was impractical to test every piece of equipment in an analog computer every day. Generally if a particular piece of equipment failed, the dynamic check case would not be correct. The amplifiers had to be balanced almost daily (remember these were vacuum tube devices) in the mornings (after having been turned off all night), and sometimes they had to be balanced several times before they would stabilize enough that we could use the simulator. The integrators were the worst culprits, since the slightest offset in just one integrator could result in incorrect dynamic tests.

The early analog computers required the programmer to make the appropriate changes to the implementation to run such static and dynamic tests. The later-generation computers, with the paper tape set-up, allowed for these test cases to be

---

[14] "Alpha" is engineering shorthand for angle of attack. "Beta" means sideslip. Accelerations in alpha are increases in the change of the angle of the relative wind with respect to the line of the aircraft's fuselage or airfoils. Those in beta are increases in the rate of the aircraft's sideward motion.

set up and run by the computer itself. The programmer still had to establish the test case(s) initially and then program the computer to repeat the tests on a regular basis. This really speeded up the process of getting an analog computer changed over between simulations.

Analog Programmers—No More

Looking back on those simulations and comparing them to today's, I can see that there are differences that are not obvious to those who were not a part of both eras. In the early days, those of us doing the programming were just analog programmers. Since at many times we did not have enough equipment to mechanize a complete 6 DOF model, we were forced to implement something less. The equations changed from simulation to simulation. The chore of mechanizing a fairly complete simulation was the full-time job of the analog programmer and not the research engineer. After the FSL got its own analog computer and hired programmers, the research engineers quit doing their own programming. They were quite willing to have us to do that job.

Early on, the analog programmers were not usually responsible for the model (i.e., the equations of motion being implemented). The research engineers doing the study knew which set of equations they wanted to use and were responsible for the correctness of the model. The analog programmer was responsible for programming the equations correctly. The same thing is true of all digital computer programs. One has to prove that what has been programmed is both doing the right job and doing the job right—the purposes, respectively, of verification and validation testing. Back then, the research engineer was responsible for the completeness and correctness of the model, while the analog programmer was responsible for the completeness and correctness of the implementation of the model.

Many of these early simulations were really research studies investigating some particular feature or characteristic of a particular airplane. Not all the simulators were for pilot training or flight planning. And in a few cases our research pilots were never even asked to fly the simulations. In addition, many of the research engineers we worked with were pilots and were quite adept at flying the simulations themselves. We in the simulation branch had the task of implementing the models correctly. This is one of the reasons that we did not need to have degrees in aerodynamics. Having knowledge in aerodynamics certainly helped, though. It also helped to have an understanding of basic electrical circuits. For some of us, these were learned on the job. Programming the analog computer was a full-time job, and we took great pride in doing this job.

This changed when simulation became all-digital. By then, after the Cyber 73 (the FRC's digital mainframe computer) was operational, the need for a quick change-over from simulator to simulator was a requirement, and the digital computer provided this capability quite well. Also, the Cyber was large enough that a single complete set of the equations of motion could be implemented and used for nearly every model. Once this model was proven to be correct, it was then used for all simulations. Many of the earlier sets of equations used small-angle approximations and a flat earth. The new model changed that and was necessary for the newer aircraft being flown at the FRC. The major difference between airplane simulators was the set of derivatives and the physical characteristics unique to each plane. This factor — along with the increasing sophistication of the aircraft and especially their onboard systems, including their control systems — led to the desirability of the simulator programmers having a greater understanding of aerodynamics and control-system design. The era of the analog programmer was over, replaced by the simulation engineer. Analog computers were demoted to cockpit interface, and this too eventually phased out as this method of interface was transferred to the in-house-built interface units.

By this time, most of the first analog programmers had either left or had become hybrid computer programmers. Computer maintenance and cockpit set-up activities were being performed by contractors. The need to quickly switch from one simulator to another and the automation that had been developed to make this happen had also brought about a change in the entire development process of a new simulation. Just like the differences between the early automobile and today's high-tech vehicles, the hands-on ease of fixing and maintaining yesterday's hardware has been replaced with highly sophisticated automation equipment and methods.

The same thing that happened to analog programming also happened to the simulator cockpits. Early on, almost everything that went into simulator cockpits was built in-house. The technicians' job evolved in much the same way as the analog programmers' changed. The technicians and the analog programmers spent many hours developing, testing, and programming the instruments, pilots' controls, and anything else that went into the simulator cockpits. I have many memories working with all the technicians during these early days. The esprit de corps was great. Nowadays, in the RAIF, there are as many as six different full-time simulations in operational status at any one time. I suspect that there are times when the people working on any one simulator hardly know the folks in the next lab. There is a lot of demand for simulators for the many aircraft projects being flown at the Dryden Flight Research Center. There has been tremendous progress in the state-of-the-art in simulation development. There has been a corresponding increase in the size of the staff to build, maintain, and operate all these simulators. It is extremely difficult, if not impossible, to be proficient in all aspects of today's aircraft simulator development and operations.

Simulation's Firsts—Christmas Buffet

As all of this would suggest, analog simulation development was a group effort involving all of the Sim Lab folk. There was a lot of cooperation, team spirit, and willingness to help out among those of us in that group. And not just at work, but also after work. Initially, many of us were bachelors, with similar outside interests. Softball, golf, fishing and backpacking in the High Sierras, basketball, tennis, and bowling are some of the many activities that we engaged in. The Sim Lab has the distinction of starting a number of Dryden firsts. For example, it was the Sim Lab that started an annual Christmas buffet. We were the first office at Dryden that had a sit-down potluck Christmas buffet to which spouses and children were invited to participate. This was a very special event and later duplicated by other offices within Dryden.

Bi-Weekly Poker Game

The guys in the FSL started a bi-weekly poker game that was very popular amongst not just us in the FSL but others around the Center. I am sure there were other similar poker games involving specific groups of workers from the Center, but I don't recall any of them being open to anyone who wanted to participate. Those other games were, for the most part, closed to outsiders. Our games were originally on Thursday nights, which was when we got paid. These bi-weekly poker nights began in 1959 at the large apartment that one of the FSL technicians (Serge Kostrakopf) and I shared in Lancaster. After work, Serge and I would go to one of the local liquor shops and buy a pony keg of beer and drag this and a large washtub and lots of ice up the back stairs to our apartment. Later, just before the local pizza joint closed, we would call and order several large pizzas (with everything) to go with our beer. There were really only two places in those days to buy pizza in Lancaster. Barones, on West Avenue I, was the best in

Lancaster and that is where we got ours. The poker games later moved to Friday nights and were hosted by other FSL folk. The games eventually stopped when the fellow that had been hosting the games for the last couple of years left and went to work in Los Angeles. By then, almost all of us were married with children and had other interests that interfered with playing poker. The stakes were not high (penny, nickel, and dime chips) and rarely did anyone win or lose more than a couple of bucks. I'm sure this factor was a big reason for the popularity of the games. But, it was fun while it lasted.

Deep Sea Fishing Trips

It was also the Sim Lab folk who started the annual Dryden deep-sea fishing trips. Dick Musick did most of the organizing and scheduling. The first several ocean fishing trips were out of San Diego, south into the waters offshore from Mexico, and were primarily for tuna. Later on, these fishing trips went out of Oceanside, San Pedro, and then Oxnard. There was one particular boat and captain that we really liked. He kept moving his base of operation from one port to another. So we did, too. He really worked hard to find us schools of fish. In addition, his boat and crew were the nicest of all those we rented, and his wife and daughter ran an excellent galley. We went with this particular boat for several years, until he sold his boat and retired. That was when the fishing trips changed from looking for tuna to bottom fishing around the Channel Islands. Fishing for tuna was exciting if we got into some good-sized schools. But we never really had very good luck finding those larger schools of tuna. The bottom fishing trips were more productive—and became quite popular. We had no trouble getting the 45 people needed to reserve a nice-sized all-day boat. These fishing trips were later organized and scheduled by the Dryden Activities Committee and are still scheduled about once a year.

Moving-base Simulators

The FSL never had any moving-base simulators. We did investigate this technology, though. One such investigation (if you can call it that) involved several of the FRC engineers and a couple of the FSL folk (Jim Samuels and Dick Musick). They actually scheduled a trip to the Disneyland Park in Anaheim to investigate a ride that was there (in those days); it had a number of flying-saucer-type ground-effects vehicles for people to ride—much like bumper cars or boats. If the person sitting in the seat leaned in one direction, the saucer would move in that direction. There was a skirt around the saucer that held pressurized air, which kept the saucer off the ground—like ground-effect boats. Leaning caused some air to leak from under the skirt and propelled the saucer in the opposite direction. This air cushion was provided from a large air chamber under the surface of the saucer. The surface had a large number of air ducts that would open when the saucer was directly overhead. The ducts were small enough and close enough together that the saucer was always over enough of them, thereby providing an adequate amount of pressurized air to support the saucer. This technology was actually considered as something viable for moving-base simulators! I remember thinking at the time that this trip was just a boondoggle. The group that went got a very extensive tour including a lot of behind-the-scenes looks at a number of the rides and attractions at Disneyland.

Another (unfulfilled) venture into moving-base simulators was the acquisition of a 6 DOF cockpit that had been surplused an airline companies' simulation facilities. This was a typical two-seat passenger transport cockpit. It included the hydraulic actuators and everything needed (except the computers) to mechanize a 6 DOF moving-base simulator. It was installed in the hangar lean-to that later housed the F-8 Digital fly-By-Wire (DFBW) iron-bird simulator. However, this piece of equipment was never used. For some reason, the decision to actually do something with this cockpit was never made. We rarely mechanized simulations of airplanes with that type of cockpit (two-seat transports) in those days. The cockpit was eventually surplused and sat in the AFFTC surplus lot for many years before someone bought it for its scrap metal.

Portable Analog Computers

The FSL had several analog computers that were portable and were meant to be loaned out for research engineers to use in their own offices or labs. The ones we had were from EAI (TR-10s, TR-20s, TR-48s and TR-58s). These were all ±10-volt transistorized systems. The first ones we bought were the EAI TR-10s, and they originally did not have removable patch panels. The components were built with patch cord holes right on the front face of each component. These components plugged into the cabinet in a rack similar to a standard instrument rack. The standard components included amplifiers, pots, multipliers, and diode function generators. The TR-10 and TR-20 cabinets held about three dozen components each. These components were interchangeable, so it was possible to change the configuration to meet the needs of the user. Each TR-20 had a removable patch panel, which was also reconfigurable, just like the components behind it. The TR-48s had patch panels that could not be reconfigured. The numbers in the model number indicated the approximate number of amplifiers available in the analog computer. We also bought small portable strip-chart recorders and flat-bed plotters to be used with these portable analogs. Research engineers used these portables for small studies and generally did all their own programming. We in the FSL taught courses on how to program the portable analogs. These portable analogs became quite popular and were constantly on loan.

Generally the more amplifiers one had to use, the bigger or more sophisticated the simulation became. On several occasions we used these portable computers to add to the larger ±100-volt analogs for those few simulations when we needed just a few more amplifiers or such. For a couple of simulators, such as the Lunar Landing Research Vehicle (LLRV), several of the portable analogs were needed because all the larger analogs were in use. The TR-10/20 analogs did not have trunk connections on their patch panels. Connecting them to some other analog(s) was done with a lot of very long patch cords, which were usually made up just for that reason. The portable analogs used a different patch cord than the larger analogs, so the cords between the two different computers had to have different ends. Cords of this style could not be bought and had to be made in-house by the FSL technicians. These particular simulations had the appearance of a big ball of spaghetti. It's a wonder they ever worked. The simulation programmer usually spent a lot of time each morning in check-out to make sure there were no loose connections.

Larry Caw's personal account contains a description of the LLRV simulation. This simulator used several of the portable 10-volt analog computers with one or more of the 100-volt EAI analogs.

The function generators in the TR-10/20 analog computers required a special shelf-like attachment to be used when setting the pots for the nonlinear function. The DFG was first removed from the rack and the shelf installed. The DFG unit was then mounted in the shelf. This exposed the pots (mounted on the side of the unit and normally hidden from view) that were used to generate the nonlinear function. These pots were set using a screwdriver. After all the pots were set, the DFG unit was removed from the shelf, the shelf removed from the computer, and the DFG unit re-installed in the computer. How's that for convenience?

Four-Stage Boost-Vehicle Simulation (1958-1959)

Of all the simulations that I worked on, the four-stage boost-vehicle simulation was easily the most interesting. It wasn't the biggest or even the longest-running simulation, and it wasn't even an airplane. Maybe that is why I remember it so well. I actually implemented this simulation four different times over a period of about two years. The third time was on one of the first analog computers ever built. This computer, as I remember, was built for the U.S. Navy during World War II. I got to use it in the spring of 1959. It was connected to a large centrifuge that provided motion with appropriate velocities and accelerations. This facility was at the Navy Aviation Medical Laboratory (a part of the Naval Air Development Center) in Johnsville, Pennsylvania. This is only a few miles north of Philadelphia. The centrifuge was capable of providing accelerations in excess of what the human pilot could endure. Our launch profiles normally went to just over seven Gs (seven times the force of gravity at sea level) and simulated the acceleration forces experienced by a four-stage rocket-powered launch vehicle during lift-off and entry into an orbit around the earth. During the latter days of our simulation, this acceleration was doubled (to over 14 Gs) and flown at this level of acceleration by most of the pilots. This was the same centrifuge used by NASA for the X-15 Program for pilot training, and by the Dyna-Soar pilots for verification studies of piloted control during launch.

The purpose of this particular simulation was to determine if a human could manually control a launch vehicle and put it into an Earth orbit while being subjected to the high G forces that occurred during such a launch. The alternative method was to use computers to control the vehicle during the launch and injection into orbit.

The equations of motion that we implemented were the 6 degrees of freedom (DOF) equations of a four-stage rocket launch vehicle, such as the Apollo launch vehicle. The longitudinal equations were mechanized completely, since the piloting task was concerned primarily with the longitudinal modes. The lateral-directional equations were simplified with constant aerodynamic characteristics. We also implemented a two-stage version, which was flown by all the pilots. The first two mechanizations were done using the EAI 31R and EAI 131R analog computers (the ones shown in photo E-4967). The last mechanization used the newer EAI-231R analog computer (which was later used as one of the X-15 analog computers; see photo E-5810).

The pilot's cockpit was actually a couch on which the pilot lay, with the instrument panel overhead. (See photo E-4548.) This positioning was intended to provide the

Components of the X-15 Simulator Analog Computer (September 1960). The EAI-23IR has the chair in front of it. (NASA photo E-5810)

Boost Simulation Couch, Panel, Controls (in FSL—April 1959). (NASA photo E-4548)

actual orientation that would be experienced in the real vehicle. The Mercury, Gemini, Apollo, and Shuttle vehicles all had this orientation for the pilots during launch. The pilots lay on their backs with the G forces almost perpendicular into their chests. Our simulator was built to provide this same configuration. This was quite different from all other simulations we had ever built in the FSL. In addition, because of the accelerations that would be experienced during an actual launch, the pilots used a side-arm controller. The right-hand controller provided 3 DOF (roll, pitch, and yaw). The launch vehicle was configured with gimbaled rocket engines to provide the control inputs needed by the pilots to steer the vehicle along a predetermined path that, if followed accurately, would put the vehicle into the correct orbit.

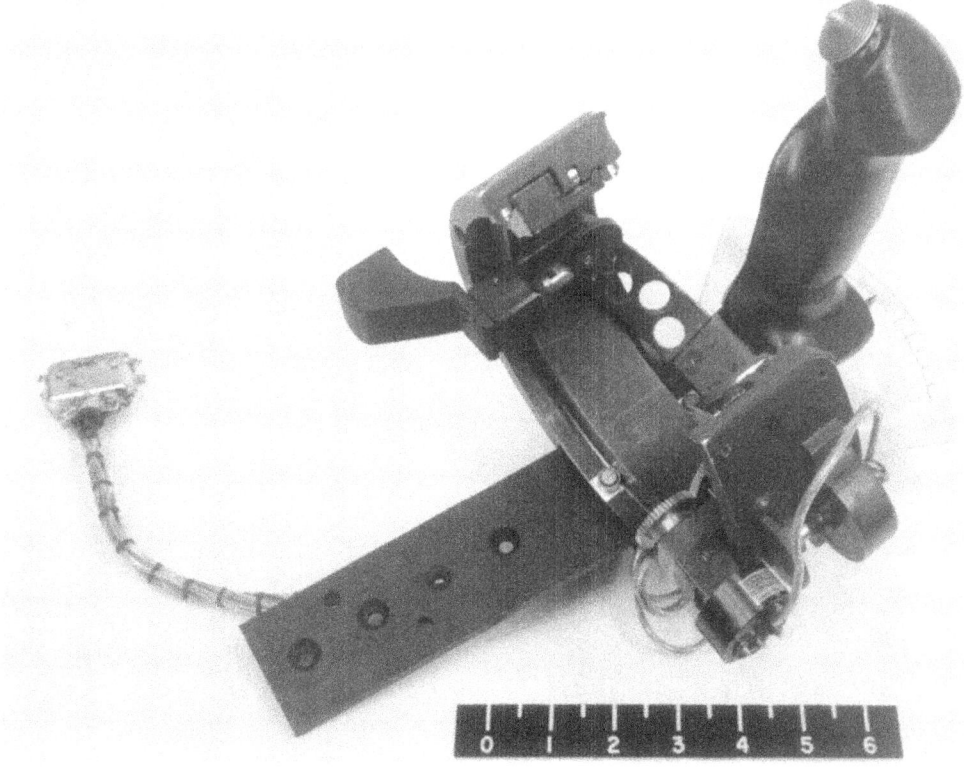

Boost Simulation Side-Arm Controller (July 1959). (NASA photo E-4725)

Three-Axis Side-Arm Controller

The simulator cockpit had a three-axis side-arm controller that was designed and built in-house at the FRC. This controller was definitely one-of-a-kind. Photo E-4725 shows this unit. It was mostly aluminum and had been made in the machine shop downstairs. Again, these guys in the shop did an outstanding job in building this controller. Dick Musick spent many hours working with them to get it in its final form.

There were seven different pilots who participated in this centrifuge simulation. From the FRC, there were Neil Armstrong, Stan Butchart, and Navy pilot Forrest Peterson. The other pilots were Bob Innis from the NASA Ames Research Center (ARC) in Mountain View, California, Bill Alford from the NASA Langley Research Center in Hampton, Virginia, and Captains Walter Daniels and Robert Rushworth from the Air Force Flight Test Center (AFFTC) at Edwards Air Force Base, California. Each pilot made a series of runs in the centrifuge and had his own form-fitting foam insert. Each insert had to be installed in the seat

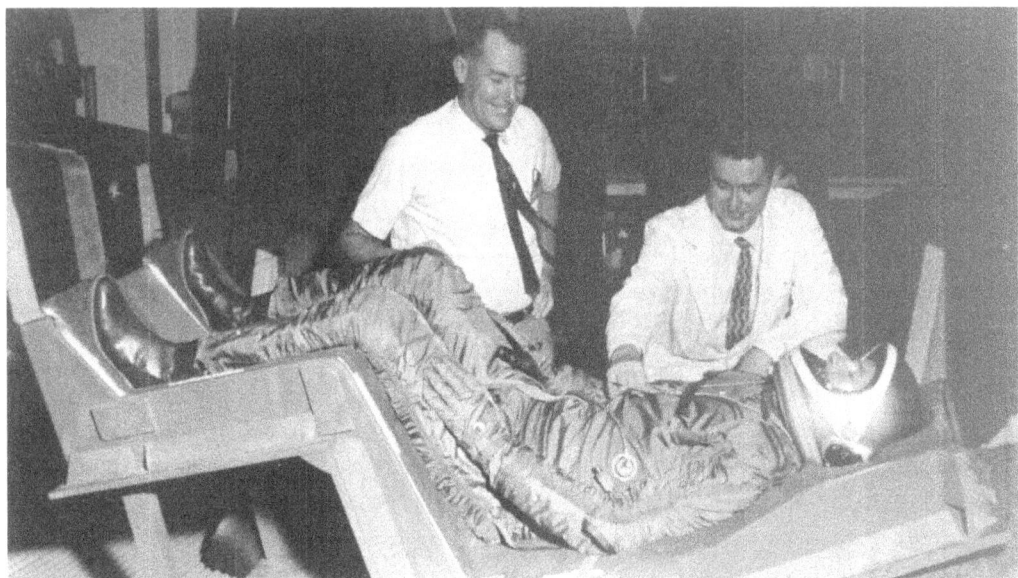

Centrifuge Seat Insert with Ed Holleman, Randy Chambers, and Forrest Petersen (July 1959). (NASA photo E-4661)

Centrifuge Gondola (July 1959). (NASA photo E-4662)

Boost Program photo (September 1959). (NASA photo E-4870)

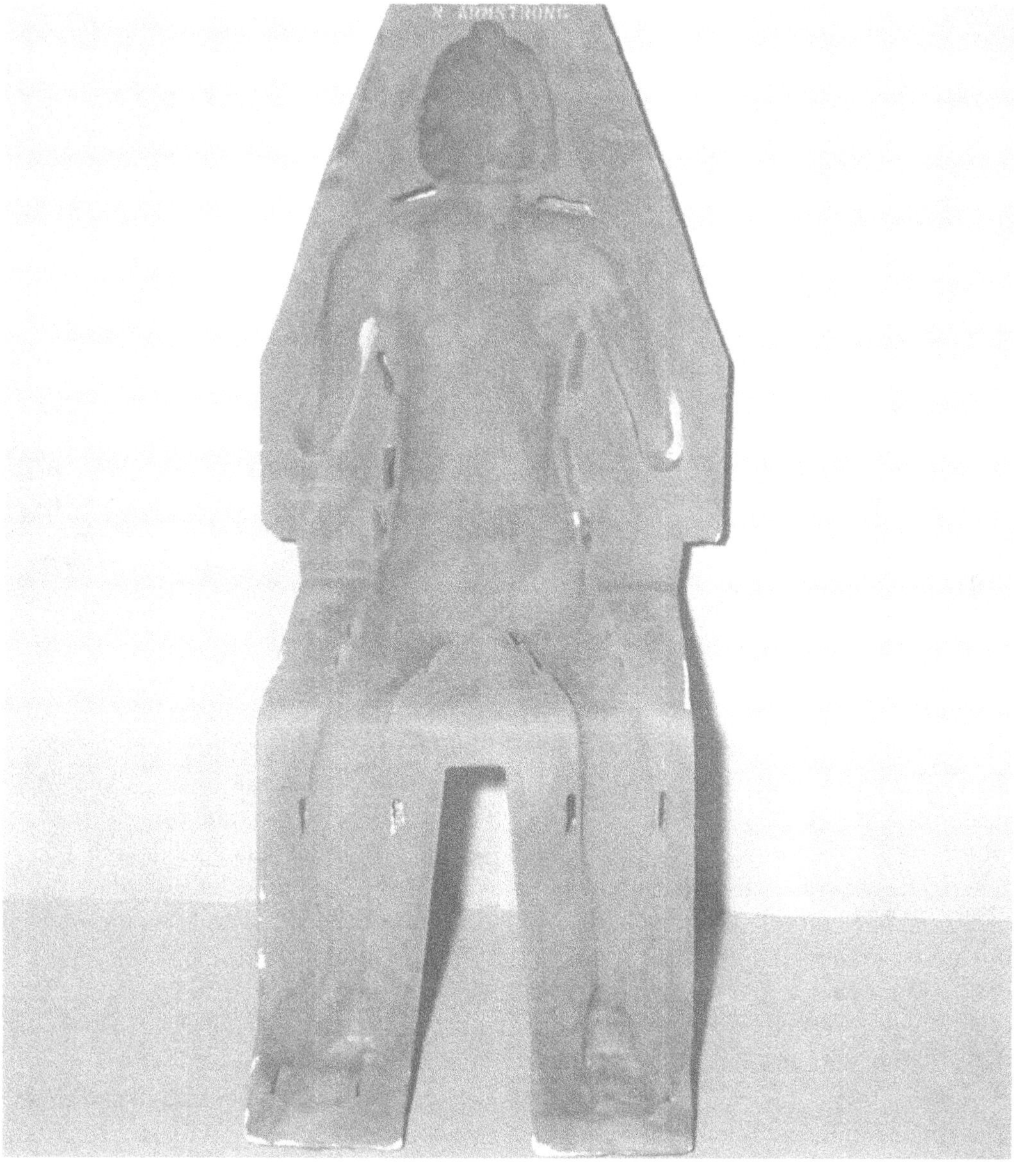

Boost Program Centrifuge Seat (October 1959). (NASA photo E-4990)

in the centrifuge's gondola before the pilot could "fly." This seat-exchange process took a while. We worked many days and evenings before all the pilots finished their allotment of runs. (See photos E-4661, E-4662, E-4870, E-4990, and E-5040.)

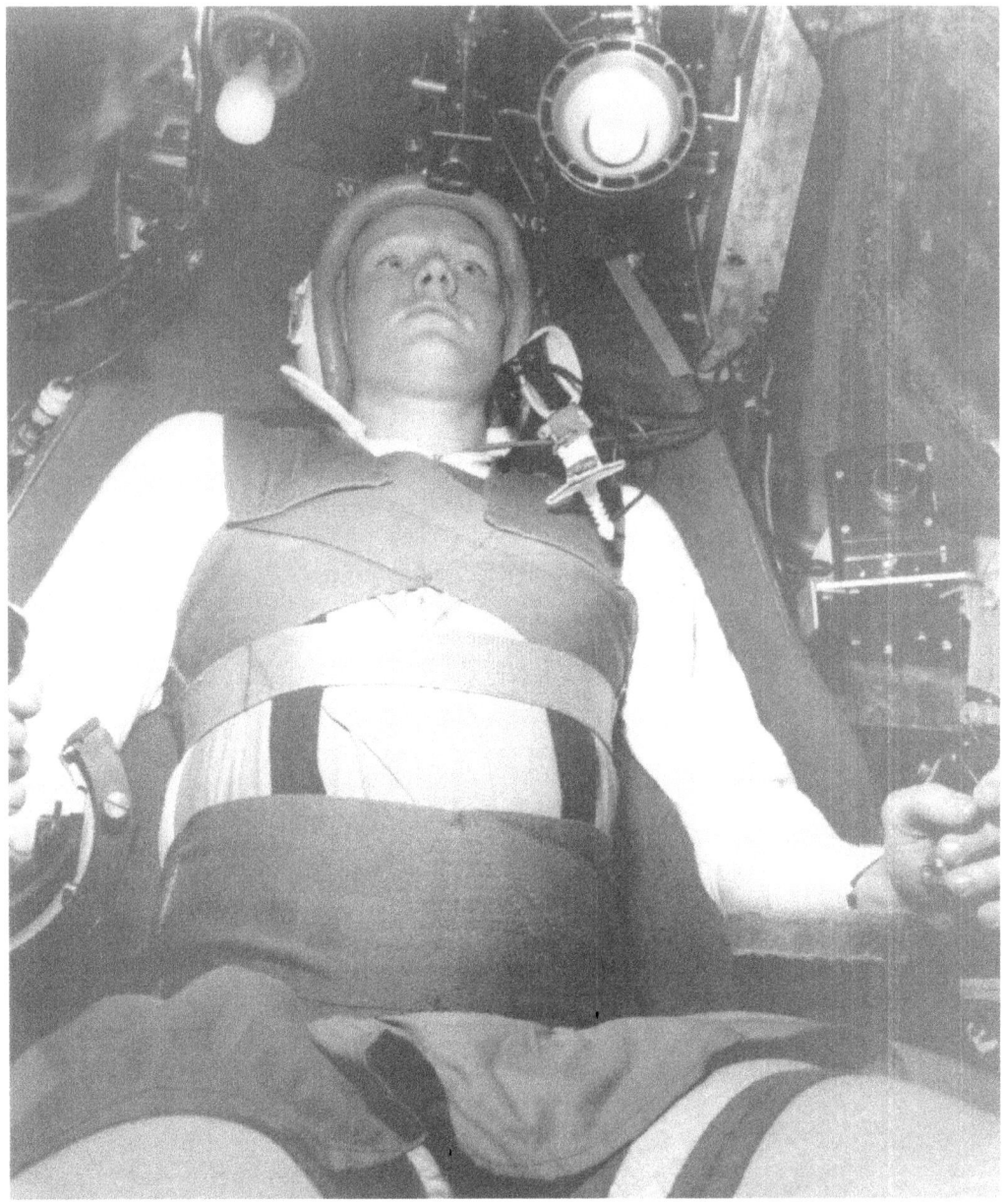

Neil Armstrong in the Boost Program Restraint Straps (December 1959). (NASA photo E-5040)

The first two fixed-based simulations at the FRC were in preparation before we went to Johnsville, Pennsylvania. This is where we got everything ready, including fine tuning the equations, the instrument panel and related switches and controls, the pre-programmed flight paths (for both the four- and two-stage versions), and building the three-axis side-arm controller to be used in the centrifuge.

The simulation lab at Johnsville was over half a mile from the centrifuge building. Since I had to be in the computer lab during the actual runs, I never really had a front-row seat during any of our simulation runs. We did have intercom, but this just wasn't the same as being there when the centrifuge was in motion. I did get to see the centrifuge in action, though. Our scheduled time period for using the centrifuge followed a study by the Ames Research Center. That study took longer than planned, because bad weather prevented the Ames group from flying. Its investigation involved comparison between actual flight and simulated flight and required the pilots to make a run or series of runs in the centrifuge and to then fly those same pre-planned flights in an actual airplane. I did get to watch several of those ARC "flights" in the centrifuge.

Compared to our study, their centrifuge runs were boring.

Anomalies/Aborts

There were times that I was glad that I wasn't in the centrifuge building. During each simulation run, I had to do the actual staging. This was done using two multi-wafer switches that changed the many parameters needing to be altered for each of the four stages. I would stand in front of the computer console and watch a timer. At the appropriate staging times I would switch to the next stage. In addition, I had also to input random flight anomalies. These anomalies were wind-shear, time-delays for rocket ignition, or other related inputs. Many of these happened during the first-stage burn or at staging between first and second stages. These were designed to see how the pilots could cope with such anomalies while under the stress of piloting the vehicle

On several occasions, the pilots lost control and the vehicle would deviate off course. When this happened, the gondola would hit one of the physical or electrical stops that were built in to prevent damage. The centrifuge would immediately shut down, the gondola would "snap back" to its home position, slow down, and then stop. This "home" position was with the pilot sitting up rather than with the pilot lying on his back. This immediate rotation of the pilot seat to an upright position was quite a jolt to the pilots. Fortunately they were well restrained in the seat with wide web belts over their legs and torso, and their helmets were restrained to prevent sudden movement. All this restraint was necessary because of the high accelerations during the typical run in the centrifuge. Nevertheless, I was the one they blamed when they lost control.

Patch-Panel Update

The old analog computer that we used did not originally have a patch panel. All components were originally connected using patch cords that varied in length from about 2 feet up to 50 feet. Each amplifier was built on a metal plate measuring about 8 inches by 19 inches. These amplifiers and all the other components were mounted in standard-equipment 19-inch racks (of that era), which were about 12 feet high. A ladder was a necessary piece of equipment during the process of wiring up a simulation. There were actually two of these computers. I believe the one we used was named Typhoon. The other one was named Cyclone, and the two computers had originally had been identical in configuration. The Typhoon had just recently been modernized and a patch panel had been added. Now, all the components could be connected using a patch panel and patch cords very similar to the EAI analog computers we had in the FSL. The patch panels were not silk-screened to help identify the location of the components, which made patching an interesting chore—kind of like putting a jigsaw puzzle together that has nothing printed on the pieces. Several of the programmers from the facility had been assigned to help us, and they did all of the patching. It was our simulation, but it was their computer and we were not really allowed to touch the hardware, which was probably a good thing.

Everything else in the Typhoon computer was as originally built, with the exception of a couple of recently added high-precision resolvers. (A resolver was a multiplier where one input was an angle and the output product was the sine [or cosine] of that angle multiplied by a second input.) A ladder was still needed to set the many pots used in the simulations. Actually, there were two complete sets of pots, which could be switched (all at once) to allow two different sets of parameters. This feature made for a quick switchover to a second set of coefficients. We never used this feature for our simulation.

The amplifiers were ±100-volt units, but were capable of over ±150 volts. Each amplifier had a small red light that came on when the output voltage exceeded about 120 volts. On almost every run, a number of these lights would come on. In spite of this, the computer seemed to be working OK. I don't remember ever re-scaling any of the parameters to eliminate these overloads. We just worked with the scale factors we had used during the earlier fixed-base simulations. The local programmers seemed to take this in stride as an everyday experience. Apparently they only re-scaled if the outputs exceeded 150 volts most of the time. The circuitry that was needed to do the coordinate transformation for the centrifuge motions and forces was mechanized by the local programmers and was generally the same for each simulation that used the centrifuge. I suspect that a few of the red lights (amplifier overloads) were from the amplifiers in this circuitry. They weren't worried, so we just accepted it too.

Rocket Staging

Switching of equation parameters (for each rocket stage) was accomplished using two specially built manual stepping switches. These switches were ganged four-position rotary devices, mounted inside a small metal box with the appropriate number of plug holes for the patch cords. During each simulation run, I watched a timer and turned by hand the two stepping switches by one position at each of the correct staging times. This changed the parameters (by switching pots) that needed to be changed for the next stage. This included such parameters as weight, thrust, fuel flow, inertias, and stability derivatives to correspond to the particular stage. There were about a dozen individual wafers (switches) in each box. I also had a number of other switches to throw to introduce anomalies such as windshear, ignition delays, and thrust misalignments.

The fourth time we implemented this simulation, back in the FSL, the stepping switches had been rebuilt and used an electric stepping motor to switch positions. Analog circuits to generate and measure time and provide the necessary switch-motor inputs replaced the manual switching that I had previously done. But I still had to be there to throw the other switches.

Most of my memories of this particular simulation have to do with the long hours I had to put in. There were seven pilots, but only one of me. I had to be in the simulation lab during all of their runs. Videan, Musick, Bill Andrews, and Ed Holleman were normally in the sim lab with me, but they also got to go watch the centrifuge runs. Towards the end of our stay, those of us in the sim lab were working 12- and 16-hour work shifts. We got up, ate breakfast, went to work, worked the morning shift, ate lunch at the base cafeteria, worked the afternoon shift, ate dinner (fortunately we had to go out, since the base cafeteria was not open for dinner), came back and worked another shift. Then we went back to our motel rooms, slept, and started it all over again—day after day after day, including several Saturdays and Sundays. The pilots came and went according to their individual schedules. They actually got bored between their turns in the simulator.

Ames Delay

The Johnsville facility had never previously scheduled two back-to-back analog simulations that both required the centrifuge. We learned the hard way. The change-over period between when the Ames folk left and the time we could really get running was almost a week. This time was spent in reprogramming the analog computer and in re-configuring the cockpit with a new seat and instrument panel. We never knew from day to day just when Ames was going to be finished, so we spent almost two weeks, day by day, waiting for our chance to get started. Once we got started, we worked our tails off to make up for this lost time. Getting the cockpit changed over took a lot more time than reprogramming the analog. We had everything ready in the analog computer lab. It only took a couple of days to check out the simulation and have it ready for when the cockpit was ready. We had lots of help from the folks in the simulation lab.

At the time, we were so busy getting ready that I never really gave much thought to the analog computers we were using. They were at least 15 years old, at the time, and still in use. The amplifiers were chopper stabilized, and these choppers were no longer being built. (The chopper was a device that helped to keep the amplifier stabilized. The vacuum tube amplifiers of those days would "drift" [deviate] due to the heat they generated.[15]) The lab had two full-time technicians who had the job of rebuilding these choppers. That is essentially all they did. They would disassemble and replace worn out parts with new parts that they manufactured in their own shop! They couldn't even buy these parts. They had to make whatever was needed. Amazing! We kept the analog computers we bought for the X-15 simulation for about 10 years, and we thought those analogs were really old and out of date when we finally surplused that equipment.

TDY Pay

In addition to the seven pilots, there were six more of us, all involved with the simulation in some way, all on travel status. Travel expenses in those days were quite meager. We were allowed $12.00 a day per diem (for both lodging and meals) for the first two weeks, $11.00 a day for the next two weeks, $10.00 a day for the following two weeks, and $9.00 a day thereafter. I guess the government expected those on TDY to rent an apartment if they were going to be on travel for extended periods. Since Ed Videan and I were there for 7 weeks, we were getting only $9.00 a day for that last week. The motel room I was sharing with Ed Holleman cost me $8.00 (plus tax) a night. I essentially lived on my own salary. I actually had to move out of my apartment in Lancaster so that I could afford to make that trip. Dick Musick and Ed Videan stayed at the BOQ at the Navy's Willow Grove Station, just down the street from the Howard Johnson's Motel the rest of us roomed at. They only paid about $3.00 a night for their quarters. That was a Navy Reserve training facility. I thought about doing this, but chose not to. It was too much like my old college dorm—small rooms, central bathroom facilities, etc. Maybe if I had been married and had kids (like Ed and Dick) I might have been more inclined to stay there. The motel room was satisfactory with me.

Government travel in those days was not something to look forward to. On top of this, the finance officer (John Yoshida) at the FRC would only send me one week's travel advance at a time. Getting these checks (and my paychecks) cashed back there was quite a chore. These were both government checks. Yet, I have never had so much trouble getting government checks cashed as there, just north of Philadelphia—the founding seat of our nation's government. Who would have thought it? Fortunately, Forrest Peterson had just recently gotten an American Express (AE) travel credit card. (AE had started its credit card service only the year before.) We were able to use this to get checks cashed at the motel office. I was so impressed with this, I sent away for my very own AE credit card as soon as I got home from this trip. This was in 1959 and credit cards such as Diners, AE, and Carte Blanc were new and not yet accepted all over. I used my AE card for both personal

---

[15] For a complete technical definition of analog computer amplifier drift, see the book by Rajko Tomovic and Walter J. Karplus, *High Speed Analog Computers* (New York: John Wiley & Sons, Inc., 1962), or any of the other sources on analog computers that are referenced in that book.

and government travel purposes for many years—until I retired 34 years later.

The Fun Stuff—Before the Hard Work

In spite of these long hours and meager travel expenses, all of us who were there still talk about this simulation. It was unique for the FRC. It was fun (at times). While we were waiting for Ames to get through, we did have some time to do some sightseeing. We soon found all the really great eating places in the area, including Bookbinders (famous for great seafood) in Philadelphia. Otto's, a German-style beer Haus, with an outdoor patio, for use when the weather was nice, was also very popular. Otto's served large steins of a variety of good German beers. Great goulash and Wienerschnitzel, too. Most of us stayed at a Howard Johnson's that had its own cafe. We ate breakfast there almost every morning, and after several weeks of this, the waitresses always had a large table already set up when we showed up for breakfast.

There was a par three pitch-and-putt golf course that we were able to play in the evenings during the first couple of weeks we were there, before the extra long work shifts began. We were back there over the Memorial Day holiday, and because the base was closed that day, Dick Musick and I drove over to Valley Forge and spent most of the day looking around there. Interesting! Especially since I later found out that a number of my distant forefathers (second generation Waltmans, including the Waltman I am descended from) were at Valley Forge with George Washington during the Revolutionary War. One Sunday, several of us rode the local commuter train into Philadelphia and sat through a double-header at the Phillies' baseball stadium.

Several of the bosses, who happened to be on travel in the area, stopped and visited with us to see the centrifuge simulation. I remember Deputy Center Chief De Beeler stopping by on at least two occasions. We also got to know and become friends with many of the folks at the lab. The doctor assigned to our project, Randy Chambers, invited us all over to his house one Sunday afternoon for an outdoor barbecue dinner.

The Old Mill

There was one particular restaurant, in the little community of Hatboro, only a couple of miles south of the lab, that we all got to know quite well. This restaurant was named The Old Mill. That is exactly what it had been. It was a converted grain mill, with a water wheel, on a small creek. There was a large glassed porch overlooking the creek that was very pleasant, especially for Sunday brunch. The main dinning hall was on the ground floor, which was where the large grinding wheels had been located. The ceiling beams were large and at just the right height to hit your head, if you didn't duck. This restaurant had just started a Thursday evening all-you-can-eat buffet dinner the first week we were back there. We quickly made this buffet our favorite place for Thursday's dinner. The food was both excellent and varied. Several of the folk from the lab joined us on more than one occasion. So, too, did the FRC bosses who happened to be on travel to Headquarters and stopped by to see the centrifuge runs. I remember De hitting his head on the overhead beams at least twice the first time he went there with us.

We also had many other meals, and drinks, at the Old Mill. In fact the bartender, who also happened to be the owner, was nice enough to drive over and pick us up for one last dinner before we left. We had the FRC C-47 with us and had finished up our work on a Thursday. We were intending to fly out on Friday morning. We had already turned in the two GSA cars we were using and had no other transportation. Dick Musick had already left for New Jersey to pick up his family for the drive home. There were still eight of us left, sitting around our motel rooms that Thursday evening, when Roger Barnicki got the idea to call the owner and ask him if he would give us a ride to his Old Mill for one last buffet. And, by golly, he did. But then we had spent so much money there I guess he felt he owed us this courtesy.

If you ask any one of us who participated in this particular simulation just what we remember most about the area, I'm quite sure that all will mention the Old Mill. It was definitely one of the bright spots in our stay at Johnsville. I heard later that our last dinner was also the last time the buffet was served. It's hard to believe that the 10-15 people in our Thursday night dinner groups were that critical in the life of these dinners. We certainly enjoyed them. So, in spite of the many long hours in the sim lab, we did have a few pleasant times. We still talk about this trip, even now, whenever we happen to see each other.

The Simulation

The group from the FRC consisted of Ed (Euclid) Holleman and Bill Andrews, who were the research engineers conducting the study, Ed Videan, Dick Musick and myself (Gene Waltman) from the FRC Simulation Laboratory, Roger Barnicki from the pilot's equipment office, and Neil Armstrong, Stan Butchart and Forrest Peterson, the FRC pilots.

Ed Videan and I flew out a week early to help get the simulation ready. Dick Musick drove his own car with his family and left them with relatives in New Jersey. The others from the FRC flew out in its C-47. They also used this plane to go to the Langley Research Center and pick up the foam inserts that the pilots used in the gondola's cockpit. These inserts were of a Styrofoam-type plastic, light but cumbersome because of their size. They provided extra protection during the high-G runs. I doubt, if we were to do this simulation over, that these foam inserts would be used today. Modern fighter-type airplanes subject pilots to similar G forces, and they do not use individually fitted foam inserts in the pilots' seats.

Toward the end of the simulation runs, we began to experiment with higher G-force runs. We multiplied the signals that determined the G force the pilot experienced by two. This meant that the pilots would be subjected to twice the G forces of the normal launch. Their bodies were not exactly prone, but with a 15-degree heads-up tilt. At the higher G forces, the blood drained out of their heads due to this 15-degree angle, and their field of view became quite narrow (like tunnel vision). I remember Neil Armstrong saying that at 14+ Gs, the only instrument he could still see clearly was the one meter that provided the error signal they used to guide the vehicle. This meter was in the center of the instrument panel. (See photo E-4550.)

Error Signal Mechanization

We used a standard ILS (Instrument Landing System) meter to display error signals in two directions. If the pilot flew the correct (launch to orbit) path, the error signals would be zero. The "correct path" had been determined during the early simulation studies at the FSL. This path was either the desired flight path, or the desired pitch angle. We used a special function generator to provide this signal as input during the simulation runs. This function generator was actually an 11-inch by 17-inch X-Y flatbed plotter. The required trace was first plotted on paper (desired flight path or desired pitch angle versus velocity) and then this trace was covered with a special "ink" that was conductive. This ink was a silver paint, and the pen was replaced with an electrical pickup that would sense an electrical signal in the ink. This signal was applied to the metallic ink trace through connectors attached with a metallic solder-like adhesive. Vehicle velocity as computed during the simulation runs was used to drive the plotter arm (in the X direction), and the pen would follow the ink trace in the Y (or vertical) direction. This signal was then used to generate the error signal for the ILS instrument the pilots used during each flight. What a kludge!

Looking back on what we had to do to get this special function generator operational, along with the black-box switches used for manual staging, and those really old NADC analogs, I am reminded of those old cartoons of the Rube Goldberg contraptions.[16] It is amazing that there was any repeatability in simulations of this nature. Another simulation, of similar Rube Goldberg construction, that comes to mind is the lunar lander simulation that Larry Caw put together several years later. The LLRV simulation was by far the most Rube-Goldberg-like that I can remember being mechanized at the FSL. If Erector Sets and Tinkertoys were your kind of toys when you were growing up, then analog computers were the thing for you. This is what made analog computers fun to program. It helped to be something of a masochist, too. I feel sorry for (digital) computer programmers who have never had the chance to program an analog computer. Since I did both while at the FRC, I can easily say that programming a digital computer is boring compared to programming an analog computer. They are as different as Tinkertoys and Pick-Up Sticks.

Upside-Down Centrifuge Run

Not only did many of the pilots fly the high-G runs, but so too did a representative from the company that had designed and manufactured the restraint system that was used to secure the pilots in the cockpit seat. These straps can be seen in photo E-5040. This manufacturer's representative not only flew the simulation in the normal manner, but he also had the gondola re-positioned such that the G force would be in the opposite direction—with his body being forced out against the straps. He was that sure the straps would support him at 14+ Gs. I believe we mechanized a simple autopilot that flew the mission for him so that he did not have to do that task. He went along just for the ride. Gutsy! But he was right. There were no problems. I would have liked to have seen that run.

We had lots of problems with the weather. There were several violent thunderstorms that came through the area during our centrifuge runs. There was quite a lot of lightning, and there were several power outages. On these occasions, we had to shut down rather than chance an outage while the centrifuge was moving. The few times we had a power outage during a run, the centrifuge would just coast to a stop, with the gondola in the rest position. There were no back-up power generators. We just had to wait till the storms moved on. The gondola did not always return to the staging dock after a power outage. When this happened, the technicians in the centrifuge lab would have to bring out a special platform to get the pilot out of the cockpit.

There were several reports or papers written about this simulation. The paper entitled "Utilization of the Pilot in the Launch and Injection of a Multistage Orbital Vehicle" (Citation 289) by Euclid Holleman, Neil Armstrong, and William Andrews, presented at the IAS 28th Annual Meeting in New York City in January 1960, is the most complete. One of the photos (E-4870) was taken during the centrifuge study. The photo (E-4548) of the couch was taken in the FSL during the last fixed-base simulation, which followed the centrifuge study.

The couch used for the fixed-based simulations was built of plywood in the FRC model shop. Roger Barnicki had one of the AFFTC's shops do the upholstery for us—a really nifty tuck-and-roll royal blue Naugahyde upholstery job that would have made those who ever had similar upholstery in their old '50s classic

---

[16] Rube Goldberg was a cartoonist known for his comical drawings of very complex machines that did very simple tasks. For more information and examples of his artwork, see the web site: http://www.rube-goldberg.com/

hot-rods drool with envy. We kept this couch long after the boost simulations were over. Some employees would occasionally spend their lunch breaks sacked out on it. Great on-the-job anti-stress therapy. I wonder where it went. It just disappeared one day.

The trip home from Johnsville was another interesting experience in itself. Two whole days, flying west, in the C-47. We refueled in Indianapolis, the first day, and spent the night in El Paso. Apparently it was customary for the FRC pilots who were returning from duties back east and who had to lay over somewhere to do so in El Paso. El Paso was just across the river from Juarez, Mexico. Booze bought there and brought back into the U.S. did not have liquor taxes added to the total price, providing you did not exceed a limit of two bottles per person. Consequently, we all were requested to help the pilots carry back as much booze as we were allowed to carry. I don't remember which pilot paid for the whiskey, but all eight of us marched across the footbridge to a small liquor shop in Juarez, bought our quota, and trudged back to the hotel with our duty-free booze. I think the toll for the footbridge across the Rio Grande was two cents per person. A fitting conclusion to a very interesting simulation experience.

The X-15 Simulator (1960-1969)

The X-15 simulator was the largest analog simulation ever mechanized in the FSL. It also became the first hybrid computer simulation when we added a digital computer to the simulator in 1964. The simulator was in use from 1961 until after the last X-15 flight on 24 October 1968. This simulation was used for many purposes, including pilot training, flight planning, systems hardware design and checkout, emergency procedures development and practice, and many different research programs. From the programmers' perspective it was, in many ways, the most complicated and frustrating mechanization that we had to contend with. For most of us who had to deal with it on a daily basis, we were both glad and sad to see it go. The X-15 Project was both exciting and rewarding, and the simulator played a big part in the overall accomplishments of the program. For that reason we were glad to be a part of the X-15 team. By the same token, we were sad to see the X-15 simulator go, in spite of all the grief it had inflicted over the years. It was like losing a favorite pet, even though that pet was part gremlin.

There were numerous different programmers involved with this simulation throughout its lifetime. John P. Smith began the process by working with the project office to select the original set of equations for implementation. He also worked on the procurement of the new analog computers. Much of this early preparation work was done using the North American Aviation (NAA) X-15 simulation as a guide. Shortly after John began this process, he was promoted to section chief. At that time he passed the X-15 programming job along to me. The computers had already been ordered by then and were installed in the fall of 1960. This was right after I had finished the fourth and last simulation of the four-stage boost vehicle, which is described above.

NAA X-15 Simulator

North American Aviation built the three X-15 rocket-powered aircraft. NAA implemented an analog simulation for use in designing and developing the vehicles. The simulator was used for some time and included the iron-bird cockpit. The X-15 simulation at the NAA facility near Los Angeles International Airport was used for flight planning for the initial 20 flights of the X-15. Dick Day spent a considerable amount of time there during 1959 and 1960 for this flight planning and for pilot training purposes. During this period, the original engineering analysis was done that resulted in the removal of the lower vertical stabilizer on the aircraft.[17] Dick Day also recalls that upon his proposing to have the ventral fin removed, Bikle said "Dick, pilots have always wanted more tail and now you want to take it away." The first flight with the lower ventral removed was the 42th flight on 4 October 1961. The NAA simulator was used for these and other purposes for the first 31 flights. The initial envelope expansion flight planning was also completed with the NAA X-15 simulator.

Computer Room False Floor

The computers used for the FRC's X-15 simulation were installed in the area currently occupied by the Center Director's office and conference room. A false floor was built, in-house, of 2x4s, plywood, angle iron, and metal rebar (reinforcing metal bars). It was covered with an ugly brown linoleum tile. Holes

---

[17] The large, wedge-shaped vertical stabilizers on the X-15 were a solution to the difficulty of stabilizing an airplane at high angles of attack. The lower half of the lower vertical stabilizer had to be jettisoned before landing because it extended below the landing gear, and eventually the X-15 team (notably, Dick Day as discussed below) discovered that it was not really needed for stability and in fact made the airplane less controllable, so the program stopped using it.

were cut where needed for the circulation of cold air and for the many cables between the computer racks. The design of this false floor made it quite difficult to string cables. The under-the-floor support structure was a lot like a cheap bridge and really interfered with getting our analogs connected. Years later, the good store-bought false flooring materials were installed, but not in the X-15 analog area. One of the photos (see E-5808) showing the X-15 analog computers was taken before the plywood flooring was covered with linoleum. The linoleum was standard GSA supply and obviously not intended for fancy offices. It was thin and flexible and molded itself to the uneven plywood floor. You could even see the nail heads in the plywood under the tiles. After being used for several years, it became quite worn and always looked dirty, no matter how often it was cleaned. This lab was where we did some serious work and was not one of the fancy "glass-walled" computer rooms that some companies had for their big, fancy digital computers. That ugly brown tile floor was somewhat symbolic in that sense.

The analog computer air conditioning (A/C) units were mounted on the roof directly above the X-15 simulation lab. Large holes were cut in the raised floor, ceiling, and roof for the air ducts. The A/C units were located in an aluminum shack for weather protection. There were two large blowers in the X-15 analog room to distribute the cold air. These blowers were in sheet-metal boxes. The fans in them were large and, when the bearings wore out, got very noisy. The blower boxes were about three feet tall and were used as tables for many different items. Because of the large amount of heat generated by the analog computers, the air temperature in this room would get quite warm in the afternoons. In the mornings, though, it was very chilly before we turned the analogs on and all those vacuum tubes started to heat up.

Wiring Diagrams

It took the last three months of 1960 to do all the tasks involved with the actual mechanization of the X-15 simulation. This included drawing the wiring diagrams, wiring the three main patch panels, setting all the pots, programming the many function generators, and running many types of tests for check-out. It was the wiring diagrams for the X-15 simulation that forced me to convert from large drafting paper to 11x17-inch drawing paper (see above). There was one page for each of the main equations, and there were many more for the auxiliary equations. The many function generators required several pages of their own. Later on, when we were simulating the two different control systems, several more pages were added for those equations. It was quite a chore to keep this folder of wiring diagrams up to date. It was too easy to make temporary wiring changes and forget to make the appropriate changes to the wiring diagrams. This happened quite frequently and caused many problems.

The simulation was declared fully operational on the first working day of 1961 (which was Tuesday, 3 January 1961). The first X-15 flight that occurred after this date was number 32, which was on 1 February 1961 and was flown by Jack McKay.

When we went to two and three shifts of operation, with a different analog programmer on each shift, the accuracy of this folder of wiring diagrams became an important issue that we all had to deal with. This was especially true for the second-shift programmers, since that was the shift when the research engineers were always trying new things. The day shift was used almost exclusively for flight planning and pilot training. Fortunately the shifts overlapped one-half hour, which allowed the oncoming crew to get a brief update from the departing crew about any changes that had been made.

In spite of all this coordination between programmers and careful diligence to keeping the wiring diagrams correct, there were many instances of unlabeled, loose, or missing patch cords. We were always searching for one more missing patch cord or the one that shouldn't have been there (according to the diagrams). Fortunately these computers were not time-shared with any other program. This meant that the patch panels were not removed from their patch bays very often. This process of changing patch panels was often the reason for loose or dislodged patch cords. If the wired panel was accidentally set down on a small object, such as a pencil, one or more of the patch cords could be pushed loose from the backside of the panel. And it wasn't always obvious until something did not work as expected.

Function Generator Set-up

A large portion of this three-month set-up time was spent in programming the many nonlinear diode-function generators (DFGs). The DFGs were used to generate functions of angle-of-attack (AOA). These were then connected to the taps on the pot-padder multipliers that were driven by Mach number. The resulting outputs were functions of both AOA and Mach number.

The DFGs used for this simulation were not the store-bought version available from EAI. These DFGs were designed and built in-house and installed in standard 19-inch racks. They can be seen in the photo E-5809 and were located between the D and E consoles. There were 15 pots for each DFG. The pots were the 20-turn type, quite small, and were set using a small jeweler's screwdriver instead of a knob. It was quite a chore to set all these pots. We also had some of the EAI DFGs and pot padders for other nonlinear functions.

Nonlinear Functions Updates

During the first part of the X-15 program, the data used for the nonlinear functions came mostly from wind-tunnel tests and theoretical studies. As the X-15 flew, and the collected flight data were analyzed, the coefficients in the X-15 simulation were modified to agree with true flight-determined data. In this way, the simulator was kept up-to-date and became an even more useful tool.

SAS & Adaptive Controllers

One of the most useful features of any iron-bird simulator was the capability to connect actual flight hardware and use it just as it would be used in the real aircraft. The fixed-gain Stability Augmentation System (SAS) and the variable-gain Minneapolis Honeywell (M-H) Adaptive Controller were the two different control systems that were initially simulated as a part of the X-15 simulation. Later, the simulator used actual hardware just like what was installed in the real airplanes. There were many reports written about these various studies. The report *Adaptive Control and the X-15*, written by Lawrence W. Taylor and Elmer J. Adkins in1965, describes the M-H Adaptive Controller, its development, and the role of the X-15 simulator. The authors commented: "It should be emphasized that all of the problems were encountered and corrected before the flight article existed, by virtue of the extensive and realistic simulation possible with the X-15 flight simulator," indicating yet another use of analog simulations. In this case, the concept and design of the adaptive-control and stability-augmentation-system capabilities were thoroughly tested using the simulator before any actual hardware was built and flown. Both the SAS and the M-H Adaptive Controller required many hours of simulation time during the design and testing phases of their development.

A lot of this simulator time occurred on second shift with Jim Samuels (one of the FSL programmers) working with the research engineers to mechanize and test the different X-15 stability-augmentation systems. Jim was the only FSL analog programmer, during those early years, who had a college degree in aerodynamics. He was the one we all turned to when we had questions concerning the equations of motion or matters relating to aerodynamics. Jim was a happy-go-lucky person who enjoyed regaling us with tall (real tall!) tales of his (supposed) past experiences. According to him, he was a combination of Indiana Jones, Sir Francis Drake, and Kit Carson. Jim was very imaginative and would creates his stories on the fly. If you added up the time spans of all these adventures, Jim would have had to have been at least 150 years old to have done all the things he told us.

Simulator Cockpits

The first cockpit we had for this simulator was the one used for the full-scale X-15 simulation on the Navy's computers and centrifuge at the Johnsville, Pennsylvania, facility. That simulation was operational long before we had our computers. All of the original X-15 pilots were able to fly the simulator and experience the G loads expected in the real flights. The hardware we got at the FRC included the seat, the instrument panel, and the pilots' controls. Later on, we also received the full-scale iron-bird simulator from North American.

This iron bird was a replica of the X-15, including the complete cockpit, and had simulated control surfaces (rudder, elevator, and ailerons). The control surfaces were simulated using weighted beams, but the hydraulics and other components were the real things. This eliminated having to simulate those mechanical and hydraulic components. (See photos E-4969, E-5808-10, E-15330 & E-16219 of the computers, cockpit, and the X-15 iron bird.)

The first cockpit was installed in the same room as the analog computers. We used this cockpit for many months until the iron bird could be delivered and installed. The iron bird was located inside the calibration hangar along the east wall. A wall was built around the iron bird to divide the hangar and provide the security and protection needed for this project. The windows in the hangar door had to be painted over to eliminate the glare on the instrument-panel meters. The cockpit faced away from the hangar door. The door faced southeast and the morning sunlight caused a lot of problems for the pilots until the windows were painted.

Black Box (F-104) Cockpit (October 1959), "flown" in preparation for the X-15. (NASA photo E-4969)

X-15 Simulator (Iron Bird) with Bill Dana (August 1966). (NASA photo E-15530)

X-15 Simulator (Iron Bird) with Bill Dana (August 1966). (NASA photo E-16219)

Patch Cords and Trunks

We never kept a count of the total number of patch cords used in this simulation, but there were at least 500 on each of the three main analog computers. With that many patch cords, the panels weighed a lot. Later on, other analog computers were added, as needed, for special purposes, such as control-system development and interface to the digital computer. We had as many as six analog computers connected together at one time. The main three computers were used for the basic equations, two for control-system simulations, and later on another one was needed for the interface to the SDS 930 digital computer (see below). They were connected together with hundreds of signal trunks. There were at least two occasions when—for some small short-term experiment—one of the portable analog computers was also connected to the simulation. There were also many trunks to connect to the cockpit.

Cockpit Trunking

After the iron bird was installed in the hangar, we had to connect it to the computers. There were several hundred trunks to/from the cockpit. These trunks were routed in cable trays originally hung on the outside wall of the second floor of the mezzanine. These went to the X-15 iron bird. The trunks eventually were relocated to cable trays that hung above the false ceiling of the mezzanine offices.

This length of trunks (over 200 feet) for that many analog signals always caused difficulties due to grounding problems. In fact, grounding problems were a real headache for a number of years in our simulation lab. The FSL technicians spent a lot of time working this particular problem. A separate grounding buss of copper pipes and large copper wires was eventually installed to help alleviate grounding problems. The copper pipes were under the false floors of the simulation labs and were mounted on special stands that provided signal isolation. Large-core copper wires were then attached to these pipes and to the computers and equipment racks as needed. These large-core copper wires were also strung to the cockpit(s) in the labs or in the hangar. The pipe and wires were all shielded with a thick plastic covering.

X-15 Simulator Hydraulics

The hydraulics stand for the iron-bird cockpit was originally located next to the mockup inside the hangar. The hydraulics unit was later relocated into its own shed, outside the Calibration Hangar. As with the early black-box simulators, someone from the facilities maintenance group had to start and stop the hydraulics unit. On second and third shift, we sometimes waited 30 minutes or more after calling before he would show up and power up the hydraulics. We also had to allow time for him to shut down the hydraulics before we left at the end of the night shift.

The X-15 simulator was used so much during the day shift by the pilots and the flight-planners that we frequently had a second shift for use by the research engineers, and especially those developing the different control systems that were being investigated for use in the X-15s. Later, after a general-purpose digital computer was added to the simulation, almost all of the time needed for programming of this digital computer was on third shift (midnight to 8:00 a.m.).

Earlier X-15 Simulations

The X-15 had been simulated using analog computers at other facilities before we started our simulation. Besides North American's complete 6 DOF analog simulation described above, the Ames Research Center had a simulator that used a 3 DOF moving-base cockpit. The Langley Research Center also implemented a fairly complete simulation but without the iron-bird cockpit. The centrifuge at NADC was also used for X-15 simulations, as already discussed in part. There were actually three different such simulations at both the LaRC and NADC during the years in which the X-15 was being designed and built. There were several conferences having to do with the X-15 development beginning in the mid-1950s. Some of this happened before I started working at the NACA HSFS in 1957. Each simulation, as you might expect, got better and better as the development of the X-15 progressed. Our simulation took a lot from those earlier efforts, and it too evolved over the years.

The digital computer added in 1964 was used to generate the nonlinear coefficients for the re-built No. 2 X-15. This was the X-15 that was damaged during an emergency landing on one of the back-up landing sites. The airplane was rebuilt, with external tanks and other modifications for the higher-speed flights. Because of the modification to the No. 2 X-15, the original set of equations was also modified to include the additional dynamics due to the external tanks. John Perry was the lead programmer at the time, and he did this upgrade. This was after I had left the X-15 simulation group and was involved with other FSL projects.

Energy Management Computer

The SDS (Scientific Data Systems) 930 was originally bought to simulate an airborne computer that Minneapolis Honeywell was building for installation in the X-15-3. The M-H Energy Management Computer was designed to calculate the landing area (or footprint, as it was called) available to the X-15 in case of an early engine malfunction. This footprint was essentially a map of the surrounding ground area with dry lakebeds that the X-15 could land on. The footprint gave the pilot a schematic, shown on a scope in the cockpit, of the attainable landing sites based on the speed, altitude, weight, attitude, etc., of the X-15 at the time the engine shut down. If this engine shutdown was premature, the X-15 did not always have enough energy to make a landing at Edwards Air Force Base (EAFB), and the pilot (and control room personnel) had to make a quick decision as to which emergency landing site the pilot would head for. There were always several emergency landing sites selected, and they had emergency crews standing by in case of such an event.

Before the actual airborne M-H computer was built, there was an interim system built, under contract, to be used in the mission control room during flights. This Energy Management Console (EMC) was an all-analog unit. Unfortunately, the company that built it did not stay in business very long. The unit had lots of problems. Charles Wagner, one of the FSL simulation engineers, inherited the job of trying to make it work, right after he started working at the FRC in 1964. In his PA, Wagner describes his efforts with the unit. Wagner spent a lot of time getting the EMC unit to work, but by then it wasn't really needed. The mission control room personnel had enough experience from having used the simulator to predict the best emergency landing site, anyway.

The pilots spent a lot of time in the simulator practicing these emergency landings. There were ten of these real-life emergency landings that were required during the actual flights. Without the extensive practice in the simulator, there could easily have been several more-serious emergency landings than really did occur. I'm sure that each X-15 pilot who had to make an emergency landing was quite thankful for all the hours he spent in the simulator practicing those very same maneuvers. There is no doubt that this type of emergency-procedures practice is one of the big reasons that real-time simulators are still being built and used by all the major airlines.

A malfunction panel was added to the simulation after the iron bird was operational. This panel contained about 3 dozen switches that allowed the flight planners to turn off signals going to the X-15 cockpit instruments or to many of the aircraft systems, such as the auxiliary power units, SAS, M-H adaptive controller, reaction control system, and the engine. The pilots spent many hours practicing emergency procedures that could occur during their flights. A number of these emergencies did in fact occur, but the pilots were always able to cope and either continue the flight or make a more or less successful landing at one of the back-up lakebeds. Before the panel was installed next to the iron-bird cockpit, someone in the computer room initiated these "emergencies." The malfunction panel just made this task easier for the flight planners who frequently were there and sitting alongside the cockpit.

My tenure as lead X-15 sim programmer/operator lasted only a couple of years. Because of the multiple shifts needed to provide an adequate number of hours each week for the many users, several other FSL programmers very quickly became full-time X-15 sim operators and programmers. John Perry, Larry Wells, Jim Samuels (and others) were drafted to help operate and program the X-15 analogs. Dick Musick, Gerry Perry, Bill Sebastian, Art Suppona, Billy Davis (and others) were the sim technicians who supported the maintenance and development of the X-15 analogs and iron bird.

When I got very involved in programming the SDS 930, I was put on graveyard shift and John Perry took over as the lead X-15 analog programmer. The graveyard shift was the only time available for the SDS-930 programming activity. The first two shifts were used for pilot training and flight planning (day shift) and control-system studies (swing shift) and other such research studies that the FRC research engineers were involved in doing. Any time the second shift was not used for research studies, I gladly used that time for the SDS 930 programming. I much preferred swing shift to the later graveyard shift. I had a hard time getting enough sleep while working graveyard. It took a long time to adjust my internal clock to working a graveyard shift. It was also hard to find a car pool, to keep from having to drive the hour-and-a-half round trip to the FRC every day.

Monday Morning Blues

The daily operation of the X-15 simulator was quite a chore. We spent a lot of time each morning getting the simulator ready. Monday mornings were always the worst because of the time it took for the computers to warm up after a weekend of non-use. The X-15 Project Office quickly learned not to expect much "up-time" before noon on Mondays. It usually took us that long to get the analog computers warmed up and stabilized. There were several "checkout flights" that we (the X-15 sim operators) would fly to see if the simulation was ready to go. We all got quite proficient in flying these check flights—both in the first cockpit (the one we got from NADC) and later in the iron bird. After we installed the iron bird, daily checkout of the simulation became a two-person operation because of the distance between the cockpit and the analogs. Several of the technicians also got proficient in flying the checkout flights, while the operators were upstairs observing the analogs and various output displays in the sim lab. There was an intercom we used to talk back and forth between the sim lab and the iron bird.

Plotters and Strip-Chart Recorders

The analog computer output devices included several 8-channel strip-chart recorders and a large X/Y flatbed plotter. This X/Y plotter had two independent pens. One pen plotted the X-15's position on a map of the area. The second pen showed the X-15's altitude along a north-south axis. (See photo ECN-1456.) These two traces

Larry Caw with X-15 Simulation Analog Computer and Plotter (August 1966). (NASA photo ECN-1456)

were plotted on special maps that were made specifically for this job. These maps were also used on the mission control room's X/Y plotters during the actual flights. There were different maps depending on the launch site chosen for a particular flight. These maps showed the launch site and the emergency-landing dry lakebeds available for such landings and the dry lake at Edwards Air Force Base, along with the more prominent landmarks in the vicinity of these dry lakebeds. The plotter would take maps up to 36 inches in both directions. The maps we used were that size. The flight planners spent a lot of time draped over the edges of this plotter in our sim lab, looking at the traces. There were thousands of sim runs flown during the life of this project. The plotter had ink pens which caused many problems, as they tended to clog up when not used for some time (like over the weekend). The pens were also quite messy and got ink on everyone's elbows or shirtsleeves and ties. The plotter was just the right height to rest your elbows on. A lot of coffee got spilt there, too!

One of the jobs of the X-15 flight planners was to prepare for each flight, which included selecting the launch site and practicing emergency landings. Later in the program, the M-H energy management computer aided in the emergency-landing-site selection. The flight planners had to do this job as a part of each flight preparation. Flight planning also included the job of trying to integrate all the maneuvers the many research engineers wanted the pilots to perform during the flights. In addition, the flight planners were trying to "expand the envelope." This envelope expansion process was an important "step-by-step" investigation of the performance limits that the FRC has used in most all of its flight programs. There were several flight planners, over the years: Dick Day, Warren Wilson, Jack Kolf, and others from the FRC, and Bob Hoey from the AFFTC.

SDS 930

The X-15 sim was used for many years and underwent several major modifications. The first major mod was replacement of the initial cockpit with the iron bird. The next was the addition of a SDS 930 general-purpose digital computer. This was a state-of-the-art small-scale digital computer. It was originally intended to be used to simulate a special purpose airborne digital computer that M-H was building for the X-15 aircraft. We never programmed the SDS 930 for that particular job. Later, a special purpose computer was built to simulate the airborne M-H computer.

Originally, M-H had planned to build another of its airborne computers (just like the ones planned to go in the X-15) for use in the simulator. M-H was behind schedule and the extra airborne computer never got built. At about the same time, we in the FSL were thinking about buying a general-purpose digital computer to provide the extra function generation capability needed for the No. 2 X-15. When we learned of the M-H problem with its airborne computer, we offered to buy the digital computer and connect it to the X-15 simulator, provided that the Air Force buy us another analog computer and the interface equipment to connect the two different computer systems. The Air Force (AF; actually, it was an AF contractor that was also involved in the X-15 Project—Litton Data Systems as I recall) bought the interface equipment and had it delivered to us in the FSL. This simulator was not only a strange collection of hardware but also had an even stranger collection of participants. Many different companies around the U.S. were involved in the X-15 Project throughout its many years of existence.

I was sent to SDS programming class and set about programming this new set of non-linear functions for our real-time all-analog X-15 simulation. Combined analog/digital simulation techniques were just then being developed within the simulation community. This was a whole new ball game—an environment that no one at the FRC had any previous experience with. I had taken some introductory classes in hybrid (combined analog-digital) simulation at EAI and UCLA. So as the lead X-15 programmer, I had the job of integrating this new technology into our analog simulation. It took a while, but I did get the job done. The analog simulation was modified so that it could be switched between the old set of non-linear functions (using the analog function generators) and the new set of No. 2 X-15 digital functions. We now had an X-15 simulation that could be used for all three X-15s again.

SDS Fortran

The use of digital computers in hybrid simulations was still new. The Fortran programming language was also quite new, and very few computer vendors had a real-time Fortran compiler and run-time package available. Fortunately, many SDS customers were buying their computers for real-time applications. Consequently, there was a lot of pressure on SDS to develop a real-time Fortran (RTF) system. We acquired this system, which we used for a number of applications. This turned out to be quite a challenge, due almost exclusively to the state-of-the-art of real-time SDS software.

Real-time software packages (such as the RTF from SDS) were designed to respond to real-time interrupts from external events. There were several of these signals used in the simulation program on the SDS 930. The RTF, being so new, had many bugs in it. We found more than our share and spent many hours programming work-arounds until SDS fixed its software.

SDS 930 Characteristics

The original SDS 930 used 1.75-microsecond silicon-logic circuitry. It had 8K of 24-bit (word) memory. The memory was state-of-the-art iron-ferrite magnetic core. The CPU (central processing unit) had an arithmetic register, an index register, and an auxiliary arithmetic register. These three registers were 24-bit and used octal (3-bit)

arithmetic. The 930 was the first small pseudo-parallel computer of its time. Previous computers of that era, in this class, were serial computers. In serial computers, arithmetic and other operations were performed one bit at a time, in serial. The 930 actually used a combined serial, parallel process that did its operations on octal characters in a serial manner. This structure allowed the 930 to run about four times faster then the previous (SDS 920) computer, while using the same speed silicon logic. This was state-of-the-art in those days. Today, you can buy school calculators that are faster and have more memory than the 930 we used in our X-15 simulator.

The operating system was not memory-resident. It was loaded into memory whenever it was needed. The system software programs—Fortran, real-time Fortran, Assembler, Utilities, and Libraries—were all stored on magnetic tape. (Actually, the original system was delivered with all this software on paper tape. Was that ever slow!) We had one 8-track magnetic-tape unit, one card reader, one paper-tape reader and punch, and an IBM Selectric typewriter. These were the only input/output (I/O) units that came with the original SDS 930. No printer or cardpunch or hard disk. We did not add a line printer until some time later. The original program was written in the SDS Assembly language. All arithmetic and function generation was done using scaled fixed-point arithmetic. Because the operating system was on mag tape, we wrote the binaries of the programs we developed onto paper tape. It took over an hour to assemble and punch out (on paper tape) the original X-15 digital simulation program. It took several hours to list this program on the typewriter. It was probably a good thing that there was only one person programming the SDS 930 at that time, considering how long it took to get anything done.

Analog Interface

There were numerous D to A (digital to analog) and A to D (analog to digital) converters for input and output of the analog variables. There were priority interrupts and real-time clocks (connected to priority interrupts) that were used for timing and other signals that required the digital computer program to respond instantaneously. We also had a large number of single-bit on/off-type functions (which were called discretes) that could be connected to devices such as switches, lights, and relays. These discretes were connected to both the cockpits and the analog computers. This collection of interface devices allowed the two different types of computers to communicate with each other. We acquired another analog computer and added this to the X-15 simulation. This additional analog provided the connections to the digital computer. There wasn't any room on the original analogs to handle the additional circuitry and trunking required for the SDS 930. Later on, when we started to use the SDS 930 for other simulations, the availability of this interface analog computer made it quite easy to connect those simulations to the SDS 930.

X-15 Simulator Sidelights

Dick Day, one of the flight planners for the X-15 program, recalls the following:

> I can think of several interesting anecdotes that occurred while the X-15 simulator was still at NAA and we did our flight planning and training in Los Angeles.
>
> When [then-] Commander Pete Peterson [joined] the X-15 program, we had several training sessions for him at the NAA, Los Angeles, facility. There were periods during the training when Pete would become confused and suddenly pull all the way back on the side-arm controller, producing excessive indicated g-levels and halt the run. It was soon discovered that, at that time, the needle on angle-of-attack (alpha) indicators of the Navy airplanes that Pete had been flying read the reverse of the AF indicators, and every time there was a lightly damped or unstable alpha, Pete's correction was immediate and violent. Retraining Pete was unthinkable, so the solution to the problem was to reverse the polarity on the instrument both in simulator for training and on the actual X-15 for flight. This worked perfectly, Pete never PIO'd[18] again either in training or in flight. Of course, the instrument had to be reversed to the original polarity before a different pilot would fly. This is a prime example (and there are many more) of the early analog simulator's large role in safety-of-flight.

The X-15 simulator was not programmed to handle landings. The visual cues that the pilots normally used for landing any airplane (the out-the-window views) were not readily available and were quite expensive. In addition the precision needed to calculate parameters such as altitude and rate of climb/descent for landing studies was not really possible with the parameter scaling used for the rest of the flight. Analog computers were accurate to about one part in ten thousand. For the X-15 simulation, with altitude scaled such that 400,000 feet=100 volts, one tenth of a volt was equal to 40 feet. Any altitude less than this value would be down in the noise level of the analog components and barely detectable. It was not possible to accurately calculate altitudes for the landing phase of the X-15 within these scaling restrictions.

The pilots found that the F-104 could be configured to provide similar characteristics to the X-15 during the final approach and landing phases, and this became the preferred simulation method for landing practice. Larry Caw did, however, mechanize a simple 4 DOF simulation of the X-15 for studies of the X-15 landing gears.

---

[18] I.e., created a pilot induced oscillation of the airplane.

This simulation calculated the forces and moments that occurred during touchdown and rollout of the X-15.[19] This simulation was done at the request of Jim McKay. Jim was a research engineer at the FRC and, with Eldon Kordes, documents this study in a NASA Technical Memorandum (TMX-639, 1962, item 342 in the bibliography). This TM discusses landing loads and dynamics of the X-15 airplane. The paper talks about loads measured during actual landings of the X-15 and also discusses the purpose and results of the simulation. Early X-15 landings showed that the pilots landed the vehicle in a similar way on each flight. Because there was so little difference, an analog simulation study was conducted to study a wider variation of factors. The forces that occurred on the landing gear were quite significant because of the locations of the nose wheel and the rear skids. The moments that were generated by the locations of the nose wheel and rear skids caused larger forces than the actual touchdowns. After the initial touchdown on the rear skids, the nose would rotate downward and then slam down quite hard on the front wheel. The simulation was conducted to see if relocation or redesign of either part of the landing gear would reduce these loads. Changes were made to the landing gear over the years as the X-15 evolved, mainly due to increased weight.

X-15 Simulator Deficiencies

In 1964, Milt Thompson wrote a paper for a SETP conference entitled "General Review of Piloting Problems Encountered During Simulation and Flights of the X-15" (item 412 in the bibliography). In this paper, Milt talked about the differences between the simulator and the real aircraft and the problems that the pilots had to deal with because of them. Many of the differences were due to extra costs associated with including particular features or hardware and the decision(s) made to not include these additional features simply because they cost too much. For example, the cockpits did not provide any motions at all. The cost of adding six degrees of motion to the iron bird was prohibitive. Most of the first group of pilots did get to fly the simulations that were implemented using the centrifuge at the Johnsville, Pennsylvania, facility. However, the pilots who entered the program later did not fly the centrifuge simulation. This lack of real motion simulation caused some problems when these pilots actually flew the X-15s. In his paper, Milt said:

> Prior to my first flight, my practice had been done in a relaxed, head forward position. The longitudinal acceleration at engine light forced my head back into the headrest and prevented even helmet rotation. The instrument-scan procedure, due to this head position and a slight tunnel vision effect, was quite different than anticipated and practiced. The acceleration buildup during engine burn (4g max) is uncomfortable enough to convince you to shut the engine down as planned. This is the first airplane I've flown that I was happy to shut down.
>
> Engine shutdown does not always relieve the situation, though, since, in most cases, the deceleration immediately after shutdown has you hanging from the restraint harness, and in a strange position for controlling.

Milt went on to discuss other differences between flight and simulator, and concludes his report with the following paragraphs:

> Although relatively sophisticated fixed-base simulation of the X-15 was generally satisfactory for flight-mission studies and flight-envelope-controllability investiga-

---

[19] Since the X-15 used rear landing skids rather than conventional landing gear, the "rollout" was really more of a slideout.

tions, it was unable to predict all of the flight problems experienced, particularly when differences in aerodynamics, control system, or cockpit equipment existed between simulator and airplane. A constant updating of the simulator is therefore required. Absence of acceleration, motion, or visual cues in the simulator has limited the adequacy of pilot training for specific flight phases and sometimes resulted in surprises or in-flight problems.

The actual flight environment must still be investigated, since the effects of apprehension and anxiety on the pilot cannot yet be simulated. It is simple to evaluate a flight condition on a simulator, rate it subjectively, and reset when you lose control. Until a reset capability is provided in the airplanes, the success of a mission is still up to the pilot.

These words from Milt's paper point out the love-hate relationship that frequently existed between the pilots and the simulators. They really appreciated the simulations for what they did but were the most outspoken about what they didn't do. And heaven help us if there was something implemented incorrectly,[20] as happened on many occasions. It was at the insistence of the pilots that we got the money (directly or indirectly) to include those capabilities that originally were neither budgeted nor even considered. This paper by Milt is included in the appendices and is well worth reading in its entirety. I was not able to interview Milt for his inputs to this paper. He died only one week after I retired from NASA in 1993. I suspect that if I had been able to interview him, many of his comments would have been the same or similar to what is in that particular publication. Milt wrote a number of other publications during his career at the FRC, several of which are included in the bibliography.

---

[20] While reviewing this part of the study, Bob Kempel made the following comment: "We found in the lifting-body program that it was far better to give the pilots no impression . . . than [to give them] the wrong impression."

General Purpose Airborne Simulator (1960-1975)

In May 1960, the Center acquired a Lockheed JetStar, a small jet passenger transport, and equipped it with an onboard computer system to simulate the flight characteristics of a wide range of aircraft. The JetStar was also equipped with an electronic variable-stability flight-control system. It was called a General Purpose Airborne Simulator (GPAS), and the aircraft could duplicate the flight characteristics of a wide variety of advanced aircraft. It was used for supersonic transport and general aviation research. Later on, it was used as a training and support system for the Space Shuttle Approach and Landing Tests at Dryden in 1977.

No matter how sophisticated our ground-based simulations were, they could not provide the visual and motion cues that are a part of every flight. On many occasions, the visual and motion cues do influence the performance and judgment of the pilot. The GPAS was developed to provide these and other simulation capabilities. Photos ECN-1346, ECN-2399, and E-27824 show the GPAS and its computer system. The left-hand seat in the cockpit was modified to be the test pilot's seat with the modified controls and displays. The right seat was for the safety pilot and had the normal controls and displays.

My only real involvement with this simulator was to help buy the analog computer that was installed in the airplane. The GPAS was a flying simulator that had an analog computer inside. This computer was used to model the dynamics of another airplane or to mechanize another experimental flight-control system. There were special controls and other equipment that essentially forced the real airplane to follow the model programmed on the analog computer. The Cornell Aeronautical Laboratory (CAL),

Ken Szalai and GPAS Computers (1974). (NASA photo ECN-1346)

General Purpose Airborne Simulator. (NASA photo ECN-2399)

JetStar (GPAS) Simulator (September 1974). (NASA photo E-27824)

Inc. of Buffalo, New York, modified the JetStar to be the GPAS. Several reports were written describing the design, development, and validation of the GPAS. There were many reports describing the many studies that used the GPAS. The bibliography contains references to a sampling of these many reports.

This airborne simulator was flown at the FRC in the mid-to-late 1960s. After acceptance testing, the analog programming task was handled mainly by the FSL folk. Actually the FSL provided more than just analog programmers. John J. Perry of the FSL became the GPAS project engineer. Larry Caw and Dick Musick provided programming and maintenance support for the analog computers and flew on many missions. The personal accounts of Stan Butchart, Dwain Deets, Bob Kempel, John Perry,

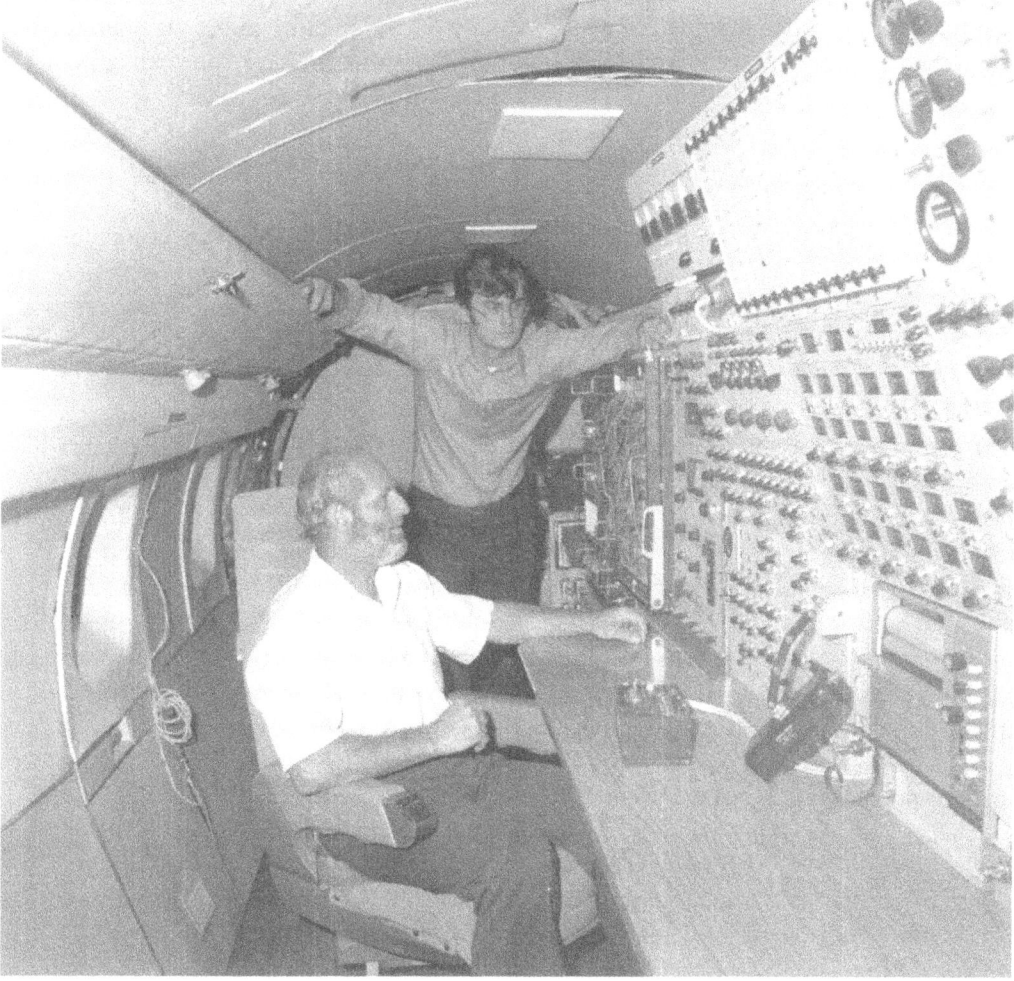

JetStar (GPAS) Computers with H. Rediess (in back) and D. Musick (September 1974). (NASA photo E-27825)

Larry Caw, and Dick Musick all include comments about their experiences with the GPAS. There are some interesting tales of events that happened with this simulator.

Process-Control Analog Computer

The analog computer that was finally selected and ordered was built by EAI using that firm's process-control analog computer (TR-5) components. Normally these components were programmed very much like the original EAI TR-10 portable analog computer. The TR-5s were ±10-volt, solid-state (transistor) analog computers. The original TR-5s did not have a patch panel. Each analog component had patch cord holes directly on the front of the component. These were essentially the same components used in the early TR-10, but "ruggedized" for harsh-environment use. These components were located in the computer in such a way that one could connect them using patch cords as if there were a removable patch panel. The photo ECN 1346 of the inside of the GPAS shows these components in the cabinet on the left and the holes for the patch cords can be clearly seen.

For the GPAS, the computer system had been modified so that all analog components were connected to a patch-panel bay, and a patch panel (visible in photo ECN 1346) was used when programming this particular computer. The EAI process-control analog components were designed to be used for manufacturing processes in which there were infrequent changes to the program. These process-control computers were usually installed inside a cabinet that could be locked. Consequently, there was no need for a removable patch panel. The process-control components were also designed to withstand the harsh environment found in a typical factory. The GPAS needed a computer that could withstand the forces and vibrations that would be encountered during flight and the temperatures inside the plane when it was in the hangar and not being used (especially during the summer months). The TR-5 process-control analog computer was suited to this environment.

The complement of analog components and their patch-panel arrangement had been determined by the engineers in the Control Systems Branch of the Research Division. These engineers (Dwain Deets and Ken Szalai) were heavily involved in the development and acceptance testing of the GPAS and did all the early programming of the on-board analog computer.

This computer was connected to the JetStar systems for input and output. One of the two pilot's controls (stick, rudders, throttles, etc) was modified to provide inputs to the analog model. The calculated outputs of the model were sent both to the simulation pilot's cockpit instrumentation and to special circuitry connected to the JetStar's control systems. This special circuitry forced the JetStar to follow the signals calculated in the model and thereby force the airplane to fly just like the vehicle being simulated in the analog computer. The other (safety) pilot's controls were unchanged, and the safety pilot was always ready to take over the controls if the GPAS got into some situation that was dangerous. There were several exciting situations that happened during some of the more risky maneuvers. They had those in the passenger compartment looking for parachutes and barf bags at the same time.

The GPAS could simulate another airplane whose dynamics were the same as or slower than the basic JetStar. It was not practical to force the JetStar to be a more dynamic airplane.[21] The GPAS was better suited to simulating larger, heavier airplanes than smaller, more maneuverable ones.

Interesting GPAS Sidelights

When the EAI TR-5 analog computer components were delivered, they were to be sent directly to CAL for installation in the JetStar, which was there being modified. Several of us went to Buffalo to discuss delivery and acceptance of the computers prior to their installation in the JetStar. As it turned out, there was another group from the FRC also there–for some work on the airplane modification process. Our flights back to California were the same morning after both groups had finished their work at CAL. Since we had the evening to ourselves, both groups decided to go to Niagara Falls for a little sightseeing and for dinner. We also made reservations for a concert by Kate Smith who was performing locally. Kate was a popular singer of that period with a powerful soprano voice. This happened to be during the winter, and the drive to Niagara Falls was quite scary because of the icy roads. The Falls were mostly ice, and very little water was actually falling.

The Seagram Tower (which overlooks the Falls) was still being built, but the restaurant at the top was open for business. Although the elevator was operational at the time, some of us (pseudo-macho types) just had to climb the stairs (at least 10 stories, as I remember) to get there. The dinner was quite good, but the restaurant hadn't received its liquor license at the time, so we couldn't have drinks with our dinner. One of the group ordered baked Alaska for dessert, and since it could not be served with the traditional flaming brandy, it was served with a (4th of July-type) sparkler. Cute.

The concert, with Kate Smith, took place on a theater-in-the-round type stage. It was superb. Our seats were in the second

---

[21] I.e., oscillate faster or respond more quickly to a pilot's or control system's input.

row, and the music with Kate Smith singing was fantastic. That was the first time I had ever seen her in person, and we all enjoyed every minute of the show.

Our flight home the next day was also quite interesting. There was a very nasty winter storm moving through the Midwest. We weren't sure when we left Buffalo if we were going to get home that day. We changed planes in Chicago. Both groups from the FRC were on the same plane. Somehow because of overbooking, or whatever, several of us ended up in first class on the flight from Chicago to Los Angeles. I was sitting next to Jim McKay (who was with the other FRC group). Our seats were near the food preparation area. Both Jim and I had noticed, as we boarded, that as the flight attendants were storing the bottles of champagne, they hid several bottles (we suspected for an after-flight party). Because of the bad weather, we had to sit and wait on the taxiway quite a while for an opening between storm cells before the plane could take off. Therefore, the champagne (excluding the bottles that had been hidden) ran out even before we took off. Or at least that is what the passengers were told—but Jim knew otherwise. He kept pestering our attendant for another glass of champagne. Although he never threatened to say anything about the hidden bottles of champagne, the attendant knew he knew.

Some time later, after we had gotten airborne and above the storm clouds and had been served dinner, our attendant decided to grant Jim's request for more champagne. She probably figured Jim would quit pestering her. All along, I had said nothing to her—in spite of Jim's many requests for more champagne. I knew we were in for a very rough trip because of the bad weather, and I didn't want any champagne. Drinks with carbon dioxide in them are not the best things to be drinking during rough flights. Not for me, at least. Anyway, she brought us what appeared to be cups of coffee (in the usual Styrofoam cups). But the contents weren't really coffee. They were mostly champagne with a dash of coffee to make them look like coffee. Jim didn't seem to mind and drank all his. I had never had champagne with coffee before, and it tasted horrible to me. I did drink some, but only because I didn't want to disappoint the attendant. It was a long, difficult flight for the attendants. They really earned their pay that night, with the weather the way it was. The plane was full with a lot of folks wanting to get out of there and just get home. The first-class seat was enough of a bonus for me. It was a luxury I rarely experienced as a government employee. Government travel regulations generally prohibit the typical government employee from arranging such accommodations.

That takeoff and climb-out was by far the steepest I have ever experienced on a commercial jet. I felt like I was lying in a hammock. And it was very turbulent. Kind of scary. But it was the only way to quickly get through and above the storm cells. I was in no mood for lukewarm coffee-flavored champagne. The first part of that trip was the closest I have ever come to getting sick on an airplane. We could look out the window and see the thunderheads all around us. There was a lot of lightning, also. As we got close to the top of the clouds, we could see the moon, which was almost full and which created a very eerie outlook between the tops of the thunderheads—pretty and surreal at the same time.

To shift from flying commercially to flying the GPAS—which in some ways was not all that different—Bob Kempel, who worked on one GPAS flight program, recalls:

> I remember when Larry Caw was assigned to the JetStar. He became a very good real-time analog programmer. We were looking at different control schemes for riding qualities as I remember it. I remember the incident when we were airborne and we were looking at different feedback schemes. I had mechanized a beta [sideslip] feed-

back. Well, as you know, signs [sign conventions] were sometimes confusing. Fitz Fulton was the pilot. The sign on beta was wrong, and we ended up with a dynamically unstable airplane because of it. We turned on the system for Fitz to evaluate, and the airplane immediately began an oscillatory divergence! Larry and I were in the back hollering to Fitz to turn it off, but Fitz was intrigued with the thing so he wanted to watch it as it diverged or maybe just teach us a lesson. He finally punched the thing off and Larry and I sighed in relief. Larry changed the beta-input sign, and we proceeded with the test.

The JetStar was a fun airplane to fly in, but I always had a feeling of impending doom or something else going wrong. Herm Rediess was my boss at the time and when he wanted me to fly in the thing all the time I told him "thanks, but no thanks," and I don't think Herm ever liked that. Don Gatlin can tell you about the incident where they almost tore the wings off. I think Musick was aboard that flight too.

The particular flight that Bob is talking about was the last flight of the GPAS. The aircraft got into a serious flutter problem that almost shook the wings off. This flight was on 7 May 1975. Following the flight, the airplane was restored to a standard JetStar configuration and used for a number of other research programs in following years. John Perry talks about this incident in his personal account. Don Gatlin, the project engineer on the GPAS at the time, provided the following in response to my inquiry about this incident:

> I was not on that particular flight. I was the project engineer and was monitoring the flight from the radio room in the pilots' office. I believe Dick (Musick) was on board and a KU [University of Kansas] grad student whose name I don't remember. [Actually, it was Dick Musick and larry Caw.] Don Mallick was the pilot, Stan Butchart in the right seat. I don't believe we even scheduled telemetry so there was no real time record of the event. As I remember, we got a call that "We've had a problem here. Get someone up to look us over." Betty Callister and I sent Gary Krier up in an F-104 to check them out. Stan told me afterward that as the limit cycle went on, he just looked out the cockpit window to see where they would crash as he believed the wings would be torn off. As I remember, there was no damage, although the airplane required a thorough inspection before flying again.

Hybrid Simulation Systems (1964-1976)

The beginning of the hybrid (combined analog and digital) era in the FSL started even before we expanded the all-analog X-15 simulator to include a digital computer. I took my first class in hybrid simulations more than a year before we started to buy our first digital computer. Also, the vendors that were making those analog computers were constantly expanding their systems to include more and more digital capabilities. Digital logic components and a separate digital logic patch panel had been added to the newer lines of analog computers. In addition, the internal mode control system had become more digital in nature. The paper-tape servo-set pot subsystem gave way to a subsystem that also allowed a digital computer to do this job. The analog mode control (reset, run, and hold) was eventually digitized and controlled from the internal circuitry, the logic patch panel, or an external digital computer. These changes evolved over a number of years and were brought on by the many users who requested more and more digital computer capabilities. The consistency and repeatability of digital computers were gradually being added to analogs. In addition, the analogs were being built so that they could be interfaced and used with digital computers.

The aircraft we were simulating were also becoming more advanced. The instrumentation in the cockpit was more complex, with digital displays and digital computers providing the inputs to the instruments. The aircraft controls were changing, with more control surfaces, and stability control systems being added to augment the pilots' inputs. The pilots' controls were also being changed and becoming more complex to simulate. The aircraft were becoming more dynamic in nature, with increased maneuverability and performance. All these factors forced the evolution of the equipment we were using to build the simulators. The basic analog computers could not keep up with these changes. At first we added digital logic and other digital-like functions to simulate the needed features, but this, too, was not enough. The only way to really simulate some of the newer features and functions that were needed was to add a general-purpose digital computer to the analog systems. The digital computers not only provided the additional computational capabilities needed to simulate the addition systems in the aircraft but also added a variety of set-up and operational functions that improved the daily use of the computer facility. All of these will be discussed in the following parts of this section.

Users were asking, moreover, that the turn-around time in getting an analog computer reprogrammed for the next simulation become as short as possible. Analog computers were expensive, and the turn-around time between simulations was taking too long and costing too much. Tying the analogs to a digital computer allowed some analog functions to be controlled by that digital computer. It also allowed the use of the digital computer for those computations better suited to the digital. We now had three different types of computational capabilities available for developing simulations: analog, digital, and hybrid. Moreover, the digital computer could now be programmed to handle set-up, check-out, and operational-run-time management. The pots could be set by the digital computer and check cases run automatically, which greatly reduced the time to change over to another simulation. The digital computer could also be used to calculate check cases, to draw the maps that were frequently used, and to handle other set-up needs. All these features now allowed the research engineers to load up their simulations and then run them without having to have a simulation programmer do these tasks for them. The simulation contractor-support staff took care of switching the instrument panels and other such tasks involved in getting the cockpit ready. So instead of a simulation being set up and kept on the analogs for weeks at a time, we now had a sim lab that could be scheduled in 2- and 4-hour segments, thereby allowing for many different simulations to be scheduled each week. It took several years to get to this point, but that is what buying digital computers and tying them into the analogs did for the FSL. The following tells how that all came about.

Many of the following paragraphs tend to be more technical than those in the preceding sections and are included for those interested in such technology. Many of the subjects to be discussed are specifically about features and capabilities of the class of digital computers and digital logic used in hybrid computers. The topics are not always related to specific aircraft but are features that were needed in the real-time simulations that we were implementing. For this reason, some readers may want to skip parts of this section. I have assumed some knowledge of digital computers and do not always define some of the terms I use. The computer industry has spawned an enormous number of new words and acronyms, and even new definitions to very common words. It is almost impossible to write about computers without using some of the terms of the trade. To avoid these terms would distract from the story, as would pausing to define every term.

In order to use this hardware in real-time simulations, we had to become intimately familiar with what the hardware did. And unfortunately, in talking about how we did this, I have to describe in some detail how it worked. Many of the problems we had in dealing with the computer's hardware, software, and vendors would be difficult to describe without this detail. We had many problems that were due to the nature of our application and the newness of the use of general-purpose digital computers for real-time use—in particular when combined with the analog computers we already had.

We were not alone. Many other simulation laboratories were also having to contend with this new technology—combined analog and digital simulation. Several of us in the FSL belonged to the Simulation Councils Inc. (SCI), a professional organization for those involved in one way or another with computer simulation. The role of SCI evolved over the years, from analog to hybrid to digital methods of simulation. We went to many different meetings, both locally (in Southern California) and nationally. The national meetings of SCI were, for many years, scheduled at the same time and place as the national computer conferences. In those years, the national meetings occurred twice a year: once in the eastern part of the United States and the other in the west. The western conference was almost always held in Los Angeles, San Francisco, or Las Vegas. Because these cities were close, we were able to go to many of these western meetings of the SCI. These conferences provided an excellent way to meet the vendors and see the newest equipment. The conference presentations were also a good way to keep up-to-date on just what others around the country were doing with their simulation equipment.

Patchable Digital Logic Units

In the FSL, hybrid simulation actually began with the purchase of a set of digital logic components that were meant to be used very much like analog computer components. They were connected with patch cords. This happened shortly after we started using the X-15 simulation—about 1963. The racks of digital logic modules were mounted in some spare rack space in the third X-15 analog computer. The digital logic included AND and OR gates, flip-flops, and digital relays. The voltage levels of these components were only 0 volts and 5 volts (which represented 0 and 1). Using these components and some black boxes (built in-house), we were able to breadboard (build preliminary logic circuitry for) simple hybrid devices such as a digital-to-analog (D/A)[22] converter. The black box

---

[22] A digital-to-analog converter converts a number in digital format to the equivalent number as an analog voltage. An analog-to-digital device does the opposite, converting an analog voltage to the equivalent digital number.

needed in this case contained the precision resistor ladder used as the voltage divider. An analog-to-digital (A/D) converter was also possible, but a little more complicated. It was essentially a high-gain analog summing amplifier with a D/A converter in the feedback. I don't remember if any of the other analog programmers ever used these units, but I had a lot of fun trying different things. It was a good way to try this digital logic with analog circuitry, which helped us to better understand the use of these capabilities.

Early Hybrid Computers

This type of digital logic was eventually added to the analog computers we bought later, such as the EAI 231-RV and the two Applied Dynamics AD-4 analogs. EAI sold a hybrid system, which was called the HYDAC (Hybrid Digital and Analog Computer). The HYDAC included an EAI 231-RV and a digital logic computer that had a large assortment of digital components. The HYDAC did not have a general-purpose digital computer in it; however one could be connected with interface equipment, such as A/Ds and D/As. We never bought one of the EAI logic computers. The sort of simulations we were doing did not use enough digital logic to justify buying that part of a HYDAC. We were able to get by with relays, diodes, and similar components to implement those functions that had unusual characteristics—such as limits or hysteresis or deadbands.

However, this type of digital logic did not satisfy all of the requirements resulting from the ever-increasing complexities of the aircraft being simulated. The only way to really provide all the needs was to interface analog and digital computers together and use each for what they were better at doing.

Photo ED00-0091-1 shows a typical Applied Dynamics hybrid system with an AD-4 analog computer on the right. This photo was taken in the early 1970s and shows just how much smaller hybrid systems had become by then. This was due to the solid-state electronics used at that time. The AD-4 Hybrid System did have a general-purpose digital computer in it. The digital logic and digital operations modules were included on the same patch panel as the analog modules. We did buy two of the AD-4 analog computers later on for use with the CDC CYBER 73-28. We did not buy the digital computer portion of the AD Hybrid System

Applied Dynamics AD-4 Computer System. (NASA photo ED00-0091-1)

(the computer rack on the left side in photo ED00-0091-1).

Integration on the Analog Computer

Until digital computers became fast enough (or the really fast ones became cheap enough that we could afford them), we were forced to go with the current-day small digital computers. Even then, these computers were not fast enough to do a complete 6 DOF simulation. There were several approaches as to just how much of the 6 DOF equations of motion would be squeezed into the digital computers and how much would be implemented on the analog computer. The approach initially chosen by the FSL was to do the integration (with respect to time) of the accelerations and velocities on the analog and to use the digital computer to calculate the actual accelerations and velocities. The digital computer calculated the right side of the equations of motion, which including doing the function generation of the nonlinear coefficients. The analog was also used for the cockpit interfaces, the output displays (strip charts, recorders, plotters, etc.), and any control-system simulations. This separation of tasks between the analog and digital computers remained constant until the FSL bought a second digital computer— an SDS 9300. The 9300 was a faster computer than the 930. It had true parallel bit processing of its 24-bit words and ran about four times faster than the 930 with essentially the same silicon logic. However, this still wasn't quite fast enough to do all of the integration on the digital. The later versions of ICARUS[23] did do the integration of the longitudinal equations. The frequency content of the lateral directional equations was still too high for digital integration. The FSL eventually got a digital computer that was both big enough and fast enough. This occurred when the FRC received the CDC (Control Data Corp.) CYBER 73 in 1973, along with the special analog interface hardware and software that also had been built by CDC. (See photo ECN-6375 of the CYBER 73-28.)

CYBER 73-28. (NASA photo ECN-6375)

[23] The ICARUS (Immediate Checkout Analog Research Unity Scaled) program is described in detail in a later part of this section.

The hybrid systems described in this document are those that were mechanized before the switch from analog integration to digital integration. This is an arbitrary point in time, since analog computers were used for many years after this date for cockpit interface and even some control-system simulation. Even today's highly sophisticated digital flight simulations still have some analog circuitry in them. But there are no general-purpose analog computers involved in the mechanization of the equations of motion. This end to the analog and hybrid simulation eras, while arbitrary, is easily accepted. However, it was really all the other problems that were characteristic of analogs that led to their phase-out for flight simulation.

Analog computers had a number of undesirable characteristics that we had to deal with—signal-ground problems, amplifier drift, limited precision, warm-up times, crosstalk, extensive set-up times, fuses, and other things. These problems that were inherent in analog computers are what eventually led to their replacement with all-digital simulations. Unfortunately, all-digital simulations still don't provide a number of the insights that are sometimes needed to understand the processes being modeled. In addition, the all-digital simulations are still sampled data systems moving though time in short but finite steps. While these time intervals are getting smaller and smaller (as the computers get faster and faster), they are not yet truly real-time or parallel in nature, as are the pilots that fly them. But they are good enough, and that is what simulation is all about.

The First FSL Hybrid Simulation

The X-15 simulation was the first hybrid simulator in the FSL. It did not begin that way. The accident to the number two X-15 in late 1962 and the resulting changes that were made during its reconstruction forced us to have to deal with a major change in the simulation. The nonlinear coefficients were different due to the addition of the external tanks to the number two X-15. The plane also had a longer body with the addition of another fuel tank for the ramjet studies planned for that particular X-15.

This need to modify the simulator occurred about the same time as Minneapolis Honeywell (M-H) was having trouble in fabricating the airborne computers that were to be used in the X-15. M-H was behind schedule in this fabrication and would not have time to build a back-up unit that was planned to be used with the simulator. Since the FSL was in a position of having to expand the X-15 simulator for the number two modifications, we agreed to buy a general-purpose digital computer, provided that the Air Force pay for the interface equipment needed to connect this general purpose digital computer to the all-analog X-15 simulator. This digital computer would be used to provide the additional capability needed to handle the different number two X-15 nonlinear derivatives. The new computer would also be used to simulate the M-H airborne computer. This was agreed to, and we set about buying the digital computer and interface hardware.

The thought of building up another set of function generators like those already in use was probably considered, but not by me or any of the other X-15 simulation programmers. We had had enough of all those fuses and dinky pots. The idea of using a digital computer to do this job was unanimously and immediately accepted. No discussion was needed. We were going hybrid.

The Digital Side of the FSL

We bought the SDS 930 computer after we had gone out with a competitive solicitation. We were not even aware that this particular model existed. It was so new that SDS had not started to advertise it. The FRC Radar/Telemetry (TM) group—on the third floor of Building 4800—had an SDS 920. Our statement of work was for a computer of the 920 class/speed/capability. The 920 was state-of-the-art for that class of small scientific computer. We were quite surprised when SDS proposed its newest model—the 930. The 930 was about four times as fast as the 920 and all the other computers in this class. This speed factor led us to select the SDS 930. I now had my very own digital computer to program.

First SDS 930 Out the Door

The 930 that SDS delivered was the first one built using its regular manufacturing production line. We got number six. The first five 930s had all been built in the engineering department as a part of the development process. Because we bought the very first 930 that was delivered, SDS seemed to bend over backwards in subsequent dealings with us. I guess it was proud of the fact that a NASA facility had bought one of its newest computers. This extra attention went all the way to the top. There were a few problems later on that involved the SDS sales or service staff. They were resolved by the president or the vice president. The fact that we could call the president directly was a useful tool in dealing with the company.

SDS 930 Characteristics

Some of the really great features of the SDS 930 were the memory access capabilities that were included in its design. It had direct memory access for its data channels. Most of the other computers (in this class) required the use of the arithmetic unit to handle memory access during data input or output operations. The SDS 930 had several types of data channels that had direct memory access and did not need the use of the computer's arithmetic registers for memory access. This meant that almost all types of input or output (I/O) could be initiated and data would flow in or out of memory without interfering with the CPU doing its work. Interrupts were tied to the data channels and would trigger when events happened—such as the end of data flow or if something had happened to stop this flow (i.e. end-of-record, malfunction, etc.). The analog interface equipment used this direct-memory feature, and thus this form of I/O could go on in parallel with CPU operations. Large volumes of data could be read or written without interfering with what the CPU was doing. This capability of the SDS 930 was a big selling point, and many of these computers were sold because of this direct-memory access feature. It provided some of the advantages that the larger mainframe computers had with respect to the smaller scientific class of computers, especially for real-time applications such as aircraft simulations.

Our SDS 930 included the basic CPU with 8,000 words of 24-bit-word ferrite core memory. The initial operating system was on paper tape and was not memory-resident. (The mag-tape version came later.) The memory-resident part of the operating system was small and included a bootstrap, a few standard constants used by all the SDS software, and a very small routine that loaded the operating system into memory whenever it was needed. (A bootstrap routine was a small program of only a few instructions that loaded itself into memory and then followed this by loading a larger, more comprehensive loader routine.) Fortunately the paper-tape unit had a winder/rewinder. The system-software paper tape filled a 10-inch reel. The bootstrap, the standard constants, and the priority interrupt transfer instructions occupied the lowest memory and used another 200 words of memory. This was the state of the art, then. Today's computers with their nanosecond instruction times, megabytes of memory, and gigabytes of disk storage weren't even imaginable then.

The silicon logic cards in the 930 were about 6 by 8 inches in size and contained one or two basic circuits, such as a couple of AND gates, flip-flops, or one-shots. There were thousands of wires running everywhere in the CPU chassis. All these wires were connected using wire-wrap equipment. When the wire wraps were installed correctly, they provided excellent connections and could be removed and refastened in the field by maintenance technicians. In addition, SDS provided diagnostic routines that could pinpoint the exact circuit board that was malfunctioning. Generally, all we had to do to fix a hardware problem was to run the diagnostic, and then swap the sick circuit board with a good board. We had bought enough spare circuit boards to fill several storage cabinets. The sick circuit boards were returned to SDS for repair.

Program Debug Process

As the only 930 programmer for many months, I had the entire computer to myself during the development and debug phase of the X-15A-2 simulation program. There were no debugging tools available—especially for real-time code. Debugging a real-time program, in those days, meant sitting in front of the operator's console, stepping through the instructions one at a time, and examining the results of each instruction. Really! Try doing that today. The computer console could display the main computer registers involved in the instruction execution. The display had several 24-bit registers, where each bit had a small light indicating if the bit was zero or one. The 930 CPU had one arithmetic register (called the A register) where an operand (the data item being operated on) was loaded before the instruction was performed. The instruction itself was first loaded into the instruction register (called the C register). There was also an Index register (called the X register) that was used to determine the memory address of the operand or storage location. It could be used for repetitive or looping operations on a sequential group of operands. And finally there was a B register that was an extension of the A register and allowed for double-word operations. These four registers (A, B, X, and C) along with the memory addresses of the instructions and operands were about all we could look at. This, however, was enough for us to actually debug our real-time programs. It took a long time, stepping through instructions one by one and checking the arithmetic, branching, and analog input or output, but that was really the only way to do this part of the checkout with the equipment we had. Not only did we have to check every instruction this way, but we had to try every different path through the code. Every option had to be tested using all the appropriate input values. Fortunately, there weren't too many different paths to test.

It was mandatory to have taken the SDS programming class. This was the only way to quickly get up to speed on the Assembler, Loader, and other software that SDS provided. The class was where I learned the many basic machine instructions and how to write Assembler code. Without this class, it was almost impossible to develop software of any kind. The X-15 program was written in the SDS Assembler language, which took the input instructions (on punched cards or paper tape) and turned them into machine-readable instructions. The input instructions were called the source code and were written by the programmer. The SDS Loader took the machine-readable instructions and put these into memory in machine-executable form. The printed listings provided by the Assembler gave us the information that we needed while we stepped through instructions (i.e. executed the instructions manually, one at a time). By knowing what each instruction was supposed to do and knowing what the operand was, we could determine if the program was calculating the right results.

Remember this was all in internal data format, which is certainly not how we learned to do arithmetic in grade school. Binary arithmetic in twos-compliment form is a long way from the decimal arithmetic we learned in school. In addition, all the equation's variables were in a scaled format similar to the scaling used in analog computer programming. We not only needed to know what the parameters were but the scaling factors that had been applied when the analog program had been implemented.

In the X-15 digital program all variables were scaled to ±1.0 as the maximum. This is similar to scaling the analog variables to the ±100-volt range of the analog computers. The D/A and A/D converters used this same scaling.[24] Consequently the input parameters were already scaled and we just used this scaling in the calculations in the digital computer.

Input/Output Routines

Some of the first routines I had to write were the ones needed to read in the data that was used in the X-15-2 simulation program. Although SDS did have a library of general-purpose subroutines for the card reader, typewriter, and paper-tape reader/punch units, we were not able to use most of these as they were too general-purpose in nature and therefore took up too much memory space. For our programs, we had to write our own shorter, simpler I/O routines. Since the X-15 program calculated so many nonlinear coefficients for the number two X-15, getting all this data into memory was an important part of the program. In fact reading the data was the first thing the program did. This data was constantly being updated as the number two X-15 flew, the research engineers wanting to update the data in the simulation to match what they were getting from flight. In the beginning, this data was read from punched cards. Once the data was read, it was converted from the alphanumeric characters to the proper internal binary format. After all the data was read, converted, and stored, it was possible to punch this data along with the entire program out on the paper-tape punch in a memory-dump format that was easily reloadable. Thereafter (until the next change in coefficients), this paper tape was all that was needed to load the X-15 simulator digital program. The entire program with all the data filled an 8-inch reel of paper tape. Reading this tape took quite a while. The program almost completely filled the 8K memory.

That's right—8K (or, to be precise, 8,192) words of 24-bit memory for both the program and all the data. That sounds sort of ludicrous now, considering the advances that have been made in computers since then. But that is all we had—and that was enough. We had to make some sacrifices in our design and coding to get everything to fit in this limited space. The only one I can remember that may have had an impact on the quality of the simulation was having to limit the data files (for all the nonlinear derivatives) to a smaller size than was desirable. The file size was quite adequate for the data we had. As mentioned above, we could not use the standard SDS-supplied I/O routines. They were just too big and had a number of capabilities that we could do without. The ones I wrote were bare-bones code that did not check for any of the possible hardware malfunctions that could happen while data was being read. If the card reader crunched a card or the paper-tape reader tore the tape, we just stopped the load process, repaired or got another copy of the card deck or tape, and restarted the load process. When you are the only user, you can make these choices. You don't have to worry about any other programs that might also be running.

Computer Program Listings

In the beginning, we only had the typewriter for the printed listings generated by the assembler. This was slow. It took hours to type out the complete program. Because of this, there were many times when the program was re-assembled without a new printout—especially if the changes were only a couple of instructions. We just marked up the last printout

---

[24] An analog value of +100 volts was converted to +1.0, zero volts was +0.0, and -100 volts was a -1.0 in the digital computer. The digital computer really didn't know what scaling had been applied to the numbers it did its arithmetic on. The programmer had to keep track of this throughout the entire program. The scaling assumed maximum values of 1.0. Therefore the numbers we were working on were really a decimal (actually, the binary equivalent), which when multiplied by the maximum value gave the correct value for the parameter.

with a red pencil and used it. This was OK if the changes were minor and did not affect the addresses (memory locations) of the instructions or operands by more than one or two locations. But after several re-assemblies without a listing, the listings got so marked up with pencil changes that it became almost impossible to determine the actual memory addresses. This made it very difficult to debug the program. We then had to take the time to assemble the program with a new listing. I tried to schedule these assemblies so that I could take my lunch break while the computer typed the printout. This situation also meant that, when I was working graveyard shift, I could not start one of these assemblies (with listing) during the last hour of the shift. That would have interfered with the day shift and the training or flight-planning activities. We eventually bought a line printer when we expanded the 930. That was a welcome improvement to the operation of the computer.

Paper Tape

There were two forms of the paper tape we used. One was a black all-paper tape for temporary files. This was oiled and this oil got all over our hands and stank like mineral oils usually do. The oil also caused the rubber bands (that were used to keep the rolled-up tapes rolled up) to get quite soft and mushy after a while. When this happened, we had to throw the roll of tape away and punch another copy from the master tape. There was also a green Mylar-reinforced paper tape. This was quite strong and almost impossible to tear. The system software and all the utility routines came on this green tape. We had boxes and boxes of these tapes in cabinets. All sorts of utility routines. The larger software programs, such as the Assembler, operating systems, mathematical routines, etc., usually came on aluminum reels. Each programmer had a personal collection of the utility routines that he or she used most. We carried them around much like today's computer nerds carry their diskettes and CDs around in their backpacks. We spent a lot of time coiling these shorter utility tapes up and were always getting paper cuts on our fingers. If you set a roll of the black tape down on a piece of paper, it would leave a doughnut-shaped oil ring on the paper. Nasty stuff!

We also used the green tape for our final output tapes, after the source-code assembler had finished its work. The green tape was not oiled, which was good. It also cost a lot more. However, the green tape was hard on the punch and caused it to wear out quickly, so we did not use it until we were ready to punch out the final memory-dump (self-loading) tapes. Because of the Mylar (between two layers of paper tape), it was a lot easier to cut your fingers with the green tape than with the black kind.

None of these supplies were stocked in the local warehouse in those days. We had to keep track and order supplies when we needed them. Fortunately the guys in the TM lab, with the SDS 920, used the same stuff, and we were always borrowing from each other when our orders were late.

SDS Programming Classes

The basic programming classes were not long enough to really cover in detail the writing of input and output routines or the individual instructions for the special-purpose analog interface. I talked my boss into letting me contract for a week of SDS programmer support. I spent two days at SDS with different programmers learning how to write I/O routines. The first day was a total waste, and I really got nothing accomplished. The second day, a different SDS programmer was assigned to help and this turned out to be most productive. His name was Rider Anderson and he was very good. We designed the digital program for the basic X-15 simulation that day. We even started on some of the I/O routines. With this start, I was able to completely write and debug all the I/O routines for the X-15 simulation program in about one week. This included the card-reader input of the data, the paper-tape routines, and typewriter routines. I also had to write routines to convert the input data from alphanumeric characters to the proper internal binary format. For someone who had never written digital computer programs before, I was quite proud of myself to do all this in about one week—in Assembly language—with the limited peripherals we had. Following this, I was also able to write, in about two more weeks, all the function-generation code that did the actual interpolation for the nonlinear coefficients and the real-time I/O routines to read the analog inputs and to write the calculated coefficients back to the analogs. It took a lot longer to actually check out all this code than it took to write the programs in the first place. I did make a third one-day trip to SDS to go over what I had done with Rider Anderson, but by then the program was nearly complete and I really didn't need any more help.

I never used the other two days of the contracted programming support. SDS did eventually offer a more comprehensive course covering its computer's data channels and peripherals. SDS also provided a one-week class devoted to its special-purpose data channels—such as the analog interface. These types of interfaces had a special class of instructions, which was not covered in the basic classes. This class was also helpful for when we got the SDS 9300. The I/Os in these two different computers were quite similar. I was able to take this class about two years after we had received the original 930.

NASA did this to me on several occasions—that is, allowed me to attend a class I needed to do my job, many years after I actually started doing that job. For example, I started buying computer systems in about 1958. That was when I wrote my first-ever statement of work (SOW) and automated data processing (ADP) acquisition plan. An ADP plan was a set of documents required by NASA Headquarters to justify a computer procurement. I finally got to go to a class on how to write statements of work in 1992, the year before I retired. Timely? By then, I had written well over 40 quite lengthy SOWs for all sorts of computer systems. Come to think of it, I never really had a class on basic analog computer programming. That was something else I learned the hard way—by doing it.

But that is the way analog computers were; you could actually teach yourself how to program one of them. Too bad digital computers weren't quite the same. Maybe that is why I never chose to defect from the FSL and transfer to the digital-programming branch in those days. Analogs were a lot more fun. It helped to have a good sense of humor and a ton of patience to cope with all their frustrating idiosyncrasies. Digital computers never had the same appeal, even though I spent more years programming them than I ever did programming analog computers.

Analog Interface

The interface equipment between the analog and digital computers was very state-of-the-art and built by SDS. There were A/D converters, D/A converters, priority interrupts, real-time clocks, and single-bit discretes.[25] The real-time clocks were programmable and allowed us to generate timing signals (connected to priority interrupts), which we used to slave the calculations to a preset interval. We were able to use a 10-millisecond frame time for the X-15 simulation. The converters were also timed by this clock-interrupt.

The analog inputs had simultaneous sample and hold circuits on each channel, which made it possible for all the analog inputs to be sampled at the same instant, then converted to digital and read in a

---

[25] A discrete is a single-bit data value (of zero or one) and is used to represent those types of data that only have two distinct values—such as on or off, switch up or down, light on or off, true or false.

sequential manner. Also, the output parameters from the digital computer were written to the D/A converters, which were double-registered, whereby the outputs were written sequentially to the first register in each D/A and then all these registers were transferred to the final output registers simultaneously. This technique eliminated time-skew differences and the problems that were associated with using parameters (in the equations) that were not sampled simultaneously.

The discretes were single-bit data items and usually connected to such things as switches (as input parameters) and cockpit lights (as output signals). These discretes were hard-wired to individual bits in a 24-bit register. There were instructions to read these 24-bit registers on input or to write to similar registers for output. The basic 930 instruction set included the instructions to test or set the individual bits or groups of bits together.

Priority interrupts were similar to discretes, in that a single input line was connected to a single interrupt. These interrupts—for example, the analog computer mode control or a timer—were connected to signals that required the computer to respond immediately. The interrupts were ordered in a hierarchical chain. This meant that the programmer had to select the order of priority for the interrupt routines. When a priority interrupt occurred, the CPU would first determine if any interrupts of higher priority were active. If so, the new and lower priority interrupt(s) would have to wait. If there were no higher priority interrupts active, the new interrupt would then become active and the routine tied to it would be run. If the active interrupts were of lower priority, the routine tied to the new and higher interrupt would be run to completion, after which control would be returned to the interrupted lower priority routine(s).

The real-time clocks were tied to priority interrupts. We had several of these special clocks, but rarely used more than one. The real-time clocks had two modes. They could be set to generate a continuous timing signal that could be set anywhere between 1 and 1x223 microseconds. The clock could also be set to generate a single interrupt signal (also between 1 and 1x223 microseconds). We rarely used this second mode, except during check-out of timed routines. Normally, we just started the timer at the appropriate interval desired for the particular simulation. In the beginning, this frame time was 10 milliseconds. During the following years, as the calculations got more complicated, the frame time grew to 50 milliseconds. This occurred during the latter days of the hybrid period and especially when we started to do all the programming in Fortran on the Cyber 72 computer in the middle '70s. This 50-millisecond time interval was about as long as could be tolerated for the aircraft simulators of those days.

930 Expansion

Several years after we bought the 930, it was expanded to its maximum size in terms of memory (from 8K to 32K). The number of D/As, A/Ds, single-bit discretes and priority interrupts were also expanded to at least twice the original configuration. We were really into hybrid simulation, and getting the digital computer expanded permitted us to do even more with it. For one thing, the X-15 program, while still the main user, was not using the 930 all the time. Since the 930 was only needed for X-15-2 simulation practice or flight-planning purposes, it was available for other simulations. Other simulations were also developed to use this 930. Having a larger computer allowed us to better support this need. Several of the FSL programmers had taken classes at SDS and were also using this computer. The SDS Fortran software was available and the computer needed more memory to handle the programs that were being written in Fortran.

A Really Hot Computer

This additional memory was a sole-source procurement, and it went OK. Or so we thought. In expanding the computer we had to add another bank of power supplies. Both banks required 220-volt, 3-phase service and the power lines in the X-15 sim lab were rewired to accommodate the expansion. What we didn't know at the time was that in wiring up the power, the electricians wired both sets of power supplies incorrectly. Besides the three phases, there were also a ground wire and a neutral wire in the incoming power lines. Somehow, the ground wire got connected to only one bank of power supplies and the neutral wire was only connected to the other bank of power supplies. Both of these lines should have been connected to both banks. In spite of this mistake, the computer worked, until one day, about a year later, when someone accidentally kicked loose the power cord from one of the banks of power supplies. The computer shut down, as you might expect. Fortunately, the power cord that was kicked loose was the one that had the neutral wire in it. If the other power cord (the one with the ground wire) had been the one kicked loose, the entire cabinet—including the outer metal skin—would have been at 220 volts! That probably would have seriously injured someone. We were really lucky, that time! The power cords were rewired.

Lots of Manuals

Another interesting (and funny) tale about the 930 expansion had to do with documentation. When we wrote the specifications for the expansion, we asked for a number of manuals. These were to be delivered with the hardware. We asked for 20 copies of the several different programming manuals and 2 copies each of all the maintenance manuals. Somehow, the people who packed the manuals at SDS for deliver sent us 20 copies of everything, including all the maintenance manuals. There were about three dozen different maintenance manuals. And we now had 20 copies of each of these—boxes and boxes full. A small truck load! I called SDS and explained what had happened, and since all these extra maintenance manuals were quite expensive, SDS agreed to send out a truck to pick them up. The SDS plant was in Santa Monica, California. The truck got to the Flight Research Center in the afternoon. We loaded all the extra boxes of manuals onto the truck and it left. The next day, the same truck was back, the same manuals were unloaded at our warehouse, and the truck left before anyone called me. (After all, the shipping labels still said these were for us.) Apparently, when the truck had arrived at the SDS warehouse the night before, the boxes were unloaded and just left on the dock. The next morning, the day-shift crew found these boxes sitting there, decided that they were ready to be delivered and sent the truck back out, but with a different driver. The driver from the day before wasn't there to stop this from happening. This time when I called SDS, I was told to throw them away. We did.

In spite of these strange happenings with the SDS computers, we had a good working relationship with the company. Its offices in Santa Monica were in a very nice locale to go to for programming classes. It was close to the beach; it was nice and cool; and there were many really good restaurants in the near vicinity of the classrooms. This included (or so we thought) the best place in all of the Los Angeles area to get prime rib—Cheerios—at the junction of Ocean and Pico Boulevards. Everyone who went there agreed with us. And collectively, among all of us, we had tried every other highly touted prime rib restaurant in the Los Angels basin. That slab of prime rib, very nicely aged, was as big as the plate, and at least one inch thick. It was so tender you could cut it with your fork. Many of us continued to go there, even after we no longer had SDS computers.

SDS was a small company, and we got to know many of the top brass, including the president and founder. I was even offered the opportunity to buy 100 shares of stock when it went public, at only $25 a share. Unfortunately, I had to turn down this offer—some sort of conflict-of-interest concern. I kept track of the stock for several years, until SDS merged with the Xerox Company in 1969. At that time the stock had gone up by almost a factor of 19. That $2,500 worth of shares I was offered was worth over $47,000. That was a lot of money in those days. It still is.

SDS Maintenance

We had a very turbulent experience with the maintenance of the SDS 930. We contracted with SDS to provide both preventative and corrective maintenance services. From Santa Monica it took several hours for an SDS maintenance man to get to the FRC after we had called about a hardware problem. Fortunately, there were computer diagnostic routines we could run, which were able to isolate specific circuit boards that were malfunctioning. These diagnostics proved to be quite handy. On many occasions, especially during night shift, I was able to diagnose and change out circuit boards to fix a problem. There were several times when the SDS repairman had been to the FRC, done his thing, and left to return to Santa Monica, whereupon the computer broke down again. Now we had to wait for him to get back to the shop before he could be sent back. This was long before cellular phones existed.

SDS eventually had a maintenance man living in the high desert. Its policy was that it would not provide a local maintenance office unless there were at least three computers in the same vicinity. The Jet Propulsion Laboratory had a tracking station at its Goldstone facility near Barstow that also had computers maintained by SDS. The FRC had an SDS 920 computer in the telemetry facility, on the third floor. Because of these three SDS computers, all in the high desert, SDS hired a technician who lived in the Palmdale area, and he was able to get to the FRC, usually within an hour, to fix hardware problems. This arrangement did improve the response time in getting our hardware problems fixed. We also bought a large supply of every type of circuit board used in the SDS 930. Unfortunately there were parts of the computer for which we did not have spares—such as power supplies and the memory units. When one of these parts failed, we just had to wait until they were replaced with good parts.

Most computer companies (in those days) took four hours to respond to maintenance calls to our area. Very few computer companies had local facilities staffed for maintenance calls anywhere in the high desert. Almost all these calls were to offices in the Los Angeles area, and it took at least four hours for those companies to respond. We had other maintenance contracts that stipulated four-hour response times. I guess SDS considered us to be good customers. The fact that SDS 930 computer we bought was the first one delivered was both good and bad, for we did have some unusual problems that were most likely due to our computer being the first one out the door. On the other hand, we did get a lot of support from the top managers at SDS. I think they liked the idea that NASA was using one of their computers for the X-15 project. This project had a lot of visibility both locally and nationally.

Salesman of the Month Club

During the next couple of years (following the delivery of the SDS 930), SDS seemed to have a lot of trouble in keeping a sales representative in our area. There weren't a lot of sales opportunities out in the desert. There was one year when we actually had 12 different sales reps assigned to the area. A couple of these I never met and only talked with over the phone. When we were getting ready to expand the 930, and had the money and specifications ready to go, I called the sales rep (of the month) and asked him if he could come up and discuss our requirements. He agreed to a date but never showed up. When I called and asked what had happened, he gave no excuse and agreed to another date about a week later. Again he never showed up. This meeting was rescheduled for a third time. Still, he never showed up and never called to say why. This time my boss called the SDS president and mentioned that we were ready and willing to buy but his sales representatives seemed to have some aversion to driving out to the desert. The very next day we had a brand new sales rep show up to help us out. I don't know what happened to the "no-show" guy. He may have been fired, because I never heard of him again in subsequent visits to the SDS facility in Santa Monica.

ICARUS

The ICARUS (which was an acronym for Immediate Checkout Analog Research Unity Scaled) program was a digital computer program that calculated the 6 DOF equations of motion of a typical airplane (see list below). The computed accelerations and velocities were output (via D/A converters) to an analog computer. There, the accelerations were integrated with respect to time to get the velocities and the velocities were integrated with respect to time to get the angles or distances. These quantities were then input to the ICARUS program (via A/Ds converters) and used in the calculations for the accelerations and velocities according to the equations of motion. ICARUS calculated a large number of nonlinear coefficients of three variables. We programmed any control systems needed by the particular airplane being simulated on the analog computer. Also the analog computer was the interface to the cockpit and all such signal conditioning was programmed using the analog components or a special-purpose cockpit interface box. The pilots' inputs were also input to ICARUS through A/D converters for use in the equations.

ICARUS was written in Assembly language, originally for the SDS 930. It was later ported to the SDS 9300 that we bought in 1967. Initially, ICARUS ran using a 10-millisecond clock. However, since most of the airplanes of those days could be simulated using a 20-millisecond frame time, we set about re-configuring the SDS 930 real-time operating system to allow us to run two different ICARUS programs simultaneously, using the SDS 930 computer. This was a big improvement in permitting the FSL to support all the many simulations asked of it.

ICARUS was written using fixed-point (scaled-integer) arithmetic. It was possible to reprogram ICARUS for airplanes that varied from the norm. That was discouraged to maintain a certain standard to the hybrid simulations. But basically, ICARUS remained as it started out to be. This was a very successful program and definitely was worth the effort spent in its development. I was able to use it for the Short Take-Off and Landing (STOL) simulations, even though the STOL aircraft had a number of nonlinear coefficients of four variables (see the section on STOL Simulations for more on this simulation). ICARUS was developed and programmed by Lowell Greenfield and Don Bacon.

Before ICARUS was put into general use, it had to be validated. This testing involved trial runs using both all-analog and hybrid simulations of the same airplane and comparing results obtained. It took several weeks, but the ICARUS implementation proved itself equal to the task and was accepted as the preferred method from then on. The HL-10 lifting-body simulation used ICARUS on either the SDS 930 or SDS 9300 and one or more EAI 231R analog computers. This particular simulation was the first to use ICARUS. Don Bacon talks a lot more about ICARUS in his PA in the section on FSL Personnel's PAs.

ICARUS was used for the following aircraft:

    Lifting Bodies (M2, HL-10)
    F-8 Digital Fly-By-Wire
    YF-12
    Hyper 3 Remotely Piloted Vehicle
    STOL
    Oblique Wing

AD-1
F-4E
F-8 Oblique Wing
F-8 Supercritical Wing
JetStar
PA-30
Shuttle (Approach and Landing Tests)
Wake Vortex research
Lightweight Fighters—YF-16, YF-17
F-18 (engineering studies)
F-104
T-33
T-37

As can be seen from this list, ICARUS was used for many different projects. Several, such as the Lifting Body and Digital Fly-By-Wire (DFBW) were very important projects for the FRC. For programs like the F-8 DFBW, the mechanization of the computer portion of these simulators was not the most important aspect of the program. The F-8 DFBW program led to the development of aircraft electronic control systems that are used in many of today's military and commercial aircraft. The software development, testing, and certification that went on using the F-8 DFBW simulator is the real story behind this simulation. This was done using the "iron-bird" cockpit that was installed in the same lean-to that had housed the X-15 iron bird. Photos ECN-7074 and E-23594 show the F-8 DFBW cockpit and some of the hardware and wiring that tied it into the hybrid computer system in the Sim Lab and the airborne computers on which the software was developed. There are many papers and reports about this project. A book chronicling this project has now been written (James E. Tomayko, *Computers Take Flight: A History of NASA's Pioneering Digital Fly-By-Wire Project*, NASA SP-2000-4224.)

The ICARUS program along with the quickly changeable EAI 231-RV and cockpits resulted in a large number of simulations sharing the same hardware and being scheduled for two- and four-hour periods each day. Weekly schedules were prepared, usually for two weeks at a time, and re-done each week because of the somewhat variable flight schedules. The early era of simulations' being able to use a computer (or computers) for weeks on end was essentially over. Projects that needed more than two-hour time periods frequently worked second shift. The ICARUS/Hybrid systems provided an almost assembly-line mode of operation that was a long time in the making. This went on for several years until those

F-8 DFBW Iron Bird Cockpit. (NASA photo ECN-7074)

F-8 DFBW Iron Bird Cockpit. (NASA photo ECN-7075)

DFBW Simulation (Early—pre Iron-Bird—in Lean-to, September 1971). (NASA photo E-23594)

computer systems were replaced by the CDC CYBER 73.

DUHOS

DUHOS (Dual Hybrid Operating System) was a special real-time operating system we had developed under contract to allow us to run two different simulations (such as with ICARUS) simultaneously on the SDS 930 computer. This was my first experience with a competitive solicitation for a software development system. We had over 20 proposals from companies all over the United States. It took quite a while to evaluate all these proposals and narrow the field to the best qualified. There were lots of small companies that were developing software systems. However, very few of them had much real-time experience, and only a couple had any experience with using combined analog/digital computers. We had asked for an operating system that would allow us to use the SDS Real-Time Fortran, Assembler, Loaders, and Libraries in a two-user (only) time-shared mode. We did not have enough memory to run more than two at a time. This was during the very early days of such time-shared multi-user operating systems. Most of the proponents had experience with multi-user, transaction-based systems that were being developed for on-line applications, but few had any true real-time simulation background or even knew what the difference was. Fortunately, there were several companies that did have the proper experience.

DUHOS was developed and written by CUC (Computer Usage Company, Los Angeles, California). The SDS 930 had been expanded to its maximum size. Its instruction format only allowed for executable code to reside in the lower 16K of memory. The upper 16K could only be used for data. There were instructions that allowed the programmer to store and access anything in the upper 16K of memory, but only as operands and not instructions. DUHOS ran two ICARUS simulations, using the lower 16K for executable code and the upper 16K for the data for the two different simulations. Each simulation used 10 milliseconds (or less), and both simulations were run at a 20-millisecond frame time (i.e., 50 frames per second). DUHOS was written so that each simulation could be operated completely independently of the other. For example, it was possible to have one simulation in full real-time operation, slaved to an analog computer for run/reset/hold control modes and the second simulation in the process of loading the data required by the program. The two simulators were completely independent and could be in any mode needed for set-up, checkout, and operation. The normal operating system for the SDS-930 was not a multi-user real-time system. It was not designed for more than one user at a time. The DUHOS required that the system routines be able to handle two different users essentially simultaneously. Most of the operating system software was neither re-entrant nor recursive, although SDS's Real-Time Fortran system had these capabilities.

Compared to today's computers, this probably doesn't sound like anything significant. But this was quite a feat for the computers of that era—especially in view of the fact that the 930's basic instruction cycle time was 1.75 microseconds and most instructions took two or more of these cycles to execute. CUC took about a year to design and implement DUHOS, working mostly on second and third shifts (and lots of weekends). Unfortunately, the lead programmer (John Swanson) quit about three-fourths of the way through the contract. Swanson had previously worked for SDS and was involved in the development of SDS's Real-Time Fortran system. He was an avid bridge player—one of the best in California—and he quit so that he could spend full time in preparation for an important national bridge tournament that was coming up. This really hurt CUC and it took an extra three months (on a nine-month fixed-priced contract) to finish the job. The company took the FRC to court in the attempt to get the extra costs paid, but to no avail. The extra costs were only about $8,000. The original contract was about $75,000 (as I remember) and should have been finished in nine months.

The DUHOS program was not written to run on the SDS 9300 we bought for the Lifting Body Program. The 9300 was a faster computer, with more of its operating-system memory resident than was true of the 930. The instruction format allowed a program to directly access any word-instruction or data in its 32K memory. Also, the 9300 SDS Real-Time Fortran was much better and we started to use it in addition to the SDS Assembly language for our digital programs. The analogs we were buying had servo set pots and could be reprogrammed in less than an hour. This meant that we could change over from one simulation to another, including the cockpit, in about an hour. Our simulations programs were getting bigger and bigger, which also prevented us sharing the 9300 between two typical simulation programs. Because of the increasing usage of the 9300 with ICARUS, the 930/DUHOS/ICARUS usage declined and the computer eventually was surplused to get it out of the old X-15 simulator area of the FSL. The X-15 Program had ended and the analog computers used for the simulator were surplused. The Center wanted the office space for other uses and the 930 was going to have to be moved. Rather than do this, FSL management made the decision to get rid of it. The useful life of the new DUHOS had also ended. One of the computer facilities at UCLA requested the SDS 930 and we donated it to the university.

I'm not sure what UCLA used this computer for. The cost of maintenance was getting higher each year as the company lost interest in providing people or parts. This maintenance problem seemed to always plague us in the FSL (and many other customers), as the computers we bought got old and the original manufacturers quit supporting them. There were many companies that sprouted up to provide maintenance of older-generation computers. The computers of those days were expensive, and not like the throw-away PCs that are being bought nowadays.

SDS 9300

When we bought this computer, via a competitive procurement, SDS's proposal included a fully developed interface to our newest analog computer. Our new analog (an EAI 231-RV) included very sophisticated digital logic and digital automatic set-up capabilities. SDS also, unfortunately for the company, bid its interface to this analog's set-up hardware at no additional cost! This turned out to a mistake on someone's part at SDS, but it was in the proposal, and was a significant factor in SDS's being selected. It was free to us. It took SDS about one whole year to design, develop, and debug this software. A lot of the analog automatic set-up circuits were relay- and servo-based, and developing digital logic and software to tie into this type of analog hardware was an extremely frustrating process. Getting the digital circuitry in the SDS 9300 to work closely with this analog circuitry was accomplished only with a lot of patience and ingenuity, a lot of sweat, and a great deal of trial and error. This digital/analog circuitry seemed to function as erratically as the temperature in the sim labs. The SDS programmers slaved for weeks to get the many digital subroutines operational. The sad part of this story is that we never really used this special-purpose software that SDS gave us. We never used that portion of the new 9300 interface that allowed the digital computer to control the mode of the analog computer, either. Our simulations were still set up so that the digital computer was slaved to the analog computer. That had been our philosophy all along, and we never changed as long as we were doing hybrid simulations.

Who's The Boss

In the world of hybrid simulations, there seemed to be two different philosophies concerning the slaving of the two different kinds of computers. The larger camp, which included most of the analog/hybrid computer manufacturers, contended that the digital computer should be the master and the analog computer the slave. The hybrid systems they were selling were designed around this philosophy, including their operating system software. The smaller group, which included the FSL, always had the analog computer as the master and the digital computer software was slaved to what was happening on the analogs. The digital computer program would just sit and wait for something to happen in the analog world. This seemed more like real life than the other way around. To us, slaving the analog world to the discrete happenings of a digital computer seemed backwards.

The special-purpose software was designed to allow the program in the SDS 9300 not only to control the operating modes of the analog (i.e., reset, operate, hold, etc.,) and the A/D and D/A interface but also to set all the servo-set pots on the analog computer. We never used that part of the digital software, either. We always set the pots either manually or with the paper-tape reader. This method was actually faster and more reliable than other methods.

SDS 9300 Acceptance

Because of this mistake by SDS in its proposal, we could not take acceptance of the 9300 computer and interface until almost one year after it was installed. Fortunately the HL-10 Lifting Body Project took a long break due to stability problems on the very first HL-10 flight. That forced the Program Office to back off and study what had really happened. Until the problem was found and fixed, the simulation was not really needed. The problem turned out to be flow separation over the afterbody, resulting in severe handling characteristics. Modifications to the vehicle were designed and tested in wind tunnels to correct the problem. Once the vehicle was modified, the pilots found it to be a very nice craft to fly, and they all wanted to do so. By then the simulator was operational.

SDS had several programmers using our computers, mostly on second and third shifts, for a number of months trying to get its software operational. It seems strange that the company would even propose such a subsystem when it did not even have the proper analog computer system to develop and test the software and interface that it proposed. SDS was forced to use ours on a time-available basis or buy its own computer. Because we could not officially accept the computer, we were only allowed to use it to convert our 930 software (that was to be used to run acceptance tests) and to become familiar with the different operating system and other software. Any other usage would have been in violation of the contract. So, the 9300 sat there almost one full year before we could really use it for anything productive. This also allowed the SDS programmers to use the 9300 during the day shift when the EAI 231-RV computer was not being used.

Applied Dynamics, Inc. AD-4 Analog Computers

The FSL bought two AD-4 analog computers from Applied Dynamics, Inc. (ADI), in 1970. These were the most sophisticated analog computers we had. Don Bacon, Larry Caw, and I attended an AD-4 programming class that was being taught by Applied Dynamic at the Atomic Energy Commission Facility in Oak Ridge, Tennessee. This facility had also bought some AD-4s and had contracted with ADI to teach the class at its site. We were able to get seats in the class. Otherwise we would have had to wait for the next normally scheduled class, which if I remember correctly would have been after our computers were delivered.

Photo ED00-0091-1 shows an ADI AD-4 Hybrid Computer System. The computer on the right is the analog computer similar to our two AD-4s. The computer on the left is the digital computer. Since we were going to use our AD-4s with the new central computer system, we did not buy the digital computer part of the hybrid system.

The AD-4 analog computer had a large amount of digital logic, including functions not previously available with the EAI analogs. After the AD-4s were accepted, they were used with the 9300 digital computer, and the EAI computers were eventually surplused. The Rocket Site[26] did opt to get the EAI analogs about a year after they were surplused.

The AD-4 analog computers were bought for use with the new digital computer that was being bought for the central data processing center, known as the CYBER 73-28. The specifications for the interface to that digital computer were based on the two specific AD-4s that we bought, which were not the standard AD-4s. ADI also

---

[26] An Air Force facility on Edwards AFB where rocket and missile testing and development occurred.

marketed a hybrid system that included an AD-4 as the analog half of that system. The standard AD-4 was built to interface easily with the ADI digital computer. Consequently our AD-4s were slightly different. This led to some problems later on, since CDC developed its analog interface on information it had gotten from ADI, which turned out to be incorrect. However, our statement of work (SOW) for the digital computer and analog interface very clearly specified that the new digital computer had to be interfaced with our specific analogs. CDC had to make some changes to the interface system after it was installed at the FRC. This caused some problems during the checkout and acceptance of the new digital computer.

Since the new software that we used (see below) was a full 6 DOF simulation, with digital integration, many of the capabilities of the AD-4s were never really used. This is particularly true of the digital logic units on the AD-4s. The AD-4s soon became just cockpit interface systems. After several years and especially after the special in-house-built cockpit interface units were put into use, the AD-4s were no longer needed and were also surplused.

The only time I can recall working with the AD-4s was during the acceptance testing that we did upon delivery. I was not able to complete all the testing, as I was reassigned to the STOL Project to handle its simulations needs. Don Bacon had to complete the testing and acceptance. I don't remember Larry Caw ever actually doing any programming of either of these two AD-4 analogs. Larry was very much involved with the GPAS and spent most of his time working on its analog computers. Don had been promoted to a management position in the Simulation Branch. There were none of the older simulation programmers left, which I am sure contributed to the poor usage of the AD-4 analogs as an important part of the hybrid simulation capabilities of the FSL. The newer FSL programmers were more inclined to use the digital computer for everything that could be done there. Even the aircraft-control-systems simulations eventually were moved into the CYBER. Analog and hybrid simulation was no longer the way to go. The FSL had started a new chapter in its evolution.

The history of that chapter will be told elsewhere, but a key figure in the transition from the period of analog and hybrid simulations to the digital simulations that followed was Al Myers, who recalled his early work at the Flight Research Center and the FSL in an interview in 1998 as follows:

> I was with NASA from 1971 through '81, for about ten years, which was an interesting ten years. I came to NASA as what I think was the last Army detailee. When NASA was originally created out of elements of the Army's Redstone Arsenal and the old NACA, there was an exchange program between the Army and the NASA to cover the technical needs over a transition period. After a couple of years, the Army decided they didn't need any more NASA people. But NASA, never turning down a free help from the technical side, continued it until the early '70's. I know I was the last Army detailee here. I think I was the last one in the program itself.
>
> When I came to NASA, I became involved with the simulation activity and what was then the Data Systems Director. And it was an interesting time in the technical history of that technology. Because we were just at the early stages of the transition between doing simulation with analog computers and moving into the realm of doing them digitally. And I just had the luck to have arrived right at the right time and kind of oversaw the transition from one generation of technology to another.

At the time I came, major elements of most of the simulation activity we were doing—particularly those that had higher frequency content to them, such as the simulation of the active control systems associated with the airplane or the actuation system—the dynamics were still being done in an analog fashion. Also, doing a simulation of a vehicle in an analog computer that would have involved all of the realm of flight dynamics at high angles of attack, for instance, simply was too complex a problem to solve in anything but what would have been a truly gargantuan analog simulation.

And we found right at this time that we were soon to be in need of the ability to simulate that. And the program that really kind of initiated that was an RPV [remotely piloted vehicle] program—one of the first research RPV programs the Center took, which was a three-eighths scale F-15. And that program's aircraft went on to become known as the Spin Research Vehicle. But then its purpose was to examine the high-angle-of-attack regime for the Air Force's new F-15 and to get some actual flight experience in that regime prior to the time the full-scale airplane was going to be flight tested in the same regime.

And initially it was felt that the ability to simulate airframe dynamics at high angles of attack with no small angle approximations and equations of motion was simply not within the state of the art of the computer systems at the time. Fortunately, that turned out to not be the case. And at the same time we were able to do that, we also moved the digital computation from the realm of Assembly language into the realm of doing things in Fortran, which had the additional benefit that a wider circle of engineers involved in the program itself could participate and understand the implementation of the simulation and the control-system code.

And we went on to simulate the F-15 through the full range of angle of attack up to 90 degrees, as a matter of fact, and to simulate the entire F-15 MCS and SCS control systems—both the mechanical control system and the electronically augmented augmentation system that overlaid the MCS, and were actually able to both develop and understand the spin modes of the aircraft and to develop recovery techniques on it. That caused a little bit of consternation initially, particularly with the F-15 prime contractor, McDonnell Douglas, who held that the airplane couldn't be spun. The contractor personnel ultimately determined that the same spin modes were, in fact, possible on the full-scale aircraft. So that was an interesting program and an interesting point in time, not only from an aerodynamic (aeronautics) perspective, but also in terms of the technology and support and the ground aspects of it—in this case the simulation.

It was also the period in which we were about at the height of our lifting-body programs. We'd been in them a few years. The M2-F3 was still flying right at the tail end of the HL-10 program and we were just getting started on the X-24, all of which were genuinely fascinating programs at the time.

Also, I came to Dryden right at the completion of the test activity of the first phase of the F-8 Digital Fly-By-Wire program. During the first phase the aircraft had been converted to a fly-by-wire system, which utilized the Apollo flight computers. These were extraordinarily reliable but rather limited in terms of the amount of memory and from the computational through-put point of view. At the time, the program was getting ready to redesign that system to a triplex system using a more modern flight computer. It turned out we picked the IBM AP-101 computer, which was an airborne-worthy system. It actually turns out to have been the predecessor of the systems that were ultimately chosen for the Shuttle. And the simulation technology activity and the F-8 Digital Fly-By-Wire program were totally intermeshed with each other.

We used the iron bird of the F-8 to do all the flight systems qualification and, of course, the simulation that provided all the simulated inputs, if you will, to the iron bird was an integral part of that. So I had the real pleasure of participating in a rather direct fashion in the qualification of that system on the F-8. We learned an incredible amount about the qualification of digital flight control systems through the experience of that whole program—an amazingly productive program—and really did an excellent job of laying the foundation for a whole new technology area in aeronautics, with fly-by-wire clearly becoming the new generation of military aircraft. And now, in the last few years, we see it also being implemented in the commercial aircraft.

And the genesis for all of that and how to go about developing and qualifying that system was right here at Dryden. It was also an interesting program, from the prospect that Dryden actually acted as its own prime contractor.

Through that activity, we had a number of subcontractors. But the basic integration and development activity was directed and done right here at Dryden.[27]

CYBER 73-28

The CYBER 73-28 was to be shared by both the simulation lab and the general-purpose data processing facility. These two different branches, up until then, had been separate and independent. That changed when we got ready to buy the CYBER. We started working on this procurement long before we even went out for bid—even before the two groups were re-organized into one division (see below). Several of us were relocated to a small office for the purpose of analyzing the uses and needs of the two computer facilities and preparing some sort of design specification that could be used for the SOW for the procurement. CDC, IBM, Xerox, Univac and others were all very interested in our upcoming RFP.[28] We talked with many different companies before we ever started to prepare the SOW for this procurement. Large hybrid computers were not the norm, and of the ones that had been developed, none were exactly what we needed.

I remember working with some IBM folks who were in the process of developing hardware and software for combined analog/digital simulations. IBM, while mostly a business computer manufacturer, did have an extensive line of scientific computers, and it also was interested in this new hybrid technology. Its hybrid research facility was at the Stanford research labs in Palo Alto, California. During a period of about one year, I made four or five trips (at government expense) with our local IBM sales representative to this facility, which had an IBM 7040-class computer connected to an Applied Dynamics Inc. AD-4 analog computer. There

---

[27] Interview of Al Myers by Peter Merlin, 14 Aug. 1998, copy on file in the Dryden Historical Reference Collection.

[28] Request For Proposal, which is a solicitation for bids on a contract.

were others from the FRC who went with me on a couple of these trips. I'm not sure that what we did was totally above board—that is, helping IBM develop the hybrid system that it most likely would propose when we sent out our RFP.

When we finally sent out the RFP, the one mailed to IBM went to its Los Angeles office. This was the address that IBM requested we send the RFP to. However, all this work we had done with IBM and its hybrid development lab in Palo Alto was handled through the IBM office in Riverside, California. This is the office that was covering the high desert area and Edwards AFB. The Los Angeles team that IBM put together to write the proposal knew nothing about what had been going on for the last year. Apparently these two IBM offices did not talk to each other very much. The proposal they submitted in response to our RFP was so far from what we asked for that we had to eliminate IBM during the very first go-around of evaluations. All that work was for nothing. I don't know if a proposal from the Riverside office would have been selected, but I'm sure it would have been a lot closer to what we wanted. After all, we had helped them build their prototype. Strange happenings! This was another instance of gremlinity.

Pot or Not?

An interesting event occurred on a trip to the CDC facility in Minneapolis to discuss our requirements with the CDC staff involved in our procurement. The group from the FRC included Ed Videan, Mary Little, John P. Smith, Ernie Dunn, Lowell Greenfield, Bob Halasey, and myself. We flew into Minneapolis and spent the night at a motel outside the city near the CDC plant. In the morning, we were to meet for breakfast with some of the CDC folks who would drive us to the plant. The motel was out in the suburbs and there were open fields nearby with a variety of farm products being grown. Greenfield and Little had gone for a short walk before the get-together with CDC.

Along their way, Lowell spotted what he thought was a marijuana plant growing in the ditch beside the road. He picked a sprig and brought it to where the rest of us were standing, waiting for the CDC folks to show up, in front of the motel's restaurant. Lowell showed us this sprig and asked if anyone else agreed that it was marijuana? Ed Videan took the sprig, looked at it, and agreed that he too thought it was marijuana. Two strangers, who just happened to be walking from their car to the restaurant, stopped, looked at the plant, and stated that it definitely was marijuana. When Ed asked why they were so sure, they proceeded to display their badges and announced that they were vice squad officers from the local law enforcement agency. These two men told us that marijuana grew wild all over that area. One of the officers then stated that picking the plant was illegal, and since Ed was the one holding it when they walked up, the officer then proceeded to (begin to) arrest Ed. He was just kidding, but Ed lost a few heartbeats before he found out that the two officers weren't serious. The officers kept the marijuana.

The CDC CYBER 73-28 included a very complete system to be used for flight data processing and general-purpose engineering and scientific computations. The new Fortran language was being used more and more by the research engineers at the FRC, and a bigger and faster computer was needed. Previously, most of the engineering programming had been done by the programmers in the data processing branch.

In addition to the standard data processing capabilities, the CDC 73 included two identical analog interface subsystems that were connected to our two new AD-4 analog computers. There was also a real-time data-communication line that was connected to the SDS 920 in the radar and telemetry facility. Unfortunately, this link was never used for its intended purpose. It had the capability of transferring real-time data directly from the radar/telemetry system to the CDC 73. That facility only had only one programmer developing software, and he never had the time to develop the software to use the link to the CDC 73. We tried this circuit during the acceptance period and it worked. That was in 1973. Dryden still hasn't implemented a similar capability even now (in 1999 when these lines were written).

The interface that CDC developed to connect to our analogs was both complex and extensive. There were two complete subsystems, one for each of the AD-4 analog computers. They included D/A and A/D converters, discretes, real-time clocks, and control circuits for the analog computers. The AD-4 analogs were the most sophisticated hybrid computers of that era and had lots of digital logic and other digital computer-like capabilities that made them particularly well suited for large complex hybrid simulations.

Larry Schilling, the Director of Research Facilities at the Dryden Flight Research Center, observed in the year 2000:

> The CDC Cyber 73-28 utilized a unique hardware/software scheme for interrupt handling and real-time I/O. It was called HRTM (Hardware Real-Time Monitor). This scheme gave full control to the programmer in setting up interrupts and linking them to real-time code. The user could specify the period and the tolerance for each interrupt. Clock resolution was 10 microseconds (2000 counts or ticks for 20 msec), remarkable for its day. Real-time input occurred at the beginning of the frame. Output occurred as specified by the programmer using the tolerance setting. For example: if the frame was 20 msec long, and the code took 10 msec to execute, the user could specify when the output would occur by setting the tolerance to a value between about 11 msec and 19 msec. The tolerance parameter also affected the CPU priority since the calculations would have to be completed before output could occur. It would technically be possible to set the tolerance to 20 msec and have the output occur at the same time as the input for the next frame. This was avoided because if several output discretes changed state (a 5-volt change), the resulting EMI could be seen on the A/Ds, so settling time was necessary. The great advantage of this interrupt scheme is that the output parameters changed state at a predictable and controllable time in every frame. This deterministic capability is of great value. I have not seen a better scheme developed since. To the best of my knowledge, CDC only sold two computers with our version of HRTM (and just a few more with a later version), so we had a rare bird.

This was probably the first time CDC had ever built such analog interface hardware, and the team it put together to do this job included not only some of its best hardware designers but also a couple of its top system programmers. Impressive. It took them a while, but they got it working.

This new hybrid system was the only one the FSL used that shared a digital computer with the general-purpose data processing group. The two branches (Simulation and Data Processing) were combined and a new division was created to use and support this new system. Besides the two different programming groups, a new Systems branch was created that included systems analysts from both original branches. I was one of about eight in this group. We had the job of overseeing the development, installation, checkout, acceptance, and initial operation of this new computer. We also got involved in the conversion of software to this CDC 73.

CYBER Software Conversion

For us in simulation, this conversion process was not difficult. All we had was the ICARUS program. Converting this one program turned out to be easy. Actually, it wasn't converted at all. Instea, new software was developed. The new simulation programs, written mostly by Al Myers, were in Fortran and were designed to use all this new capability. ICARUS had been written specifically for the SDS computers. Converting it to the CYBER wasn't necessary.

As Larry Schilling pointed out on reviewing these lines:

> The new simulation program written by Al Myers (with collaboration by Lowell Greenfield) was known as RTSIM (Real-Time Simulation). It was quickly replaced with RTSIMII (Real-Time Simulation II) which was in use when I arrived [in 1978]. There was also a batch version called SIMII. All of Dryden's current sims trace their heritage back to this work. Not only was this a 6 DOF formulation, but it avoided small angle approximations and used a full floating-point implementation. The digital integration algorithm was a modified 2nd order Runge-Kutta that was developed by Myers and Greenfield (at least I think Al said Lowell had a hand in it).[29]

Unfortunately, the ease with which those in simulation converted to the CDC 73 was not the rule for all the data processing programs. Conversion of these programs turned out to be a lengthy job. CDC provided a remote batch terminal to be used for this purpose. This was the FRC's introduction into the world of digital data communications. I remember working with the telephone companies to get this remote batch terminal operational. Edwards AFB is in Kern County, while the CDC computer facility was near the Los Angeles airport. There were three different phone companies involved in getting the telephone line between these two facilities. None of these telephone companies had much experience in providing telephone lines for use with digital data. This was quite early in the use of telephone lines for digital data, and every phone company did things differently. It took some time before they were able to provide us with a working link. This link went from Edwards to Bakersfield to Los Angeles.

The remote batch terminal did allow us to convert programs to be used on the new computer. The terminal included a card reader, printer, and cathode ray tube. The communication line was only about 110 baud and quite slow. It took forever to get a large program compiled, run, and the output listed. It seemed as if we were sharing this CDC computer with everyone else in the Los Angeles area. For those programs that required magnetic tapes, we had to either take the tapes there or use a courier service. I remember having to make several trips to the CDC facility just for this purpose.

Before the CDC computer was delivered, the FRC employees had handled the daily operations of the previous central data processing computers. I believe that this new computer was the first one for which the FRC contracted for computer operational support. Until this contract started, we in the new Division got stuck with the job of being computer operators. Most of us had no real experience doing this sort of work. CDC provided a one-week training class, which we all took. Everyone in the Systems Branch and all the programmers in the Programming Branch got drafted to be computer operators. Each day, the Systems folks worked two-hour shifts, and the programmers worked one-hour shifts as operators. Mounting

---

[29] The RTSIM program as Bacon remembers (Don was Myers' boss at that time) was written for the XDS 9300 in Fortran, and Don does not remember any airplanes that had simulators built using this program. It was done to study if such a Fortran sim could actually run on the XDS 9300 in real time and to see what problems might arise. RTSIM was ported to the CYBER, and the all-digital CYBER version (RTSIMII) was the one used for subsequent simulators.

mag tapes, changing disc packs, handling stacks of punched cards, and fussing with the printer outputs were not the types of activities we were used to. This went on for a number of months until the new service contract started and its personnel took over the job of operating our new system.

The CDC 73 was so much faster and more powerful than the previous computers in the FSL that the new simulation software included the integration of the accelerations and velocities with respect to time. This part of the simulations was no longer done on the analog computers. Those brand new, very sophisticated AD-4 hybrid computers at that point in time became very expensive cockpit interfaces. This also meant that a lot of the new digital interface hardware and software that CDC had developed for us was never really used as intended. This was the beginning of the end of hybrid simulations in the FSL. Many of the original and more experienced analog/hybrid programmers had been transferred to other jobs. New simulation engineers were being hired, many with no analog programming experience, and this too had an influence on the way things were done. From then on, almost everything was done all-digital. The analog computers were still being used to simulate the control systems, but that too was to be replaced a couple of years later with an all-digital simulation programming capability that was developed at Dryden by John Edwards. He developed the algorithms that allowed for these very complex aircraft control systems to be simulated using a digital computer in real time. It wasn't too much later that all the analog computers in the FSL were surplused. Simulation was all-digital. The cockpit interface was now handled by special-purpose hardware developed mostly by Charlie Wagner, and built in-house.

Lifting-Body Simulations (1967-1972)

The lifting-body simulations[30] were mechanized by Don Bacon, Lowell Greenfield, and Larry Caw. Initially, the simulations were all analog. However, they became hybrid with the use of the SDS 930 computer and the ICARUS program. The aerodynamic coefficients for the HL-10 vehicle were very nonlinear and could not be adequately mechanized using analog components. The Lifting-Body Project Office agreed to pay for the purchase of a new digital computer for the FSL for the purpose of implementing the HL-10 simulator. The computer we bought was an SDS 9300, and after it was accepted, the ICARUS program was modified to run on this computer.

This simulation was operational in 1967, which overlapped with the period when we were running the X-15 simulator. The HL-10 simulator did not have an iron-bird cockpit like the X-15. It used several different simulation cockpits. (See photos E-10278, E-10591, E-16464, and E-18902 of the M2 and HL-10 cockpits.) It did have a visual display device to give the pilot a rudimentary "out-the-window" display. Also, the pilots used the an F-104 airplane for landing practice, as they did in the X-15 program.

The following paragraphs are from Don Bacon, one of the simulation programmers for the Lifting Body Program. His personal account below includes much more on the lifting-body simulations.

> The HL-10 was the first one I did myself. In the early days of the lifting bodies, it was all analog. We took several consoles to do one, and you could only do one at a time. In the long run, we did the M2-F2 and M2-F3, which Lowell Greenfield was responsible for. The HL-10 was mine and the X-24 was over at the Air Force. We also did some work on the Hyper III (which was the switchblade wing design) and another one, all of which contributed to what later became the Shuttle.
>
> The derivatives were nonlinear and the aero people had constructed the family of curves. Ken Iliff did a lot of the work—and Bertha Ryan. I still remember the first time I went down to ask her a question, and she stood up and drew herself up to her full height and said "I am a theoretical aerodynamicist and I don't chase wind-tunnel data for simulation guys."

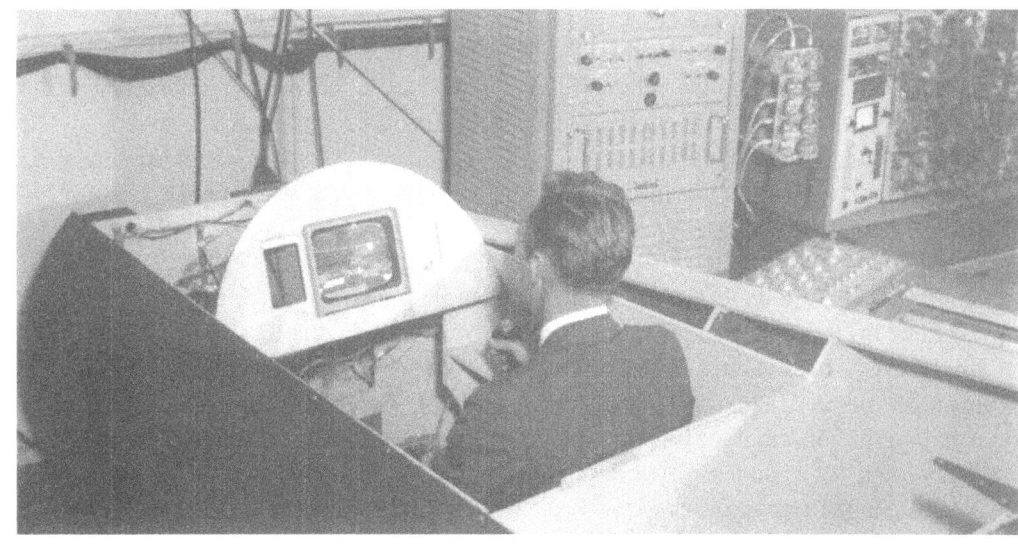

Bob Hoey in the Early M2 Simulator Cockpit (Norden Display and TR-48—October 1963). (NASA photo E-10591)

---

[30] There have been several lengthy papers and books written about the Lifting Body Program. These are listed in the bibliography.

Lifting-Body Simulator Cockpit (March 1967). (NASA photo E-16464)

The nonlinear curves were set up with families of independent variables, so every Mach number had a set of curves—and alpha and beta [angle-of-attack and angle-of-sideslip, respectively] were independent variables. They were all done on pot-padders [a type of analog function generator]. During that time, they wanted to fly each airplane every two weeks. We took about a week to get the pilot ready—to learn what to do for the next flight. It took 40 hours to reset the pot-padders for each airplane. Lonnie [Cooper—EAI maintenance support team lead] and the EAI guys worked all weekend. They worked around the clock to get the 40 hours needed between Friday afternoon and Monday morning to switch from one lifting-body simulation to the other. . . .

Static checks were done. We'd calculate the frequency and damping for dynamic checks and then run them out on the strip-chart recorders. Again, once you had done this to check them—we had plastic overlays prepared in the reproduction shop—you could lay them over the strip charts and see. One of the interesting things that happened: the process in going from paper [recording] to plastic [overlay] stretched the curves on the plastic. If you took the original and laid the overlay on it, they didn't match any more. . . .

So it was kind of a trick to get an overlay that would work. That took another 10-15 minutes. So it was common to spend an hour—after you were sure everything was all right—on just checking things. And then, of course, you flew it. You'd pick a sample mission and fly it just to make sure the computers, model, controls, and displays were all right. You didn't have those problems with simulations that were set on dedicated equipment and were flown day after day, such as the LLRV and X-15.

Lowell Greenfield was the primary digital programmer on the ICARUS project. He left NASA sometime after we had received the CDC CYBER 73 to work for an aerospace company in the Los Angeles area. He has subsequently died, and his achievements and experiences are for the most part unrecorded. After he got into digital computer programming, he concentrated his efforts in the systems programming support area, and especially operating systems, such as the CDC CYBER Operating Systems (SCOPE, etc.). Lowell took a number of courses through both UCLA and USC on computer-systems software design and programming and became thoroughly involved in that particular line of programming. Lowell and Stan Yount were sent to the Navy's computer laboratory at Johnsville, Pennsylvania, in the fall of 1972 to get hands-on experience with the CDC SCOPE Operating System. Their travel duty was before we received delivery of the CDC CYBER 73-28 that was installed at the FRC in 1973. Lowell and Stan spent about four weeks there learning about the software from a systems programmer's point of view. This is the same Navy facility that had the centrifuge used for the boost simulation described previously.

Larry Caw was a backup programmer on the lifting-body simulations (M2 and HL-10). Larry did very little digital programming; his work was mainly with the analog computer and cockpit interface. Larry was still responsible for the LLRV simulator at the time, so his involvement with the lifting-body simulation was primarily as a backup analog programmer. He did this job for only a couple of years, until he was assigned to work on the GPAS program. Larry's PA is included below.

Robert (Bob) Kempel, one of the NASA research engineers, was heavily involved with the Lifting Body Program. His PA account is included below and contains a lengthy discussion on the lifting-body simulations. Bob also wrote a document in 1998 entitled *Simulation and Modeling Support in the Flight Testing of Lifting Reentry Vehicles*. This, too, is an excellent discussion of the role of simulation in the Lifting Body Program. See the bibliography for other publications by Bob on the Lifting Body Program.

Both Bob Kempel and Don Bacon, in their PAs, talk about speeding up the simulation so that the time period was shorter than real time. This was the idea of Jack Kolf, one of the lifting-body flight planners, after talking with the pilots following several flights. Apparently the pilots felt that the events during a typical lifting-body flight seemed to happen faster than they actually did. To provide a similar feeling in the simulator, the time constant (used in integration with respect to time) was set so "simulator time" was about 40 percent faster than normal. This procedure was not used during the normal flight-preparedness simulator runs. The day before a flight, the time constant was changed and the pilots made a number of practice runs. This simulated a "faster than real-time" sequence of events. The pilots thought that these runs helped them get ready for the actual flight. The typical lifting-body flight lasted only about eight minutes, and many were less than four minutes.

Milt Thompson wrote a paper[31] that discusses his experiences with the Lifting Body Project and the role of the simulations that the FRC and the AFFTC implemented in support of this project. Milt made the first five flights of the M2-F2 in 1966. Milt also flew a large number of flights in the wooden M2-F1. This lifting body was originally towed behind a souped-up 1963 Pontiac Catalina convertible that had been modified to tow the M2-F1. Later, the aircraft was towed behind the FRC's C-47. In the book entitled *Flying without Wings* by Milton O. Thompson and Curtis Peebles, Milt describes the early flights he made in the M2-F1 and M2-F2 lifting bodies.[32] This book is a very interesting accounting of the Lifting Body Program from the viewpoint of one of the pilots involved with that project.

---

[31] The paper by Milt Thompson, which is unpublished, is entitled "Lessons Learned from Flight Research," and is available in the DFRC Historical Reference Collection, location L1-5-11B-10.

[32] Milton O. Thompson and Curtis Peebles, *Flying Without Wings: NASA Lifting Bodies and the Birth of the Space Shuttle* (Washington, DC: Smithsonian Institution Press, 1999).

STOL Simulations (1971-1972)

This set of simulations comprised the last ones I did. A special Short Take-Off and Landing (STOL) Project Office had been established to study STOL aircraft technology. The office was located where the X-15 simulation computers had been. Jim Adkins was the project manager. Fitz Fulton was our project pilot. Harold Washington, John Gibbons, Bruce Powers, Dave Kier, Terry Putnam, and I were also assigned to the project. I was about halfway through the check-out and acceptance of two brand new Applied Dynamics, Inc. AD-4 analog computers that had just been delivered to the FSL. Don Bacon had to complete this acceptance testing after I was re-assigned to do the STOL Project simulations.

There were two different STOL aircraft configurations, an externally-blown-flaps configuration, and an augmentor-wing configuration. (See below for explanations of the two configurations, and see the reports written about these simulations, citation numbers 738 and 770, for further information.) This simulator, with two different sets of nonlinear coefficients, was one of those that we implemented for airplanes that did not really exist. There were models developed for wind-tunnel studies and the like, but the real planes were never built. (See photo E-22756.) At least not the ones we simulated. The two we simulated were just models of what STOL airplanes might be. Airplane manufacturers have, I'm sure, benefited much from such studies by NASA.

The STOL Project seemed to have sufficient clout to do most of the tasks that were planned; however, the STOL simulation did not share in this high priority. I had to work around all the other simulations that were being run. This also manifested itself in such a way that I had little help in getting the cockpit set up. I was essentially on my own, and could not depend on much help from any of the sim technicians, because they were all busy working on other simulation tasks. They helped out whenever they could. We used an existing cockpit, with few or no changes. I either did all of the cockpit scaling by myself or enlisted the help of one of the engineers in the project office. For the first implementation, this wasn't too difficult, since the cockpit we used was in the same lab as the SDS 9300 and

STOL Wind-Tunnel Model (February 1971). (NASA photo E-22756)

the EAI 231-RV computers. Later the cockpit was moved to another room as this particular sim lab was reconfigured.

Many Nonlinear Functions of Four Variables

What I remember most about these two simulations was that I had to implement a large number of nonlinear derivatives of four variables. Analog computers were not well suited for functions of four variables. One- and two-variable nonlinearities were not difficult. Three-variable function generation took a lot of equipment and was avoided, if possible. Four-variable function generation had never been done in the FSL. I used the ICARUS program, running on the SDS 9300, and two different analogs for two different implementations. The 9300 was connected to an EAI 231-RV. This analog was used for integration of the accelerations and velocities calculated by the digital program. It was also used for the fourth variable interpolation of the derivatives, which were read back into the 9300 program for use in the calculations of the equations.

For the first implementation, the EAI 231-RV was also used for the cockpit interface. The second implementation used a Comcor portable analog computer for cockpit interface. The second implementation was required when the cockpit was moved to a different room. This necessitated the use of a second computer for cockpit interface. The ground-based cockpit is shown in photo E-23281. The simulation equations were very typical for this type of vehicle. ICARUS was set up to do a large quantity of functions of three variables. By using this capability and interpolating for the fourth variable (coefficient of thrust [C_μ]) on the analog, I was able to do this four-variable function generation. Not very difficult, just never been done like this before. The cockpit that we used was configured for a typical transport aircraft with a yoke, rudder pedals, and two or four throttles. Both of the STOL vehicles we simulated had four engines.

STOL Simulation Cockpit, Displays, and Controls (June 1971). (NASA photo E-23281)

The cockpit shown in photo E-23281 is the one we used for the STOL simulation. Besides the SDS 9300 and EAI 231-RV, I also had to use one of the FSL portable analog computers, a Comcor 175. This was the only time I used this particular analog in any of my simulations. The Comcor analog computer was a solid-state computer. It had about 100 amplifiers but limited function-generation capability. For this simulator, it was used primarily for interface to the cockpit instrumentation and pilot's controls. An out-the-window display was provided by the Norden Contact Analog. It generated a fake ground plane consisting of random checkerboard squares or other repeating patterns. It also had fake oval clouds in the sky. The display patterns moved and changed, depending on the aircraft's position, velocities, and attitude.

Two Different STOL Configurations

In the two different STOL configurations, the big difference lay in the design of the wings to provide additional lift. For the augmentor-wing version, a portion of the jet engine exhaust was deflected down by large flaps, thereby providing additional lift during takeoff and landing. The externally-blown-flaps aircraft diverted bleed air from the jet engines over the wings, thereby creating additional wing lift during takeoff and landing. In both cases, this additional lift was mechanized as the derivative $C\mu$ [coefficient of thrust, deflected downward to increase lift]. Many of the aircraft nonlinear coefficients were mechanized as functions of alpha (angle-of-attack), beta (angle-of-sideslip), $C\mu$, and Mach number.

STOL Simulation Cockpit (ARC Moving-Base Simulator—January 1971). (NASA photo E-22438)

Ford Tri-Motor Flights

Besides flying this simulator, Fitz was also able to fly several aircraft using STOL-like approaches and landings. He got to fly one of the few Ford Tri-Motors that was still in use. This plane was being used for short ferry hops to islands in Lake Erie that were being serviced by a small commuter airline in the area. The runways on the islands were quite short and required a STOL approach and landing. The Tri-Motor was capable of doing this. Fitz also got to fly some larger commercial jets that flew in and out of a number of small islands in the South Pacific. Most of these islands had short runways and the jets also had to use STOL-like approaches and takeoffs. Normal takeoff and landing procedures could not be used for the short runways.

ARC Moving-Base Simulator

We also used the moving-base simulator at the Ames Research Center at Moffett Field, Mountain View, California. It had a large 6 DOF motion simulator for such studies, with a commercial-jet-type cockpit. The ARC had implemented a similar configuration STOL simulation on the computers connected to the motion-based cockpit. (See photo E-22438 of the ARC STOL cockpit.) I still remember the day we went to Ames so that Fitz could fly the moving-base simulator there. We flew up in one of the small airplanes that the FRC had. The weather over the San Joaquin Valley was extremely bad, with clouds, rain, lightning, you name it. The local FAA vectored us clear out over the Pacific before we could turn north for Ames. Fitz was flying. He then spent almost all day flying the simulator. When we flew home, we were vectored east almost to the high Sierras, to get around the weather over the valley, before we could turn south for Edwards. It was nice and clear here. So, guess what? Fitz decided to shoot some touch-and-go landings before he finally landed! Almost 11 hours after we had taken off that morning. These test pilots are a hardy breed!

My Last Simulation

This was my last complete simulation of any kind. My career as a simulation programmer was coming to an end. Shortly after this, I was transferred into a different group to help buy a new computer system for the central computer facility. Several years later, I got drafted to do some programming for the HiMAT (Highly Maneuverable Aircraft Technology) and DAST (Drones for Aerodynamic and Structural Testing) simulations, but that programming task was to decommutate the real-time telemetry data stream from these two RPVs (Remotely Piloted Vehicles) for both the Simulation and the RPV laboratories. Also, I was getting more and more involved in buying computers. Computer procurements always took a long time in the government. Shortly after the STOL simulators were no longer needed, we began to reconfigure the entire simulation laboratory. The FSL offices moved into the area where many of the simulation cockpits had been located. It was also about this period of time that we began getting ready to replace our SDS 9300 computer. The SDS 930 had already been donated to UCLA.

Personal Accounts of the FRC Simulation Laboratory Personnel

The following personal accounts (PAs) of members of the FRC Simulation Laboratory were prepared from responses to letters, phone calls, and electronic mail. The inputs received varied widely both in format and content. Some were dictated onto audio cassettes either by the people themselves or during interviews. Some were pieced together from letters and e-mails. A few of the FSL personnel were not located and have moved and left no forwarding addresses with friends or the FRC personnel office. Several of the FSL personnel chose not to return any information, which is unfortunate, for some of them were very active participants in the development and use of the FSL. At least one has died, and his account will never be written.

The following sections are, for the most part, as written or recorded. I have taken few liberties in transcribing and editing the material and then only to try to maintain a certain approach in this publication. I have also added information, suggested by the individuals, when their recollections were dim and they could not recall events exactly. In some cases information has been added by other FSL members during the review process. For the most part, the PAs are the individuals' own words.

The many reports that were written about the results of the various simulations have also provided data. The many research engineers who used our simulations and wrote technical papers have also provided information, not only about the simulations, but about the FSL personnel who implemented those simulations. I have tried to mention all those people, but I am sure I have missed some. I have spent many hours in the DFRC Research Library reading and scanning as many of these technical reports as possible, in an attempt to collect as much information as possible about the actual simulation implementations. Unfortunately, most of these reports only mention the use of analog computers and do not provide details. Many of the reports only list the equations that were programmed. Almost none of them actually discussed the specifics of how the simulation was implemented. Since we in the FSL were not required to write reports about how we mechanized these simulations, very little remains that could be used in the preparation of this study. So far as I can determine, analog computers are no longer manufactured or used for real-time simulations,[33] so the details of how we implemented ours is perhaps no great loss, except to those of us who were there.

In many cases the data presented in these PAs overlaps what is written in other sections. This is particularly true when a FSL member was very much involved in the development of one of the more important (and bigger) simulations that are discussed in detail. But, even though there is some repetition of data about specific simulations, what follows are the words of the different participants, and an important part of this monograph. We all see and experience things differently, and our memories are as different as we are.

Edward N. Videan

Ed Videan was the first chief of the original Simulation Laboratory. This

---

[33] I based this statement on considerable research on the Internet. I also talked with Mike Najera (who heads the sim hardware group in the RAIF), and he says that there are still some analog circuits in almost all of the simulators being built today. The newer "glass cockpits" with the computer-driven displays have eliminated most of the analog circuits that were used in simulators built since this building opened. *However, there are no analog computers in use with the simulators.* Just analog circuits (i.e., variable voltage devices) as opposed to digital circuits—digital computer I/O words of some number of bits (1s or 0s). The electric stick used in all the cockpits is an analog device and so are some of the instruments, and these instruments still use the SIMLINK interface that Charlie Wagner designed and had built to replace the use of analog computer components (amplifiers, pots, etc.).

organization had several different names throughout the years, and as mentioned earlier, is referred to as the FRC Simulation Laboratory (or the FSL) throughout this monograph to avoid any confusion caused by the different names.

The History of the First Analog Computer at the FRC

The analog computer (or more properly, the electronic differential analyzer) first came into use at the HSFS in 1956, as best I can remember. The date might be as late as 1957. The requirement which drove the introduction of the analog computer was a need to analyze a dynamics problem troubling the then-current jet fighters, known as roll coupling. The F-86 fighter (and others, I believe) were exhibiting large uncontrolled excursions in angle of attack and sideslip in response to high-speed rolling motions. At this time there existed at the HSFS no practical way to solve the differential equations of motion which describe such a complicated dynamics problem. Digital computers were in their infancy, and the limits on speed and memory ruled out any practical way to solve the equations.

Both Langley and Ames Laboratories were beginning to use analog computers and had acquired some facilities. In addition, the AFFTC had recently purchased a modest facility built by Goodyear. This machine was known as the GEDA (Goodyear Electronic Differential Analyzer). The heart of the analog computer system was a high-quality operational amplifier, which, suitably configured, could sum several electrical signals and also integrate the resultant sum. This capability was exactly what was needed to solve a set of aircraft differential equations of motion.

Other required functions such as the multiplication of two independent variables and function generation were performed by servo devices.

When the AFFTC acquired its first analog computer (the GEDA), the HSFS made arrangements with the AFFTC to use this system to start investigating the roll-coupling problem. I believe it was Richard Day who led this effort along with several others. I believe Albert Kuhl was also working on this problem. After two or three months of successful work, the HSFS decided to acquire its own computer system. During the procurement cycle, a small delegation of people from the HSFS traveled to the Ames Laboratory for a week of training on the programming and use of an analog computer. Those from the HSFS were Richard Banner, Richard Day, Richard Musick, and Ed Videan. Our host at Ames was Stanley Schmidt, who headed up the Ames facility. Shortly after this, the FSL received its first system, the EAI 31R, built by Electronics Associates, Inc. I believe this early system contained about thirty amplifiers, two servo multipliers, plus a complement of scaling potentiometers. The cost was about $60,000. I am not sure about the number of amplifiers, but this is the number that comes to mind.

Since the analog computer was able to solve the aircraft equations of motion in real time, it was recognized to be a natural for aircraft simulation with a pilot in the loop. However, in these early days there were no controls or displays which in any way looked, acted, or felt like anything found in an airplane. There were no commercial sources known, and no resources available to develop suitable devices. For the early roll-coupling investigation, the stick input was provided by a wooden stick attached to a potentiometer. Displays were provided by voltmeters with a scale and pointer calibrated for the appropriate quantity. Some side-arm controllers were borrowed from the space program at a later date to be used as pilot input devices. Through the years, FSL personnel designed and developed a rather full range of general-purpose displays and controls which could be tailored for use in a wide variety of applications. Richard Musick, Charles Wagner, and others were key to this effort and can supply much more detailed info. I believe this was one of the genuine innovations which the FSL made to the art of simulation.

Here is an anecdote which might be of interest. It concerns the rivalry which developed between the analog and digital computer approaches to simulation during those early days. A simulation conference was held in El Paso, Texas, in 1958, I believe. I attended this conference along with Stanley Schmidt of Ames. One speaker described early efforts to solve the aircraft equations of motion utilizing a digital computer. Because of the limited speed and memory of the [then-]current digital machines, this effort did not demonstrate any practical capability. However, the speaker predicted that one day, digital computers would supercede analog machines in the field of flight simulation. The conference attendees were mainly a very partisan group of analog-computer loyalists who then heaped ridicule on the speaker. In addition to the problem of limited digital computer capability, there existed no analog-to-digital and digital-to-analog converters. General Dynamics in San Diego had built an experimental model which was not really practical because of size, cost, and very importantly, reliability. As I remember, it was almost the size of a washing machine. I guess the moral of the story is, sometimes it pays to listen to the dreamers.

In 1958, I believe, the FRC became interested in the piloting aspects of the manned space program, specifically, the problem of piloting a space vehicle from launch to orbit. The Navy possessed a human centrifuge at its Johnsville, Pennsylvania, facility, and the FRC obtained the Navy's cooperation to utilize this facility for a piloted launch investigation. This program was the largest simulation attempted by the FSL up until this time. A special function generator was developed and built at the FSL to simulate atmospheric density from sea level to space. The full simulation was designed and tested in the FSL prior to traveling to the Johnsville facility. The Navy had a large simulation facility at Johnsville which was devoted principally to investigating submarine warfare. The FSL program was installed on the Navy computers and interfaced to the centrifuge. If I remember correctly, NASA, Air Force, and Navy pilots participated. I think Neil Armstrong was a participant. The program required seven weeks of time at Johnsville plus all the preparation time at the FSL.

The next large program was the X-15 simulator. John Smith and others were much closer to the program and can supply more details. One episode stands out in my memory. I believe the X-15 was the first time we attempted to include an airplane and its systems in a simulator loop. While the simulation was successful, I remember how we struggled to solve the [electrical-signal] ground loop problems between the aircraft (hangar ground) and simulation facility (facility ground). As I recall, we finally ran a ground cable from the [analog computer] laboratory to the airplane and lifted the hangar ground.[34] The solution sounds so simple and logical now.

Richard (Dick) O. Musick

Dick Musick was the first FSL technician and was assigned to this job from his previous position in the instrumentation shop. He also provided support for the data-reduction equipment that was in use at that time. Most of this PA is from a letter that Dick sent me. Photo ED97-44197-1, taken in 1957 (from the 1957 AFFTC Year Book), shows Ed Videan and Dick Musick in front of the first analog computer in the FSL.

The simulation laboratory was formed after the NACA moved from the south base to north base. I believe that to be 1955 or thereabouts.[35] My duties during the pre-move period and shortly after were building special flight-data instrumentation, repairing standard flight instruments, and maintaining the data reduction equipment. At that time the data reduction equipment was composed of three telereader/telecondex machines, typewriters, and IBM relay-operated card reader/punch machines. [See photo E-2145.]

An interesting sidelight to the data-reduction process and a definite credit to the ladies operating the equipment involved the conditions [under which they worked]. All units were crowded into a small, darkened room with no special air-conditioning equipment (it was quite warm.) Each telereader/telecondex had well over 200 tubes consuming a lot of energy and converting it into heat. I would

Ed Videan (on left) and Dick Musick at EAI 31R Analog Computer (1997—from AFFTC 1957 year book). (NASA photo ED97-44197-1)

---

[34] There was almost a 1/2 volt difference between the hangar's signal ground and the computer's signal ground. To get around the problems this difference was causing, all the trunks had their shields grounded only at the computer end. The hangar end of each trunk had to have its shields disconnected (i.e., not connected to the hangar's signal ground). The computer ground was also connected to the hangar equipment. Consequently the electronic equipment in the hangar was using the same ground as the computer equipment in the simulation laboratory.

[35] Actually, it took place in 1954.

Dick Musick with film reader (December 1955). (NASA photo E-2145)

go in there periodically to perform some duty and within 15 minutes, I'd be sleepy. The operators had to stay in the room eight hours a day.

The analog equipment and I first made contact when it arrived at the HSFS. Since I had the best electronic background of all the technical people in the instrumentation division, the finger was pointed at me, and I was told "From now on, you are a computer specialist." And so it was!

Since our new equipment—an EAI 31R—used tubes, it had a heat problem, which required attention. A plenum chamber had to be fabricated upon which all the equipment would rest to blow refrigerated air through it. I can't recall all the initial installation, but it seemed to me to be an EAI 31R console, a rack of amplifiers, a rack of servo multipliers that also contained several resolver units, and a rack of pot padders.

Following the decision to set up a flight simulation facility at the HSFS, we assessed our on-board equipment and talent and found it lacking. Like nada.[36] We started

---

[36] Spanish for "nothing."

from scratch. Ed Videan drew the short straw as simulation engineer, and I was informed I was the tech for the project. At the time, I was the sole support for the research-film-data-reduction equipment and was to continue in that capacity. I didn't think I could do it.

Ed arranged for the computer equipment to be purchased. I just twiddled my thumbs (and worked on telereaders) while waiting for the EAI technical manuals, my source of training, to arrive.

The equipment arrived and it was installed on a plenum chamber for cooling. I guess we did OK because when Ed Videan, Al Wilson, the electrician, and I finished fumbling around, the system worked. I don't remember in the slightest if we had any major problems.

OK, we had our computer in place and working; now all we needed was to provide a simulator cockpit. Our first effort was, as best I can recall, a cutoff broomstick, which was spring-loaded to represent an aircraft control stick. The instruments were an oscilloscope display to represent the horizon, and micro-ammeters with limited needle displacement to display necessary flight parameters. This was crude (pre-caveman stuff) to say the least, but it was a start. [This control stick is shown in photo E-1841 and the display is shown in photos E-2950 and E-3395A.]

Instruments

I'll start with the instruments, which were the highest priority in coming up to speed on our physical aircraft simulators. In looking at the instruments locally, we found our stockroom grossly lacking, but we adapted. Although we were not able to match the aircraft instrument in

Reaction Control Stick (April 1957). (NASA photo E-2950)

appearance, we faked it as best we could. The instruments in stock were micrometers, low-level voltmeters, and milliammeters,[37] all of which were single-needle, limited-needle excursion and of course not scaled for flight simulators. [The earlier instruments can be seen in the photos mentioned in the previous paragraph and also in photo E-2626.]

We enlisted the aid of John Bostain and the photo lab to produce a more realistic face. At first, the simulation techs would draw up an oversize instrument face and John would downscale the size as required. It worked OK. [Several of these instruments with the photo background can be seen in the photo E-4969.]

Later on, the photo lab employed a draftsman, Jerry Lyons, who did the artwork for the instrument faces.

As a matter of interest, the instruments we used at first were manufactured by Triplett, Simson, and GE. The greatest needle movement was about 100 degrees stop-to-stop.

Knowing that the in-house-supplied meters were inadequate from the start, the technicians started searching for a better unit with a larger face and greater needle movement. A meter manufactured by Weston was found, which met our immediate needs. It was larger in diameter, had better damping, and had a needle excursion of 300 degrees. It was the answer to our prayers for a single-turn instrument. We invested in the Weston meter for quite a few units over the years. [Several of these instruments can be seen in the Boost Simulator Instrument Panel in photo E-4550.]

The next priority in instruments was for multi-turn-needle units such as Mach-meters and altimeters. We ended up taking several steps in the development of a totally satisfactory unit. We went over to the Air Force surplus and talked the people there into contributing some altimeters and Mach-meters as well as other things that looked interesting. No paper work!

We delivered the instruments (unmodified) to Rebel Harwell and the machine shop for modifications per oral directions (plus a pseudo work order). Rebel and his technicians were to adapt the altimeter to be driven by a Kerfott synchro unit. They did this both expertly and quickly. We then drove the synchro receiver with a synchro transmitter, which was in turn driven by a shaft-to-shaft coupling with a servo unit responding to the analog altitude signal. There was a lot of slop in this arrangement but it did the job. [Three of these servo-synchro units can be seen in photo E-14648.]

The next step up was the purchase of a cylindrical-shaped servo unit with the power and input plug located on one end and a rotating output shaft on the other. They were manufactured by Spectrol. We adapted the output shaft to the input gear of the instrument being fabricated. The overall unit was big but operated better then the synchro-driven instruments.

As a final step in producing panel instruments for single- and multiple-turn needs, we designed and built, in-house, a DC servo unit that was both small and easy to inte-

---

[37] Instruments for measuring electric currents in milliamperes (multiples of one-thousandth of an ampere).

Servo to Synchro Units (LLRV Sim Cockpit—April 1966). (NASA photo E-14648)

grate into the instrument. Not only was it compact; it also operated smoothly throughout its entire range and cost a small fraction of the Spectrol servo's price. This was the final phase for the development of a universal DC servo, which was used throughout our aircraft simulators thereafter.

Much credit has to go to Bob Ballard and Robby Robertson of the machine shop for their expertise in putting life into our instrument servos.

One other instrument problem which required attention was how to drive the three-axis 8-ball [attitude indicator] without modifying the instrument itself. Built by Bendix, it was flight-qualified and would be too expensive to physically modify for our needs. The answer turned out to be very simple, since it took a synchro signal to be the input (one for each axis); we would drive one of our servo units with a computer output representing the parameter. We then mechanically connected the servo output shaft to a synchro transmitter drive shaft and wired the three-phase output to the input plug on the back of the 8-ball. Voila! The servo unit we created solved many of our instrument problems and found a lot of other uses as well.

Cockpits

Our cockpits were a little slow in getting started. The first was a common chair (with no lap belt) for the pilot to sit in and a spring-loaded cut-off broom handle to provide (simulated) flight inputs. [See photo E-1841.] The flight instruments (all electrical) were located in a narrow aluminum pseudo panel, which bridged a large Dumont CRT that represented an "out-the-window" view. We got by with this by using a lot of imagination.

The first real attempt at simulating a cockpit came about a bit later. We made contact with Flight Operations and borrowed blueprints for an F-104 cockpit. Using this, we recorded critical measurements around which a semi-realistic "black box" could be built: our aircraft cockpit. The cockpit was fabricated in our model shop by Ernie [Lowder] and Chuck [Garvey]. They did a hell of a job in making all the measurements we gave them to meet. The first major cockpit was built of 3/4-inch plywood with the plywood edges finished with oak strips. It came complete with a removable seat mounted on rails for fore and aft seat movement. Two other features need to be mentioned. The floor was about 12 inches above the base floor and was hinged for access. It was all painted flat black. The unit was basic and needed a control system, instruments, and other electrical and mechanical devices, which were added later. If I remember correctly, the stick and pedals were spring loaded.

Several instrument panels were manufactured by our model shop and configured to represent the instrument layout for specific aircraft. Panel exchange was quite easy.

The final aircraft simulator control system was fabricated using DC torque motors provided by Inland Motors of Roanoke, Virginia, the same manufacturer that provided our instrument servo torque motors.[38]

John P. Smith

John Smith was the first FSL programmer/engineer and was initially a lieutenant in the U.S. Army Signal Corps who had been assigned to work at the NACA HSFS in 1957.

I reported to the High-Speed Flight Station on 4 April 1957. The first analog computer had been installed early that year, around January or February. The log for use of the computer had as the first application a program, which Harriet[39] provided in February, solving an integral and not a true simulation. She says it didn't work too well, which is not surprising, considering the poor repeatability and low accuracy of the analog computers at that point in time. My first simulation was a derivative matching program with Chet [Wolowicz].[40] We used a pen follower as the control input in a five-degree-of-freedom simulation program. Chet said we did the work in one hour that it used to take a mathematician a month to accomplish.

During that period we did either five-degree- or three-degree-of-freedom simulation programs. That was because of limited computer

---

[38] Following his reading of this study in manuscript, Robert W. Kempel appended a note at the end of this PA: "One thing that really made FRC 'tick' was the fact that there were so many talented people who were willing to apply their talent to unusual jobs [in places like the] photo lab, machine shop, etc. Inventiveness, innovativeness, and the common cause. Dick was one of the greatest!" Kempel also commented, "I remember going to Dick with some problem, and Dick would pull out a shelf from his desk with a sign on it that said 'pound here' [meaning, if you were frustrated, you could pound your head there and get rid of your frustrations without bothering him further]. Dick had a great sense of humor!"

[39] Harriet Stephenson (who later married John Smith) was a research engineer at the HSFS.

[40] Chester Wolowicz was a research engineer at the HSFS. He wrote a number of reports on such subjects as stability characteristics of aircraft, stability derivatives, a simulator investigation of orbital derivatives, and operational and performance characteristics.

capability. The equations were ones that had been developed at Langley several years before. For pilot-in-the-loop simulations we used a classroom chair, which had a writing surface on the side. We mounted a B-17 formation stick on the writing surface. The display system was a CRT for the horizon and up to three voltmeters mounted on the side of the CRT for critical cockpit instruments. We used grease pencils to calibrate the CRT and the voltmeters. When we had to have a center stick, Dick would fix up a pipe with springs and mount it on a plate. [See photos E-1841 and E-2950.]

One of the early simulations I did was on the X-1B. It was a program Wendy [Stillwell][41] tried [in an attempt] to refine the reaction-control-system design for the X-15. The objective was to define a zoom maneuver, which would give the maximum amount of time at low q [dynamic pressure] where the reaction control system would be effective, and to develop the best control laws. This was a three-degree-of-freedom simulation, and we got some strange results. We found that when we pulled to high angles, the airplane would just keep going up. That is when we found out that the Langley equations were small-angle approximations. After that experience, we derived our own equations.

We also did several simulations in support of the future space program, including looking at various concepts for multi-stage rockets to use for orbit and reentry systems. For our first visual simulation, which was for orbital docking, Dick [Musick] modified a projector aperture so that we could control it with a servo. We programmed the system so that the size of an image projected on a wall would represent the size of the docking target as it was approached. [See photos E-5035 and E-5037.].

In 1958 we started our work on the X-15 simulator. One of the major things we did was the development

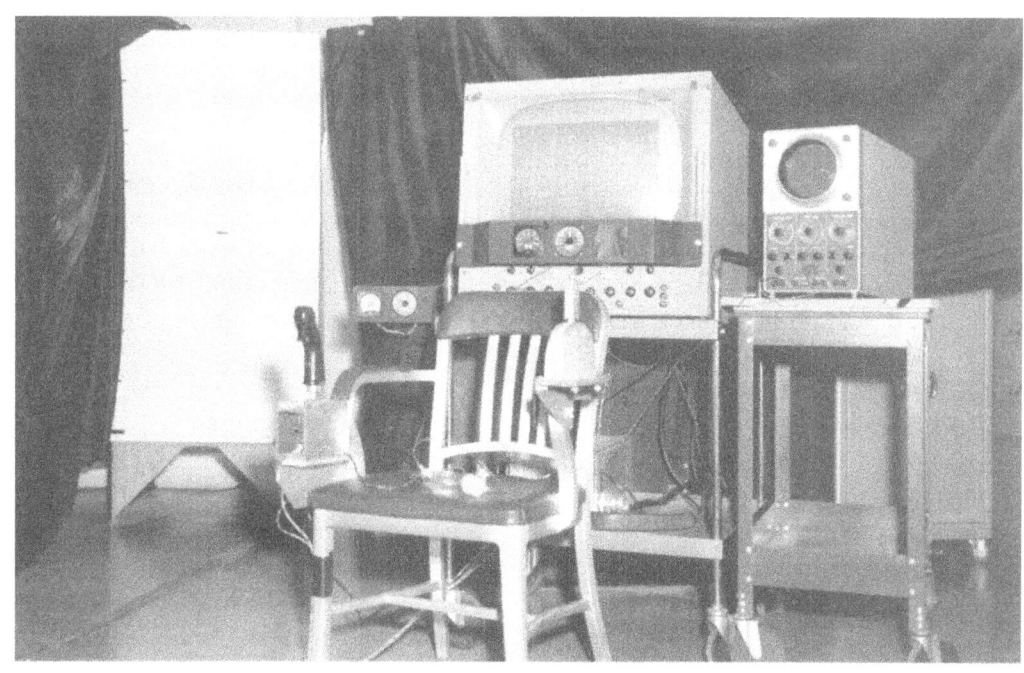

Orbital Rendezvous program simulation equipment (October 1959). (NASA photo E-5035)

---

[41] Wendell Stillwell was a research engineer at the HSFS. He, too, wrote a number of reports on such things as flight measurements, reaction controls, and simulator studies of reaction controls, plus several studies on the X-15 including one well-known special publication.

Orbital Rendezvous program simulation equipment (October 1959). (NASA photo E-5037)

of the round-earth equations. That was a major step in being able to predict the maximum performance of the vehicle. I also did the simulation with Jim McKay on the landing-gear problem. That turned out so well that when the Air Force needed to define runway width for the Dyna-Soar Program, its engineers asked us to develop the dynamic simulation of their landing gear and its run-out characteristics. J. L. [Samuels] and [John] Perry developed the equations of motion, but we did not have the equipment to do the simulation. So the simulation was done at FDL [Flight Dynamics Laboratory].

In the early days, the time needed to bring a new simulation on line was about one to two weeks. We made a big use of transfer functions, which involved the use of the S-plane technology. We would come up with black boxes that used electronic components in the feedback and input of amplifiers to simulate non-linear functions. The checkout and validation of simulations was a new and changing environment.

Gene Waltman

Since much of what I did has been discussed throughout the other parts of this monograph, this is just a brief summary, listing the major tasks, accomplishments, and other facts related to my career in simulation. I have included a number of the computer procurements in this list because they were an important part of the FSL history. I worked at NACA HSFS-NASA DFRC from July 1957 to July 1993.

- Worked in the FSL from July 1957 to about 1975, plus a brief period for HiMAT and DAST Real-Time TM decommutation software for Sim and RPV labs in 1978.

- Worked as an analog programmer, hybrid programmer, and systems analyst during that period and
  - Implemented several X-1B and X-1E simulations: 1957-1960
  - Implemented a number of F-100 series aircraft simulations: 1957-1960
  - Implemented 4 different 4-stage-boost simulations (3 fixed-base and 1 moving-base):1958-1960
  - Programmed the X-15 simulation, all-analog:1960-1964,
  - Programmed the X-15 hybrid simulation:1964-1968
  - Programmed the STOL simulations: 1970-1972
  - Programmed several other moving-base simulations, 1958-1972, at the

Ames Research Center
- Programmed several heat transfer programs—analog (1958-1960), and digital (1964-1968)
- Taught analog computer programming classes

- Investigated the early hybrid computer technology: 1960-1975
  - Programmed in Assembler, Fortran, and real-time Fortran languages for the SDS, CDC, HP, and Varian computers

- Procured at least one major computer system (hardware or software) each year from 1958 through 1975, mostly for the FSL, but also several systems for other computer facilities at the Center. I was actually involved in such procurements until I retired in 1993—but not all for the FSL. Many of these procurements were for one-of-a-kind systems and not off-the-shelf systems, due to the unusual needs of the FSL.
  - Computer procurements: 1958-1975
  - Including collecting requirements, writing the SOW, and working with Procurement on the request for proposal, proposal evaluations, negotiations, and selection
  - Working with vendors during system buildup, installation, and acceptance testing
  - Working with users for conversion and startup of new equipment.
  - Searching out new equipment and technologies for possible use in the FSL

John J. Perry

I started 1 September 1959. That was my first day. I had two interviews—I interviewed with John Smith [in simulation] and Ken Sanderson [in instrumentation] . . . and John took me. He took me on a tour and showed me the digital computer, which at that time was an IBM 650. This was a room full of computers. I had never seen a computer up close and personal. I didn't even know what an aeronautical research engineer did.[42] They offered me a job, and I figured if they thought I could do it, I could do it. So, I accepted.

Orbital Rendezvous Simulation

My first involvement with simulation was really primitive. I had been at the FRC about 6 weeks. My first simulation was an orbital rendezvous. We were supposed to simulate two bodies orbiting in space, rendezvousing. And of course, we had nothing, hardware-wise. All we had were the equations that described the phenomenon. So it was my job to use either the TR-10 or the EAI 31R, that first analog with the rotary voltmeter.... I don't remember which I used. I was working with Dick Musick to develop the hardware. What we ended up with was a strange-looking contraption. He went out and built this cylindrical screen that couldn't have been more than five feet tall. We took one of the metal wastebaskets, turned it upside down, and mounted a hand controller on it. Then he put a couple of dials on a makeshift instrument panel. He also modified a slide projector aperture so that as we closed on the target, the picture on the screen got bigger. And he projected the image on a servo-driven mirror to simulate attitude. That was the first simulation I worked on as a young engineer.

---

[42] John Perry graduated from Florida A&M University, Tallahassee, Florida, in 1959, with a BS in Mathematics. He got an MBA in Management Decision Systems from the University of Southern California in Los Angeles in 1977. He also received a Certificate in General Business Management from the UCLA Extension in 1973.

[See photos E-5035 and E-5037 for the final set of equipment used in this simulation.]

We had pilots come in there, sit, and try to dock, and it was amazing. We had a distance meter, just a simple little voltmeter dial, showing distance from the target. And the picture got bigger as we got closer, and we could rotate. It was very primitive, but it was effective. Orbiting in space is a no-brainer these days, but it was an interesting challenge as I think about it now. Back in those days we wondered, "How are we going to do this?" I'm sure we didn't contribute to the big solution that NASA finally came up with, but we were probably among the first to figure out, "How can we do this?" And what kind of system do we need to practice this, before we have to do it live. I think I worked on this simulation up to the time I got assigned to work on the X-15 simulation.

X-15 Simulator

At that time the X-15 simulation was on the EAI 31R and 131R computers. We then went "big time" and got three brand new EAI 231Rs. The voltmeter on the 131R had digital panels, and the numbers would come up on the different panels. I thought that was the craziest voltmeter I had ever seen. I thought that was an improvement over the dials. Then, we got the 231Rs with the newer voltmeter—I don't know what the technology was, but the numbers were all on one plane: the numbers just changed around. That was great.

I remember having the job of working on that X-15 simulation, with all of those patch cords. I think I still have a couple of the multiples that I keep just to remind myself of how it used to be. Those patch cords were hanging off the patch panels, some connected by all of those multiples. As I recall, we were still using the 131R. I remember how the servo resolvers used to get stuck. I used to have to go in the back to put some torque on the shaft to get them unstuck. One day I was in there, and I put my hand back there to unstick a resolver and touched something hot. The natural reaction was to jerk my hand away, but there was a bar above the opening. Since it was in a pretty tight space, my hand just bounced back and forth between the hot source and that bar. It beat the heck out of the back of my hand before I was able to remove it. We had to do a lot of things to make those simulations work. But they worked!

As the project engineer on the X-15 simulator, my job, first thing in the morning, was to make sure that it going to play that day. As you know, with analogs, sometimes they would play and sometimes they wouldn't. We had those two test runs that we did—the one was an altitude run and the other was a speed run. Every day, before the pilots came down, we had to be sure it was going to work right that day. We had this little fudge factor on a pot—we'd twist that factor until it came out right. I'll never forget, that altitude flight was 314,000 feet. If the computer would do that flight, then we could practice altitude flights that day. If we were planning to practice speed stuff, where we wanted constant dynamic pressure or constant altitude or something like that, then we would have to do the low-altitude speed runs to see if that was going to work. We would play with it and play with it until we were ready. Then we would call Flight Ops and say, "OK, we are ready to go." The pilots would then come down to practice.

Some of the pilots were more excited about practicing than others. Jack McKay never wanted to practice. But people like Joe Engle would practice until they were blue in the face. They just wanted to get it right. Bob Rushworth was another one; he was probably the most precise low-altitude pilot we had. If we told Bob we wanted a certain dynamic pressure for a certain number of seconds, that is what we got. He would practice on the simulator until he was sure he could do that in flight. So, it was fun working with those guys.

I don't remember when I came into the program. I just remember that I worked on it for six and one-half years. I started before we got the SDS 930. I never really made the hybrid transition. I went to the GPAS from the X-15. Other people were working on the 930, and later on the 9300.

We had some significant challenges, but we were up to them. That is what made working for NASA so much fun. Because NASA was the glamour agency of the federal government, we could attract and retain the best and brightest. We believed we were good, and we set out to prove it every day. That didn't mean we didn't have conflict and didn't fuss and fight, but we brought our best every day. We didn't leave anything on the practice field.

Derivative Matching

I remember Glenn Robinson and I were doing derivative matching[43] on swing shift. Glenn and I never got along, but we rode together to and from work. We would fuss from the time he picked me up until we got to work, and as soon as we got in the computer room, all our arguing stopped, and we worked well together. We used Sanborn recorders, with the red ink flying everywhere. We had overlays, and we put them on the inked paper to see if we were matching the derivatives. When we were off at midnight, and as soon as we got to the car, we started fussing again. However, we did some serious business during our work shift. That was a part of my simulation career when I was basically supporting Stability and Control in the derivative matching process. I wasn't doing anything other than making sure the computer was working. They were the ones doing all the work, but I think it was important work that I did as well. We were trying to refine the wind-tunnel data so that we could make the simulations more accurate.

X-15 Landing Simulation

That was true up until we got to the point where we decided that, because of some problems we had with some of the landings, we wanted to write a simulation of the X-15 landing. I was given the responsibility of coming up with the equations to do that. I'll never forget—it was right before I was getting ready to go on vacation, and I was going to be flying to Florida. I took that stuff with me, and on my flight back to Florida, I did a lot of work on those equations. It turned out it was 10 degrees of freedom (DOF) because

---

[43] As explained more briefly above, derivative matching, on an analog computer, was a process of determining the nonlinear derivatives for a particular airplane. Most of the X-15 derivatives used in the simulator were originally obtained from wind-tunnel tests and were not always accurate or complete. Derivative matching was used to update the wind-tunnel data using actual flight data. Over the years, derivative matching was done using several different analog computers and for many different airplanes. This analog process was eventually replaced with digital parameter-estimation techniques developed by research engineers at the FRC.

we had to do the 6 DOF for the airplane and four for the landing gear. We had to include sliding friction for the skids, rolling friction for the tires on the nose gear, and the torque created by the struts. I was working with Jim McKay on that project. We ended up getting that job done in terms of the design of the system to simulate the landing of the X-15, and then the FRC lost interest. However, it was implemented at Wright-Patterson. I never got to see it, but I heard that it worked really well. That was probably the most challenging job I had ever had to do in applying the math I had learned in college, primarily because we had to do it from scratch. We already had 6 DOF equations for the aircraft, but we had to add the 4 DOF for the landing gear and integrate them. We also had to add ground effects. I never got a chance to play with it after I had done it, but I was told that Wright-Patterson did and thought it was successful. It would have been a real challenge for analog computers, and I believe we were still analog at that time. It might have been a lot easier if we had had faster digital computers.

I think my last major piece of work on the X-15 was that landing gear problem. Although that wasn't the end of the program, it was basically the end of my active involvement in it. I had been kind of moving into supervision, and watching Larry Caw with the TR-48s and the LLRV thing he had—that mess he had. Man, he had the messiest hook-up I had ever seen—wires running everywhere. Larry had a hornet's nest over there.

GPAS

I then moved on to the JetStar. Bikle basically made that decision to take it out of the hands of Research and Dwain Deets and Ken Szalai, who were working on it, and put it back into simulation. GPAS was fun work, too, because it basically was the same thing we had done, but in the air. It was a different kind of challenge because we had to try to make the GPAS—the JetStar—fly like other kinds of airplanes. Again, we were playing the programming role because Herm Rediess and those guys in Stability and Control and Handling Qualities were designing the experiments. We were just trying to make sure that we turned their designs into effective simulations. And we got to fly and run the computer in the air while they were doing the testing. It was fun work, and it was exciting work.

The first couple of flights we went up on, I took Dramamine. I sure didn't want to get motion sickness up there because I knew we were going to be all over the sky. I could tell from the work we were doing in the hangar that it was going to be a wild ride. But Dramamine just wiped me out. We usually tried to fly in the morning when the turbulence was low. I decided I'd just rather be sick because once we landed, I was worth nothing for the rest of the day [because] I was so lethargic. I stopped taking the Dramamine. When I was a kid, I fished. I'd go out in the Atlantic in a rowboat and fish all day; yet I never had motion sickness. I don't know why I thought an airplane would create some. I never got sick on the GPAS, but most of the other folks did. Larry Caw did! Owen Parish used to brag about how he was a pilot and never got sick. I saw him walk off the GPAS one day with that [barf] bag full. The GPAS got him. I don't remember if Musick ever got sick. I know Herm did. Herm would get sick at the drop of a hat. The thing is, they were always looking at these low-static-stability configurations, so you knew the thing was going to be unstable. The pilots were always interested in seeing just how unstable it was before ever trying to control it. I would tell them "we're ready," and they would take their hands off the controls to see how quickly it would go divergent. They were saying, "That is interesting," and I was saying, "Come on—somebody control this thing." We'd be all over the sky. Herm couldn't handle it; he'd get sick almost every flight when we were flying low-static-stability configurations.

We had several interesting experiences. One, we were looking for turbulence for Ken Iliff to work on his doctoral dissertation and were down in these canyons looking for rough air.[44] The pilots were up there talking about "this is just light chop," and I couldn't even keep my feet on the floor in the back of the airplane. I was saying, "Hey, wait a minute, this is light chop? What are we looking for?" We finally found some good turbulence that Ken did, in fact, use for the parameter estimation part of his dissertation. He did give us acknowledgement for having gone through that. In fact, I still have a copy of his dissertation in my office.

The second thing was when we added those side-force generators to the fuselage and the direct-lift devices to the wings. The modifications were done at Lockheed Georgia. We were flight testing them, and we got into a flutter situation. I wasn't flying. Larry was in the airplane, and Stan Butchart was flying. That was scary. I was sitting in the control room, and from what I could determine from what they were saying on the aircraft, it was going to be a disaster. When they landed and we went out to look at the airplane, we had buckled some skin and popped some rivets. We had probably come very close to a situation where the airplane would just come apart. In fact, Butchart said that he was looking for the spot where they would likely crash.

So we had some interesting times with the GPAS. I think Bob Baron took over [as project manager] after I left. They did some more interesting things with it. I was more into managing the hardware when I was working with Charlie [Wagner] and those guys. Charlie developed the first effective version of a variable-feel stick: the electric torque motor stick. He did a great job on that. The interesting thing about Charlie [was that] his degree was in mechanical engineering. He had to teach himself electrical engineering to make that work. And of course, he did it, and it worked very well.

So, I got into that part of simulation where we were developing and testing hardware. My primary role was that of managing that operation. Charlie was the primary engineer, and Dick [Musick], Art Suppona, Gerry Perry, and Billy [Davis] were doing all the building and testing. My role became one of coordinating with the project managers, negotiating for resources, including time. My deal with those guys was this: [as stated by John,] "I don't know how to do what you do, so you tell me what

---

[44] Ken Iliff is a research engineer and is currently the Chief Scientist for the DFRC. Actually, the JetStar was not flying as an airborne simulator when it was gathering data for Iliff's dissertation but just gathering data about turbulence. The reference for the dissertation is K. W. Iliff, "Identification and Stochastic Control with Application to Flight Control in Turbulence," UCLA-ENG-7340 (Ph.D. diss., University of California, Los Angeles, 1973).

you need and how long it is going to take. I'll take that to the bank. All I ask you to do is, if you find out that you need more or are going to take more time, let me know as soon as you know. I don't want to get blindsided out there." We worked that way for years. They'd tell me what they needed, and I'd go out and get it from the project managers. If the project managers said they needed it in six months, and those guys said it would take nine months, I'd tell them they could get it in nine months because we can't do it in six. So, that was my job. Gerry Perry usually overestimated his time, so I learned how to calibrate his estimates. Gerry always wanted about 50 percent more time than he thought he needed, just in case. We had a good group of folks, and Charlie was the main man. He developed some wonderful stuff and he did so up till the end of his career.

That was basically the end of my career in simulation because I moved up to become John's deputy. I still managed that part of the organization up until I got ready to go to graduate school, which was '76. As John's deputy, I was still managing Charlie and that crew. That was getting to be a no-brainer because those guys were so good that they didn't need anything from me. The Division pretty much ran itself. And there wasn't anything I could do for the digital side. I didn't understand what they did anyway. So, I knew it was time to do something else if I wanted a reason to get up each morning. At that time, I could disappear for an afternoon and go play golf, and no one would miss me. There was nothing for me to do. My job was simply dealing with Procurement, dealing with John Yoshida[45] on budget issues, and trying to make sure the guys had what they needed to do their job. I was doing no technical supervision and was primarily working with the project managers to make sure that we understood their requirements and negotiating with them for extensions in schedule or money. That wasn't a frequent occurrence because those guys were so good at estimating what they needed and how long it would take. That is basically the reason I applied for full-time graduate study. I was getting bored with that job because there was nothing for me to do. I never thought they would accept me as a full-time graduate-school candidate, but they did. Then I had to figure out what I wanted to do once I was accepted. That was basically the end of my simulation career. When I came back from graduate school, I went into Administration.

Donald C. Bacon

I arrived on 1 September in '64. The 930 was just delivered. In the first six months or so I did things to get familiar. One of the things was that Jim Samuels[46] sat down with me to teach me to derive the equations of motion, beginning with $F=ma$ from basic physics.[47] We worked on that for a couple of

---

[45] John Yoshida was the chief financial officer at the FRC.

[46] Jim Samuels was the first analog programmer in the FSL who had a college degree in aeronautical engineering.

[47] Newton's second law of motion asserts that the rate of change of momentum of a body is proportional to the force acting upon the body and is in the direction of the applied force. This is usually stated as the equation $F = ma$, where F is the vector sum of the applied forces, m is the mass, and a is the vector acceleration of the body. The equations of motion for an aircraft can be derived starting with this basic equation.

weeks. He'd say to me, "Think about this How does that work; what assumptions did you make?" The example he used, and one of the simplifications we made, was that forward velocity was greater than vertical velocity. If you ever get into an airplane and it is dropping faster than it is going forward, then you've lost terms [from your equations that] you now need. And particularly, there were different kinds of airplanes that were experimental; you constantly had to keep in mind the assumptions that you made in the equations you were using.

Lifting-Body Simulations

The first one I was assigned to do was the HL-10—in '65. Lowell Greenfield was the guy assigned to help, and Gene Waltman was the technical advisor. By that time, Jim Samuels had either just left or was in the process of leaving. He wanted to do more "hands-on" work and John [Smith] wanted him to do more management work. They came to a parting of the ways over how much time he spent on the 930 and how much he spent with the guys. [Jim went to work for the Lockheed Rye Canyon Simulation Facility.]

The HL-10 was the first one I did myself. In the early days of the lifting bodies, it was all-analog. We took several consoles to do one, and you could only do one at a time. In the long run, we did the M2 [both the M2-F2 and M2-F3], which Lowell was responsible for. The HL-10 was mine and the X-24 was over at the Air Force. We also did some work on the Hyper III,[48] which was the switchblade wing design, and another configuration [of the Hyper III]. All of these contributed to what later became the Shuttle.

The all-analog, I still remember, was drawn out on one sheet of paper the size of a table—so you could see all the connections for the basic simulation. And then each section was on 11 x 17 pieces of drafting paper—grid paper—with all the inputs and outputs carefully labeled so you could look at one section. You could look at the big picture as well as the individual pieces.

Testing

There was a lot of work involved in testing. I still remember the first time I got it all ready to turn the HL-10 on. Ten or twelve simulation guys gathered around. I said, "What I've done is set the basic parameters for the initial conditions[49] to zero so that I won't have any trouble when I turn it on." And half the group snickered, because they knew what was coming. So I said, "OK, I'm ready" and turned it on. Whistles went off, bells went off, servos went winding, and amplifiers' alarms screamed all over the place—and they said. "Shut it off, shut it off." So I shut it off. They said, "Think about it—you set velocity and weight to zero, didn't you?" And I said, "Yes." "Well, you divide by those numbers and that screwed everything up—what do you get when you divide by zero?" So everybody had a good laugh—but it was a lesson learned: Sometimes what you think is the simplest way to approach something is not really going to work.

---

[48] There is an excellent description of the Hyper III project in the book by R. Dale Reed with Darlene Lister, *Wingless Flight: The Lifting Body Story* (Washington, DC: NASA SP: 4220, 1997), pp. 158-166

[49] Initial conditions are the values for those parameters in the equations that are normally not equal to zero when a simulation run is started. Velocity, altitude, weight, heading, etc., are examples of calculated parameters that have initial values at the start of each run.

The derivatives were nonlinear and the aero people had constructed the family of curves. Ken Iliff did a lot of the work in getting the data ready—as did research engineer Bertha Ryan.[50] I still remember the first time I went down to ask her a question—and she stood up and drew herself up to her full height and said "I am a theoretical aerodynamicist and I don't chase wind-tunnel data for simulation guys!" She left soon after to go to work at China Lake. They wouldn't let her do the theoretical work she wanted to do and they wouldn't let her in the hangars near the planes, so she left to work at China Lake.

Simulation Switch-over

The nonlinear curves were set up with families of independent variables—so every Mach number had a set of curves—and alpha and beta were independent variables. They were all done on pot-padders. During that time, they wanted to fly each airplane every two weeks. We took about a week to get the pilot ready—to learn what to do for the next flight. It took 40 hours to reset the pot-padders for each airplane. Lonnie [Cooper—EAI maintenance support team lead] and the EAI guys worked all weekend. They worked around the clock to get the 40 hours needed between Friday afternoon and Monday morning to switch from one [lifting-body simulation] to the other.

And then we checked the derivatives out by sweeping them using the Rep Op[51]—we had plastic overlays and the Rep Op scope that we had for derivative matching. We used that to sweep through the independent variables and be sure, 'cause every now and then we'd get a spike in one [of the derivatives].

Static and Dynamic Checks[52]

Static checks were done first. Next, we'd calculate the frequency and damping for dynamic checks—and then run them out on the strip-chart

---

[50] Bertha Ryan and Harriet Smith were the research engineers responsible for the earlier M2-F1 analog simulation. Al Readiger was the FSL programmer for this simulation. There is an excellent description of this simulation in Dale Reed's *Wingless Flight*, pp. 26-31.

[51] Rep Op (which is short for Repetitive Operation) was a feature available on most analog computers. Rep Op allows the operator to reduce the problem solution time by a ratio of 100:1 and the computer alternates between the RESET and OPERATE modes, causing the solution to be produced many times a second. This allows the calculated outputs to be displayed on an oscilloscope at a rate (usually) that is fast enough that the entire solution can be seen at one time. The operator can make changes to almost any of the parameters in the equations (usually via one or more pots) and the effects of the changes can be seen immediately. Once the desired solution is attained, the time constant can be returned to normal and the solution calculated in normal time, with the results plotted on a recorder. Although not really intended for the use described, Rep Op was a very convenient method of displaying the nonlinear derivatives. If one or more of the data points in the functions had been incorrectly programmed (or if there was a blown fuse), the bad data point(s) would be immediately visible on the oscilloscope.

[52] Static checks on an analog computer provided a method of determining if the implementation was correct (i.e., were all the components correctly connected and were all the pots and function generators correctly programmed?). Static checks were done with the computer in the RESET mode (i.e., computer time was equal to zero and not changing.) Dynamic checks were performed with the computer in the OPERATE mode (i.e., computer time was changing.) Normally, for a dynamic check, a known time history solution (with known initial conditions and known inputs) was used to determine if the implementation was working correctly. If the results of the dynamic check were different (with the same inputs used in the known solution), then there was something wrong with the implementation. This problem was usually some analog component that was malfunctioning, as might happen if a fuse were blown. Many hardware problems did not always show up when the computer was in the RESET mode and would only be noticeable when the computer was in OPERATE. Both static and dynamic checks were run during the initial implementation of the simulation. Thereafter the daily dynamic checks were adequate to determine if the simulator was working correctly for that day. If changes were made to the implementation, then new static checks were calculated for checkout purposes.

recorders. Again, once we had done this to check them, we had plastic overlays prepared in the reproduction shop; we could lay them over the strip charts and see where we were. One of the interesting things that happened [was that] the process in going from paper to plastic stretched the curves on the plastic. If you took the original and laid the overlay on it, they didn't match any more.

The same thing happened on all copiers—everyone doing engineering work and using the copiers knew that the copiers stretched the scale. So it was kind of a trick to get an overlay that would work. That took another 10 to 15 minutes. So it was common to spend an hour—after you were sure everything was all right—just checking things. And then, of course, we flew it. We'd pick a sample mission and fly it just to make sure the computers, model, controls, and displays were all right.

We didn't have those problems with simulations that were set on dedicated equipment and were flown day after day, such as the LLRV and X-15. One of the powerful uses of the simulations was that you could take pieces of hardware off the airplane and tie them in [the simulation]. I remember we took servos from airplane stock and instruments and tied them into the simulations as a way of being sure they were ready for flight. Of course, there were some things that were very difficult to simulate. Now the whole aircraft is tied in at the RAIF routinely. We had iron birds for the X-15, PA-30, and F-8 DFBW. The JetStar flight vehicle was tied to its computers for systems development and model checkout.

Landing Simulation Capability

One of the problems we always had was simulating landings. There was a lot of work done on visual displays and techniques to simulate landings. Our group finally adopted the policy: with the equipment and the technology we had, we could not adequately simulate landings for research airplanes. So what was worked out was to take the airplanes that were closest to the research airplane in performance and use them to practice landings. The F-104 in a very dirty configuration[53] was used to practice landings for the lifting bodies. The Grumman Gulfstream II was used for Shuttle approach studies. This [landing simulation] was always a terribly difficult problem—even though a lot of work went into trying to provide better visual displays to the pilot.

Another thing we did with the simulation was prepare the pilot for whatever was new. Typically, pilots flew 40 hours of simulation for a 4-minute flight of a lifting body, though the pilots—Bill Dana, Milt Thompson (who flew the first M-2 flight), and Bruce Peterson (who flew the first HL-10 flight)—could better tell you how long that was in effect. And of course there were surprises. The airflow over the back end of the HL-10 wasn't as expected. It was a year between the first and second flights. Bob Kempel and Wen Painter did a lot of work as the controls guys, and Iliff was the aero guy on the HL-10.

They also used the simulator in later years to draw the maps that were used in the range. We'd go in

---

[53] This is the term used to describe an airplane that is not aerodynamically clean, which usually means that the landing gear is down, or the speed brakes are extended, or the flaps down, or for some other reason something is causing a reduction in the airplane's performance.

early on the morning of a flight. We'd call the Air Force and get the weather data, plug it in as extra velocities [i.e., as crosswinds in the appropriate directions] and their altitudes, and then fly that day's mission and draw the expected ground-track maps for the control room.

Faster than Real-time Simulation

It was only a 4-minute flight to go from 45,000 feet to the ground; they were falling like a rock. The pilots were [extremely] busy during the actual flight, and as I recall it was Jack Kolf who came up with the idea of making the simulation run faster than real time. We did that and as I recall it was about 40 percent[54] faster than real time. The pilots said that it now felt like the workload they were seeing in flight. They didn't do the research that way. What they would do is, the day before a flight we'd change the time constants by changing the gains on all the integrators and run the simulator about 40 percent faster than real time with the pilots flying the next day's mission. That way, they were sure to get enough time to do everything on the checklist of research tasks the engineers wanted them to do each flight. This was late in the program. It wasn't that way in the beginning.

Use of SDS 930

The first thing we did when the SDS 930 became available for the lifting-body simulations was to use it for generation of the very nonlinear derivatives. We had derivatives as functions of control surfaces, alpha, beta and Mach number—four or five independent variables for some of these. Some of them were very unusual. Derivatives that you'd expect to be all one sign crossed the axis and caused roll reversal, for example, at certain conditions. Coupling between roll and yaw also occurred. The table lookup [nonlinear function generation] was the first thing we did. Of course that completely changed the load on switching from one sim to another.[55]

The next thing was the calculation of the longitudinal or slowly changing variables. So now we are talking about velocity, dynamic pressure, and altitude—parameters that were very difficult to do on an analog computer, because they had large ranges of variables. We always had a precision problem with altitude and velocity when the aircraft got near the ground.

There was a lot of experimentation that was done coming up with the integration schemes. A lot of tests were run; we'd set it up and let it run all night. We let it calculate analytic functions like $sin^2 + cos^2 = 1$, and the derivative of one is the other, so we could take derivatives, and integrate and square and let it run all night and see how close to one

---

[54] Several different values were tried, from 20 percent to as much as 50 percent faster. The pilots seemed to prefer a value of about 40 percent faster as being the one most like what they experienced in flight.

[55] The use of the digital computer for function generation of the lifting-body nonlinear derivatives eliminated the use of much of the analog-function-generation hardware. This also eliminated the need to reprogram these analog function generators whenever the simulation had to change from one vehicle to the other. This function-generator-reprogramming job was usually done over a weekend by the simulation support contractor, as described above. The simulation could then be changed from one vehicle to the other in a matter of hours, rather than days.

we still were. 'Cause one of the problems with digital integration was phase shift. Another problem was predicting what a parameter was going to be at the beginning of the time frame—so that we were calculating with the correct variables.[56] Our solution—it was Lowell Greenfield's idea—was, instead of using a complicated integration scheme, as they were teaching in the classes, we used a very simple integration scheme and ran it very fast. We were running at 100 samples per second where other people were running at 10 or 20. This was done by taking advantage of the fact that a lot of the parameters only needed engineering precision.[57] So a lot of the terms in the power-series calculations were dropped out of the standard digital functions.

The next thing that was done on the 930 involved sines, cosines, and square roots[58]—since those were noisy operations on the analog. And we worked on powers (exponents) so [calculations of] things like dynamic pressure and altitude were a piece of cake since we didn't have functions of altitude to worry about [any more]. Another early use—in table lookup—was to do the atmospheric tables. We could go in with altitude and temperature and get the parameters needed to calculate dynamic pressure and Mach number. That was a big advantage.

We were very concerned about doing anything that was high frequency—anything that was faster than 3 cycles a second (because we needed 30 samples per second), which we got from the theoretical work we did taking courses and working with professors at UCLA and USC.[59] Many courses were taught at Edwards and others were taught in Los Angeles. In those days, the young engineers had car pools going to UCLA one night a week. Or taking classes out at Edwards, which were usually taught by USC. You must realize that in the middle '60s, digital computers were not fast enough to do what they do today. And they didn't have the parallel architecture that they have today—where we could take a problem and divide it up among a bunch of computers that were yoked together. So people were working all kinds of

---

[56] This refers to one of the problems with combined analog and digital (hybrid) simulations. The digital computer calculated parameters using inputs read in from the analog at the start of each digital time frame. The parameters calculated during that frame were then sent out to the analog at the beginning of the next frame. This resulted in a time delay, which usually affected the accuracy of the simulation. The shorter the time period, the smaller the error. One method of dealing with this time delay was to try to predict, at the beginning of each time period, what the input parameters would be at the end of the time period. These predicted values would then be used in the calculations (instead of the actual inputs).

[57] Engineering precision means that the degree of exactness (or refinement) of the measurement being made or the calculation being performed is both adequate and sufficient to provide the accuracy needed for the task at hand. For example, in combined analog/hybrid simulations, there was no need to calculate mathematical functions in the digital computer to a degree of exactness that exceeded the analog computer's accuracy (which was only about one part in 10 thousand.) This was a waste of the digital computer's time and memory, both of which were quite limited and better used for more significant calculations.

[58] There are numerous terms in the equations of motion of an aircraft that require the calculation of mathematical functions such as sines, cosines, and square roots. We used algebraic series, such as: $Sine\ \alpha = A_0 + A_1\alpha^1 + A_2\alpha^2 + A_3\alpha^3 + A_4\alpha^4 + ... A_n\alpha^n$. We did these kinds of approximations whenever we could, since it was faster to do so than to do a table lookup. On the other hand, there were no such simple equations for approximations of the density parameter needed in the calculation of dynamic pressure, so we had to do a table lookup in the 930. We did this since it was better than doing so on the analog (as we had to do earlier with the all analog sims).

[59] University of Southern California.

schemes to do integration and to try to do other things where there were time frames, time shifts, and phase shifts that had to be dealt with.

There were lots of Simulation Councils Inc. meetings where the analog guys and the digital guys were basically calling each other crazy, and those doing hybrid—like us—would say: "Well, you're both right and you're both wrong." Our view was to take the strengths of the digital and the strengths of the analog, with due respect for the time delays, time shifts, and phase shifts that were inherent in using a digital and the precision constraints inherent in using an analog. 'Cause 100 volts represented whatever it was—whether it was 50,000 feet of altitude or ±5 degrees of beta. The ±100 volts had to be spread[60] over that calculation. So we took the strengths of both systems. We kept the control systems on the analog to take advantage of parallel processing and instant results. We kept the lateral equations on the analogs and the longitudinal equations—such as altitude and velocity—on the digital. The analogs by now had logic components that were programmed on a separate panel. This allowed decisions to be made and alternatives selected. For example, gear up/gear down could be more accurately simulated.

In the middle phase of all this— from '64 to '68—we began specifying a faster digital computer. In the early '70s, Gene Waltman's team specified and bought a time-shared digital computer. It was a Control Data CYBER 73-28—in which we put everything. In those days, it was a good strategy to get the biggest, fastest digital computer and put everything on it. We had business on it, we had batch on it, we had range on it, and we had simulation on it. We had one processor dedicated to batch and one processor dedicated to real-time. I don't remember how many, but there were 10 or 12 small processors that just fed stuff in and out of the big processors.

As I recall, there were only five of the CYBER 73-28s built. We had one; the Army Missile Command had one; there was one in Europe—and they wouldn't even tell us on which side of the Iron Curtain it was located.

These special 73-28s (with the real-time front ends) collapsed of their own operating system weight[61]—it was so expensive that the customers had to pay for all the system upgrades. And when we got tired of doing that, the design group went on to other things. So the support wasn't there. Everyone else (to the best of my knowledge) ran batch and real-time on different shifts. We were the only ones who ran real-time and batch at the same time— and not time-sharing but in true parallel processing, because there

---

[60] This refers to the scaling of parameters on the analog computers. Depending on the dimensional units, variables could have values or rates of change that went from very small to very large numbers. Scaling is the process of setting the expected maximum values to be equal to the ±100 volt range of the analog. For example, if the maximum altitude is 100,000 feet, then its scale factor would then be 100 volts/100,000 ft. or $0.001H$(volts/foot), where H = altitude (in feet). To convert a value to the corresponding analog voltage, we would multiply the value by the scale factor. If the altitude was 40,000 feet, the voltage would then be 40,000 feet times 0.001 volts/foot—or 40 volts. To convert an analog voltage to the corresponding value, we would divide that voltage by the scale factor. A voltage reading of 50 volts would therefore be equal to 50 volts/ 0.001 volts/foot—or 50,000 feet.

[61] This refers to the large size and complexity of the special software that CDC developed to manage the real-time front-end hardware connected to the two analog computers in the FSL. CDC had a very limited set of customers.

were two processors running. We simply forced CDC to make it work. The acceptance testing that was supposed to take 30 days took a year.

At the same time we acquired the CYBER, we acquired two Applied Dynamic Inc. analog computers. They had a lot of digital logic and what today would be called firmware. One comment—all the programming we've been talking about was done in Assembly language, although Fortran was available. There was real-time Fortran, and Fortran designed for simulation. But it was so slow we couldn't use it for the kind of vehicles we had. At that time you could write Fortran routines that ran batch. So basically you were solving the same set of equations two different ways—one in Assembly language and using the analogs and the other in Fortran. If they didn't match, we knew something was wrong in one of them, but we didn't know which one. If they did match, we had a fair confidence that the check worked, since we were using the computer in two different modes and with two completely different languages.

It wasn't until we got the CYBER in the '70s that the computer was fast enough—what with two main processors and 10 small processors feeding it—and the Fortran compiler was efficient enough that we could actually write simulations in Fortran. It was Al Myers who wrote the first Fortran simulation to run in real time on the CYBER. There were lots of thought processes, a lot of agony, a lot of gnashing of teeth—if you will—over whether we were really ready to switch. It turned out it really was a viable way to do simulation, and it turned out to be a powerful tool.

ICARUS

Another thing that happened about that time was the ICARUS simulation. ICARUS started with Ken Iliff's idea of using the digital computer to help set up the analog computers and help run the check cases to minimize the load on the simulation engineer. He suggested this because in addition to the research engineers and the pilots, we needed a simulation engineer present anytime a simulation was running to handle set-up problems, to be sure the analog computer was running right, and to be sure the digital and analog were in sync, plus all the kinds of things that could go wrong with the cockpits, which were the displays to the pilots. The thought was if we simplified the set-up and the checking by moving them onto the digital computer, then use unity scaling—in which we took the biggest value of a variable and called that 100 volts—and let the digital computer do the scale factors for us, research engineers could then set up the simulation and run it for a basic engineering problem. That would also allow us not to need all those other people there, which would permit us to run off-shift or on weekends.

There was always a problem when we had emerging projects. They didn't yet have any money or priority, but there was a lot of hard work that was needed to get going, and there were usually two or three excited research engineers and pilots who were ready to get going. The structure wasn't there to support them, 'cause they weren't ready to fly.

ICARUS meant Immediate Checkout Analog Research Unity Scaled. We started with the word ICARUS, and we sat around the office one afternoon and made the words fit.

The idea was that Icarus, the son of Daedalus, escaped from prison with his father, using wings made of wax and feathers. He got so excited with what he was doing that he flew too close to the Sun, melted the wax, and fell into the Aegean Sea. That is what we told the research engineers. It's wonderful and you can really use it, but if you lose track of the assumptions, if you lose track of the simplifications that say you can do this and that, and you can't do other things, you'll get too close to the Sun and fall into the sea of misleading results. That was a graphical way of telling them not to forget about those terms that were taken out to simplify the model.

So, that was a project that I did—making it a practical thing to use the digital. You could put in the maximum values of the parameters; you could put in a simple set of the derivatives. We had functions of Mach number, alpha, and beta. The tables were predetermined—we could set the breakpoints wherever we wanted—but the numbers of tables, the kinds of derivatives, and which ones we had were all pre-set up. So if an engineer wanted to use it, he could bring in a simple set of wind-tunnel data. That is usually all he had in the very early stages of the project—a few wind-tunnel runs. Then he could make some linear adjustments on them—out in the maximum values for the parameters. ICARUS would scale it and set it up. He could then type in the initial conditions for the run he wanted to make.

By then, switches had been installed in the cockpit. Gerry Perry did that. He was the one who figured out how to run the analog from the cockpit. Ken Iliff was confined to a wheelchair and couldn't jump in and out of the cockpit. It was his idea to put controls in the cockpit so that a guy running a simulation by himself could control the analog and therefore control the whole simulation by resetting it or stopping it in the middle of something. Later he gave up on HOLD and there were only OPERATE and RESET. There wasn't any point in going to HOLD in the middle of something since there wasn't anything to get out and look at. Gerry Perry designed that, and by this time Charlie Wagner had designed the cockpit setup. It had a card reader, which used a punched card to turn switches on or off and set the pots (initial values) on that interface computer that was built at the FRC together with the electric stick, with torque motors to provide forces.

So now we had a system in which an engineer could come in (having had a simulation setup), load a copy, turn it on, go sit in the cockpit, and fly the simulation. The criterion now was 30-minute setup, and simulation time was scheduled by Dick Webb in 2-hour blocks. Because now, in 30 minutes you could change the cockpit and computer. So, ICARUS was used for dozens of projects, particularly those in the early stages and also where there was control-system work to be done. At this time, the FRC moved to many projects that involved control-systems work—as opposed to performance work. A lot of the guys were setting up fairly straightforward, simple control systems on the analog patch boards themselves. 'Cause they were Control Systems guys and were turning the computers on and running the system. We were running 16 hours a day and frequently on Saturdays and Sundays, if needed. Typically, if a pilot was preparing for a mission, that was done in the daytime. Even the high-priority guys would bring in their requirements. They were scheduling on a two-week basis, with the first week being firm and the second week preliminary. At the end of the week, we would redo the preliminary schedule into a firm schedule and make another preliminary schedule for the following week.

ICARUS allowed a lot of work that did not have the priority and would never have gotten any time to be done under the previous arrangement. This resulted from these two simple ideas: Immediate Checkout using the digital to run the static and dynamic checks, and Unity Scaling, again using the digital to set up the scale factors for all the variables that had to be displayed in the cockpit. We still had the control systems with the high frequencies on the analog—but now we were doing the derivatives and equations on the digital.

The period we are talking about was the late '60s and the '70s. It was about '73 when the CYBER came on-line. So we're talking about '69 to '72. Then, with the advent of Fortran and with the CYBER running the simulations, two things happened. The flight data (from Telemetry) was in terrible trouble; it was taking two weeks to get flight data turned around, and simulation was a breeze.

The decision was made to take the guys who had been in simulation and move them to solve the flight-data problem. Larry Caw was the first. Gene Waltman was one of the early ones. John Perry moved over, and Lowell Greenfield became the systems guy on the CYBER. So the simulation group was broken up (except for a couple of younger guys) and moved in to attack the flight-data problem. In a couple of years we were getting 24-hour turn around [on the flight data]. We were getting 90 percent on-time delivery with that kind of criterion.[62]

And I was one of the ones who switched over, too. At the time the CYBER was being specified, I took a look at Mary Little as she was running the flight and business data and John Smith running simulation, both on the same computer, and I decided that was not going to work—that somehow, someway we were going to have to have one group that ran the machine and specialists who ran the applications. The Systems Analyst Group—under Dave Hedgley—was also founded then. I went off and took a lot of work at UCLA in statistics—in mathematical statistics 'cause no one else was doing that. I was working towards a certificate in numerical analysis. About that time a Ph.D. was hired—under contract—to do statistics.

So I shifted over to the kinds of things needed for operations. On my own—while taking some classes—I did a lot of work talking to people and looking at what kinds of problems there were in running a computer center. Because at that time, it was all magic. I remember going to the guy who was head of programming and asking how long it would take to do a job. He said, "Well, you know, it's a creative process. It might take a week or it might take a month." And he leaned back in his chair and puffed on his pipe and said, "You can't push creativity," and of course in those days that was a long-standing argument whether software was an art or an engineering practice. There were lots of attempts to come up with criteria—they did things like "count lines per day" and it was all a big game. And in my perspective,

---

[62] The goal was to get the data collected from a flight processed and ready for use by the flight project personnel within 24 hours after a research flight was completed.

there was no way to predict—based on IBM studies—who would be a good programmer. You couldn't predict based on education or intelligence, and the only thing I ever saw that really worked was that, in general, people with music backgrounds made good programmers. And I've been told that is also true with people working in the early days of communications.

In my own view, it does make a difference. My son studied music in college. The idea came to me while talking with him about this. A musician has to pay attention to both the theme and the flow of the piece of music—as well as the details of the structure of the music. For example, on a keyboard you have to pay attention to what every finger is doing and at the same time to the whole flow of music in terms of the quality of the music. My son is a drummer, so he had both hands and both feet going, six or seven pieces of equipment. So that's my own thought on why music can be a predictor of success in software— because you have to pay attention to both the big picture and the details.

So at that point I became the chief of the operations group when the two divisions were combined—that is, the whole CYBER organization was realigned into a software group, a hardware group, and an operations group. Within the operations group that I headed, we saw a major loss of simulation engineering capability because simulation required all three: operations, engineering, and software. We did all those. We had a technician assigned who was an expert in all areas of electronic and mechanics. To the extent that it was a separate skill area to be a simulation technician, simulation was out of control in my view at that point. First of all, we had taken the people and sent them to do other things— systems work or whatever. And secondly, the structure didn't really allow for a simulation engineer. So one of the changes that was made in the latter '70s, which went on for several years, was that a simulation group was re-established within the software part of that structure. Larry Schilling and others became what we would call simulation engineers again—or what NASA calls specialists in theoretical simulation techniques.

One of the interesting things was that in the early days, around the '60s, we were classified as mathematicians. To give an indication of the flavor of the work positions, we had mathematicians, aerodynamicists, and physicists—there weren't any computer degrees. They didn't know what to do with the computer people. In the later '60s and early '70s, if you were more software than hardware, you were considered a mathematician, and if you were more hardware than software, you were an electronics engineer. My own classification changed several times during that period. I used to say I became an engineer by act of Congress just like officers became gentlemen. They didn't know what to do. There was no computer scientist series among civil service job classifications. The only thing there was for a person who did data entry, or keypunch, was a clerical work category. It wasn't until the computer scientist's series was created that there was any semblance of order.

Lawrence (Larry) Caw

Larry worked in the FSL from 1962 to 1975. I (Gene Waltman) wrote this PA from a number of notes, letters, and various other inputs provided by Larry, with additional information from others in the FSL.

X-15 Landing Studies

The first simulation Larry had as his own was an X-15 landing-loads-analysis study for the research engineer Jim McKay. Jim was the twin brother of John (Jack) McKay, the X-15 pilot. Jim wrote several reports dealing with the landing characteristics of the X-15. This simulation did not involve any cockpit and only had four degrees of freedom: main-gear motion, nose-gear motion, airplane pitch, and vertical translation. A brief description of this simulation is in an appendix to the report: (Citation No. 342) *Landing Loads and Dynamics of the X-15 Airplane* by James M. McKay and Eldon E. Kordes, NASA TM X-639, March 1962. This simulation used a single EAI-231 analog computer. Larry also worked as a programmer on the X-15 simulation. Photo ECN 1456 shows him standing in front of the X-Y plotter used by the simulation to display ground track and altitude during flights. Larry and several other FSL programmers were assigned to help out with the X-15 simulator when we went to two and three shifts of operation.

LLRV Simulation

The next significant simulation Larry Caw did was of the Lunar Landing Research Vehicle (LLRV). This simulation earned Larry the dubious title of the FSL Kludge King. It was implemented using an unusual collection of different analog computers, including an EAI 31R, EAI 231R, and several portable analogs (TR-10s, TR-20s, etc.). Because of the differences between the larger analogs (31R and 231R) and the portable analogs (TR-10s), there were many home-made patch cords connecting the two different types of computers together, giving this particular simulation the appearance of one huge Rube Goldberg kludge. Photo ECN 637 shows one of the LLRVs. Larry spent many morning hours making test runs and trying to get this mass of patch cords and computers to work before he could call the project office and tell the pilots to come fly. The portable analog computers were situated on one of the air-conditioner blower housings in the X-15 simulation lab. This housing was in a corner of the lab and across from the EAI 231R that was also used in the simulation. The extra-long patch cords were hung from the ceiling. The wood flooring used in the X-15 lab interfered with running the trunks under the floor. The cockpit was in the next room, which had no false floor, and also required the use of some overhead trunking. Photo E-10840 shows the simulation cockpit. Unfortunately, no photo was ever taken of the computers. If there had been a photo taken, I'm sure Larry would have had a copy mounted on

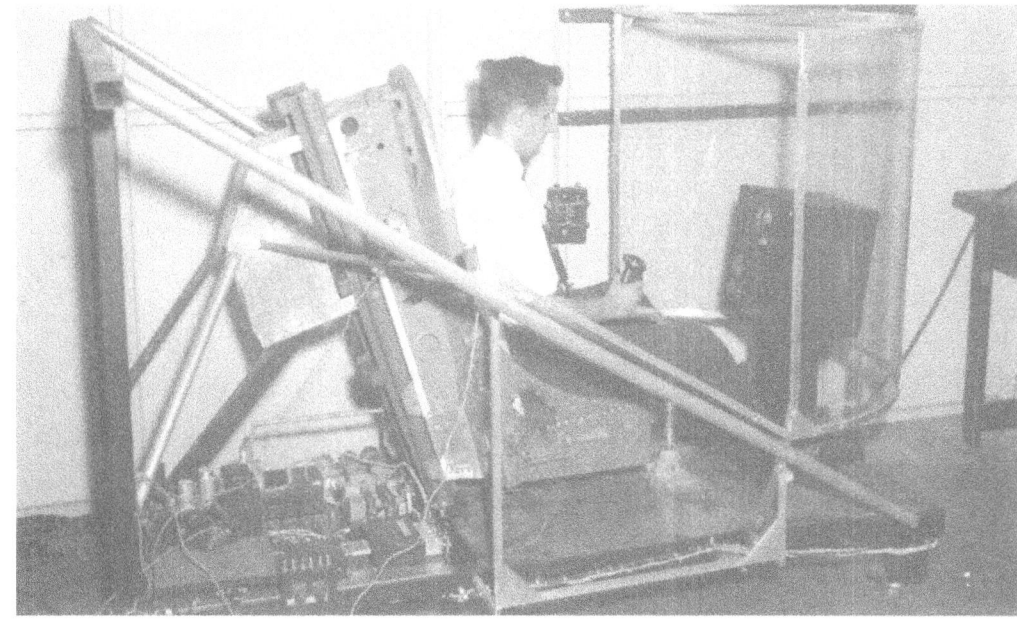

Frank J. VanLeynselle in the LLRV Simulator Cockpit (January 1964). (NASA photo E-10840)

a dartboard in his office. This simulation shared the lab with the X-15 simulation computers, and there were many mornings, when I would be in the process of checking out the X-15 simulation, that I heard all sorts of grumblings emanating from the other corner where the LLRV simulation was situated. Thinking back on this simulation and the overhead mass of patch cords, I am reminded of the Munsters' mansion and all its vines and cobwebs in a popular TV program from the 1970s.

This simulation was unique in that it was a simulation of a simulator. The actual LLRVs—there were two built by Bell Aerospace—were eventually used by the Apollo astronauts to practice Moon-landing maneuvers on the Earth. The actual LLRVs had the capability of simulating the Moon's gravity (one-sixth that of Earth's), thereby allowing the astronauts to perfect their landing techniques before ever going to the Moon. The two LLRVs were first flown at the FRC during the early check-out and development phases of the landing studies. The on-board avionics system was designed and built by Bell and tested using the simulation. Later, these vehicles were transferred to the Manned Space Flight Center (later redesignated the Johnson Space Center) in Houston, Texas, for use by the Apollo astronauts. NASA also had three more of these vehicles built for training use. The training vehicles were called Lunar Landing Training Vehicles (LLTVs) exclusively.

Besides Larry Caw, the FSL technicians involved in this simulation included Art Suppona, Gerry Perry, and Leo (Dick) Webb. This simulation lasted for about three years. The research engineers included Gene Matranga, Cal Jarvis, and Wilt Lock. Many reports were written about the LLRV program. A number of pilots flew the simulation and the simulator, including Joe Walker and Don Mallick from the FRC, and Jack Kluever from the Army. See photo ECN-637 of one of the LLRVs with the FRC pilots. Houston pilots Joseph Algranti and H.E. Ream also flew the LLRVs during the early days of the program. Deke Slaton and Neil Armstrong were two of the astronauts who also flew the LLRVs (in

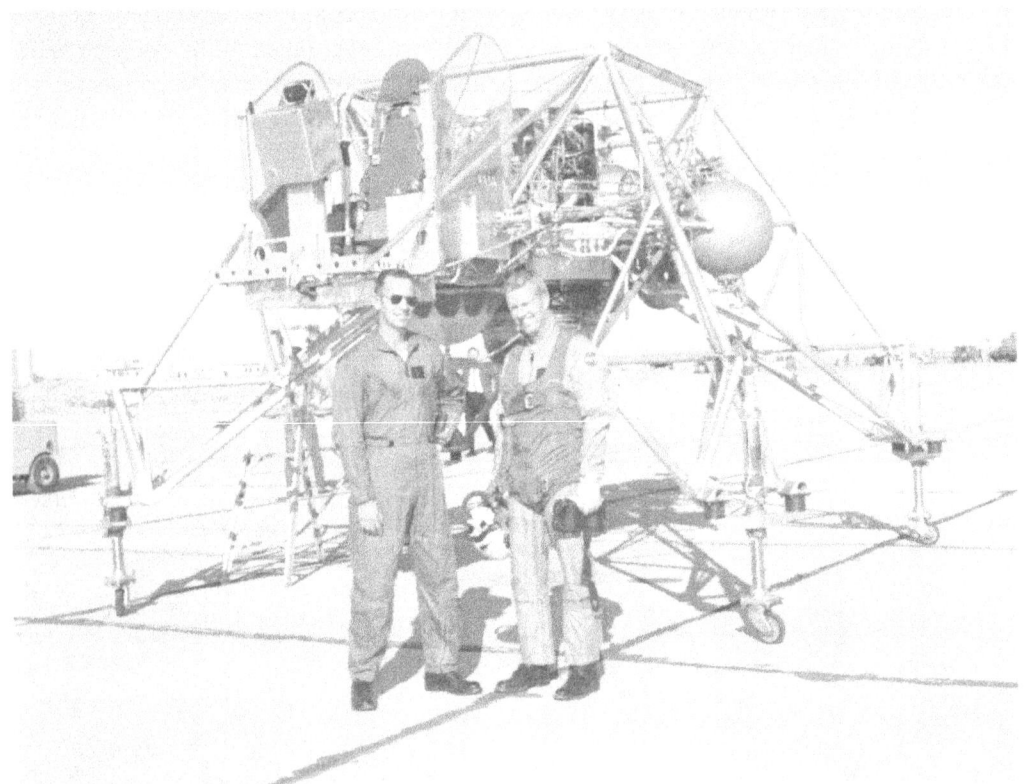

LLRV with Joe Walker (on right) and Don Mallick. (NASA photo ECN-637)

Houston) and the ground simulation.

This ground simulation also had flight hardware tied into the analog mechanization. This particular black box was a prototype of the electronics used in the LLRV. The engineers were trying to duplicate actual system responses as closely as possible, and rather than try to simulate this particular piece of hardware, a prototype unit was connected to the simulation. It was several years later before aircraft were connected to FSL simulators. Once the FSL moved into the mezzanine in the Calibration Hangar, this began to happen more and more. Our experiences with trying to simulate onboard computers was never good. It was far easier to actually connect the real hardware, either in an iron-bird cockpit or the real aircraft. The new Integrated Test Facility (ITF) was built with this concept in mind. There were many simulations in the FSL that used real avionics. In the current facility (now called the Research Aircraft Integration Facility [RAIF]), entire aircraft are connected just for this reason.

The LLRV was a unique simulation with somewhat unusual equations. At that time, the FRC was heavily involved with the X-15 Program, and there weren't a lot of resources available to devote to this simulation. The oddball collection of analog computers made it an especially difficult and frustrating simulation to keep up and operational from day to day. Larry and the FSL technicians who worked on this simulation have a lot to be proud of. We kidded Larry a lot about this kludge, and the other sim programmers (that filled in for him when he was on leave) did not look forward to having to work on his simulation. It definitely had its own personality, and Larry was its only "recognized and accepted" owner. But it was so temperamental that it gave even Larry fits at times. It was like having a Tasmanian devil as a pet.

The attitude rockets on the LLRV made quite a bit of noise. At first the pilots complained about this, since it was distracting. Later on, they found that there was a pattern to the noise and they could use this as an indication of just how the vehicle was doing with the control system engaged. Because of this, a study was conducted with the simulation using a white-noise generator to simulate the attitude rocket jets to try to determine if the noise patterns could, indeed, be of any use. I don't know what the results of this study showed but I doubt if it had any impact on the ultimate purpose of the LLRV—which was to train the Apollo astronauts to land their lunar lander on the moon and to provide data for the design of the actual lunar lander. But this little ancillary study shows just another of the interesting things that our simulators were used for.

Lifting-body Simulation

The next major simulations that Larry Caw was involved with were those for the lifting bodies. There were several different mechanizations during the Lifting Body Program. The first simulations were all-analog implementations. As the X-15 Program was winding down, the SDS 930 digital computer used in the X-15 simulator became available for use with other implementations. The lifting-body simulations also began using this digital computer. Because of the many different lifting-body configurations, it became necessary for the simulation to be easily and quickly re-configurable. Using the SDS 930 for the many different nonlinear coefficients helped in achieving the rapid changeover needed by the Lifting Body Program Office. Larry Caw was a backup programmer to Lowell Greenfield and Don Bacon on this simulation. Larry programmed and operated the analogs and never got involved in the digital side of the implementation. I don't remember Larry ever going to any of the SDS programming classes. These lifting-body simulations overlapped with his support of the LLRV, which was his main concern at the time. Like the X-15 simulation, the lifting-body simulations originally used pot padders for the many nonlinear functions in the equations of motion. Pot padders were very time-consuming to set up and check out. Larry spent a lot of time working with these components. The integration of the SDS 930 (see below) into the simulation was a definite improvement and resulted in a significant decrease in the time needed to re-configure the simulation. Even so, the Air Force and the FRC split the simulation effort, with the Air Force providing the early M2 simulations (while the FRC was installing the SDS 9300) and the X-24 simulations. The FRC implemented the HL-10 and the latter M2 simulations (which used the SDS 9300 digital computer instead of the original SDS 930). Larry worked with the lifting-body simulations from 1966 to 1969.

There are several excellent publications about the Lifting Body Program that include discussions of the simulations. I particularly recommend: (1) NASA RP-1332, by Robert W. Kempel, *Developing and Flight Testing the HL-10 Lifting Body: A Precursor to the Space Shuttle*, (2) Dale Reed's book with Darlene Lister, *Wingless Flight: The Lifting Body Story*, and (3) the Bob Hoey study, "Testing the Lifting Bodies at Edwards." The publication by Reed is available on the DFRC Web page at URL http://www.dfrc.nasa.gov/History/Publications/WinglessFlight/. The Hoey publication is also available on the DFRC Web page at URL http://www.dfrc.nasa.gov/History/Publications/LiftingBodies/contents.html. There is also a document on the website by Bill Dana, which is his talk to the National Air and Space Museum, Smithsonian Institution as a part of the Charles A. Lindbergh Lecture at URL http://www.dfrc.nasa.gov/History/lifting_bodies/lifting-1.html. This document contains many really great photos of different lifting bodies. These photos are all downloadable, and many are in color.

GPAS (General Purpose Airborne Simulator)

As a simulator of different aircraft configurations, the GPAS was as unique in its own way as the LLRV simulation. Larry worked on these simulations from 1968 to 1973. The various simulations were all analog and included studies of the concept of a flying simulator. This was done both here and at CAL (Cornell Aeronautical Laboratory in Buffalo, New York). CAL was the organization that was selected to build the airborne simulator. These studies helped determine the feasibility of such a flying lab and to design the appropriate control systems. After the JetStar was modified and the on-board analog computers installed, there were closed-loop simulations that used the on-board analogs and external ground-based analog computers. There were also simulations that used ground-based analog computers tied into the airplane control systems. The analog computers used in these different phases of the simulations were EAI 231Rs and EAI TR-58s. The section on GPAS further describes the on-board analog computer system.

The GPAS was used for a number of years in many different types of studies: handling qualities, stability and control studies, parametric studies, noise turbulence studies, and variable stability control systems studies. During the latter years of the program, direct-lift and side-force surfaces were added to extend the simulator capabilities. The GPAS employed a modified Lockheed C-140 JetStar. Photos ECN-2399 and E-27825 show the airplane and the on-board computer system. There were many technical reports written covering the various studies and the results.

Larry Caw worked on this project with John J. Perry and Dick Musick from the FSL. Herman Rediess, Dwain Deets, and Ken Szalai were the control systems engineers, and the FRC pilots included Stan Butchart, Don Mallick, Hugh Jackson, and Fitz Fulton. Many guest pilots also flew the GPAS, including Wernher von Braun, who stated that flying the GPAS was like dialing an airplane. The GPAS did have the capability of simulating many other aircraft in actual flight. Larry flew 176 flights in the GPAS as the simulation specialist.

Art Suppona

I got there—Computation and Simulation [the FSL]—the day after Labor Day in 1961. The big simulation then was for the X-15 Program. And, of course, all of us technicians were either under the floors pulling cables or pulling parts of the EAI analog computers apart, every day, doing maintenance on them, and trying to do preventative maintenance. Most of that effort was with the operational amplifiers, which were tube types, and trying to keep them free of noise, basically, in that the doggoned machines would integrate on noise and they were chopper stabilized amplifiers.[63] Ninety percent of that work was trying to check the tubes and to check that the chopper stabilization circuit was working.

Cleaning Spirits

The resolvers were another big thing, which entailed cleaning the various parts using 200-proof alcohol, which only Dick Musick was authorized to withdraw from stock. He was the only one authorized in Computation and Simulation to sign for it, in pint bottle quantities. Needless to say, some people just might have a temptation to have a little stronger refreshment during the day, but that was one thing we never saw happen.

Floor Tiles

We ended up having to get under the floors for all the cables. That was always a fun thing. Sometimes someone came up with a radical change in programming; and we would literally have to tear the floors up as much as we could. Luckily, they came out in two-foot squares, and we were able to do our work rather unimpeded—except we had to always be on the alert as to where we were stepping as it was very easy to stumble on the steel supports, which were threaded arrangements, each one of which supported the corners of four floor tiles. The idea was to get those tiles adjusted precisely so that there were no edges sticking up for someone to stumble over later.

Glider Simulator

Now, the X-15 having all the funding, when someone from another program came up with a bit of an oddball request of some kind, we had to do a lot of improvising. And my first experience with that was when an individual—I cannot remember the guy's name—had a private project (if you will); he came in with some kind of a glider program that he wanted to establish. Lowell Greenfield was the programmer for the simulation. But I built the simulator for him. They wanted absolute simplicity; the objective of the simulation would be achieved strictly by instruments. The only reason I bring this up is that the control stick was a cutoff broom handle and the rudder pedals were also made from a part of the broom handle. Everything was strictly tension-type springs, for providing the force and maintaining a zero position. There were pots, of course, for stick-and-rudder-position indicators and for input into the portable computer, which was a TR-10 analog computer. It only took a few days to jury-rig this thing up. This guy and Lowell were very anxious to show it to Paul Bikle.[64] Paul got in and operated it as Lowell and this engineer looked on. Paul flew it, with the ever-present cigar in his

---

[63] Choppers are described in the section on Four-Stage Boost-Vehicle Simulation. See also glossary.

[64] Paul Bikle was a world-class glider pilot as well as the center director.

mouth, and then he got up and said that it was totally unrealistic—and stomped out. That was my introduction to the frailties of simulation. We thought we did pretty well in getting that thing cranked out in such a short time and achieving the objectives of the project engineer. We really got shot down, but good!

F-104 Stick Kicker

There was another simulation that was, more or less (shall we say?), not done on a formal work request and involved making do with what we had or getting around the normal methods of procurement, if you will. Joe Walker came in one day and expressed a desire for a simulation of the "stick kicker" function of the F-104. As I remember, when the F-104 was put into a certain climb or nose-up attitude, it would fall flat and get unstable unless the pilot reduced the stick position. [The stick kicker was a device that vibrated the control stick to remind the pilot that he was getting into an undesirable situation.] I had no engineering guidance on this, just his verbal request. I remember that I had to buy an electro-mechanical clutch. For the life of me, I don't remember how I got that through the mill. I think we put it on some other program's charge number. It only took about 10 days of work in the machine shop; we already had a stick of some kind that needed some minor refinements. The biggest thing was getting a function generator that would respond to the attitude of the airplane. This time things worked out a little bit differently in the end. We busted our butts getting what Joe wanted. Anyway, I forget the name of the programmer I was working with. As I remember, we got things ready, and we gave Joe a call and said we think we have what you want. By the way, the cockpit we used was an old one that had been sitting there, alongside the equipment in the analog room, but it served the purpose. Anyway, Joe got in there, flew it for about five minutes, got his questions answered, and that was the end of that![65]

Early Lifting-Body Cockpit

Once again, working in simulation was an education to us, at least for this guy [himself] who was new to this type of work and making his first endeavor in any kind of research work. It was a good precursor of things to come. And of course, when the lifting bodies came along, this was (for me) an introduction from beginning to end in getting a simulator built (I mean from scratch). The program wanted it as nearly realistic [as it possible could be], not only in the handling of it but in the visual environment for the pilots. The first heavy-weight lifting body—the one Bruce Peterson got hurt in—[was the M2-F2]. We had the square box simulator cockpit, but everything else was pretty good as far as the handling qualities went, and of course the programming was pretty straightforward. To get the stick forces, we used surplus aircraft parts. Dick Webb and I were sent to buy an assortment of parts from surplus aircraft shops in the L[os]A[ngeles] basin. We bought quite a few items we thought we would be able to use in simulators. The first lifting-body simulator used quite a bit of that stuff. We acquired a fiberglass cockpit that Northrop had used to configure the vehicle. This was used for the simulator. It provided a very realistic environment.

Electric Stick

It was just a few years later that Dick Musick and Charlie Wagner came up

---

[65] The simulator was flown only that one time!

with the design for the electric [control] stick. There was one cockpit that Dick Johnson [not in Simulation] had designed that used hydraulics and was built by Northrop. It was a typical hydraulics thing. By golly, if you weren't leaking hydraulics fluid, you were fighting to get it in tolerance.

Dick and Charlie came up with the design for the electric force generator, which everyone called the electric stick, and we also had one for the rudder pedals.[66] This really was a better unit and got rid of a lot of the mechanical problems in the old stuff.[67] It was a close-tolerance design that provided better forces and travel and feel. We originally did most of the construction and computer circuitry in-house, but eventually we had to contract this out, which was a first. We either had to do this or hire more people, and NASA was reluctant to hire more people for this job. The design kept getting better, especially as solid-state devices came along. This was used quite extensively for the various RPV (Remotely Piloted Vehicle) simulations and every simulation thereafter.[68]

Visual Displays

Then there were the video displays that started out being pretty crude but got better as we went along. Since we weren't allowed to buy more than one of the big monitors, we had to design and have built a rather elaborate hoist system to move this heavy monitor around between the different cockpits. We got to be experts at moving these heavy loads around the lab. Another big thing then was when Charlie [Wagner] got the patent for the rotating video display, which made the visual presentation much better for the pilots.

Soldering Standard

In '79, I got tasked by our boss to come up with a soldering standard. Headquarters had come up with a directive that simulation was a part of the "system," and should have a soldering standard, just like the aircraft technicians used. Simulations, even though they were ground-based, still had to have the same quality standards. So we had to develop the specifications for this. We took what was being used downstairs by the aircraft technicians and adapted it to simulation. I don't believe anyone was ever put in charge of enforcing this standard.

F-8 DFBW Iron Bird

I was also involved in the modification of the F-8 iron bird for the Digital-Fly-By-Wire simulator. This was a real F-8 airplane, and we spent a lot of time getting it ready for use as a simulator. It was located in the lean-to that was attached to the side of the calibration hangar. This modification of the F-8 took a lot of our time, but once it was done and connected to the computers, we

---

[66] The "electric stick" was put into operation about 1971. It was first used for lifting-body simulators and almost every simulator after that.

[67] The "old stuff" mentioned here is in reference to all the pilot's controls that have been discussed in previous sections; it includes the various hydraulics and spring- and bungee-loaded sticks and rudder pedals that were used in the earlier cockpits in the FSL. These hydraulic and mechanical devices had undesirable characteristics that made their use a very frustrating experience. The electric stick was a major factor in the on-going development of the simulation capabilities and had a lot to do with the FSL being one of the best sim labs in the world.

[68] See Charles Wagner's PA in the following section for further discussion of the electric stick.

hardly ever had to go back down and make changes. It worked quite well for many years.

Tools

We spent a lot of time waiting for our stuff to be manufactured in the sheet metal and machine shops. Simulation did not have a lot of priority there. We got to thinking about this and just how much time we wasted waiting for things to be built. It occurred to us that if we had some of our own equipment, we could make a lot of the stuff we needed. John Smith approved the purchase of a metal lathe, milling machine, and a band saw. Unfortunately, this was when Dave Scott was center director and had been directed to reduce unnecessary duplication. He had procurement go through all outstanding PRs and canceled those that appeared to be duplications. Our orders for the lathe and milling machine got canceled. Some time later, one of the buyers in small purchases called and said that the order for the band saw had been misfiled (at the time that the other two had been canceled) and was still there and she wondered if we still wanted the band saw. So we did eventually get our (Sears, Roebuck, and Co.) band saw.

Charles Wagner

I started working for NASA in late 1964, right after Thanksgiving. My first assignment was to try to help get an EMC [Energy Management Console] up and running.[69] This was an all-analog device that was supposed to provide a real-time display in the control room during X-15 flights. It produced a heart-shaped display on a CRT [Cathode Ray Tube] that outlined the area where the X-15 could glide to at all times during its flight. A transparent map, attached to the CRT face, depicted the available landing sites. The EMC received real-time flight data, including altitude, speed, and direction.

Energy Management Console

Unfortunately, the EMC had been built by a start-up company, which apparently went belly up right after it was delivered. I was told the company consisted of two guys in a garage. The EMC was poorly constructed, even by the standards of its time, and a technician and I spent many hours finding and replacing hundreds of defective parts. We finally got it to working (sort of), and it found its way into the control room. The feedback I got indicated that the EMC worked, but the flight controllers did not need it by the time it became available; they already knew by experience which landing sites could be reached at any time during the flights. Simulation had been involved in the original research to determine the database needed to define the X-15's landing area, and I believe John Smith had been responsible for ordering the device. So, when it arrived and did not work, his group inherited the responsibility of trying to fix it.

Dalto Visual Simulator

My next project was the Dalto Visual Simulator. It was on order when I started working at the FRC, and when it arrived I became its

---

[69] The X-15 was launched from a B-52 mothership long distances from the Flight Research Center and Rogers Dry Lakebed, its intended landing site. Flight planners identified intermediate dry lakebeds for emergency landings when necessary. Flying at speeds up to Mach 6.7 and altitudes up to 17 miles, the X-15s had a lot of energy that needed to be managed carefully so that the airplane could reach a lakebed and land at the proper speed.

caretaker. This device was intended to provide an out-the-window view of the area around Edwards. It was probably funded by the X-15 project (the only one with any money), but it was never used for the X-15. The Visual Simulator (VS) was an all-analog device that took a vertical picture of a terrain transparency (something like an aerial photograph) and distorted the picture to make it appear as if it were being viewed in perspective from a flying aircraft. It used a now-obsolete camera known as a flying-spot scanner to view the transparency. It seems the military had ordered a bunch of these devices for its flight trainers and had quickly discarded them when they did not work well. I must have spent a couple of years on this gadget and learned a lot about electronics in the process. I even wrote a couple of technical papers on it. Like the EMC, the VS was built by a not-too-reputable company that delivered something that was unreliable and performed poorly even when it did work. I eventually got it working better than the factory had been able to, but the technology was inadequate for it to provide a useful picture. At high altitudes, the visual range was limited to about three miles, which is fairly useless. At low altitudes, the picture resolution was too poor for it to be useful as a landing aid. It turned out to be an expensive toy that never really did much useful work for the various simulations.

Norden Contact Analog

The visual device that was actually used for many years by several of the simulations was the Norden Contact Analog. It usually worked, and it generated a fake ground plane consisting of random checkerboard squares or other repeating patterns. It also had fake oval clouds in the sky. [See photo E-10591.]

Simulator Cockpits

Then, [it was] on to the simulation cockpits themselves. The earliest cockpits I can remember working on were little more than wooden boxes with spring-loaded sticks and panels consisting mostly of simple, cheap meter movements with dials printed in the photo lab.

Altimeters were a particular problem. Dick Musick put together homemade altimeters that worked pretty well, considering what he had to work with. But because of their very high amplification (20 millivolts represented 1,000 feet, or one full revolution of the fast hand), small electrical errors looked really big. A typical problem was that the altimeters were jumpy, with the fast hand oscillating constantly over 50 or 100 feet. They were annoying when they did that. The problem was that even a slightly noisy amplifier on the analog computer would make a good altimeter look bad.[70]

Another type of instrument that was used fairly extensively was the synchro.[71] It was used when the total movement of the needle had to exceed the limits of a simple meter movement. A synchro could revolve through a full revolution (or many revolutions). The problem was that the available drivers that could convert DC voltage to synchro were expensive and unreliable (a common

---

[70] Due to the high scaling normally used for altitude, if the amplifier that was providing the input to the altimeter was even a little bit noisy (i.e., not steady, but jumping around) the altimeter's needle would also jump around. The vacuum tubes in the amplifiers would get old and cause this noise. This was distracting to the pilot. For most signals to the cockpit instruments, a little bit of noise in the amplifiers (that provided the signal) did not have such an effect, but the altimeters seemed unusually sensitive to this noise.

[71] The synchros used were three-phase 400-cycle alternating current motors. Many of the aircraft's instruments were synchro-driven.

problem with early solid-state devices). I remember seeing many burned synchro converter boards. They were always burned in the same place, indicating that it was the same component that always failed.

Cockpit Interface Equipment

Another early problem was that we had both 10-volt and 100-volt analog computers driving the cockpit displays. The interconnects were made via patch panels. If an incorrect patch was made, or the wrong patch panel was put in place, 100-volt signals could get into places such as the output of a 10-volt amplifier, and the result was usually a blown component. I got the assignment of trying to prevent these disasters, and I came up with an interface console that could withstand 100-volt signals at both the inputs and the outputs without damage. The original interface console was programmed using a punched-card reader. The card reader was very difficult to wire up without short circuits, and the switch contacts were unreliable. Even so, the interface consoles usually had enough working channels to be useful. A follow-on model eliminated the card reader and was more reliable. We constructed several copies of this version and used them for many years.

The spring-loaded sticks were a constant problem. The pilots said that they did not feel like [those on the] the airplane. They also usually had a lot of slop (free play). I began work on a better spring-loaded stick that was adjustable, but before I got very far, Dick Musick had begun to demonstrate some success with an electric-powered stick. He and Art Suppona put one together using TR-5 and TR-10 computers to program it. It was fairly successful and was used for some early simulations. (I don't remember for sure which ones, but I think it was used on a lifting-body simulation.) One of its problems was that if the trim integrator drifted, it could drive the motor hard against the mechanical limit and eventually burn out the motor. These were expensive gadgets to replace.

Electric Stick

I inherited the job of refining the electric stick. I repackaged the physical stick assembly and hooked it up to a more sophisticated program on a TR-48 computer. I began incorporating safety features to eliminate the motor burnout problem and to relieve some fears of some of the pilots. It seems that there was an old hydraulic-powered stick (or maybe it was a control wheel) around that had a habit of going hard over right into the pilot, where it threatened his physical safety. (I remember seeing one pilot leaping out of the seat, fearing for his life!) This gave powered sticks a bad reputation, and some pilots said they would never get into a cockpit with one. Eventually, I was able to make the electric stick safe enough for pilots that there were no threats or close calls. Gradually, they began to accept it as safe and began asking for more variable feel characteristics to more closely model the aircraft. I eventually developed a self-contained equipment rack that included all of the electronics required (including the power amplifiers) and eliminated the clumsy TR-48 and external power amplifiers. This was the most successful project I ever worked on. Eventually, six copies of the stick were built, and these were in use for many years on virtually every simulation.

More on Sim Cockpit Instruments

I remember working on cockpit instrument panels to make them interchangeable. This was so a single box with an electric stick could be used for several different aircraft simulations. Thus, a standardized cockpit was born, and panels could be arranged in many different ways. The standardized panel interface was matched to the interface console described above, which incorporated all of the stuff required to run 8-balls and other specialized aircraft instruments.

We began buying simulator instruments from a small company in New Jersey. (I don't remember the name, but there are a lot of its instruments still around.) They looked like actual aircraft instruments. Our first purchase was for altimeters, and they were quite successful. It seems we finally found a company that knew what it was doing. With the better amplifiers and some filtering in the cockpit interface, the altimeter noise problems disappeared, and the pilots were happier. We bought dozens (maybe hundreds) of various simulator instruments, ranging from simple one-turn instruments with replaceable dial faces to altimeters and converted 8-balls that ran on DC inputs instead of synchro.

Trunk Switches

Because we had a variety of analog computers and a variety of cockpits that needed to be interfaced, there was always the problem of connecting the correct cockpit to the correct combination of computers via the many trunk lines running around the lab. Dick Musick came up with an early solution by using (I believe) motor-driven rotary switches to select the correct computer. While this solution worked, a rotary switch has the characteristic of touching intermediate voltages of unknown origin on its way to the correct position. This was another one of the causes of the blown components described earlier, and it helped spur on the desire to develop an overload-proof interface console. Eventually, the rotary switches were replaced with a massive patch-panel assembly known as DISPATCH [Distributive Patching]. It was built in-house. I designed it and Gerry Perry built it. I believe it contained somewhere around 20,000 wires, and Gerry built it without a single wiring error!

The world of analog computers, requiring a trunk line for every input or output variable, and analog cockpits with the same requirement led to literally miles of cables under the floor. Art Suppona, Gerry Perry, and the other technicians spent years of their lives fabricating trunk cables. Working hard, one man could make about two cables a day. Thus, every time some major change was required, much work went into making new cables.

A cockpit usually required about 20 cables, so there were about two weeks of solid cable building required just to hook up one single cockpit. I remember Don Bacon once remarked that it sure took a long time to build a cable. Various connector manufacturers began to introduce connectors that could be installed in less time. Unfortunately, every analog computer maker had its own favorite trunk connectors, so we had no choice about which ones we could use. Even worse, those connectors were usually both expensive and difficult to install. So we had to stock a large variety of connectors and tools to build all of those cables.

Personal Accounts of FSL Users (Research Engineers and Pilots)

This section contains personal accounts of research engineers and pilots who programmed, used, or flew a number of the different analog and hybrid simulations. These PAs are in a somewhat chronological order with the first group being the engineers in the order that they were involved with the analog sims throughout those early years. The same is true for the pilots' PAs. The PAs are in somewhat different styles, depending on how the information was collected. For some of the people, the PA is in the form of a narrative or story. Several of the people have sent me information via e-mail and letters, and their PAs have been pieced together into narratives. A couple of these are from interviews, and the PAs are in more of a question-and-answer form. Again, I have tried to edit what they say as little as possible and to keep their information in their own styles.

Richard (Dick) D. Banner

The following is from several e-mails and notes from Dick Banner:

The Very First Analog Simulation

I don't remember the dates, but [what I am about to relate occurred] not long after we moved from the main base to the new facility.[72] De Beeler, then Director of Research, asked Al Kuhl and me to look at the subject of vertical tail loads in rolling pullout maneuvers. He apparently had been in contact with someone at the Air Force Flight Test Center and had arranged for Al and me to look at its new analog equipment in hopes of using it to simulate flight conditions. When Al and I saw the equipment, it was just being uncrated, and the Air Force lieutenant who was assigned to work with us didn't seem to know much about it. The lieutenant, Fred Smetana, was very willing to let us help unpack it and assemble the parts. It was manufactured by Goodyear and called GEDA (Goodyear Electronic Differential Analyzer).

The Douglas X-3 airplane, before being turned over to us at the NACA [High-Speed Flight Station], had undergone the usual Air Force acceptance testing, which included rolling maneuvers. Flight data was available for the aircraft motions from these maneuvers. I went to Douglas and got the time-history data and the flight derivatives that were available. Al and I "programmed" the GEDA analog computer to simulate the flight conditions, and we were struggling with the high angle-of-attack simulation when an F-100 crashed somewhere between Lancaster and Rosamond. We were asked if we could simulate the F-100 on the GEDA. We did, and as we did, we discovered that the lateral-directional period simulated with the derivatives given us did not match the flight data. Al took a look at the way the in-flight directional stability parameter was obtained and decided that it was not correct. He went on to derive a new set of equations which would give us a better method of obtaining the in-flight directional stability parameter, allowing us to simulate the F-100 flight conditions. [See the appendices for a copy of the in-house memo written by Banner and Kuhl on this study.]

---

[72] The move from the South Base facility took place in June 1954. The new facility marked the beginnings of the present facilities at Dryden Flight Research Center.

To the best of my knowledge, we were the first at NACA, Edwards, to simulate aircraft motions on a computer. The usefulness of aircraft motion simulation was becoming obvious to many of us at the time Al and I were working on the GEDA, but I had no sense of what it would become. Langley had much more capability at the time, and Joe Weil went there to work with Ordway Gates on problems of other aircraft similar to the F-100. Al and I continued to support their simulation studies, sending them our GEDA results for the F-100. The results were published in a paper given at a conference at Langley, with all four of us as authors. After that, Al and I were reassigned to other work, and Dick Day was assigned to the GEDA.

I worked a little with Ed Videan (some kind of a committee) to choose the first type of simulation equipment we were to use at our facility, REAC[73] or something like that, using ±100 volts DC. I even attended classes at Ames [Aeronautical Laboratory] with Ed Videan, Dick Musick, and Dick Day on programming the equipment. My first simulation (not documented) on the new equipment was a simple heat transfer problem, which I bungled at first. Your [Waltman's] recollection of using the wrong time constant on a heat transfer problem probably came later than this, but I don't remember. I did no more documented aircraft motion simulations after the GEDA experience, but I remember that Chet Wolowicz worked on aircraft motions simulations on the REAC in those early days, and we consulted occasionally. My recollection is that Dick Day was working mostly on getting the pilot into the simulation at that time. I had at first thought that the REAC equipment would be useful in the coming heat-transfer and aerodynamic heating studies that I had been assigned to, but as it turned out, I worked mostly with Ray Jackson on the IBM digital computers, setting up methods to predict aircraft skin temperatures in flight and backing out heat-transfer data from the measured skin temperatures. Somewhere along the line, I supplied the equations to program the X-15 simulation to read out skin temperature, but I don't remember the details.

Richard (Dick) E. Day

I started at the NACA High-Speed Flight Research Station in 1951. I left to go to Houston in February of 1962. I came back in 1975 to do Shuttle work and retired at Dryden in 1981.

Initially, when the X-2 came to the desert for its flight tests, Walt Williams assigned me as the NACA Project Engineer. At this time, we served in an engineering advisory capacity to the Air Force prior to that service's turning the airplane over to the HSFS for flight research. The Air Force had engineers, but they were not sufficiently acquainted with the research aspects of flight test, so Joe Weil and I went down and programmed (mechanized) the Goodyear Electronic Differential Analyzer (GEDA) with the equations of motion and the airplane's aerodynamic and physical characteristics to make the X-2 simulator. We used an iron pipe with centering springs for the control stick and control position transducers (CPTs) to provide control-surface-position input to the analog. Rudder control

---

[73] REAC (Reeves Electronic Analog Computer) was an earlier acronym for the EAI analog computers.

was not provided because the X-2 rudders were locked at supersonic speeds. The display was a CRT, and I believe Ed Videan provided the equations for that. They were pretty simple, but at the time, I didn't know how to do that. So we had a wing as viewed from the rear on the CRT. The wing would indicate sideslip, angle of attack [AOA], and roll, and that was our first simulator. [See photo E-1841.] The simulations were all performed using 5 DOF. We didn't have the capability to calculate 6 DOF, so we would set the aerodynamic parameters to the various Mach numbers and altitudes predicted by performance calculations. Because this was only a 5 DOF lateral-directional simulation, there were no meters, such as a Mach meter or altimeter. We used the GEDA for many aerodynamic programs prior to acquiring our own analog devices and going to Ames for analog programming instructions.

Pete Everest made all the powered flights except five. He incrementally increased Mach number on each flight until he reached Mach 2.4, and after burnout, he would get aileron pulses while decelerating. We made analog matches to the flight data and plotted the flight data along with the wind-tunnel and theoretical calculations. We then came up with a curve for the C_{n_β} [yawing moment coefficient with respect to sideslip] vs. Mach number [X-2 paper: TM X-137 (Citation No. 246), Fig. 7].[74] Using these data, the simulator showed that beyond Mach 2.4 the airplane entered into uncontrollable divergences when increasing angle of attack beyond four or five degrees. So when Pete made his Mach 2.8 flight, after burnout he kept the angle of attack to almost zero—maybe one degree—until he slowed to Mach 2.2. He then started turning (increasing angle of attack), but Pete was not painted into a corner as Mel Apt was going to be on the final flight.

Oh, something that is pretty important, these are all at one Mach number—5 DOF at one Mach number—because we didn't have the capability to do 6 DOF. So we did [Iven] Kincheloe's at different altitudes up to the altitude he finally got to, and a little higher. I think he had 19 pounds of dynamic pressure. [Mel] Apt was the third and final X-2 pilot to be trained on the simulator. Then we'd go to Mach 2.6, 2.8, 3.0. I'm not sure if we went to 3.2; I think 3.0 was the highest we got. We showed him if he increased AOA to about 5 degrees, he would start losing directional stability. The tail would be in the shadow of the wing. He'd start this, and due to adverse aileron, he'd put in stick one way and the plane would yaw the other way. We'd say all you had to do was push over. We showed Apt this, and he did it many times.

Unfortunately, on the final flight, the unexpected increase in performance to Mach 3.2 positioned the X-2 farther from the landing site (Rogers Dry Lake) than planned, placing the airplane at a possible point of no return. Apt was now literally painted into a corner. He had to decide whether to decelerate to Mach 2.4, as briefed, to make a safe turn, thus increasing the distance even farther from the landing site, or try to make the turn immediately and risk the instabilities that had been predicted and "flown" on the simulator.

Well, the simulator was a new

---

[74] C_{n_β} is the yawing moment coefficient with respect to sideslip.

device that had never been used previously for training or flight planning. Most pilots had, in fact, expressed a certain amount of distrust of the device. Whether distrust of the simulator or a fear of not making it back to the landing site affected Apt's decision, he opted for the turn. His radio message was, "OK, she's cut out. I'm turning." There was an ominous silence of 20 seconds before Apt uttered an almost unintelligible, "She goes. . . ."

You can see his aileron input here [TMX-137, Fig 6]. He started a right turn. Then he put the stick in left and he still kept rolling to the left. Then he put the stick in 10 degrees to the right. He kept staying at a constant roll velocity, until he hit here, and that is when he got this AOA and beta[75] and he hit roll coupling. On his final flight, he was so far out because he went so fast (Mach 3.2). He may have been at what he thought was the point of no return. He thought, "Gosh, I'd better get back." But he knew, from the simulator, if he made the turn and increased his AOA, he'd get in trouble. So, anyway, he chose to make the turn and got in trouble. That's the Apt story.[76]

The foregoing is a fairly condensed history of what happened with NACA's use of the Edwards Air Force Base GEDA prior to NACA's obtaining its own analog system. I think it also indicates the impact of the first analog simulator at Edwards and the HSFS on the conduct of flight-test and flight-research programs.

Larry Taylor and I did some work with his theory and my piloting and analog work [see NASA TN D-746-*Flight Controllability Limits and Related Human Transfer Functions as Determined from Simulator and Flight Tests.* (Citation No. 304)]. [This report discusses the results of a simulator study and associated flight and centrifuge studies that were performed to determine the levels of static stability and damping necessary to enable a pilot to control the longitudinal and lateral-directional dynamics of a vehicle for short periods. Novel piloting techniques were found which enabled the pilots to control the vehicle at conditions that were otherwise uncontrollable.]

We had a pretty good X-15 centrifuge program that lasted about two months. That was all analog. [This is in reference to a X-15 simulation using the NADC centrifuge at Johnsville, Pennsylvania.]

I made one statement, that the GEDA down at the AF was the very first flight test simulator; however, I qualified it quite well by saying [it was] used for pilot training, obtaining aerodynamic data, derivative extraction, and flight planning. Other people had analogs and they were doing design work, and other such things, but I don't think an analog had ever been used as a flight-test tool to the extent that the GEDA was. It was the first of its kind, even with all these qualifications. There were the old training simulators—the Link simulators—that were only training simulators and not research simulators. I guess research would go with these others. It had fixed derivatives, all servo-driven, and

---

[75] Angle of sideslip

[76] Apt lost control of the X-2 due to roll-coupling and lost his life when the aircraft's nose section hit the desert floor.

even 50 years ago there was a simulator that was the same thing—all servo-driven displays and that sort of thing.

One of the first jobs I did on our analog was to run an F-104 3 DOF climb program. The last time I used the GEDA was after Apt's flight, to get some data to put into the accident report. It was after that—in 1956—that we got the (analog) simulator. I was using that simulator to try to duplicate the flight. I did the programming on it. Dick [Banner] did his own, and I guess Videan did some. I always programmed my own.

I did all my own mechanizing. Here's what I did at FRC with our new computer [he refers to TMX 137]. The input was silver ink.[77] The rest of them are the actual flight records and the analog records. That's at the end of that report. I used it for that. I think we got it very quickly—around the first of 1957. All I had was the Boeing B-17 side-arm controller. We got it from Ralph Sissle. It was a formation stick. I don't know if you know the details of it, but the copilot had one and the pilot had one, and there was a red button on top. When you wanted to take over, you'd push the button and start flying. It was a good thing, but I never tried landing with it. There weren't many others with it then. I think the reason I got it was because I'd had so many hours flying in the Canadian Air Force. I guess they figured they'd let this old geezer use it, and. . . .

One note I had, after we had the X-15 simulator, with the iron bird downstairs: Bill Johnson of North American Aviation called up and asked—now that we had the X-15 simulation—if we would do a favor for him. He wanted us to see what we could do if we were to attach a so-and-so rocket to the X-15 and launch it near the maximum height. So I did that for him. I took different heights and launch angles—and we didn't have any dynamic pressure; it was pure space. It didn't get to orbit, whatever the rocket was. It was a North American missile of sorts. John Perry was doing the simulator work for me. This is when we were still in the X-15 program. I had to sneak that one in for Bill. He had always been generous with his time when the X-15 simulator was still at the North American Aviation site at the Los Angeles International Airport.

Donald Reisert

I found two reports on projects that used analog computers to help guide the flight programs: TM-137 [X-2, Citation No. 246] and ARS No. 1674-61 [F-104A, Citation No. 297]. Both reports mention the use of computers to provide simulation of the aircraft.

X-2 Simulation

I don't have dates but I believe about six or seven of the thirteen powered flights of the X-2 were made during 1956.[78] Dick Day and

---

[77] This term "silver ink" is in reference to a method of implementing a nonlinear function using an X-Y plotter. This had the ink pen replaced with a sensor that follows a path drawn on a piece of plotting paper with silver ink. An electrical signal was transmitted through the ink path by means of wires attached at each end of the path. The plotter arm was driven by the independent signal (in this case, time) in the horizontal direction, and as the pen arm moved across the paper, the pen sensor followed the "silver ink" path. The output of the pen arm was then the signal that represented the input parameter (in this case a time history of the pilot's input) that was used in the simulation model. Not very elegant, and it took some time to set up; but it worked.

[78] The correct number of flights in 1956 for the X-2 was 12.

I started the computer program about this time. This work was performed on the Air Force computer and was to help guide the Mach-altitude flight-envelope expansion. The X-2 was in the Research Airplane Program that was paid for by the NACA, Air Force, and the Navy.

The Air Force pilots were to fly these flights to obtain the Mach number and high-altitude records before the NACA was allowed to fly it. Bell Aircraft supplied people to maintain the vehicle and help to train some NACA mechanics and rocket people. NACA instrumentation people performed the installation and maintenance of the instruments to measure the flight data.

The computer was only large enough to perform the three-degree-of-freedom equations for the speed and altitude runs or some five-degree-of-freedom equations (for stability and control) with the Mach number held constant. The constants and coefficients of the equations were installed by setting rotational resistors that were all connected together with plug-in wires. When ready to run, it was a mass of wires on top of a shelf about waist high. Some values were put in using pots (about 100) that covered a vertical panel above the shelf.

The cockpit simulation was very sparse. I think we calibrated voltmeters with a grease pencil. Dick Musick made a two-axis control stick using a broomstick and two pots. There was a strip chart that had six or eight pens to record the data. A photograph was taken of me at the controls demonstrating the setup. I was growing a beard for some contest and looked pretty bad. For the later runs, Dick Day brought in a B-17 formation control stick to replace the broomstick and made things look better.

The early flights were made by Lt. Col. [Pete] Everest, and after one visit to the simulator when we were having some trouble because we didn't believe data, he declared that machine no good. (The problem occurred when presenting the stability data at the higher angles of attack. The wings would not remain level after starting the run, and the aileron inputs to level the wings made things worse until the roll mode was lost after full aileron input.) I remember one meeting with the Air Force, probably after some flights were made where Col. Hanes[79] strongly suggested to Lt. Col. Everest that he go back and fly the simulator again as we tried to present the flight conditions for each flight before the envelope expansion to higher Mach number. He did fly the simulator again.

The flight program went slowly. I think the X-2 was designed to go to Mach 4; however, the wind-tunnel data indicated a low directional stability at the Mach numbers below 4.0.

Our procedure was to use the directional period[80] at the highest flight Mach number to calculate

---

[79] Col. Horace A. Hanes, Director of Flight Test and Development, AFFTC.

[80] The period (length of time) between peaks in the oscillations that occurred after a disturbance (such as a stick or rudder pulse by the pilot) that caused the aircraft to oscillate about one or more of the aircraft's axes. For the case mentioned, the pilot would put in a small rudder pulse and the plane would oscillate about the vertical axis—the nose would move from side to side, and this motion would then die out over a short period of time. Using the recording of this motion, the research engineers could determine the appropriate aircraft derivatives for the corresponding conditions (i.e., Mach number, attitude, etc.).

the coefficient C_{n_β} (using the Dick Banner-Al Kuhl equation); use the flight data to modify the computer inputs; fly the simulation to the next safe, highest Mach number; write a flight plan to obtain flight data at this point; then continue until the flight envelope was fully expanded.

The X-2 did not have any stability augmentation, so after it went supersonic, the beta (sideslip) vane would start to oscillate and the period would lengthen as the Mach number increased (indicating a decrease in directional stability). We did not ask for many specific flight-data maneuvers and requested periods of fixed controls, especially at the higher speeds near engine burnout, so we could measure a clean period of beta oscillation.

Lt. Col. Everest made about four flights, the last two achieving Mach 2.7 and Mach 2.87 (shown as flight B in TM X-137).[81] He must have believed some of what we said about not going to high lift at high speeds as flight B data show he pushed over slightly after engine burnout, even though the aircraft was speeding away from the landing site and started to turn about 35 seconds later near Mach 2. We had a problem getting our lateral-directional period for the flights above Mach 2.4 to calculate the C_{n_β}. The period was getting longer, and we could not find even a half cycle without some lateral control inputs to invalidate the data.

As Lt. Col. Everest was preparing for the last two flights, he was also preparing for a new assignment with relocation and had only a limited amount time to fly the X-2. This was during the summer of 1956. At this time, Capt. Iven Kincheloe was assigned to perform the high-altitude flight, and Capt. Mel Apt was assigned to finish the Mach-number expansion. Another time constraint was that the aircraft was to be delivered to the NACA on 7 October 1956.

Capts. Kincheloe and Apt came by to fly the simulator often and were very cooperative. I don't remember how many flights Capt. Kincheloe performed, but he did have more than one and was exposed to the X-2 gliding characteristics before he made the high altitude flight.[82] On 7 September 1956, Capt. Kincheloe very successfully performed the high-altitude flight (flight A of TM X-137). With the turn-around time required, there was time for one more flight before delivery of the aircraft to the NACA.

The last Air Force flight was to be an introductory and high-speed flight for Capt. Apt. The drop,[83] engine start, and rotation for the climb out were very important for the success of the high-speed flight (as it left more fuel for the high-speed end of the flight). I remember being at the simulator with Capt. Kincheloe guiding Capt. Apt in the launch and climb-out as he flew the three-degree-of-freedom performance setup. Capt. Apt flew a very efficient engine start and climb-out in his flight. I was on the lakebed for this flight and remem-

---

[81] Everest actually made ten flights, the last one going to Mach 2.87.

[82] Kincheloe made four flights, with the fourth reaching 126,200 feet on 7 September 1956.

[83] From a modified Boeing B-50 mothership.

ber watching the flight after engine start. As the X-2 passed over the south lakebed, I was impressed with the speed, as I had never seen a contrail laid down that fast. After burnout and the contrail stopped, the chase planes could not find the X-2, and there was no response to radio calls. The Air Force had a small tower, I believe on the east side of the lakebed, with personnel who had watched the flight with high-powered glasses and witnessed the rolling as the wings flashed in the morning sun. The people [in the tower] also were able to see the capsule dropping (there was a small stabilizing parachute that inflated after the capsule separated from the aircraft) and reported its location.[84] A helicopter with a medic on board was sent to the capsule.

The aircraft survived pretty much intact as with the weight of the nose capsule and pilot removed, the center-of-gravity traveled aft and allowed the aircraft to recover from the inverted spin that was indicated by the over-the-shoulder camera. The aircraft glided and contacted the ground at a shallow angle. It landed to the east of the base. I got a ride out to the wreckage. The aircraft was upright and the vertical tail did not touch the ground (some people felt the tail would break off if high-Mach-number maneuvers were performed).

The instrumentation was in the nose capsule and the aircraft, and it survived to let us plot a time history of the flight, as shown in flight C of the report. After the flight data was worked up, a six-degree-of-freedom analog computer simulation was performed at the NACA HSFS. Also, The Langley Laboratory performed some more wind-tunnel tests on the X-2 models to provide higher Mach number C_{n_β} and $C_{n/\text{aileron}}$.[85]

Large overlays of the data were made and the control inputs were plotted to this large scale and then covered with soft wire.[86] These wires (elevator and aileron only) were then used as control inputs starting at burnout. Small mouse-like items ran over the wires in real time, making control inputs to the six-degree-of-freedom simulation. Dick Musick made the wire inputs and Glenn Robinson and Herman Rediess performed the computer program.

F-104 Reaction Control Analog Simulation

The F-104 program studied the use of reaction controls at low dynamic pressures. The F-104 was outfitted with small rocket motors to control the three axes as described in report ARS-1674-61 [Citation No. 297].

As the aircraft was being modified, a three-degree-of-freedom analog program was started to determine the performance characteristics of the F-104 at low dynamic pressures. We also had to define a task for the pilot to perform using the reaction controls.

---

[84] The X-2 featured a nose capsule in which the pilot could eject from the aircraft. Once it stabilized, he would then separate from it and descend to the ground using a seat-pack parachute. Unfortunately, Apt never got out of the nose capsule before it hit the desert floor.

[85] Yawing moment coefficient with respect to sideslip and aileron deflection, respectively.

[86] This refers to a method of generating a nonlinear function that was very similar to the "silver ink" method described earlier. In this case, the plotted trace was covered with a piece of soft wire that was bent to match the trace. This wire was glued to the paper, a signal was transmitted through the wire, and the sensor on the arm would follow the wire as the pen arm moved across the paper.

We wanted to provide a familiar computer cockpit for the pilot, so I measured the F-104 instrument panel and gave Dick Musick a cardboard cutout of the panel, and he had one made in aluminum. Dick also made up an open box about the cockpit size with a seat at the proper distance from the panel. A center stick for aerodynamic controls and a three-axis reaction stick on the left side of the instrument panel were installed. Dick also had the panel and the cockpit painted a flat black, which did a lot to clean up the presentation. To start the program, Dick installed gauges to show angle of attack, bank, and sideslip as located on the aircraft panel. Airspeed, altitude, and g meter were also installed so the zoom maneuver could be flown. After the initial performance data were defined, the simulator was changed to six degrees of freedom. Joe Walker (the project pilot) flew the simulation and commented that it was better than our usual simulations.

The F-104 instrument panel was modified to include an X-15 three-axis ball, and we were able to also get one for the simulator, which helped in keeping the simulator as a valid tool. The three-axis ball was a new design, and NASA wanted to get some experience with it. [Photo E-4287 shows the first cockpit with the reaction-control stick but before the three-axis ball was installed. This photo was taken in late 1958.]

Other NASA and Air Force pilots flew the F-104, but I don't remember if they flew the simulator. The program didn't last very long, as the X-15 was coming along and everyone was assigned to that project. We never got to modify the simulator or the aircraft to use the reaction controls as rate dampers or combine the aerodynamic controls and reaction controls on the center stick.

Comments on Don Reisert's F-104 Simulation

[I believe Don is talking about three different F-104 reaction-control-simulation mechanizations, with some time in between. There were two different simulations that happened before I got there. The first one was mechanized on the AF GEDAs (see NACA RM H58G18a, Citation No, 214). The second simulation was done using the HSFS's new EAI 31R. In his PA, John Smith mentions doing an F-104 simulation for Wendell Stillwell, which Don worked on, too. The cockpit Don describes was already here when I got here. Also, the analog computer that was here (an EAI 31R) did not have enough equipment to do a 6 DOF simulation. I suspect that for his first mechanization, Don did his own analog programming, with possibly some help from Videan or Day. The third mechanization was done after we had bought more analogs. I remember doing such a simulation about that time, which must have been the one Don mentions. I also remember the 8-ball being installed in the black cockpit and getting to use it. There were no true 6 DOF simulations implemented from when I got there until after we had bought our third analog. There was at least one 5 DOF with a time varying velocity parameter (i.e., velocity was input as a function of time, which I refer to as a 5 1/2 DOF simulation) being used in the other equations. Again, the lack of good records interferes with being completely certain about these facts.

This 5 1/2 DOF simulation could have been the one Don is talking about. This study had the pilots doing a zoom maneuver until the F-104 got to its maximum altitude and went into almost a zero-g ballistic type arc—during which the pilots did a number of maneuvers using the reaction controls (i.e., under near-zero dynamic-pressure conditions). This particular simulation was done using the 31R and 131R analogs.

The report *Simulation Studies of Jet Reaction Controls for Use at High Altitude* (NACA RM H58G18a) by Wendell H. Stillwell and Hubert Drake references another report entitled *Study of Exit Phase of Flight of a Very High Altitude Hypersonic Airplane by Means of a Pilot-Controlled Analog Computer* (NACA RM L57K21) by Windsor L. Sherman, Stanley Faber, and James B Whitten of the Langley Aeronautical Laboratory. This report has an appendix written by Robert E. Andrews that describes the analog mechanization in complete detail. This is by far the best such documentation I have been able to find of any analog mechanization from those early days. The study is also very similar to the 5 1/2 DOF that I did. The only real differences are the particular airplane used and the cockpit mechanization. The HSFS study used an F-104, while the Langley study used a hypothetical hypersonic aircraft.

Since I have not been able to find a similar document written by anyone here, I have included many of the pages of that specific appendix in the appendices to this monograph. In his appendix, Robert Andrews not only describes the details of the analog mechanization but also talks about certain equipment inaccuracies that plagued all of us who had to program those computers. He also describes the special testing and work-arounds that he used to deal with these problems. This mechanization happened during those early days in the use of analog computers for flight simulations and is a good example of the state-of-the-art of analog programming at that time. The techniques employed at Langley and Ames had an early influence in the way similar simulations were programmed at the HSFS in the beginning.]

Robert (Bob) W. Kempel

Bob Kempel is an aeronautical research engineer who spent a lot of time working with the simulation lab. He started at NASA in 1960 and left to work for the AFFTC in 1963 because he wasn't allowed to program the analogs as much as he wanted to. He returned to NASA in 1966 and worked on the Lifting Body Program. There has already been a lot written about Bob and his involvement with the Lifting Body Program, both in papers by Bob, and in Dale Reed's book *Wingless Flight*. In April 1994, Bob, along with Wen Painter and Milt Thompson, published the NASA Reference Publication 1332, entitled *Developing and Flight-Testing the HL-10 Lifting Body: A Precursor to the Space Shuttle*. This publication is an excellent and informative history of the HL-10 flight-test program. Dale Reed, in his book, tells about all the lifting bodies that were flown at the FRC. Both of these publications discuss the involvement of the FSL simulations of the different lifting bodies. The AFFTC also implemented simulators of the M2-F2 and X-24B. This division of tasks was due in part to the FSL simulation capabilities being so tied up with the X-15 program. Like the X-15 Program, the Lifting Body Program was another example of the FRC-Air Force team working together to accomplish the goals requested of it.[87]

Bob's activities at NASA include working on the X-15 program during his early years at the FRC. Following this job, he was heavily involved with the Lifting Body Program as the principal stability-and-control, handling-qualities, and flight-simulation engineer on the HL-10 and M2-F3 lifting bodies. He has also been actively involved with the Highly Maneuverable Aircraft Technology (HiMAT) and Controlled Impact Demonstration (CID) programs, both of which

---

[87] The Navy and North American Aviation were also part of the X-15 team. The lifting-body team also included Northrop and Martin.

involved RPVs, and the GPAS flying simulator.

The lifting-body simulations in the FSL began as all-analog mechanization and became hybrid in the late 1960s, first with the use of the ICARUS program on the SDS 930 and later on the SDS 9300. The SDS 9300 was bought to improve the simulation capabilities because the lifting-body nonlinear derivatives were, in fact, too nonlinear for analog-computer implementation. Fortunately for the FSL, the HL-10 was down for such a long period of time between the first and second flights that the extended SDS 9300 checkout and acceptance period (of almost one year) did not affect the flight program. The SDS 9300 had been accepted by the time the HL-10 Project group had resolved the problem encountered on the first flight.

In one of the e-mails I got from Bob, he recalls:

> As I remember the situation, after the HL-10's first flight on 22 December 1966, we grounded the vehicle. We went to the Langley Research Center (LaRC) and told the involved engineers there about the aerodynamic problem. Once a modification was proposed, or I should say two possible vehicle configuration changes were proposed, they wouldn't choose either. They insisted that we at the FRC do that. I did all the plotting by hand and picked one based on all my comparisons, and then I remember Larry Caw doing something with all the data. I remember Larry and John Smith coming to me, indicating that the data were too nonlinear to mechanize on the analog. That was when we approached John McTigue [the Lifting Body Program manager] to buy us a digital computer to do the function generation. We did that. Then one day, Lowell Greenfield came to us and wanted to demo[nstrate] a mod to us in the sim mechanization. We flew the sim, and it looked OK to us. Then Greenfield told us that it was all-digital. That is the first all-digital sim I remember working with. I remember ICARUS, but I don't think we did [much] with that in the sim. ICARUS, as I remember ,used linearized (simplified) aero[nautical] derivatives. I really can't remember, though. I never used it very much. It was a good idea, but I had the full nonlinear HL-10 to work with and I worked with that a lot.

Both of these documents mentioned above [*Wingless Flight* and *Developing and Flight Testing the HL-10*] refer to the ICARUS simulation program performing the integration (with respect to time) of all the calculated accelerations and velocities on the digital computer. The early version of ICARUS did no integration on the digital computer. A later version of the ICARUS program used by the HL-10 simulation did digital integration of only the longitudinal equations— such as horizontal and vertical accelerations and velocities. The natural frequencies of the lateral-directional equations were too high for digital integration on either the SDS 930 or the SDS 9300. The integration of these parameters was always done on the analog computer. The M2-F3 was the last simulation to use the 9300/ICARUS hybrid system. This was followed by a new all-digital 6 DOF Fortran program that used the XDS 9300 (formerly SDS 9300) and a new set of large-angle equations for the three-eighths-scale F-15/SRV (Spin Research Vehicle) in the early1970s. The program was later ported to the CYBER 73.

The following paragraphs are also from Bob:

Acceleration due to Gravity

> Then there was the story about daily checks of analog computers because they were known to

possibly be different from day to day. One day the dynamic checks didn't come out quite right. Differences between the standard dynamic check and that day's dynamic response were very subtle. Don Bacon, the sim engineer, insisted that everything was OK and nothing had changed. Upon further investigation, I remained unconvinced. I determined that the acceleration due to gravity (32.174 feet per second squared) was wrong! Don said this was impossible! Don looked at me and said, "How could this be?" I insisted that the only thing I could determine from the dynamic responses was that the acceleration due to gravity had to be wrong. Don went back and did more checking and then came to me kind of sheepishly and admitted he had found the mistake. It was indeed the acceleration due to gravity that was wrong. He never did tell me how it was incorrectly mechanized. We just never said anything more about it. Looking back, it was kind of humorous, though.

The "Midnight Patcher"

Analog computer mechanizations were very precarious . . . in that the computer mechanization consisted of a myriad of various-length wires on a front patch panel, which linked the various analog components. To the uninitiated, this panel looked like multicolored spaghetti. A complex simulation patch panel was typically a real mess. Once a simulation was mechanized and thoroughly checked, the wires in the patch panel were not to be touched by anyone but the simulation engineer. Analog mechanizations were required to be statically and dynamically checked quite frequently (like daily) due to the problem of occasional component failure. If a component failed, the simulation could be mildly or grossly invalid, depending on the criticality of that particular component.

It was always suspected that we had a "midnight patcher" due to some of the problems with patch panels found by some simulation engineers on their next shift, the midnight patcher being a real or mythical person who would either pull or rearrange a wire on a patch-panel. These problems were typically unusual and unexplained, ones that could only be attributed to the "midnight patcher".

Electric Stick and the "Blue Box"

Significant innovations were pioneered in the FRC simulation lab. The electric stick was one. The development of this stick enabled engineers to duplicate the stick characteristics of many different airplanes. These sticks had the capability to vary stick breakout force, force gradient, mass damping, range of deflection, etc. This was a significant development and many aerospace agencies across the USA were interested in using this technology in their labs.

The "blue box" (so called because of its color) was a generic cockpit enclosure that had interchangeable instrument panels representing different airplanes. Cockpits could be reconfigured from one airplane to another in about 30 minutes. With more than one blue box, a tight simulation schedule could be maintained.

JetStar

I remember when Larry Caw was assigned to the JetStar. He became a very good real-time analog programmer. We were looking at different control schemes for riding qualities, as I remember it. I remember the incident when we were airborne and we were looking at different feedback schemes. I had mechanized a beta (sideslip) feedback. Well, as you know, signs (sign conventions) were sometimes confusing. Fitz Fulton was the pilot. The sign on beta was wrong, and we ended up with a dynamically unstable airplane because of it. We turned on the system for Fitz to evaluate, and the airplane immediately began an oscillatory divergence! Larry and I were in the back hollering to Fitz to turn it off, but Fitz was intrigued with the thing so he wanted to watch it as it diverged or maybe just teach us a lesson. He finally punched the thing off and Larry and I sighed in relief. Larry changed the beta-input sign, and we proceeded with the test.

The JetStar was a fun airplane to fly in, but I always had a feeling of impending doom or something else going wrong. Herm Rediess was my boss at the time and when he wanted me to fly in the thing all the time, I told him "thanks, but no thanks." I don't think Herm ever liked that. Don Gatlin can tell you about the incident where they almost tore the wings off. I think Musick was aboard that flight too.

The following is from Don Gatlin in regard to this particular flight:

> I was not on that particular flight. I was the project engineer and was monitoring the flight from the radio room in the pilots' office. I believe Dick [Musick] was on board and a KU [University of Kansas] grad student whose name I don't remember. [Actually, it was Dick Musick and Larry Caw.] Don Mallick was the pilot, Stan Butchart in the right seat. I don't believe we even scheduled telemetry, so there was no real time record of the event. As I remember, we got a call that "We've had a problem here. Get someone up to look us over." Betty Callister and I sent Gary Krier up in an F-104 to check them out. Stan told me afterward that as the limit cycle went on, he just looked out the cockpit window to see where they would crash as he believed the wings would be torn off. As I remember, there was no damage although the airplane required a thorough inspection before flying again.

Dwain A. Deets

Waltman: I'd like to get your comments on some of the simulations that you might have been involved with; talk about what they did or didn't do, their capabilities, and any problem areas, or anything that you thought might have been lacking, or any of their good features.

Deets: OK. Do you want me to start with the F-8, or does it matter?

Waltman: The GPAS.

Deets: OK. I can even go back before the GPAS—you're starting in which year?

Waltman: In 1955—that's when the simulations started. Were you involved with the X-15?

Deets: No, I was thinking about a precursor to the GPAS—the F-100 airborne simulator, our first variable stability airplane. Are you interested in airborne simulators in your study, or are you restricting your study to ground-based simulators in support of research airplanes.

Waltman: This publication is about

simulators/simulations that used analog (and hybrid) computers, which includes the GPAS, but not the F-100 airborne simulator. It also includes some moving-base simulations that we implemented at other computer centers.

GPAS

Deets: The things that come to my mind are where you had analog computers, general-purpose analog computers in your office, the portables—like the TR-10 or TR-48—those kinds of things, where you could work with them in your office and then take them down next to the airplane and tie them in somehow. But it wasn't anything like the X-15 simulator—they weren't that grand and capable and in a sim lab like that. The GPAS, all along, when I was involved with it, used analog equipment. And as we progressed to the more capable computers—like TR-48s that were upgraded—we started getting more user-friendly function generators. And that became an important thing. How easy is it to change your breakpoints and function generators? What kind of mechanism is it? It became sort of a mechanical issue—did the jitteriness of the mechanics of the function generators show up when you turned the knob? It was those kinds of issues that we stewed about.

A lot of things I remember about the GPAS (the JetStar) involved getting to the point of having an analog computer on board the airplane. It served as a model of the airplane you were trying to simulate. We actually specified a good share of that system. So, it was kind of built to our specs. The layout of the patch panel was as we requested, and things like that. So, that certainly was part of the whole simulation.

Waltman: Did you ever fly in and use it—go up in the airplane?

Deets: Oh, yeah. I definitely did. If you want to consider the GPAS as one of your simulation tools rather than how did simulation support GPAS, one of the stories occured as we were checking out the system—back at CALSPAN [Cornell Aeronautical Labs]. Basically, we were hooking up a ground-based simulation outside the airplane to actually try everything before the first flight. We spent the whole summer checking everything out so that we had complete confidence that we had done everything right with the model and hooking up the airplane. There were some points where you couldn't use the actual hardware, like the sideslip vanes. You couldn't actually flow air over any of the vanes. So you bypassed the vane itself and tested the sim model of the vane as best you could. We did a lot of worrying about the dynamics of the vane and whether you needed to model it or not. We stewed about that a lot.

So, when we were finally ready to fly, I was test engineer for the first series of flights. The first time we engaged the lateral control system so that we were using feedback from the sideslip vane, among other signals, we obtained an estimate of the sideslip rate [beta dot] using analog circuitry. Its purpose as a feedback was to provide damping to the Dutch roll. As I turned up the gain, after the system was engaged, we started veering off as I was turning it up. The more I turned it, the more the airplane started to wobble back and forth—more and more unstable in the lateral directional axis. This was not supposed to be happening. My reaction was: I am doing something wrong. I'd better crank it up some more. I actually considered this a PIO, although I as the test engineer was in effect the pilot. And I was in the back of the airplane doing this, and the pilots were calling out, "What's going on back there?" So they shut it down and called me forward to have me explain what had happened. (They were supposed to be "hands off" to let the system respond alone.)

Well it turned out, through that whole summer, we had been working with reverse polarity in our signal for the sideslip. The person who calibrated it set it up wrong. It wasn't clear in his mind which way was positive when the vane moved for positive sideslip, and we didn't have a carefully reviewed calibration procedure throughout a summer-long checkout. So, everything we did was based on that wrong sign. And we never knew about it until we actually turned the system on in flight.

Ken Szalai was the other person flying about that time. There was a series of flights as we were expanding the flight envelope. One person, as I remember, who was a Cornell person responsible for overseeing the flutter clearance—I can't remember his name, but he always insisted on wearing the parachute when he was in the cabin. We had a special [escape] chute that would allow crew egress by dropping down through the floor of the cabin. It always unnerved me that he thought he couldn't take time to put his parachute on if we had a problem.

One of the other stories that comes to mind is that one of our real challenges was getting a strip-chart recorder that (1) was rugged enough for the aircraft environment, (2) had a read-out that we could see soon enough—that didn't have too much delay between when something happened and when we could see something in the records—and (3) could be seen right away because of the type of paper and pen. The pen was some sort of heat thing, but what it wrote wouldn't necessarily be really vivid right away and we would have to wait for the record to develop. So, that was always a challenge.

Another thing I remember was just in the analog computers. This is more in the ground checkout around the airplane. Sometimes when things weren't quite checking out when they had been working previously, the first step in troubleshooting was to take your hands and push against the patch cords, hoping that by doing that, suddenly it would start working. And sometimes it did start working. You had some connections that were pretty unreliable. That's the analog days.

F-8 DFBW (Digital Fly-By-Wire)

I'll now move to the F-8. This is just simulation and support of advocacy stuff. In the early days, we used TR-10s or TR-48s. Ken Szalai and I were trying to sell the idea of a CCV (Control Configured Vehicle), and so we had the idea that you could put a canard up there somewhere near the nose of the airplane and take the tail off. We were going to demonstrate the fact through computerized fly-by-wire, although at the time we only had analog flight control. We weren't bold enough to think about digital. But we were bold enough to think about taking that horizontal stabilizer off. Our main argument was that the force of the rear tail was in a direction that was down in order to trim things up, which meant that the wing had to offset that or carry more lift and therefore more drag because of the lift. So, we thought that if we put the canard up in the front, we could actually be using the lifting surfaces of the canard for part of that lift. We kind of analyzed that to the point where that would be a better airplane. Not so much in the savings in weight, but just where the lift was being applied.

So we hooked up the TR-10 with a model of this, and we concocted a side view of the airplane display that showed where the canard would have to be [located] to stabilize the airplane. We had just a stick figure of the fuselage and where the canard would have to go. So we did some very early conceptual research, I guess, using this mechanism, to see what that canard would be doing under any kind of maneuvers. It never went anywhere, but it was instructive to us and we were always looking for a way of using some dynamic visual representation to help sell the whole idea. We put it on a scope. It was just Ken Szalai and me. If there was someone from the sim group, I can't remember who [it was]. I know there was interest in it.

That's applying simulation to the world of advocacy. And then when we actually got into the F-8 Digital Fly-by-Wire [Project] itself, we made use of a lot of the Apollo simulation capability that was back at Draper Laboratory. And in my own case, I became educated in a big way on what was already being done in the world of simulation, all in support of the Apollo Program. The engineers at the Draper Lab were very methodical about the way they would do things. They were very systematic in testing a software load. A lot of what they did in the F-8 program was basi-

cally brute force—the flight control system was a fixed-point digital computer. One of the primary concerns was overflow. All parameters must be scaled relative to the maximum value the parameter could take on. But they had to check what happened if something overflowed in some register in there. So, you had to do hundreds and hundreds of cases to see what broke down and how that impacted the closed-loop system. So, much of what we did wasn't piloted simulation; it was batch simulation. We ran so many cases, and then we examined every case to see whether what had happened was reasonable. We didn't try to predict everything, but rather we would just look at it and see if it all made sense. Did the things seem to be happening that ought to be happening?

So, that was a learning experience on how to use simulation. And then we came back here and basically tried to do the same type of thing but using a lot more pilot-in-the-loop as compared to the batch stuff—and tying in more and more hardware to the simulations. So many of our simulations were a build-up to get more and more of the hardware—actual actuators and hydraulics. So, that is what was really happening with the F-8 iron bird that was down in the lean-to. Each one was kind of a step progression towards more and more completeness of our simulation to the point where we were ready to go out and fly. Some of the big issues involved components that were digitally embedded within things that still had to be analog. We were trying to understand any effects that the digital [systems had]—the sample rate, any latency. Also, we had simulation up in the mezzanine and the iron bird downstairs and we had the communication lines between these, all artifacts of the simulation that wouldn't necessarily be in the real flight world. We probably spent more attention on all those simulation artifacts than we did in the elements that would be in the real flight environment.

The step from analog to digital on the flight-control side brought in a lot of other issues. One of the aspects of that is trying to bring the whole management system [together]—it is more of a cultural thing than anything else. It involved the different types of people, whoever it was, such as the head of the safety office, people with their own particular past experience that they felt comfortable with—which [consisted of] all-analog type systems, whether they were computers or whether they were hardware, mechanical hardware that was analog in nature. So [we had] to bring that set of people along to being comfortable about this box that they didn't understand. They only knew that it had zeros and ones, and a one could turn into a zero, and so they could imagine the worst things that could happen. So, that was a very important thing. I'm trying to think whether the same concern was shared by those types of people towards the simulators that they depended on as building confidence towards what was going on with the airplane. I don't know if they had the same worries about the simulators.

GPAS Again

On the GPAS, we did studies in the effects of motion—where we had the real-world motion to some degree—if you want to say whatever the JetStar did in the way of motion was the real-world motion. Then we had it exactly. If we were trying to simulate some other airplane, we had some degrees of freedom matched and we didn't have others. But still, we were interested in trying to figure out what were the effects of washout filters and those things that would have to be in a moving-base ground simulator—a motion simulator—which would have to be taken into account. We didn't have any of the motion simulators here at the FRC because that was not highly important to us. But when we got interested in the research aspects of it, we did some of it in the airplane, and some of it we'd go up to Ames and use its moving-base simulators. But that was a pretty small part of what we did.

[The following comments are] on the subject of the controllers—the stick or the wheels—and how important that is in having a good overall simulation. I was involved with a lot of research studies from the standpoint of how the differences in feel affect the pilot—in terms of the net results or evaluation of the airplane. So, [we dealt with] topics such as: should you pick off the force that the pilot applies to the stick or the [control] wheel as your input to the simulator, or should it be the position of the stick? How are these two different? [What are] the dynamics between the two of them? Should you use mechanical devices such as bungies, springs, and [similar] devices in order to give [a simulator] the right feel, or should you have servo actuators that are moving the controller? . . . If you have something that is programmable, . . . you are going to have to use some sort of actuator to move the stick according to the pilot's input. That gives you the flexibility to change it easily so that you can go from one simulation of an airplane to a different one. The problem with mechanical systems is that you can't make those kinds of changes easily. So, much of the debate over GPAS requirements struggled with that issue because we had to figure what to put in the GPAS. A lot of what we were struggling with was also a major item of concern to the ground-based simulators for other reasons—issues such as whether you needed a hydraulic actuator for the servo controlling the stick; whether electrical-mechanical was better or worse, [or at least] adequate, [and] how did that affect the dynamics of the controller? I'll leave it at that. That was a major topic of interest and, therefore, research.

Stanley P. Butchart

Stan joined the NACA HSFRS in May 1951 as a research pilot. Most of the aircraft he flew did not have flight simulators, since there were no such simulators in those days. Some of the simulators he did fly were the Iron Cross[88] [see photo E-2581], F-100, F-104, GPAS, and the Boost Program.

Waltman: Let's start with anything you want to say about the Iron Cross simulator.

Butchart: On the Iron Cross—from the pilot's point of view—the first thing was getting the controls in the right direction. Roll was pretty straightforward, twisting the wrist, [as was] yaw. [See photo E-2906 for a picture of the pilot's control stick.] When it came to pitch control, the engineers had set it up to go one way—I can't remember which way it was, now—like, for the nose to go up, I think they had it so that you went down [with] the stick. It soon became obvious to us that the normal way of thinking was to get the nose up, you lifted—rather than the logical way, as if you had a normal stick for pitch control.[89] So, that sort of thing didn't take too long to straighten out.

The development of the amount of thrust that was required to control it took a lot longer. It seemed like it took a long time to determine the

Iron Cross with Stan Butchart (September 1957). (NASA photo E-2581)

---

[88] The Iron Cross was a mechanical device to simulate reaction controls designed for flight research on the X-1B airplane. Most of the flight research actually occurred on an F-104, as discussed above, because of fatigue cracks in a propellant tank of the X-1B. Then, further research occurred on the X-15.

[89] In typical aircraft with the usual control stick for pilot's inputs, the pilot would pull back on the stick to get the nose of the aircraft to go up. Thus, going down with the stick was the opposite of what the pilots were used to.

Iron Cross 3-axes Side-arm Controller (April 1957). (NASA photo E-2906)

right amount of thrust to get the proper response. As with any simulator, there was quite a learning technique—how to beep it, how long to beep it. Fortunately they had the crash bars on it, so if you hit them, you'd start over again.

Waltman: Do you remember any other simulations?

Butchart: I don't really recall what we had. For the early simulations, the biggest problem I had was with the displays. They didn't seem real. It wasn't a true-life thing. It was hard to correlate between real life and looking at a meter. The fellows who rigged them up were the pinball experts who could run them better than we could when we got in and tried to fly 'em.

In the early days, too, there was no motion or feel to it. And I think an awful lot of the ability of a pilot flying an airplane has to do with his feel of the motion and of the degree of motion and that sort of thing. Until they got the advanced part of it where you could get the motion and the feel of it, it was just a pinball game. I didn't get much out of 'em.

Waltman: That was one of the things we looked at in the early days—whether or not we should have moving-base simulators. I did some simulation at Ames, where we used moving-base simulators. But it just never happened at the FRC.

Butchart: Probably a money thing?

Jack McKay and I participated in a simulation at Ames on the centrifuge there. There you have all the motions. It was a whole lot more realistic. We would go up there on Monday on the Gooney Bird and stay there three or four days using the centrifuge. We did this for a number of weeks. I don't remember what the Ames engineers [were after]—it was a general-purpose thing they were doing. You had the ability to dial in all the parameters—to develop the best airplane you could—by yawing moment coefficient or whatever the derivatives were. You could dial it in—up or down—until they all matched and you had the best airplane you could fly. But we got up there one morning and they weren't quite ready. We crawled into the simulator and were looking at it, and all of a sudden we noticed there was a Mach meter that goes up over 3, and an altimeter that goes up to 100,000 feet. And we wondered, what are they looking at? Lockheed was using the thing on weekends. We had seen Lew Shock of Lockheed there. They were developing early SR-71 [actually A-12, in all probability] stuff—before they flew—and they were using the Ames simulator for that.

I always had the feeling that the best thing you could do was to get motion. The centrifuges seemed to have an awful lot, because you could get the G inputs, all of the real-life feels to the thing.

I guess we could on and talk about the program we did back at Johnsville on the centrifuge. When was that? The spring of '59. I was the only one who had two chairs made, one for my regular flying suit and one for my T-100 pressure suit. I could get up—it seemed like—to 14 or 15 Gs in the pressure suit—2 or 3 Gs above what you could do without it. We made those chairs back at Langley. We went back there and took our suits. It was kind of interesting how they made them. We would lie in sand and they would shoot some kind of gas into the sand to harden it. And [they would] make the Styrofoam seats from that. I have a photo from back there that shows all of us sitting in our seats, except for [Neil] Armstrong; he was off somewhere and not in the picture.

One of the things that struck me, and I guess all the pilots about the same, [was that] as I remember we did a single-stage, a two-stage, and a four-stage [launch]. The pilot's job was to keep the needles centered [on an instrument that was usually used for instrument landings]. There were vertical and horizontal needles and we had to keep those centered, and they were programmed with what your trajectory should be. You just kept them centered and you went through the whole thing. But between stages it was very critical. From my recollections, if it was more than half a second, you'd lose it. The whole program, as I recall, was aimed at looking at whether or not a pilot could be in the loop, fly it, and launch it into orbit.

Waltman: The control stick was built here—the three-axis controller—it was one of the things we did during the first two fixed-base studies at the FRC.

Butchart: Was that made out here?

Waltman: Yes.

Butchart: That may have been why Joe [Walker] and I went up to MIT and stopped at Johnsville on the way back. We were looking at a three-axis controller that they were developing at that time. It seemed to work pretty well, considering that you had 10 or 12 Gs on you and you were able to sit there and control the thing through your wrist motion.

That time at Johnsville was an interesting one. We had a lot of fun, going out to dinner and places. As we talked about earlier, we went to the Old Mill. I guess every Thursday night we'd wind up out there for dinner. De [Beeler] was going to buy us all dinner one night, and I've still got the check that he signed with a fictitious name so it wouldn't go through. I roomed with Neil Armstrong back there and he got in trouble when they lost his laundry one time and we were busy buying shirts and underdrawers and the whole nine yards.

I can't think of much more since I didn't use many of the simulators. The first simulators that I remember, in 1957, were so simple that I couldn't see from the pilot's point of view where it was going.

Waltman: That's the way it was in those days. We spent a lot of time those first couple of years working out the cockpits and problems with the cockpits, and hydraulics and instruments and developing new instruments and such.

Butchart: Looking back, I remember that you were doing more work on the instrumentation—was it real and so [forth]?

Waltman: That was part of growing up during that period. Once we got started, we had one of the best facilities in the country, and now it probably is the best.

Butchart: I think it is amazing what they have now, where they can tie the airplane right into the computers upstairs.

I flew the X-4 and the X-5 and the Skystreak and Skyrocket [two different version of the D-558]. I didn't have any simulation work because there wasn't any in those days. Then I did most of the work on the B-47 when we had it instrumented at Langley and brought it out in '53, I guess it was.

I did a lot of work on the F-100—the roll coupling stuff that I got into kind of by accident. I was doing a series of rolls for—I don't remember who the engineer was—but we had straps attached to both sides of the cockpit with a chain and a piece of metal with holes drilled in it for two degrees, four degrees, eight degrees, etc., for aileron throw. We would put a pin in the stick and you could pop it over—and it would be exactly six degrees or eight degrees or whatever you needed. One of the funny incidents that happened one day: [Iven] Kincheloe was chasing me, and I was at 40,000 [feet] at the speed I should have been for 30,000 feet (it was my mistake as much as the engineer's), and when I popped it over, it uncoupled like crazy. It went in such a direction that you couldn't sit and tell anyone which way it went or what happened. It was just over with. Kincheloe was flying chase and he laughed and he thought that was the funniest thing he had ever seen. He said, "Do that again." And I said, "No thank you." When they uncork, they really go ape. Gene Matranga was running that program. Early on, the F-100 had 30 degrees of plus and minus aileron and about two inches of stick throw. It was very sensitive. Two inches and you got 30 degrees. Later on, they doubled the stick throw to four inches on each side for full aileron. But his study was to see if we really needed the full 30 degrees of aileron. I'm quite certain they changed that later on, 'cause it was a whole lot more aileron than you could live with. I don't remember if there were any simulations about that.

William (Bill) Dana

Note: These comments from Bill Dana's interview have been edited to eliminate some discussion that seemed unrelated to the main theme of the personal account. The original interview—along with all the others that are included as personal accounts in this document—are available in their original form and will be (with any other pertinent information collected) in the Dryden Historical Reference Collection.

X-15 Simulators

Dana: I came here the first of October of 1958. To put that in a time perspective, it was about two weeks before they rolled out the first X-15 for a press conference at El Segundo. And I remember Vice President Nixon was there. I wasn't at the press conference, but Vice President Nixon was there. And it was interesting that at that time I was working on the X-15 simulation that Dick Day had. I don't remember how many degrees of freedom it was. It was probably only three. It was probably pitch axis only. Because Dick was looking for the maximum Mach number and maximum altitude he could get out of the X-15 with the interim engines [two XLR-11s instead of the single XLR-99 designed for the X-15] in it. That was the program he was doing, and I was his cockpit pilot.

And about the only thing I remember about the technology was that Dick had to run a check case every morning to make sure the analog computer was putting out the same output it had put out the day before. And as soon as we got that check case done to Dick's satisfaction, then generally the simulator worked all day reliably. I remember one of the sim engineers, of course, was you and one was John Smith. And the third one I remember was J.L. Samuels.

Then about 1961, as I remember, we moved the X-15 simulator [iron bird] up from El Segundo. You might remember exactly what year that was. And then we became really pretty sharp in our simulation. We had the inertias of the control surfaces simulated and real hydraulics driving the actuators. So we had actual hysteresis in there. And it was a very good simulation. I didn't fly the X-15 simulation that came up from El Segundo much until I got in the program much later, in mid-1965. So from about the time the simulator moved up from El Segundo to when I checked out, I did not fly the X-15 simulator very much. But it was considered a high-fidelity simulator at that time.

And I remember one anecdote about it. The electronics for the X-15 simulator were up in the room presently occupied by the center director's office and the executive conference room. And there were literally about 1,000 fuses in that analog simulator. And every time we'd have a summer electrical storm, why it would blow every one of those 1,000 fuses. And J.L. [Samuels] would walk down the back of that analog computer with one bucket full of good fuses that he was putting in and another bucket he was filling up with burned out fuses that had been shot by the lightning system. And the only technicians whose names I can remember from those [days were] Dick Musick and Bill Sebastian. I guess we had Gerry Perry. And then from '65 till the end of the X-15 program in 1968, I worked on the X-15 simulator on an almost daily basis. Sometimes I'd spend 50 hours simulating for one ten-minute flight if I had the time available due to weather or the aircraft [being] out of commission.

There was something else I wanted to say about the X-15 simulator. Oh, it was interesting that one of the X-15s had a research instrument panel in it. It had vertical instruments, which were the rage in those days, as contrasted to the round dials that were in the number one and number two X-15s. The number three X-15 had this research panel, which was very significant research at that time. And the X-15 was a challenging airplane to do instrumentation research in. [See photo E-11778 of the X-15-3 instrument panel.]

But the interesting thing was that we had to build two separate instrument panels for the X-15 simulator. We had one with the round dials, and we had another one with the vertical tapes in it. And these were heavy. They probably weighed a couple of hundred pounds. They were more than one man could wrestle in and out of the simulator. So we had a little fork-lift—a little cherry picker that we lifted the round dial instrument panel out of the simulator with when we were going to fly ship three. And we dropped the vertical-tape instrument panel in with that same cherry picker and then "flew" our simulation. And then when the next pilot came along, why we put his instrument panel in. And it was a lot of administration, but it worked very efficiently.

And we flew the analog X-15 simulator all the way to the end of the X-15 program in 1968, and then I went into the lifting bodies— first into the HL-10 and then into the M2. And the engineer I worked with most on the lifting bodies was Jack Kolf. He was a flight planner for both the HL-10 and the M2. And the lifting-body simulator, in contrast to the X-15 simulator, was digital. And now of course, we think of digital simulators as being the Cadillacs of simulation. But it wasn't always so. At the time we made the transition from the X-15 to the lifting bodies, the analog simulator was quite mature and well-developed and the digital was a new thing. And we had a lot of trouble—a lot of reliability problems—with the digital simulator. And I think that's a little vignette that ought to be recorded because now we think of digital computers as being quite reliable and quite capable. But it wasn't always so.

Waltman: We did have a digital computer in the X-15-2. It was an interesting period going from analog to hybrid.

Dana: Yes, it was. That's right. I had forgotten the hybrids. But you were definitely right about ship two. A portion of the X-15 number two simulation was digital. And they weren't very reliable because the digitals weren't very reliable for awhile.

Other Simulations

And when the M2 program—the M2-F3 program—ended in the fall of 1973, I went on to the sub-scale F-15 program. I was alternate pilot on that to Einar Enevoldson. And I flew some sub-scale F-15 simulations.

Well, I can't remember any other programs before '75 that I flew besides the rocket airplanes. There probably were others. I guess we had a Vigilante [A-5 (1963)] simulator. Don Hughes would have been the principal investigator on that. And I think we had a Vigilante simulator up. But I don't remember much about it. And I don't remember any of the other participants in it except Don Hughes, who was the principal investigator

I think I've mentioned about all the early players that I remember from simulation. Dick Day, of course, was kind of the father of analog simulation. And I worked with him on the X-15 early in the X-15 program. He's got just about total recall. So you'll get a lot of information out of Dick. I'm having a little trouble dredging up players. You and Ed Videan and John Smith were in simulation when I got here. And I think you and John were mainly working analog.

John [Perry] was probably here in '59, if I remember correctly—'59 or '60. He was an early comer.

I remember one other little vignette about the M2 simulation. We didn't use this technique during the flight program, but we investigated it on the simulator after the flight program was over. And that was that rocket pilots always complained that the mission went faster—seemed to go by faster than the simulation did. So Jack Kolf had the idea, why not run the simulator at faster than real time and see if that reminds the pilot of the actual flight. And we did that on the M2-F3 simulator—ran the simulator at faster than real time and experimented with 1. 2 and 1. 5 times the real time and finally empirically came up with the idea that about 1.4 times real time was a good representation of how the mission appeared to the pilot in real time. And so Jack did some real ground-breaking work on the simulator. And that would have been about 1974.

Waltman: Yes. I got some stuff from Bob Kempel just the other day, and he said the same thing. This faster than real time seemed to . . .

Dana: More accurately simulate the boost portion of the flight.

Thomas C. McMurtry

Supercritical Wing Program

I came here in late 1967. The first program I really got involved in, that had any simulation associated with it, was the F-8 Supercritical Wing (SCW) program. Wilt Lock was the controls engineer on that airplane. We spent a lot of time in the simulator looking at gain schedules, looking at the modification to the control system. The simulation activity was never one that I got enchanted with [and I never] spent a lot of time looking at the approaches to simulation. Instrumental from my view was putting together a usable simulator that served two purposes. One was, we had not flown a significantly modified airplane. It wasn't a brand new airplane, but one with the new wing on it, a change in the configuration. The basic airplane had an arrangement where the fuselage moved down and changed the incidence angle for landing. And of course we didn't have that. But there were a lot of major changes to the control system that had to be done to make the airplane have the flying qualities we wanted it to have, and also to see what kind of performance we thought the airplane would have. It served the purpose of preparing for the characteristics of the airplane from a stability-and-control level and [for] me as a pilot. Wilt worked the auto-gain scheduling and everything. I obviously factored in my thoughts about the qualitative judgments of how the airplane behaved.

The second thing that the simulator provided was mission planning. The benefits I got out of the simulation—the engineering simulation approach, where we had just basic cockpits, basic controls—were adequate. I felt for my entire career here at NASA that that was all we needed. We didn't need a mockup of the cockpit with all the frills and fancy furnishings that airplanes have. The engineering simulation approach has been completely adequate, in my view, to provide the benefits that a simulation can provide to a piloted program.

Again, the first program I was involved with that really used simulation to a great extent was the F-8 Supercritical Wing Program. I also got in on the F-8 Digital Fly-By-Wire Program—participated in the simulation there—but that was driven primarily by Gary Krier as the project pilot. I'm trying to remember who led that simulation—Wilt Lock was involved in that pretty extensively, also.

Then the other program was the Lifting Body Program. I only flew two flights in the X-24B. I used to go out and fly the F-104 and practice simulated approaches with that airplane. My experience with the simulator was pretty limited. The Air Force had the simulator. I spent a lot of time practicing with Jack Kolf. By that time, the simulation had really matured. They kept enhancing the simulation based upon the results of flights. The simulation was a great preparation for me to go out and fly a couple of drop flights on the X-24B.

All of the simulations, from my view, were beneficial in that they provided the mission planning and gain settings. They gave us a good look at variances in the behavior of the airplanes, especially in stability and control. The analog systems did that well enough, I thought. We could look at some variations as to the good characteristics and changes that made us start to be sensitive or overly sensitive. I thought we were able to do that effectively with the simulations that I was exposed to. Interestingly, I made a note. The first flight of the F-8 Supercritical Wing airplane, for example, that I got to make. When I came back, I have to tell you honestly that it was so much fun and so exciting and such a thrill to fly that airplane the first time, that I probably would have said that the simulator was exactly like the airplane or the airplane was exactly like the simulator, I should say. I think that oftentimes it takes a flight or two before a pilot is able to feed back to the simulation. Well, obviously, there is quantitative data that you can use to change the simulation. But the qualitative data sometimes isn't completely effective until the pilot has had a chance to fly the airplane a couple of times. 'Cause that first time you are so excited, so enthusiastic that you could make it all work. Unless there was something that was really major, it is pretty hard to sort out the minor difference between the simulation and flight.

I mentioned that the engineering simulation approach has been an adequate approach here at Dryden. Another thing that I would add to the engineering simulation approach is that, the way we do business here, a pilot preparing to fly something that is new and unique could go out to the airplane; a lot of procedures can be developed between the time that is spent in the cockpit before the flight takes place and [time in] the simulator. So you don't need a full-up simulation to develop all the procedures that are needed to accomplish a research test-flight.

Moving-Base Simulators

Moving-base simulators add some to a simulation. I do believe that. It's another characteristic that is added to your total perspective. To say, though, that moving-base simulators add a dimension, big step, and a great dimension to simulators, quite honestly I don't feel [that they do]. They do add something.

Visual Presentations

The biggest need in simulation is an accurate visual presentation. That's the feature of simulations, in my view, that is most lacking even today. I've not stayed with simulations and looked at the most modern simulations. I did go up to United Airlines and flew its 747 simulator. They have some fairly recent technology there. It's good simulation, it's good visual presentation, but it's still not real-world; it's got a long way to go to get to that point.

So, moving-base simulators do add to a better representation of a vehicle's characteristics—both [with respect to] performance and [to] stability and control. And then the visual presentation adds another dimension. But I still say that the engineering approach taken here with a minimum of visual display and no moving base has been adequate.

Aircraft Speed Is a Factor

Another thing that strikes me: the speed of the vehicle is definitely a factor here, too. Now, the simulations that I have been associated with, with minor exceptions, are subsonic activities. I've flown the SR[-71] simulator a little bit—for several hours before I flew the airplane for one time. I've flown the F-15 at supersonic speeds, and some other vehicles. Obviously a vehicle like the X-15 had different cues to the pilot that I, think, would have [made] a visual representation more beneficial to them. On the simulations for the F-8 Supercritical Wing and others, the engineering approach was adequate without a really good visual presentation. The faster you go, I think, the greater the need is to have a really useful visual display, at least when you get down in the atmosphere and you are starting to make approaches and landings.

Finale

This is our story. It was interesting and challenging. It started in 1955 and went to the mid-'70s. Analog/hybrid simulation had run its course and, after about 20 years, was no longer the preferred method. Analog computers were not able to keep up with the advances being made in the airplanes we were simulating. Digital computers had grown up and were the better type of computer to use. We had to move on, and the present simulation laboratory is doing that.

This was the end of a very exciting period in the history of the NASA Flight Research Center. Those of us who were there (and I'm sure I speak for most of us) are all very happy and proud of having been a part of that history. In a sense, we were the "barnstormers" of flight simulations at the FRC. Looking back on this period, I will never regret the decision I made that very first day when I was given the opportunity to work in the simulation laboratory. Simulation is an important component of almost every flight project that Dryden is involved in. The analog/hybrid simulation systems of the NACA HSFS and NASA FRC were an important foundation in the development of today's capabilities. Dryden is a unique institution. So, too, is the Dryden Simulation Laboratory.

The X-15, the Lifting Body, LLRV, GPAS, the F-8 DFBW, and other flight programs owe a lot to the simulators that we built. It is difficult to imagine any of these programs having been as successful as they were if simulators had not been included.

For those of you who are a part of the present-day simulation facility, you have a strong and proud heritage—keep up the good work. I say that both as a commendation and as a challenge!

Appendices

Edwards, California
March 11, 1955

MEMORANDUM for Engineering Division Chief

Subject: The determination of the directional stability parameter, C_{n_β}, from flight data.

1. During a recent analogue computer investigation of the F-100 airplane, certain discrepancies in the results were noted. Although several particular flight motions were duplicated by assuming 5-degrees-of-freedom and using the best flight and wind tunnel determined stability derivatives available at that time, when the system was subjected to a simulated rudder pulse the period, as measured in β, was considerably different from the flight measured period of the actual airplane.

2. Since there was some doubt at that time about the level of directional stability of the airplane it was decided to vary the directional stability parameter, C_{n_β}, over a sufficient range and observe the period of lateral motion resulting from an abrupt simulated rudder pulse at an angle of attack of 5 degrees (level flight attitude for $M = 0.72$; $h_p = 32,000$ feet). The measured periods were then substituted into the single-degree-of-freedom equation which was used to determine the value of C_{n_β} from flight and the results indicated large differences between the values used and the values determined by the single-degree-of-freedom method (dashed and solid lines, fig. 1).

3. At this point it was deemed necessary to re-evaluate the method of determining the directional stability parameter, C_{n_β}, from flight data. The 5-degree-of-freedom, body axis system equations which were used in setting up the investigation were considered. A logical and systematic approach was taken in an effort to arrive at an equation for determining C_{n_β} which would combine simplicity and accuracy. It seemed necessary to include the term αp in the $\dot{\beta}$ equation. The derivation is presented in Appendix A. The simple formula below was derived to partially include this effect in the determination of C_{n_β}.

$$C_{n_\beta} = \left(\frac{2\pi}{P}\right)^2 \frac{I_z}{qSb} + \alpha_{o_{TRIM}} \frac{I_z}{I_x} C_{l_\beta} - \frac{I_{xz}}{I_x} C_{l_\beta}$$

For this case the $\frac{I_{XZ}}{I_X}$ term was neglected since the airplane under investigation had a very low inclination of the principal axis. For airplanes with relatively large principal axis inclinations, it would be necessary to include the $\frac{I_{XZ}}{I_X}$ term.

Appendix 1. Memorandum for Engineering Division Chief, Richard D. Banner and Albert E. Kuhl, "The determination of the directional stability parameter C_{n_β} from flight data," 11 March 1955.

The above equation indicated the effects of the initial angle of attack, the inertia parameter $\frac{I_Z}{I_X}$, and the effective dihedral parameter C_{l_β}, none of which were considered in the single-degree-of-freedom equation for C_{n_β} which was previously thought valid for airplanes with small principal axis inclination.

4. An analogue computer was used to establish experimental verification of the analysis and to ascertain the magnitude of the effects of variations in the effective dihedral and the initial angle of attack. An angle-of-attack range of from 2° to 7° was investigated since most flight data would fall in this range, and a range of C_{l_β} of from 0.015 to 0.24 per radian. The results of these studies are shown in figures 1 and 2 and are self explanatory.

5. As a further check on the validity of our assumptions in reducing the 5-degree-of-freedom system to the simple formula for C_{n_β} as given herein for this analysis, studies were made on the analogue computer over the angle-of-attack range from 2° to 7° with first the complete 5-degree-of-freedom system and then with the modified 3-degree-of-freedom system (holding angle of attack constant throughout the maneuver). The results verified the assumptions, indicating essentially no differences in the period of the lateral oscillation of the 5-degree-of-freedom system and the 3-degree-of-freedom system (holding α constant).

6. The periods of the lateral oscillations obtained when C_{l_β} and the initial angle of attack were varied independently, holding C_{n_β} constant, (fig. 2) were then substituted in the revised equation for determining C_{n_β}. The results are presented in figure 4 and show good agreement. For comparison the values of C_{n_β} as determined by the single-degree-of-freedom method are also shown.

7. Since current interest is largely centered around the lateral stability problems of present high speed airplanes of high wing loading and low incidence perhaps a re-evaluation of their level of directional stability would be in order, particularly for the airplane under consideration. Since it appears that the effective dihedral should also be considered, even with airplanes having small principal axis inclination, it would appear that wind-tunnel studies would be necessary. In any case analogue computer studies seem imperative.

-3-

8. It is felt that analogue studies similar to the above should be made to verify the suggested method as a generalized case, and could be published in report form as a better method for determining C_{n_β} about the body axis from flight.

Richard D. Banner
Richard D. Banner
Aeronautical Research Scientist

Albert E. Kuhl
Albert E. Kuhl
Aeronautical Research Scientist

Appendix A

Writing the 3 lateral equations of motion as:

$$\dot{\beta} = -r + \alpha_0 p + Y_\beta \beta \qquad \text{I}$$

$$\dot{r} = \frac{I_{xz}}{I_z}\dot{p} + (n_\beta)\beta \qquad \text{II}$$

$$\dot{p} = \ell_\beta \beta \qquad \text{III}$$

Taking the time derivative of equation I assuming α is constant.

$$\ddot{\beta} = -\dot{r} + \alpha_0 \dot{p} + Y_\beta \dot{\beta} \qquad (1)$$

Substituting equations II & III into (1)

$$\ddot{\beta} = -\left(\frac{I_{xz}}{I_z}\ell_\beta\right)\beta - n_\beta \beta + \alpha_0 \ell_\beta \beta + Y_\beta \dot{\beta}$$

collecting terms

$$\ddot{\beta} - Y_\beta \dot{\beta} + \left(n_\beta - \alpha_0 \ell_\beta + \frac{I_{xz}}{I_z}\ell_\beta\right)\beta = 0$$

Since the imaginary part of the roots to the auxiliary quadratic equation determines the period of the oscillation,

$$\frac{i\sqrt{(Y_\beta)^2 - 4\left(n_\beta - \alpha_0 \ell_\beta + \frac{I_{xz}}{I_z}\ell_\beta\right)}}{2} = \frac{2\pi}{P}$$

squaring and simplifying:

$$n_\beta = \left(\frac{2\pi}{P}\right)^2 + \alpha_0 \ell_\beta - \frac{I_{xz}}{I_z}\ell_\beta + \frac{(Y_\beta)^2}{4}$$

but

$$C_{n_\beta} = \frac{I_z}{qSb}n_\beta = \frac{I_z}{qSb}\left(\frac{2\pi}{P}\right)^2 + \alpha_0 \frac{I_z}{I_x}C_{\ell_\beta} - \frac{I_{xz}}{I_x}C_{\ell_\beta} + \frac{I_z}{qSb}\frac{(Y_\beta)^2}{4}$$

[For comparison between this method and the single degree of freedom method the last term was dropped

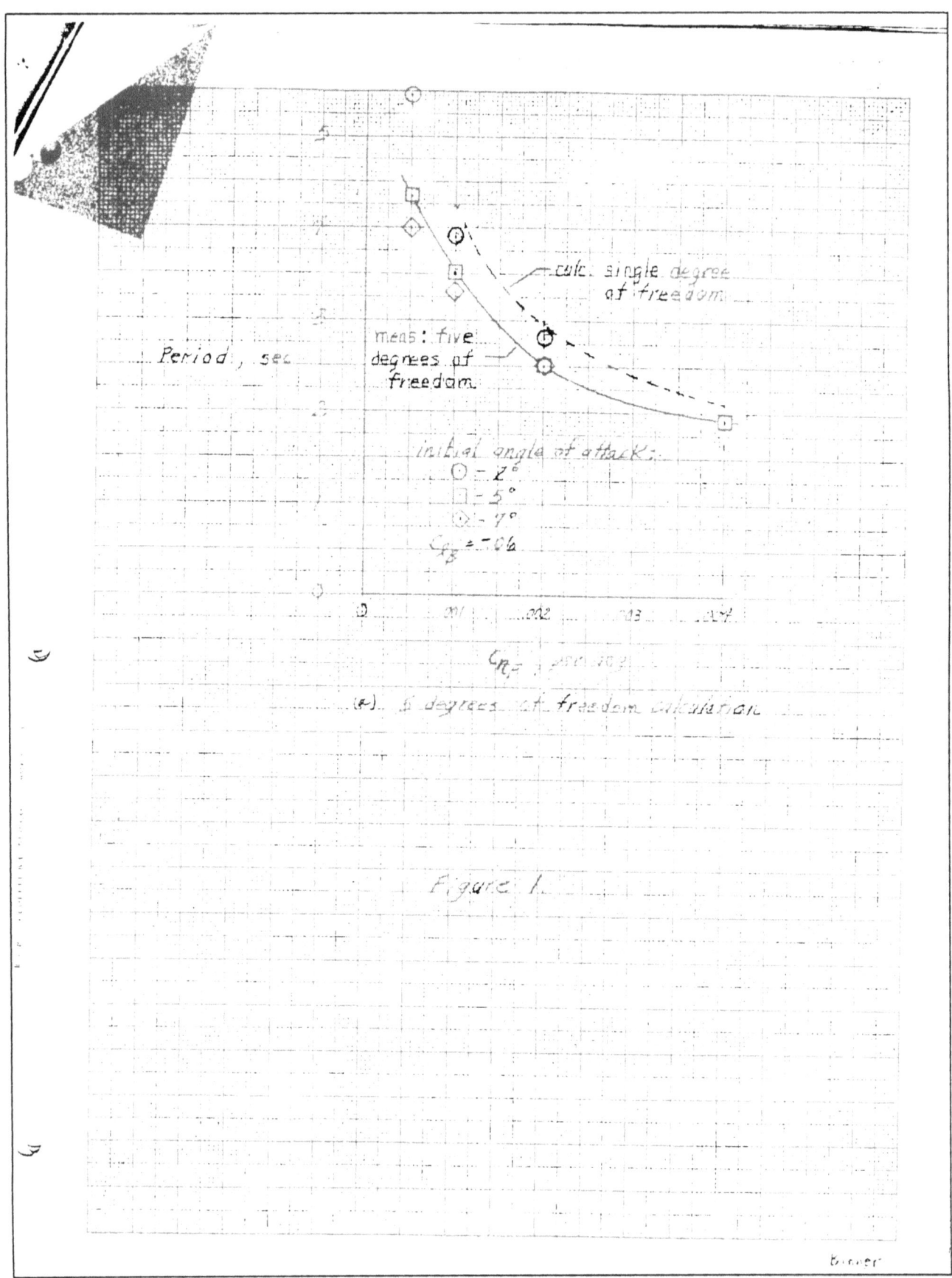

(e) 5 degrees of freedom calculation

Figure 1

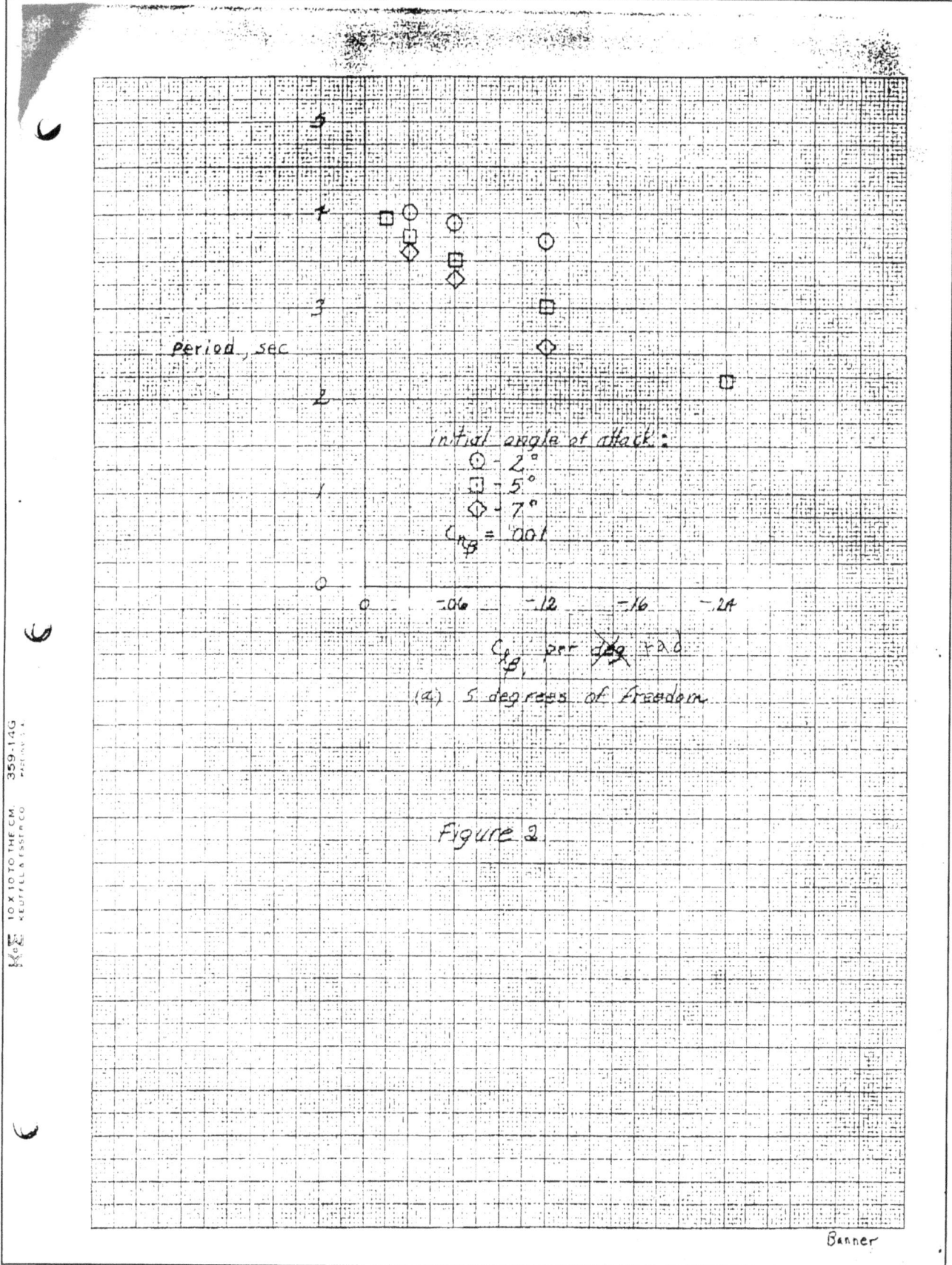

(a) 5 degrees of freedom.

Figure 2

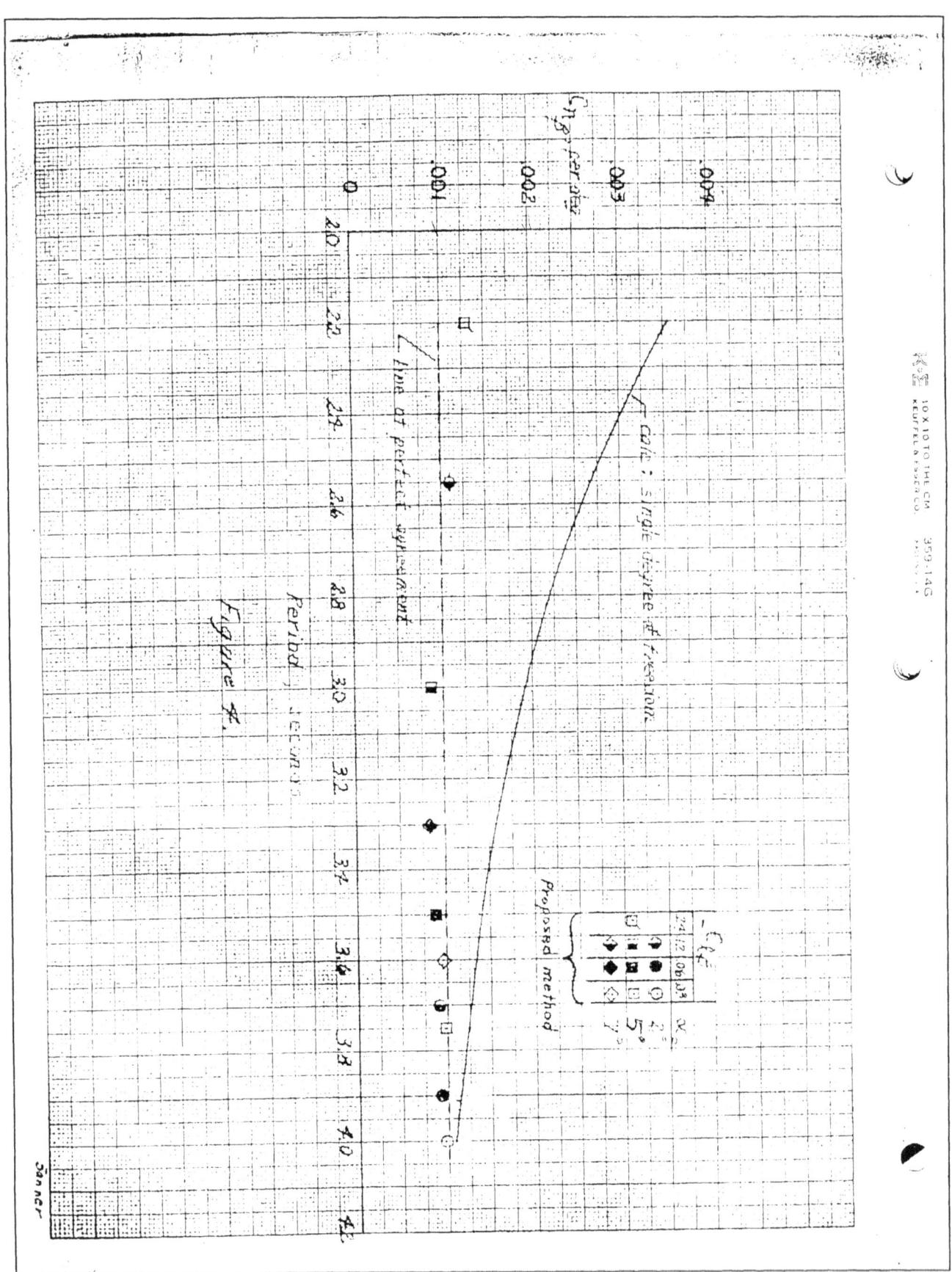

Figure 4.

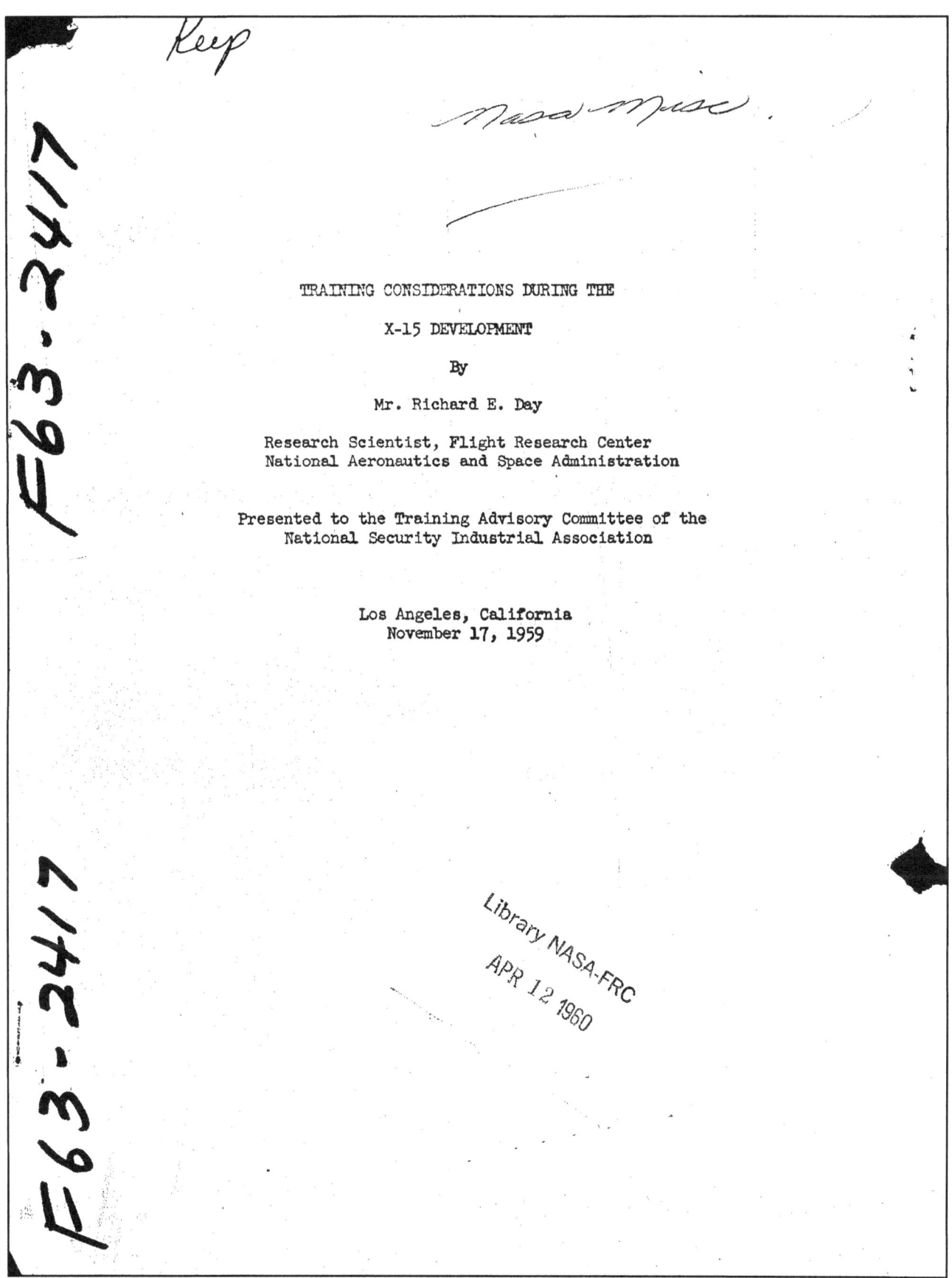

Appendix 2. Richard E. Day, "Training Considerations during the X-15 Development," paper presented to the Training Advisory Committee of the National Security Industrial Association, Los Angeles, California, 17 November 1959.

TRAINING CONSIDERATIONS DURING THE X-15 DEVELOPMENT

Presented to a Meeting of the NSIA, Los Angeles, Calif., November 17, 1959

by Richard E. Day

The NASA Flight Research Center, during its 13-year history, has had the responsibility of extending the envelope of manned flight to ever-increasing speed and altitude. In early programs it was necessary to live with a minimum of training aids in planning and conducting flight projects. As time has progressed, more and more training aids have become available for use, and it can be safely said that without some of these aids the X-15 program would be so hazardous as to be impractical. Another reason why training aids are presently of the utmost importance is the financial aspect. If the current ratio of airplane cost to the number of expected flights is considered, the cost per flight is found to be extremely high. In addition, flights may be relatively infrequent. Consequently, from the time-cost considerations, it is essential that the pilot be trained to peak proficiency in order to obtain the maximum amount of research information in the minimum amount of time.

This paper reviews briefly some of the early uses of pilot training aids in research investigations. A pertinent flight trajectory of the X-15 research airplane will then be summarized and the various training aids that have been, and are being, used in preparing the pilot for flying this trajectory will be indicated.

This paper is concerned primarily with X-15 pilot training. Implications of training X-15 support personnel will be one of the subjects of the following paper.

In developing training aids and methods for the X-15 program, the NASA has been fortunate in being able to draw upon a considerable background of experience from previous research airplane programs.

H-157

Prior to the general acceptance of the analog computer, essentially no ground-training devices were employed by the NASA in guiding flight testing of research airplanes. Rather, gradual in-flight buildup to design conditions was depended upon. However, certain types of control problems are not amenable to this approach since they are characterized by abrupt and violent instabilities. As early as 1953-54 the X-1 and X-3 research airplanes and some of the century series fighters were experiencing violent motions about all three axes during rolling maneuvers. These motions resulted from what is known as inertial roll coupling and are analogous to the instability of a slow-spinning top or gyroscope. At about this same time the electronic analog computer was coming into its own as a device for solving highly complex, nonlinear, differential equations with an adequate degree of engineering accuracy. Since the mechanics of inertial coupling was quite complex, the use of an analog was obtained to determine the causes and possible solutions to these problems.

Figure 1 shows the arrangement used in this study. The pilot observes pertinent display information that has been calculated by the computer. His control reactions to this display are then sent back to the computer for interpretation into modified display information. Thus a closed-loop solution is available for real-time operation. It should be mentioned that this procedure has definite advantages over the open-loop approach; by including the human operator in the loop, the effects of inadvertent and corrective control inputs can be evaluated. In addition, actual hardware such as stability-augmentation systems may be included in the loop. From this study a logical training procedure evolved for flight-test guidance in critical stability areas. Figure 2 lists the logical steps that were developed during the roll-coupling program:

First, preflight simulator studies were made to determine the flight conditions and roll rates that would produce divergent motions.

Second, noncritical in-flight maneuvers were made to determine the stability and control derivatives, inasmuch as a simulator is only as good as the accuracy of the parameters used.

Third, step one is repeated, using the most reliable data.

Fourth, the validity of these final simulations is then checked by making noncritical flight rolls.

The last step involves a gradual buildup to the most critical conditions.

This close coordination of simulator training and flight testing has been used in probing many critical flight-research areas. The method has general applicability and is being used in X-15 flight-test guidance.

It appears pertinent at this point to review briefly the qualifications and experience levels of the X-15 pilots. The eight pilots presently on the X-15 roster represent North American Aviation, NASA, the Air Force, and the Navy. The average pilot is 36 years old, has been flying for 15 years, and has spent half that time in experimental test flying. Each has a Bachelor's degree, and several have advance degrees. They are all voluntarily in the profession, so that creating motivation is no problem. These pilots have lived with this program since its inception and have made valuable contributions to the design, based upon their experience in previous research-airplane programs.

Before discussing X-15 training developments, perhaps it would be best to show some of the tasks required of the pilot. Figure 3 illustrates a typical design altitude mission, with various phases of the flight indicated.

The airplane is launched from the B-52 carrier airplane near Wendover, Utah. During the boost phase the pilot is exposed to as high as 4g chest-to-back acceleration and, consequently, must resort to a side-located controller. After burnout the pilot will experience several minutes of weightlessness. In this ballistic-flight regime the air is so thin that conventional controls are ineffective and reaction jets must be resorted to. The next phase of flight, the reentry, is perhaps the most critical from the standpoint of stability, control, heating, structural loads, and the pilot's acceleration environment. After recovery, the airplane is vectored to the dry lake at Edwards for a landing. To date, the X-15 has been flown to only moderate altitudes with the interim engine.

The remainder of this paper will be devoted to a discussion of the training development in the areas of boost, ballistic flight, entry, and landing.

To simulate the various phases of the X-15 mission, an extremely elaborate analog and simulator arrangement was mechanized by North American Aviation to study in detail the overall flight control problem from launch to landing. Figure 4 shows part of the vast analog-computer complex used in the X-15 program. Coupled to the analog is an exact duplicate of the complete control-system hardware, including the pilot's display and cockpit mockup. A photograph of this general equipment is presented in Figure 5, and Figure 6 is a drawing showing the arrangement of the cockpit. Note, in particular, that there are three control sticks. A conventional center stick is provided for normal flying, and, mechanically linked with it on the right is a console stick for control under high acceleration. The control stick on the left is provided for the reaction-control system.

The initial simulator studies examined the control problem in the most critical areas of the flight envelope, such as the trajectory described previously. During the pilot-training program, optimum control techniques and boundaries for reentry were established through a systematic study of pertinent variables including the effects of stability-augmentation malfunctions.

Although the relative difficulty of various types of entries could be fairly well established, based on the static-simulator program, it was known that the pilot would be subjected to extreme accelerations for considerable periods of time. Therefore, it was felt that simulation, including acceleration, should be accomplished to determine the validity of the static-simulator results. Accordingly, a cooperative program was conducted by NASA, NAA, and the Navy, utilizing the human centrifuge at Johnsville, Pa. For the first time the centrifuge was tied into an analog computer so that closed-loop real-time simulations, including accelerations, would be possible. A simplified sketch of the centrifuge is shown in Figure 7. To orient the acceleration vector properly, gondola rotations are superimposed on the normal rotation of the centrifuge arm.

It should be mentioned that during the early centrifuge tests, the original display arrangement presented a scanning problem under acceleration. Modifications were suggested by the pilots, and the improvements were verified in the centrifuge tests.

The results of the centrifuge program generally substantiated the static-simulator results from the standpoint of pilot capability and indicated that the pilot could withstand prolonged periods of high acceleration and still perform the task required of him. The pilots indicated, upon interrogation, that the most important benefit derived from this training program was that of establishing confidence. Now they knew that in the g field of the X-15 they would be able to handle the airplane. One more unknown had been removed for the pilot.

One of the primary objectives of the flight program will be to establish motion-simulation requirements for the X-15, which should be of great value in determining the required sophistication of training devices for future vehicles.

One of the unique features of the X-15 control system is the side-located aerodynamic controller. Inasmuch as little previous experience had been attained with a console controller of the X-15 type, an installation similar to the X-15 (Figure 8) was made in an F-107A airplane. The F-107 program enabled pilots to evaluate the in-flight characteristics of such a controller. Initial flight tests resulted in pilots favoring the center stick because of overcontrol due to sensitivity of the side stick. However, after a nominal training period, the pilots learned to discipline themselves to smaller control inputs and eventually favored the side stick in certain flight regimes.

The portion of the X-15 flight requiring reaction controls is made under conditions of zero g and cannot be simulated for any appreciable length of time with ground-based simulators. Consequently, the final phase of simulation training must be made in flight. Reaction-control studies at the Flight Research Center began in 1955 with crude equipment used in conjunction with an analog computer. However, this investigation established several requirements that have been substantiated by many subsequent studies.

The next development in this field was construction of what is known as the "Iron Cross". This simulator, shown in Figure 9, consists of two I-beams mounted on a universal joint at the center of gravity. To power the rockets, hydrogen-peroxide fuel is metered through a valve and is activated by a silver-screen catalyst. It should be mentioned that the Iron Cross was devised primarily to check operational characteristics of the rockets and control-system hardware and was found to be inferior to the analog as a training device.

The next logical step in the development of reaction controls was to install them in an airplane capable of achieving altitudes that would permit a significant amount of time at low dynamic pressure. The Flight Research Center has equipped an X-1 rocket research airplane and an F-104A with reaction controls for this purpose.

The last area to be discussed, that of the landing, also requires training, since the X-15 landing characteristics are not conventional. The basic geometry of the airplane is such that considerably steeper landing approaches are encountered with the X-15 than with any previous research airplane. Figure 10 illustrates a typical X-15 landing approach. For comparison, the conventional approach path of an operational aircraft is also presented. The differences in glide paths and ground tracks are readily apparent. To train the pilots for the X-15 landing phase, several methods were considered. First, an analog computer was used with an oscilloscope presentation to indicate approach attitude. This gave the pilots and engineers an understanding of the relative importance of the factors affecting the landing flare, but definitely lacked the in-flight realism afforded by the rapid approach of the ground. A more sophisticated visual display technique is now being developed at NASA for landing research on advanced vehicles. The most useful training for the X-15 program was obtained by employing a standard F-104A airplane. By suitable scheduling of thrust - and drag-producing devices, the approach path of an X-15 could be very closely simulated. In practice, the pilots were encouraged to build up to the steep paths in rational steps. Should long intervals occur frequently between X-15 flights, the pilots will practice these approaches immediately prior to a scheduled flight.

In conclusion, the potential role played by various training aids in the development of the X-15 program has been shown. Future flight data will afford the unique opportunity to assess the true value of these training aids for the X-15 and to establish training requirements for future vehicles.

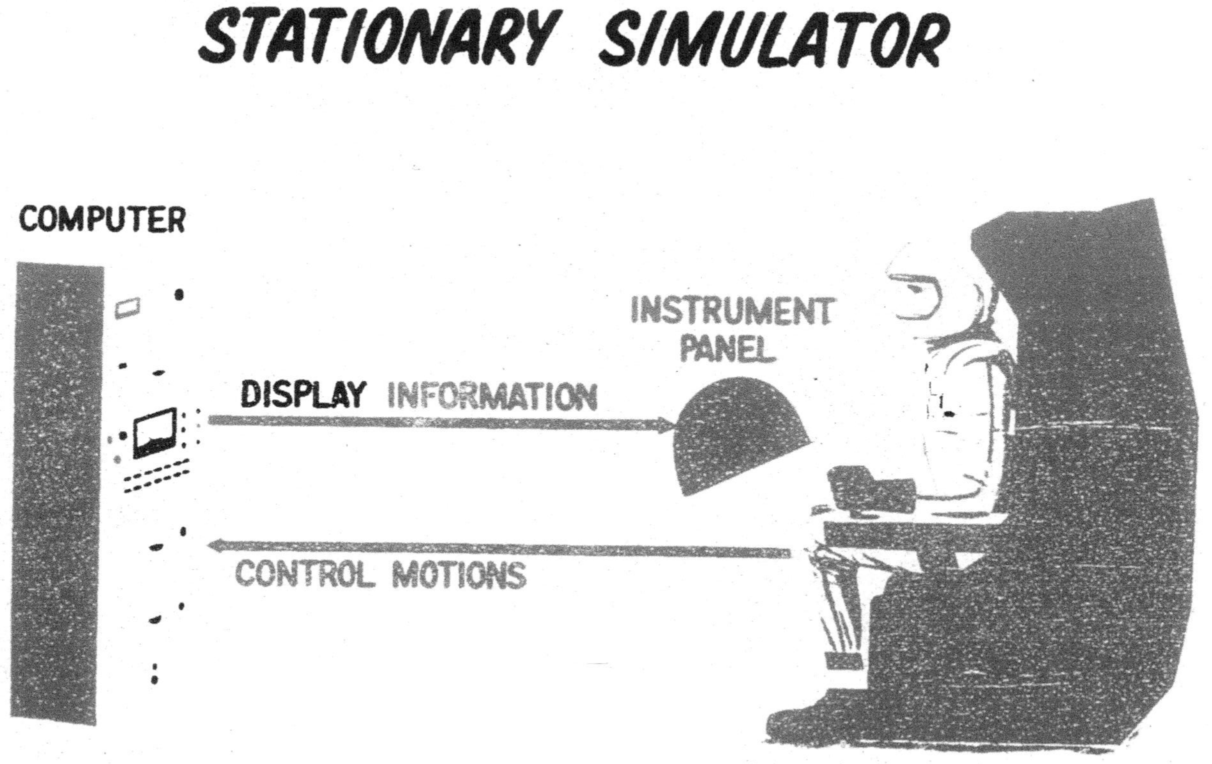
STATIONARY SIMULATOR
COMPUTER
DISPLAY INFORMATION
INSTRUMENT PANEL
CONTROL MOTIONS

Figure 1

LOGICAL STEPS IN ROLL-COUPLING FLIGHT PROGRAM

1. PRE-FLIGHT SIMULATION STUDIES TO DETERMINE CRITICAL AREAS
2. FLIGHT DETERMINATION OF STABILITY AND CONTROL DERIVATIVES
3. FINAL ROLL SIMULATION STUDIES FOR FLIGHT CORRELATION
4. FLIGHT CHECK OF NON-CRITICAL ROLLS
5. GRADUAL BUILD-UP TO CRITICAL CONDITIONS

Figure 2

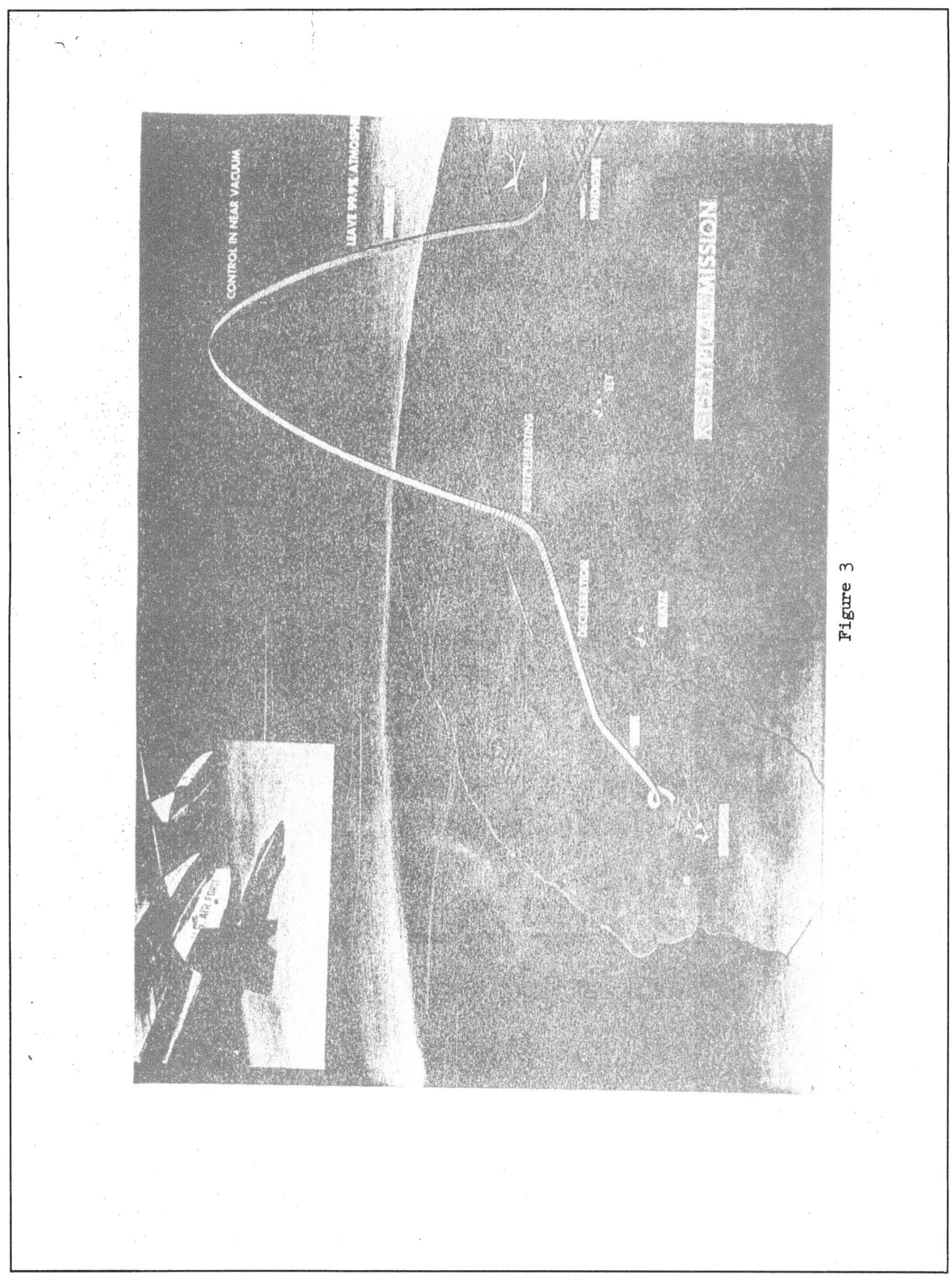

Figure 3

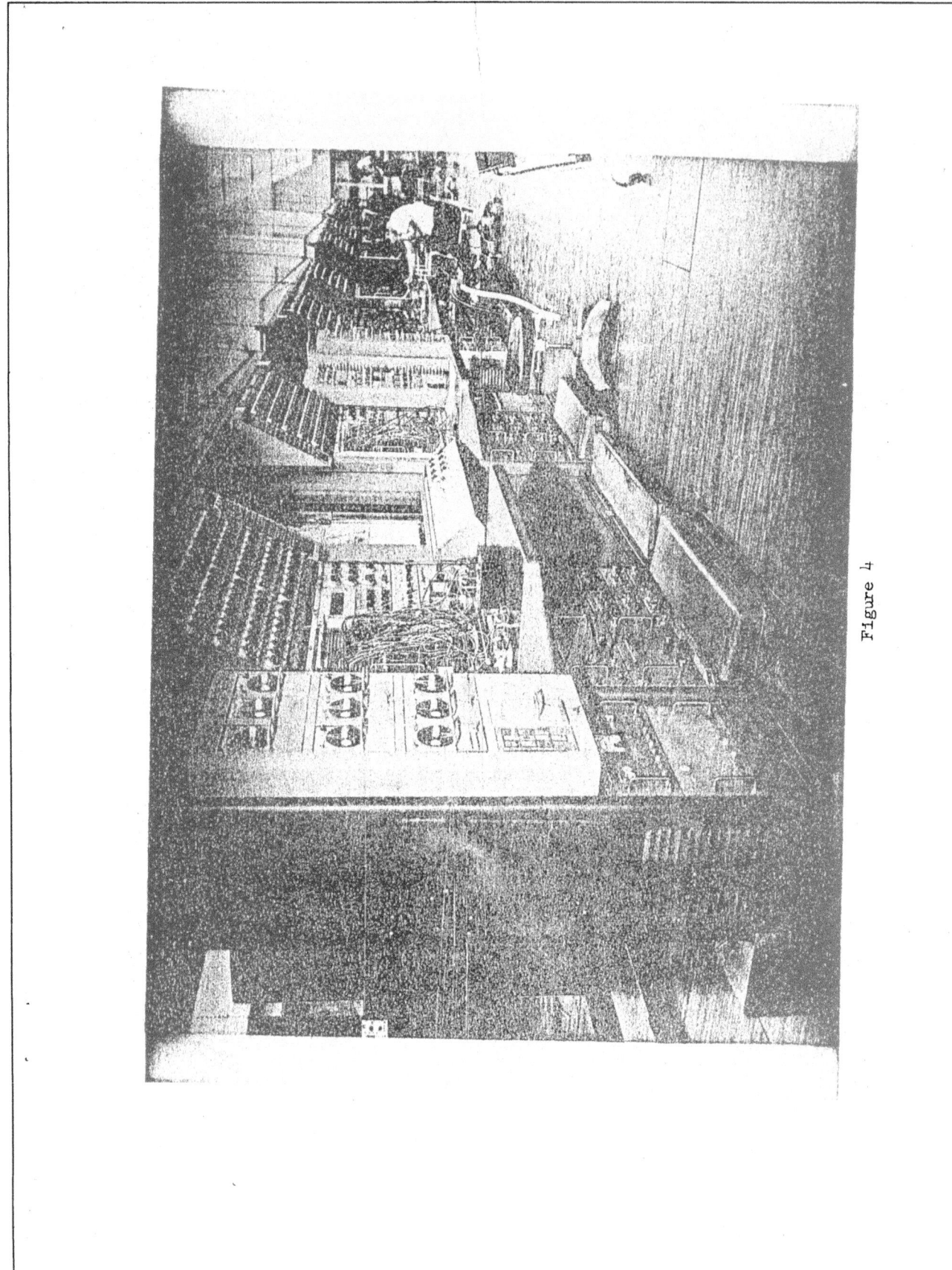

Figure 4

Figure 5

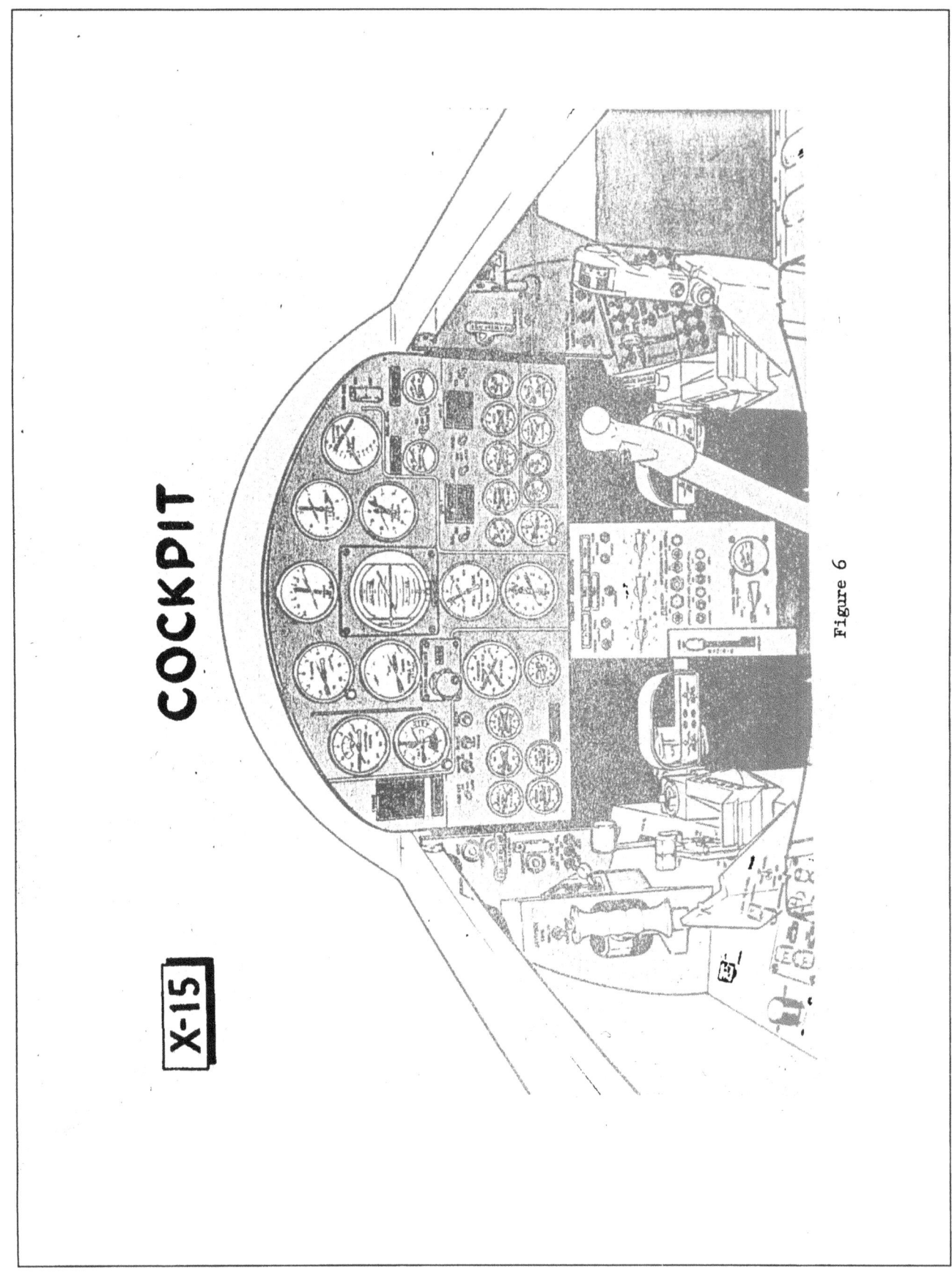

Figure 6

SIMULATION BY CENTRIFUGE

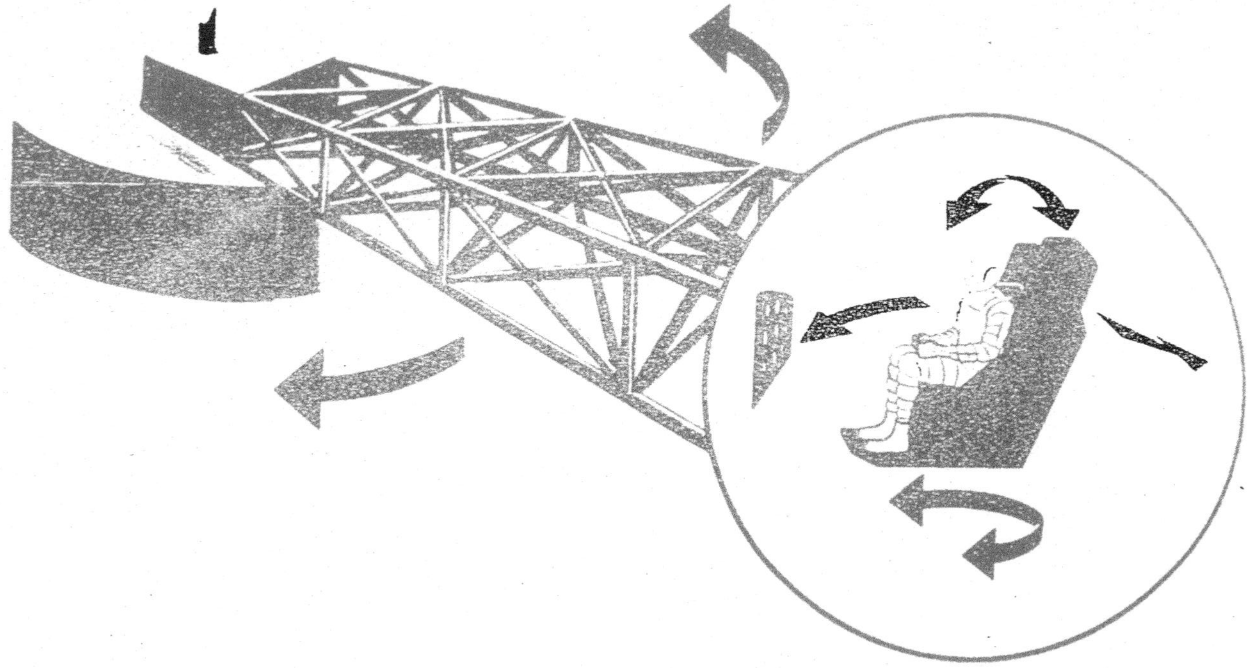

Figure 7

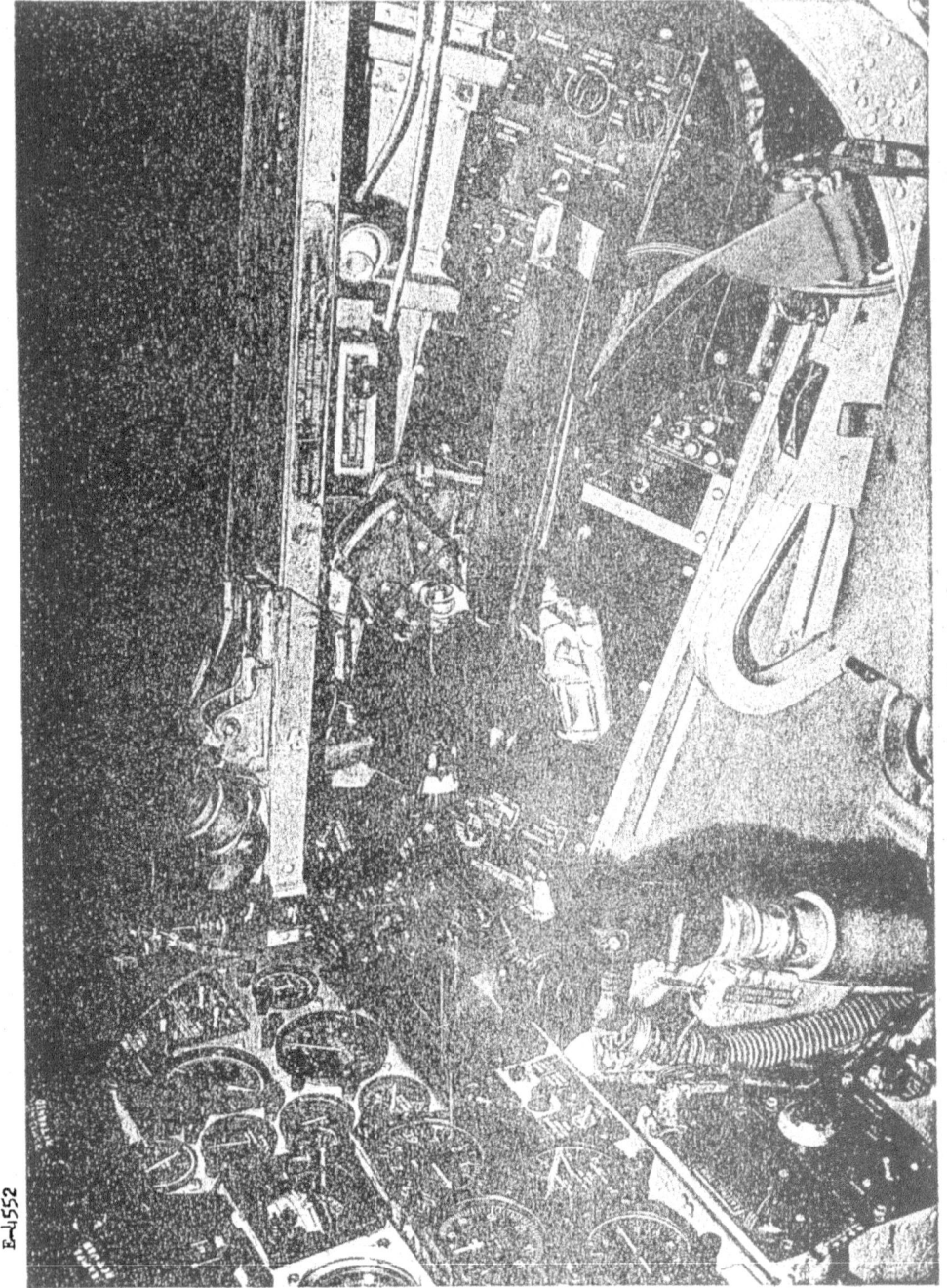

Figure 8

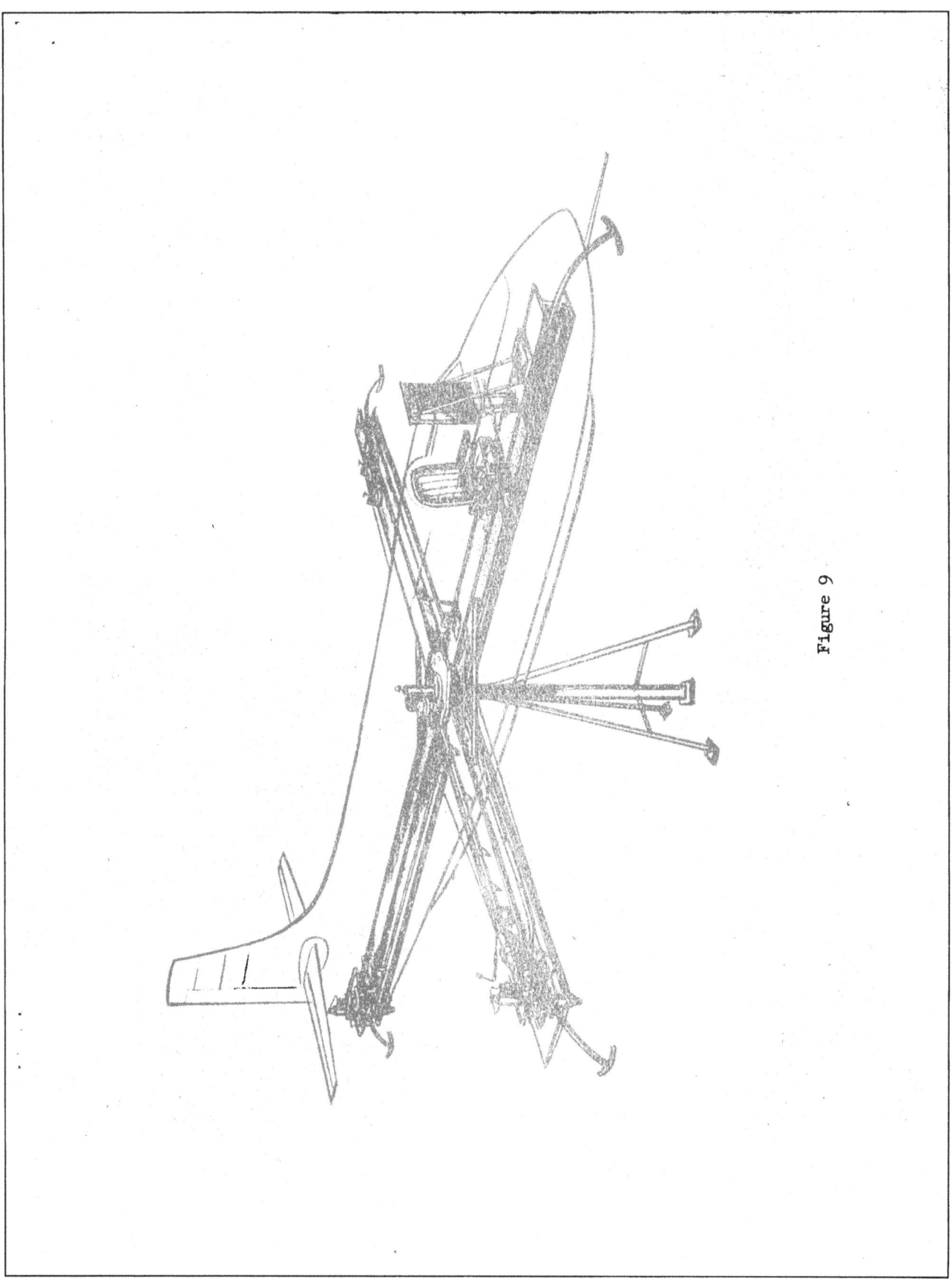

Figure 9

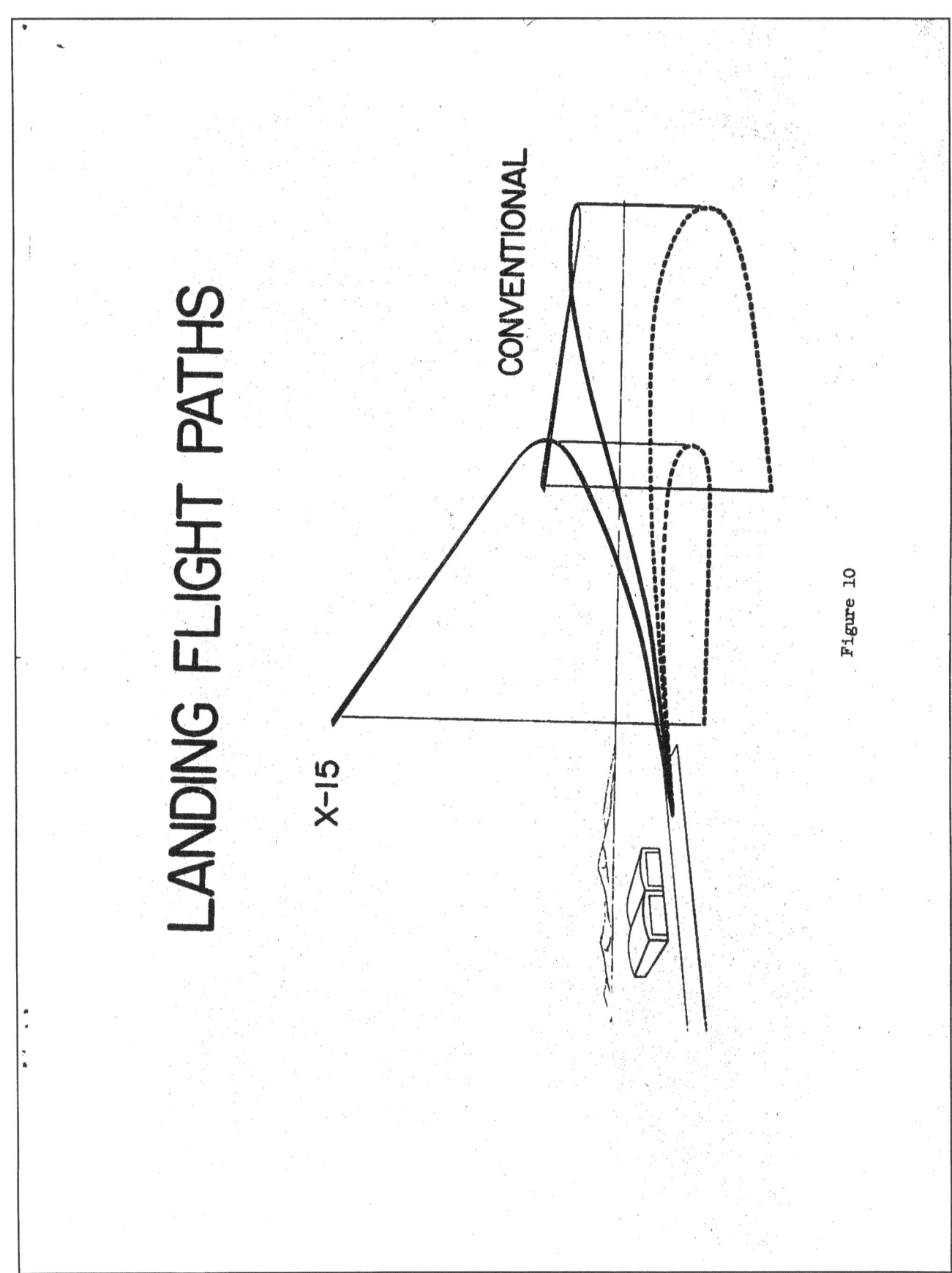

Figure 10

GENERAL REVIEW OF PILOTING PROBLEMS ENCOUNTERED

DURING SIMULATION AND FLIGHTS OF THE X-15

Milton O. Thompson
NASA Flight Research Center
Edwards, Calif.

The advantages of simulation have been expounded on for years by engineers and pilots. We cannot presently ignore or fail to take advantage of the prediction capability of simulation in the development of a new aircraft or flight vehicle. The question is: How complete must the simulation be to anticipate the many possible problems that could be encountered?

This paper describes a few of the problems encountered on X-15 flights that were not anticipated during simulation. Some of these problems were consequences of simulation deficiencies. Others were a result of simulation limitations imposed by the omission of complex and costly flight-environment conditions.

The X-15 flight experience covers a wide range of environmental conditions from high-longitudinal-acceleration boost profiles to low-lift-drag-ratio landings. This offers us a unique opportunity to comment on a number of pertinent points regarding simulation and simulation requirements.

DESCRIPTION OF SIMULATORS

Figure 1 shows the hardware mockup of the X-15 cockpit and control system with simulated control surfaces. Actual electronic control components were used as simulator hardware. Some of the analog computing equipment and the plotter and recorders used in the simulation are also shown.

For the mechanization of the complete six-degree-of-freedom equations of motion, which represented the X-15 aerodynamics, analog computers were used. Nonlinear aerodynamic variables were programed as a function of Mach number and angle of attack.

The simulator was constantly updated with flight data and hardware to insure accurate performance and controllability matching for subsequent flight simulations. The wind-tunnel derivatives, in general, proved to be fairly accurate and little updating was required to improve the simulation of the actual vehicle. Such factors as motion, acceleration, and visual displays were omitted because of the added complexity, cost, and nonavailability of the necessary equipment. Other types of simulations, such as the F-104 and the centrifuge, were resorted to in an attempt to anticipate problems resulting from these omissions. But, we still had problems. This, of course, is one of the reasons for actual flight testing--to determine whether there are problems you have not anticipated.

Appendix 3. Milton O. Thompson, "General Review of Piloting Problems Encountered during Simulation and Flights of the X-15" [1964].

EFFECTS OF IMPROPER SIMULATION

For any type of simulation, it is logical to question how complete the simulation should be in terms of cockpit duplications, systems operation, and flight-environment effects. The X-15 experience shows that, at least for pilot training, the cockpit simulation must be as complete as possible.

Cockpit

Two examples of seemingly minor differences between the simulator and the airplane illustrate the importance of cockpit duplication. Consider, for example, an incident in which the polarity of the simulator switch that energizes the trim button was different from that in the airplane. The pilot practiced his flight plan in the simulator and became proficient; however, in the airplane with a different polarity switch, the practiced technique was no longer useful. By the time he made the necessary correction, he was so far off the desired flight profile that for research purposes the flight was of limited usefulness.

On another occasion, an instrument was different in the airplane than in the simulator. The pilot checked the panel for the position of the needle rather than for the actual reading. This also resulted in the flight being off the desired flight plan. Both of these differences between simulator and airplane were readily apparent prior to flight; however, the consequences were not fully recognized until after the actual flight was made.

Systems

Failure to properly duplicate systems operation and the in-flight consequences are illustrated in the following example. The hydraulic output of the pumps used to supply the simulator control system did not match that of the airplane. During an in-flight maneuver, the pilot experienced a complete loss of artificial pitch and roll damping and an unstable control system because of control-system feedback characteristics (fig. 2). An investigation of the cause of the system instability indicated that the high gain capability of this adaptive system could not only saturate the control-surface rates, but the actuator servo rate as well. The pitch gain was at a maximum just prior to the maneuver. When the maneuver was initiated by the pilot with a relatively low-rate pitch and roll command, the system responded with a signal to the actuator servo that exceeded the rate capability. System damping of the airplane response began with the first motions and, since the gain was at a maximum, the damping signals were also asking for more servo actuator rate than could be supplied. Damping of these motions was achieved with a reduction in pitch gain, which the system eventually scheduled. This instability could not be duplicated in the simulator until the hydraulic-system output was increased to match that of the airplane.

2

Structural Environment

Another omission in duplication of the flight-environment effects almost caused the loss of an airplane. During reentry from an early altitude-buildup flight, a severe vibration at 13 cps was experienced by the X-15 for approximately 1 minute. After the pilot lowered the stability-augmentation-system gain, and with an increase in dynamic pressure, the shaking stopped. The pilot landed without further incident. An investigation into the cause of the vibration (fig. 3) indicated that at low dynamic pressure in the absence of aerodynamic damping the structurally lightly damped horizontal-tail surfaces were excited at their natural frequency by pilot control inputs. The X-15 inertial reaction to this oscillation was sensed by the stability-augmentation-system gyros which closed the loop through the control system. This problem could have been predicted on the fixed-base simulator if sufficient consideration had been given to the possibility of its occurrence in flight. The solution to the problem was developed on the simulator. A redesign of the augmentation-system filter was required to uncouple the system. The redesigned filter was checked out on the fixed-base simulator to insure proper attenuation at 13 cps. This change avoided the shaking problem.

Acceleration, Motion, and Visual Cues

Even if the cockpit and control systems are duplicated, the omission of other cues, such as acceleration, motion, and visual, can result in some serious problems. Some examples are given in the following sections to illustrate the possible effects on a mission.

Acceleration.- Acceleration cues were considered an unnecessary luxury in the X-15 simulator. The original X-15 pilots were exposed to typical mission simulations on the U.S. Navy's centrifuge at Johnsville, Pa., but not for training simulation purposes. These tests were primarily to determine the detrimental effects of acceleration on controllability during typical speed and altitude missions.

Later X-15 pilots had participated in various centrifuge programs but had not been subjected to X-15 mission accelerations during the training period.

The lack of acceleration capability in the X-15 simulator has not resulted in any serious problems during the flight program. There have been surprises, though, and some more subtle effects on pilot impressions as a result of this omission.

A typical altitude mission is shown in figure 4. Normal a_z and longitudinal a_x acceleration are shown in the lower plot. Prior to my first flight, my practice simulation had been done in a relaxed, head-forward position. The longitudinal acceleration at engine light forced

3

my head back into the headrest and prevented even helmet rotation. The instrument-scan procedure, due to this head position and a slight tunnel-vision effect, was quite different than anticipated and practiced. The acceleration buildup during engine burn (4g max) is uncomfortable enough to convince you to shut the engine down as planned. This is the first airplane I've flown that I've been happy to shut down.

Engine shutdown does not always relieve the situation, though, since, in most cases, the deceleration immediately after shutdown has you hanging from the restraint harness, and in a strange position for controlling.

Some of the more subtle effects of lack of acceleration during simulation are apparent to even experienced X-15 pilots. It is quite common to experience vertigo during various flight phases. Initial rotation to the desired climb angle requires from 20 seconds to, in some cases, 40 seconds depending on desired climb angle. The average rotational g is 2.0. It doesn't sound like much time, but it can be. The horizon is lost at a pitch angle of about 10° because of the head position and window size. The result is that the pilot swears he is going straight up and on a number of occasions has pushed over to look for the horizon. This has resulted in low peak altitudes a number of times, particularly when the θ vernier or pitch-attitude indicators have been in error or failed to operate properly.

The duration of high g (3 to 6) required to effect a change in flight path at hypersonic speeds is also hard to get used to. A pullout from 350,000 feet with a negative 40° flight-path angle at $M = 5.4$ requires an average 5g for 20 seconds. A 10° heading change at $M = 5.3$ requires 3g for 20 seconds.

On the low-g side, an initial climb angle of 25° at a velocity of 3000 fps requires 40 seconds of zero g flight to kill off the rate of climb, during which time you have climbed an additional 40,000 feet.

At low dynamic pressures (less than 100 psf), 90° bank angles for prolonged periods may only result in 10° to 20° heading changes because of the lack of g capability.

Most six-degree-of-freedom simulations will accurately predict these situations, but it is quite different when you actually undergo this, since you tend to relate g-time situations to previous experience. Subsonic flight experience shows much greater flight-path changes resulting from these same combinations and you are convinced in most high-velocity situations that you have exceeded the required flight-path change.

<u>Visual</u>.- Visual cues were also omitted in the X-15 simulator. As a result, several important phases of flight could not be realistically evaluated. Approach, flare, and landing have always been accomplished by the pilot using out-the-window information. Using visual cues, the pilot is continually adjusting his situation right up to touchdown, since his capability to judge distances, heights, and closing rates is

improving with proximity to the ground. The control rates, frequency of control input, and the amplitudes actually used during an X-15 approach and landing exceeded those used in any other mission phase. These control motions had not been fully appreciated during fixed-base or airborne simulations. Control-surface rate capability was subsequently increased to insure against a possible pilot-induced oscillation during approach, flare, and landing.

A postflare floating problem, peculiar to the X-15 with the adaptive control system, was not anticipated because of the inability to properly simulate flare and landing. This particular problem is a result of the lack of speed stability in a rate command control system. Lack of speed stability was apparent from simulation, but the effects on approach, flare, and landing were not obvious. Airspeed had to be monitored more closely during approach, and nose-down trim used to make the postflare control force feel normal during deceleration.

Main-gear landing loads were much higher than anticipated. Realistic landing simulations might have indicated this condition. These excessive main-gear loads were due to a natural pilot control response. As a result of gear geometry, on main-gear touchdown, the nose tended to pitch down rapidly. The pilot and the stability augmentation system responded with increased nose-up stabilizer. The aerodynamic loads produced by the large horizontal-stabilizer deflections added to the rebound loads following nose-gear contact could exceed by 50 percent the initial main-gear loads. A push or nose-down control input is now used to alleviate these aerodynamic loads.

Several other problems have been encountered as a result of the lack of proper simulation of the flight phases in which the pilot uses external vision. One pitfall was avoided, however, which is normally encountered in simulator evaluations of flare and landing. Flare and landing simulations not done in flight tend to indicate the desirability of a flare from maximum L/D as optimum. Even with a visual display, this is generally the result obtained. The reason for this erroneous conclusion is the inability to handle postflare float time. Heights of 2 to 3 feet are hard to judge even with the best visual displays, and closing rate with the runway, or a tendency to balloon, is not readily detectable.

X-15 performance simulations using an F-104 aircraft during approach, flare, and landing indicated the desirability of extra airspeed during approach and flare. This additional speed provided better control capability throughout and gave the pilot an extra g margin during flare to adjust his rate of flare as his perception improved near the ground. The postflare time provided by the excess airspeed preflare was useful in making final adjustments prior to touchdown and for extending the gear after flare completion. There is no problem in handling postflare float time during an actual landing. X-15 float times of 15 to 20 seconds are common and, even at the high touchdown airspeeds (190 knots), vertical velocities less than 4 fps are common.

5

A visual display is not adequate for landing simulation unless it can stimulate the pilot to respond with the same control rates, frequencies, and amplitudes as obtained in flight. It is also not realistic if it does not provide a pilot with the capability to handle postflare floating.

Motion.— Angular motion cues were also omitted in the X-15 simulator. Linear and angular accelerations can affect the pilot's control capability to respond to a particular flight condition. In certain instances the motion cues will assist the pilot in controlling the airplane. In other situations, these same motion cues may cause the pilot to induce, sustain, or feed an airplane oscillation.

A lateral-directional problem encountered in the X-15 with the original tail design gave us an opportunity to evaluate the effect of motion cues on pilot control capability. An F-100C variable-stability airplane was used to further investigate this condition in flight. The results are shown in figure 5. During the initial portion of the time history, the pilot (using a center stick) attempted to hold the stick fixed. The airplane motions caused the pilot to inadvertently apply small control inputs and increase the amplitude of the oscillation. The oscillations damped, however, with hands off. When the pilot attempted to apply conventional corrective control, the amplitude again increased. The use of a side stick in the X-15 alleviated the problem of inadvertent control inputs. An unconventional control technique, which was developed on the simulator and demonstrated in flight, could enable the pilot to control and effectively damp this type of airplane motion. The lack of motion in the fixed-base simulator prevented a full appreciation of this particular problem.

CONCLUDING REMARKS

Although relatively sophisticated fixed-base simulation of the X-15 was generally satisfactory for flight-mission studies and flight-envelope-controllability investigations, it was unable to predict all of the flight problems experienced, particularly when differences in aerodynamics, control system, or cockpit equipment existed between simulator and airplane. A constant updating of the simulator is therefore required. Absence of acceleration, motion, or visual cues in the simulator has limited the adequacy of pilot training for specific flight phases and sometimes resulted in surprises or in-flight problems.

The actual flight environment must still be investigated, since the effects of apprehension and anxiety on the pilot cannot yet be simulated. It is simple to evaluate a flight condition on a simulator, rate it subjectively, and reset when you lose control. Until a reset capability is provided in the airplane, the success of a mission is still up to the pilot.

SYMBOLS

a_x	longitudinal acceleration, g
a_z	normal acceleration, g
h	altitude, ft
q	dynamic pressure, psf
t	time, sec
β	angle of sideslip, deg
δ_a	aileron deflection, deg
φ	bank attitude, deg
$\Delta\varphi$	change in bank attitude, deg

7

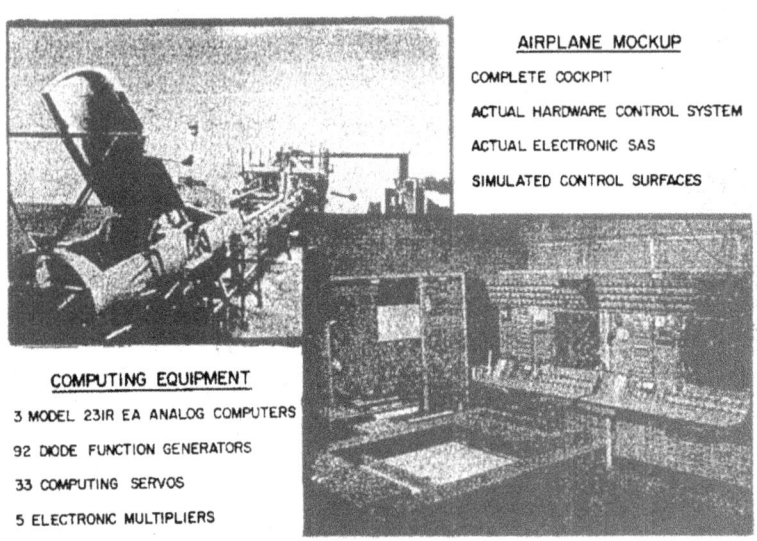

Figure 1

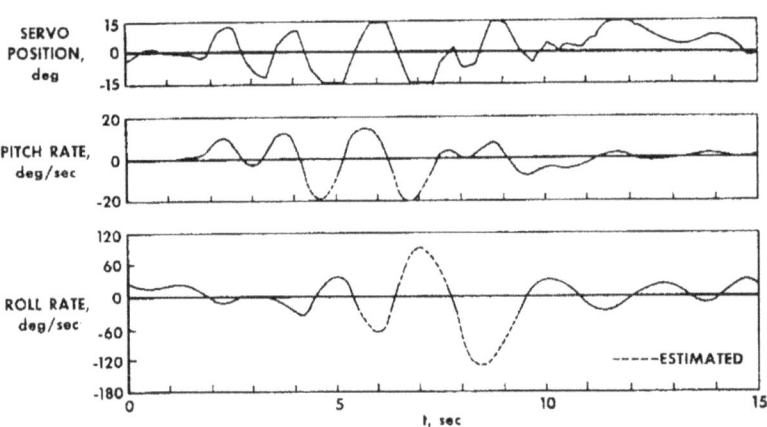

Figure 2

MECHANISM OF VIBRATION

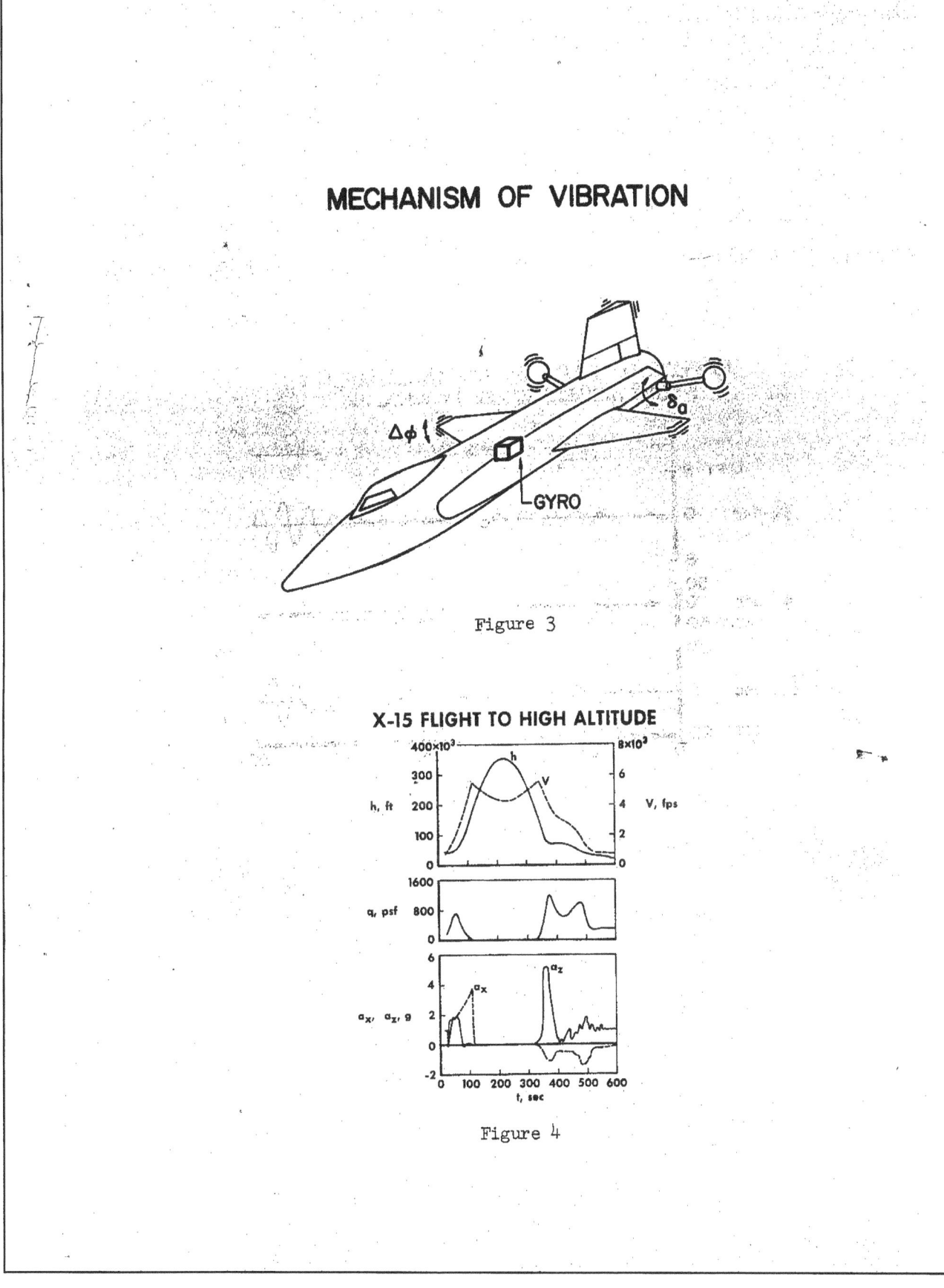

Figure 3

Figure 4

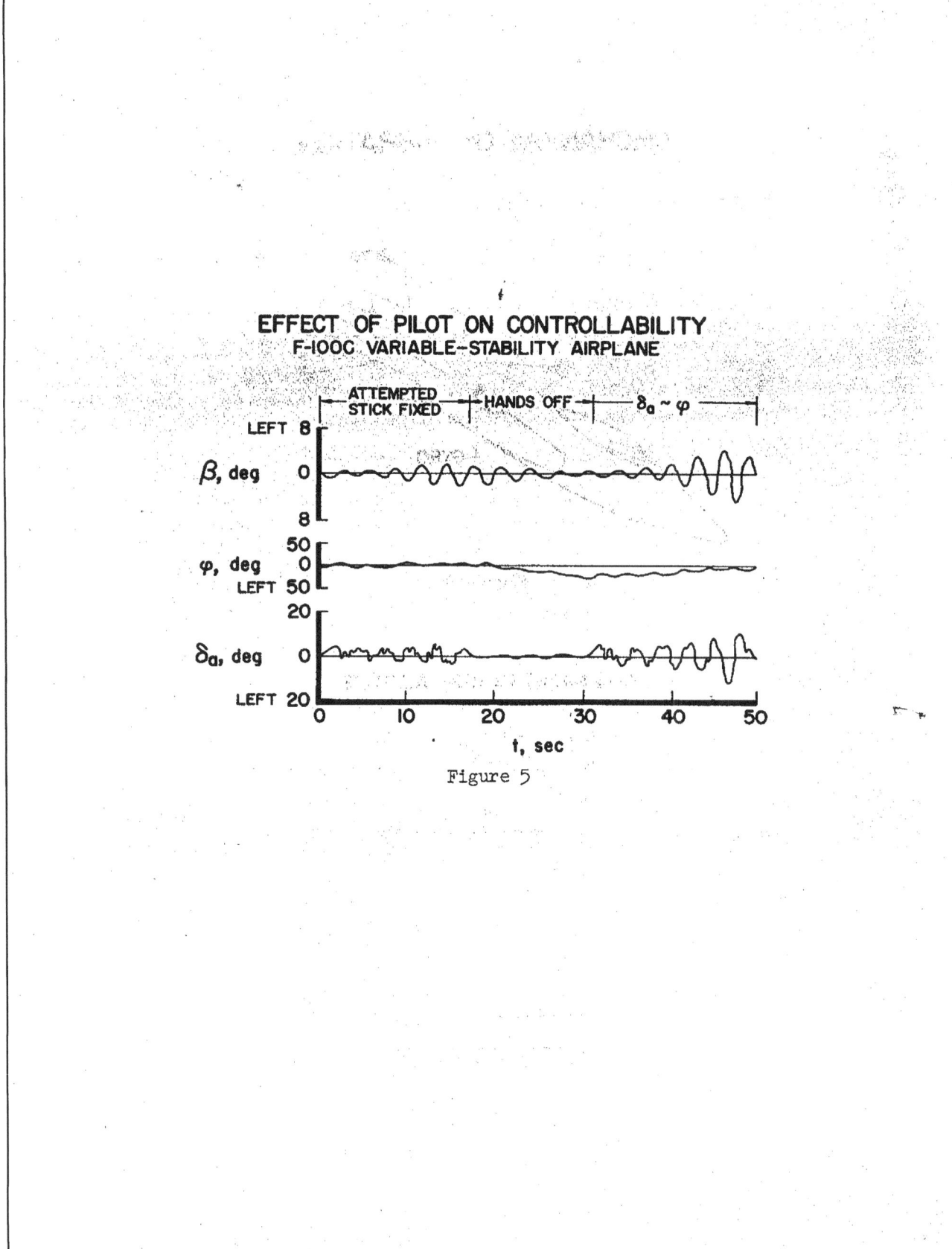

Figure 5

NACA RM L57K21

APPENDIX

THE ANALOG SIMULATOR PROGRAMING

By Robert E. Andrews

INTRODUCTION

This appendix presents the equations of motion which were simulated and a description of the mock cockpit. Also presented is a discussion of the difficulties encountered along with some of the checks performed to verify the simulator results. A complete schematic diagram of the analog simulation is shown in figure 12.

REPRESENTATION OF THE AIRPLANE

The airplane was represented by the five-degree-of-freedom equations with time-varying coefficients. The equations were written about the principal body axes and are as follows:

$$I_x \dot{p} = (I_y - I_z)qr + q_d Sb\left[C_{l_\beta}\beta + C_{l_{\delta_h'}}(\delta_R - \delta_L) + C_{l_{\delta_v}}\delta_v + \frac{b}{2V}\left(C_{l_p}p + C_{l_r}r\right)\right] \quad (1)$$

$$I_y \dot{q} = (I_z - I_x)pr + q_d S\bar{c}\left[C_{m_0} + C_{m_\alpha}\alpha + \frac{1}{2}C_{m_{\delta_h}}(\delta_R + \delta_L) + \frac{\bar{c}}{2V}\left(C_{m_q}q + C_{m_{\dot{\alpha}}}\dot{\alpha}\right)\right] + E_{M_V} \quad (2)$$

$$I_z \dot{r} = (I_x - I_y)pq + q_d Sb\left[C_{n_\beta}\beta + C_{n_{\delta_v}}\delta_v + C_{n_{\delta_h'}}(\delta_R - \delta_L) + \frac{b}{2V}\left(C_{n_r}r + C_{n_p}p\right)\right] + E_{M_H} \quad (3)$$

$$\dot{\beta} = -r + \alpha p + \frac{1}{V}\left[gm_3 - \dot{V}\beta + \frac{q_d S}{m}\left(C_{y_\beta}\beta + C_{y_{\delta_v}}\delta_v\right)\right] \quad (4)$$

$$\dot{\alpha} = q - p\beta + \frac{1}{V}\left[gn_3 - \dot{V}\alpha - \frac{q_d S}{m} C_{L_\alpha} \alpha\right] \tag{5}$$

The coefficients of these equations, which are functions of the Mach number and hence the flight time, are presented in table III. These expressions were obtained by fitting polynomials to the data presented in figures 2 to 4.

It was necessary to compute the direction cosines l_3, m_3, and n_3 so that the gravity forces could be properly included in the airplane representation. The following equations were used

$$l_3 = l_{3_0} + \int_0^t \left(m_3 r - n_3 q\right) dt \tag{6}$$

$$m_3 = m_{3_0} + \int_0^t \left(n_3 p - l_3 r\right) dt \tag{7}$$

$$n_3 = n_{3_0} + \int_0^t \left(l_3 q - m_3 p\right) dt \tag{8}$$

where $l_{3_0} = -\sin \theta_0$, $m_{3_0} = \sin \phi_0 \cos \theta_0$, and $n_{3_0} = \cos \phi_0 \cos \theta_0$.

PILOT'S DISPLAY AND METHOD OF CONTROL

The pilot's control station contained oscilloscopes to display the roll angle, sideslip angle, angle of attack, heading angle, and pitch-attitude angle. It also contained a conventional center control stick and rudder pedals. Figure 5 is a photograph of the control station.

Two different display combinations were used during this investigation. The same information was displayed in each but the location was different. The information was displayed on a 5-inch dual-beam oscilloscope in the form of an inverted T which rotated about its own axis and also translated horizontally and vertically. Two rectangular oscilloscopes, each 3 by $1\frac{1}{2}$ inches were arranged to show their displays through a mirror. One was mounted in a vertical position to the left of the main oscilloscope and the other was mounted horizontally above the main scope.

NACA RM L57K21 21

The first display combination, called the β-ϕ display, presented angles of attack, sideslip, and roll on the center oscilloscope and the pitch-attitude and heading angles on the left auxiliary and top auxiliary oscilloscopes, respectively. The inverted T rotates through an angle equal to the roll angle of the airplane, clockwise for positive angles. The angle of attack translates the T vertically, upward for positive angles, while the angle of sideslip translates the T horizontally, to the left for positive sideslip. The display on the left auxiliary oscilloscope presents a horizontal line which translates vertically with the pitch-attitude angle, upward for positive angles. The top auxiliary oscilloscope presents a vertical line which translates horizontally with the heading angle, to the right for positive angles.

The second display combination, called the attitude display, presents the roll angle, heading angle, and pitch-attitude angle on the main oscilloscope with angle of attack and angle of sideslip presented on the side and top auxiliary oscilloscopes, respectively.

The scales for angles of attack and sideslip were approximately 0.1 radian per inch for each display. The pitch-attitude and heading scales were approximately 0.4 radian per inch for both displays.

The angles presented in the display give the pilot the necessary information for orientation with respect to space as well as with respect to flight path. The Euler angles ϕ, θ, and ψ give the bank angle, pitch-attitude angle, and heading angle, respectively, with reference to space. The Euler angle equations have been simplified by setting $\sin\theta$ equal to zero and $\cos\theta$ equal to unity. These equations are

$$\phi = \phi_o + \int_0^t p\, dt \tag{9}$$

$$\theta = \theta_o + \int_0^t (q \cos\phi - r \sin\phi)dt \tag{10}$$

$$\psi = \psi_o + \int_0^t (r \cos\phi + q \sin\phi)dt \tag{11}$$

where $\phi_o = \psi_o = 0$ and $\theta_o = 31.5°$.

The inverted T was generated by using a dual-beam oscilloscope with one beam generating the wing and the other beam the tail. For the wing a sine wave was amplitude-modulated by resolving it by the sine and cosine of the roll angle ϕ, adding the translating voltage (α, β, θ, or ψ) to it, and connecting them to the horizontal and vertical plate of the first beam. The tail was generated similarly except that a rectified sine wave was used. For the β-ϕ display the four inputs to the oscilloscope were

$$W_V = \alpha + A \sin \omega t \sin \phi \tag{12}$$

$$W_H = -\beta - A \sin \omega t \cos \phi \tag{13}$$

$$T_V = \alpha - B \sin \omega t \cos \phi \tag{14}$$

$$T_H = -\beta - B \sin \omega t \sin \phi \tag{15}$$

where W_V and W_H are the signals applied to the vertical and horizontal plates of the beam producing the wing and T_V and T_H are signals applied to the tail beam. $B \sin \omega t$ is the rectified signal from $A \sin \omega t$. The details of this setup are shown in the schematic arrangement in figure 12.

The pilot's controls were a conventional center position stick and rudder pedals to provide aerodynamic controls. Roll control was obtained by the differential deflection of the horizontal tail; thus, it was necessary to combine pitch and roll commands in the horizontal-tail surface deflections. This was done by computing separate deflections for the right and left sections of the horizontal tail by using the following equations:

$$\delta_R = \tfrac{1}{2}\delta_1 + \delta_2 - K_1 p + K_2 q \tag{16}$$

$$\delta_L = -\tfrac{1}{2}\delta_1 + \delta_2 + K_1 p + K_2 q \tag{17}$$

Heading control was obtained by an all-movable vertical surface, and the control deflection is given by

$$\delta_V = \delta_3 + K_3 r \tag{18}$$

NACA RM L57K21 23

Artificial damping is supplied to the airplane by feeding signals proportional to the angular velocity to the control surfaces. The terms $K_1 p$, $K_2 q$, and $K_3 r$ are the damping terms for roll, pitch, and heading, respectively.

The control surfaces were limited in travel to $+15°$ and $-45°$ for the rolling tail and to $\pm 6°$ for the rudder. There were no rate limits nor limits on the autopilot authority. The physical properties of the control stick are given in table II.

A burnout warning lamp was included in the pilot's display. This lamp was provided to give the pilot a warning so that the trim changes that occur at burnout could be anticipated. This lamp came on 3 seconds before burnout and went out at engine thrust cutoff.

ANALOG PROGRAMING AND CHECKING

A complete schematic diagram of the analog simulation is shown in figure 12. Potentiometer settings for the diagram are given in table IV. The total amount of equipment used is as follows:

```
Amplifiers (total) . . . . . . . . . . . . . . . . . . . . . . . . . . . 102
    Integrators . . . . . . . . . . . . . . . . . . . . . . . . . . . . . 15
    Summers . . . . . . . . . . . . . . . . . . . . . . . . . . . . . . . 37
    Inverters . . . . . . . . . . . . . . . . . . . . . . . . . . . . . . 50
Potentiometers . . . . . . . . . . . . . . . . . . . . . . . . . . . . . 109
Multipliers (shafts) . . . . . . . . . . . . . . . . . . . . . . . . . .  12
    Potentiometers . . . . . . . . . . . . . . . . . . . . . . . . . . .  33
Dual resolvers . . . . . . . . . . . . . . . . . . . . . . . . . . . . .   2
Relay amplifiers . . . . . . . . . . . . . . . . . . . . . . . . . . . .   4
```

In order to check the analog setup, static and dynamic checks were made. Several digital check cases were run also. None of the check cases had any control inputs other than artificial damping.

For the program set up on the simulator, the dynamics of the problem were found to be near the critical region for the computer. Since the computer was to operate in conjunction with a pilot, a real time scale had to be accepted. In order to determine the effect of the dynamic error introduced by the analog computing elements, especially the servomultipliers, a digital check case without piloted controls was calculated. Runs made with different time scales on the analog setup showed that running the analog slow by 5:1 and 2.5:1 consistently gave the same results. Runs at a 1:1 time scale gave different results, without much consistency. By meticulous choice of variables to drive the servo-multipliers, the 1:1 time-scale runs were made to check consistently those made at slower time scales. In this particular setup to obtain the products m_3r, m_3p, n_3p, and pr, the variables driving the servo-multiplier were changed: m_3r from the m_3 servo to the r servo, m_3p from the m_3 to the p servo, n_3p from the n_3 to the p servo, and pr from the p to the r servo. A comparison of the digital and analog results for one typical check case is shown in figure 13. In this case the only disturbance is the engine thrust misalinement.

An inspection of figure 13 shows some difference between the final analog setup and the digital calculation. In order to find if this magnitude of error is within the sensitivity of the analog equipment, two check cases were made. For one case the initial angles of attack and sideslip were equal to 0.1 radian, and for the other case both angles were 0.105 radian. It was found that this 5-percent difference in input would more than account for the differences in the digital and analog results of figure 13 and that final results similar to those of figure 13 could be considered reasonable. It was felt, however, that with the availability of more servomultipliers or if electronic multipliers had been available, the dynamic error could have been reduced.

Another trouble spot was the calculation of the direction cosines. Here it was found that the static nulling error of the servomultipliers was important because of the output voltage possible for zero input to the servomultiplier when a large voltage was impressed across the multiplying potentiometer. This was found to be particularly critical in the n_3p product in equation (7). Because of the dynamics involved, this product was calculated on the p-multiplier but better static accuracy would result if the product was obtained from a servomultiplier driven by n_3. Thus, it was necessary that this multiplying potentiometer be set carefully on zero. The use of diode-type multipliers may be warranted because of their good zero output for zero-input characteristics and their good frequency response.

The static stability derivatives which were functions of Mach number could be expressed as functions of flight time (see table III and fig. 4) because of the programing of Mach numbers. Terms such as $C_{l_\beta}\beta$ and $C_{L_\alpha}\alpha$ were then written as the product of a polynomial in t and α or β. As shown in figure 12, this permits the static stability derivatives to be generated on servomultipliers driven by t and t^2 which are slowly changing variables compared with α and β.

NACA RM L57K21   25

STARTING THE ANALOG

In the check case shown in figure 13 the motions start abruptly because of the engine thrust misalinement in pitch attitude and heading. In the piloted runs which had thrust misalinement, the pilot was allowed to fly at a constant Mach number until the misalinement could be trimmed out. The flight-plan trajectory was then started. This procedure allowed a smooth controlled start on the trajectory with the only abrupt change in trim occurring at burnout.

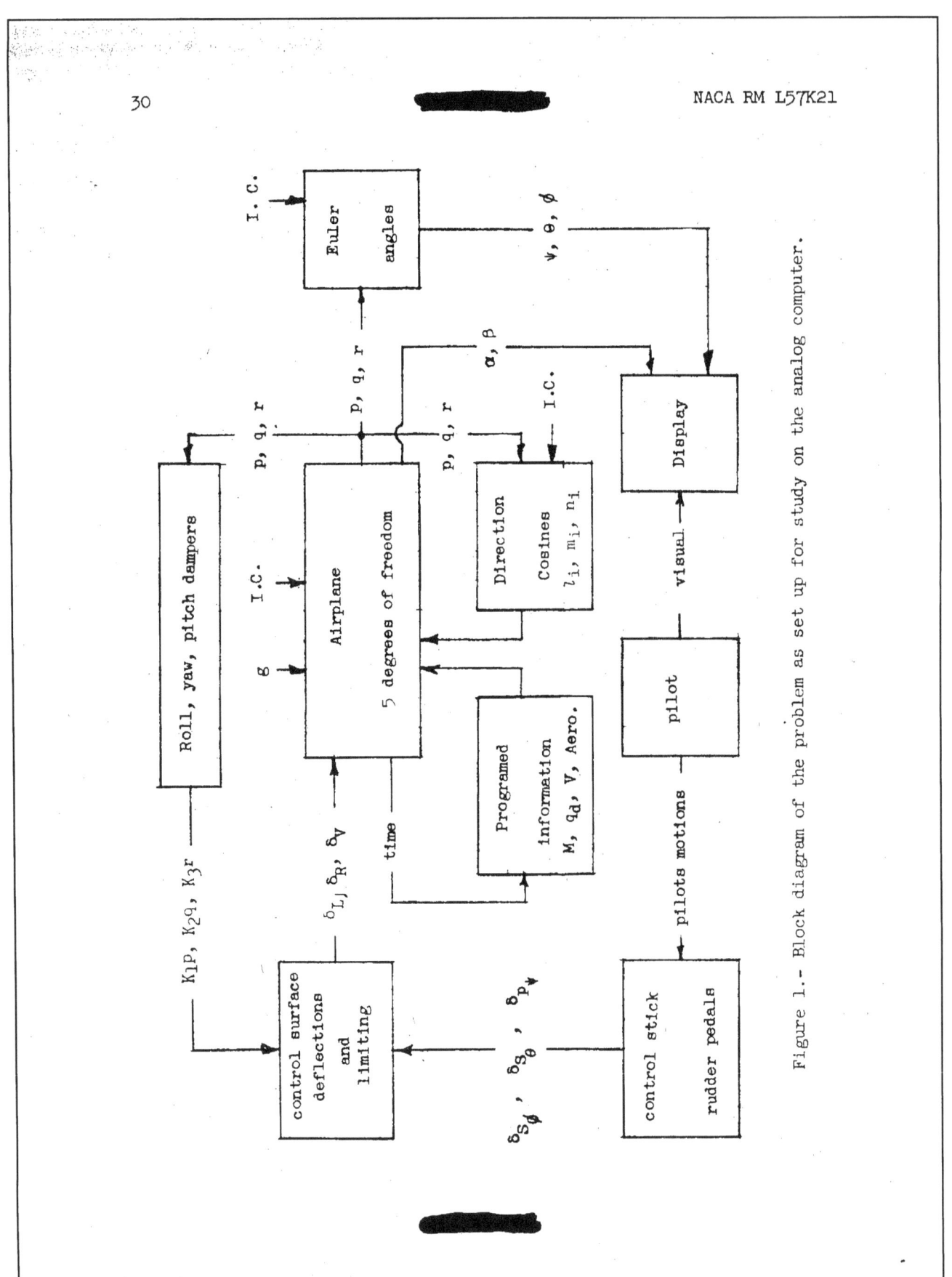

Figure 1.- Block diagram of the problem as set up for study on the analog computer.

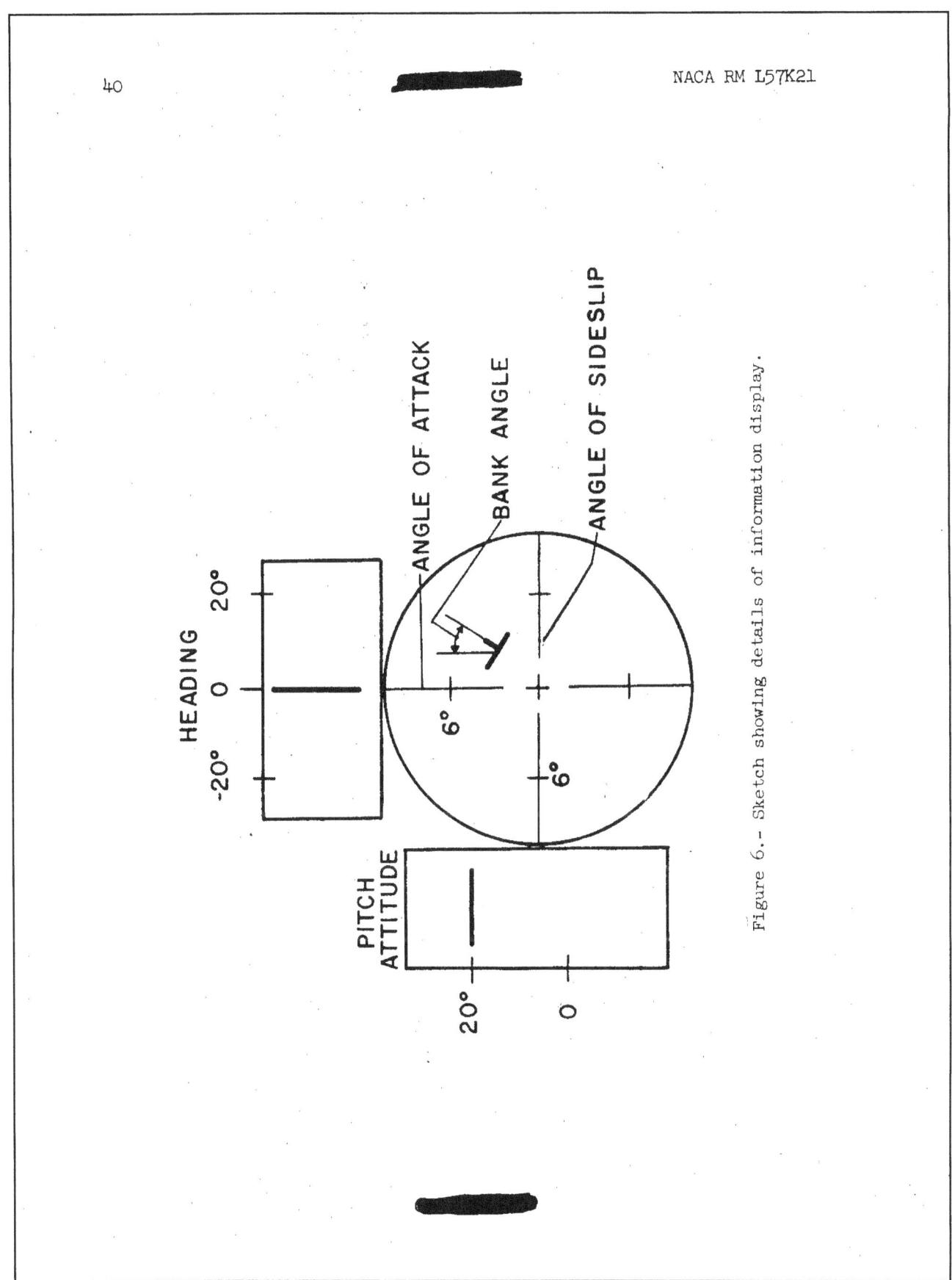

Figure 6.- Sketch showing details of information display.

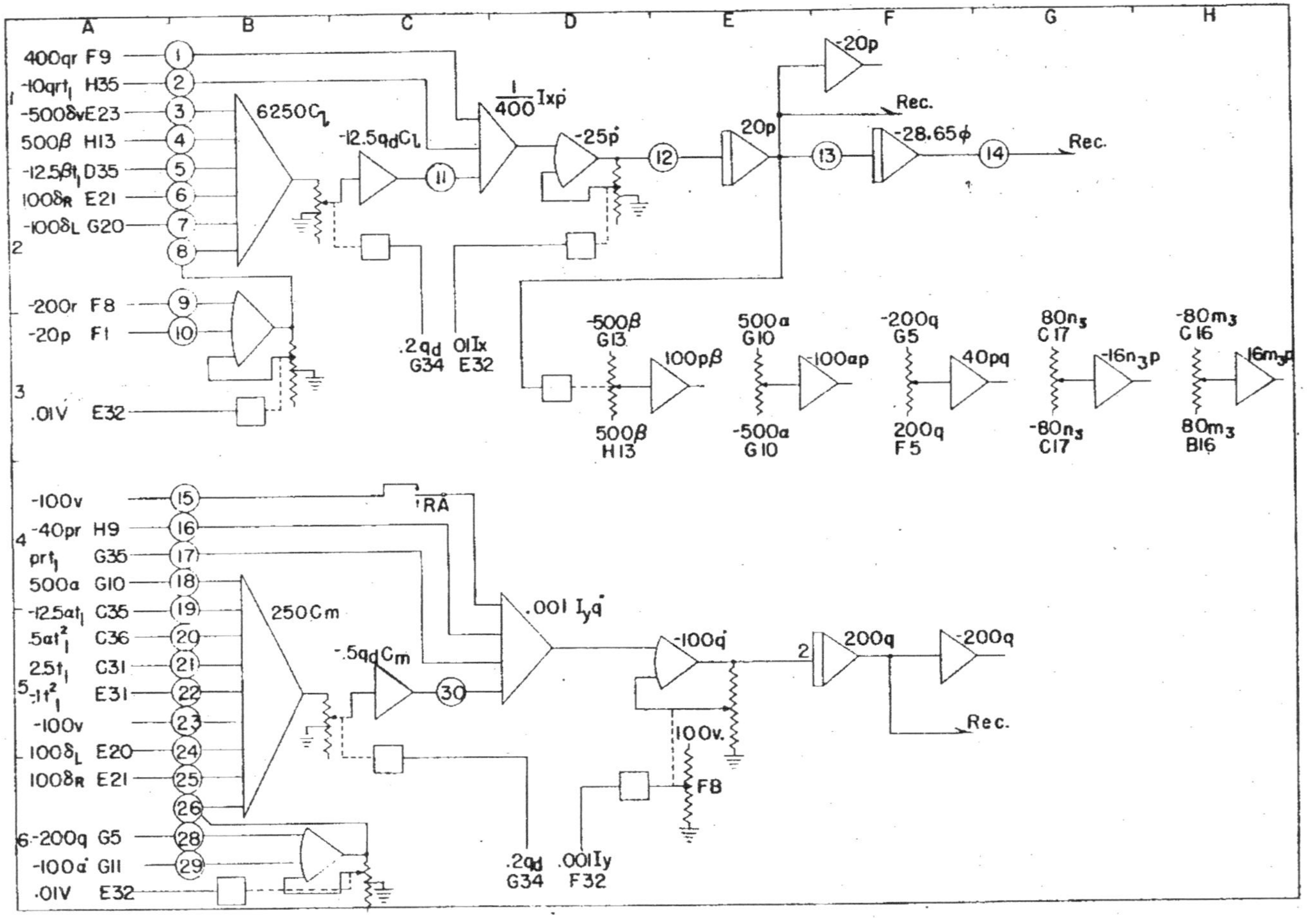

NACA RM L57K21

47

(a) Rolling and pitching circuit.

Figure 12.- Schematic diagram of analog simulation.

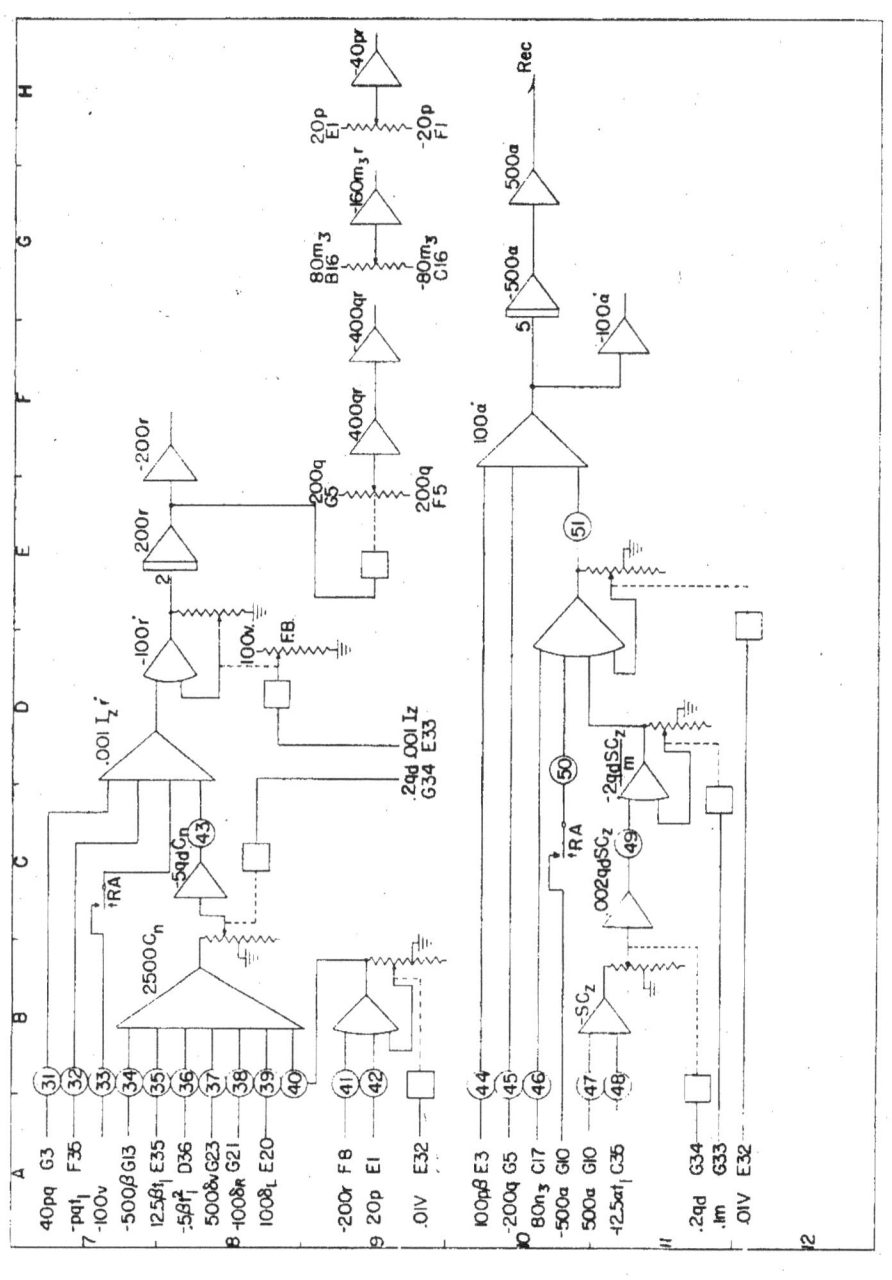

(b) Yawing and angle-of-attack circuit.

Figure 12.- Continued.

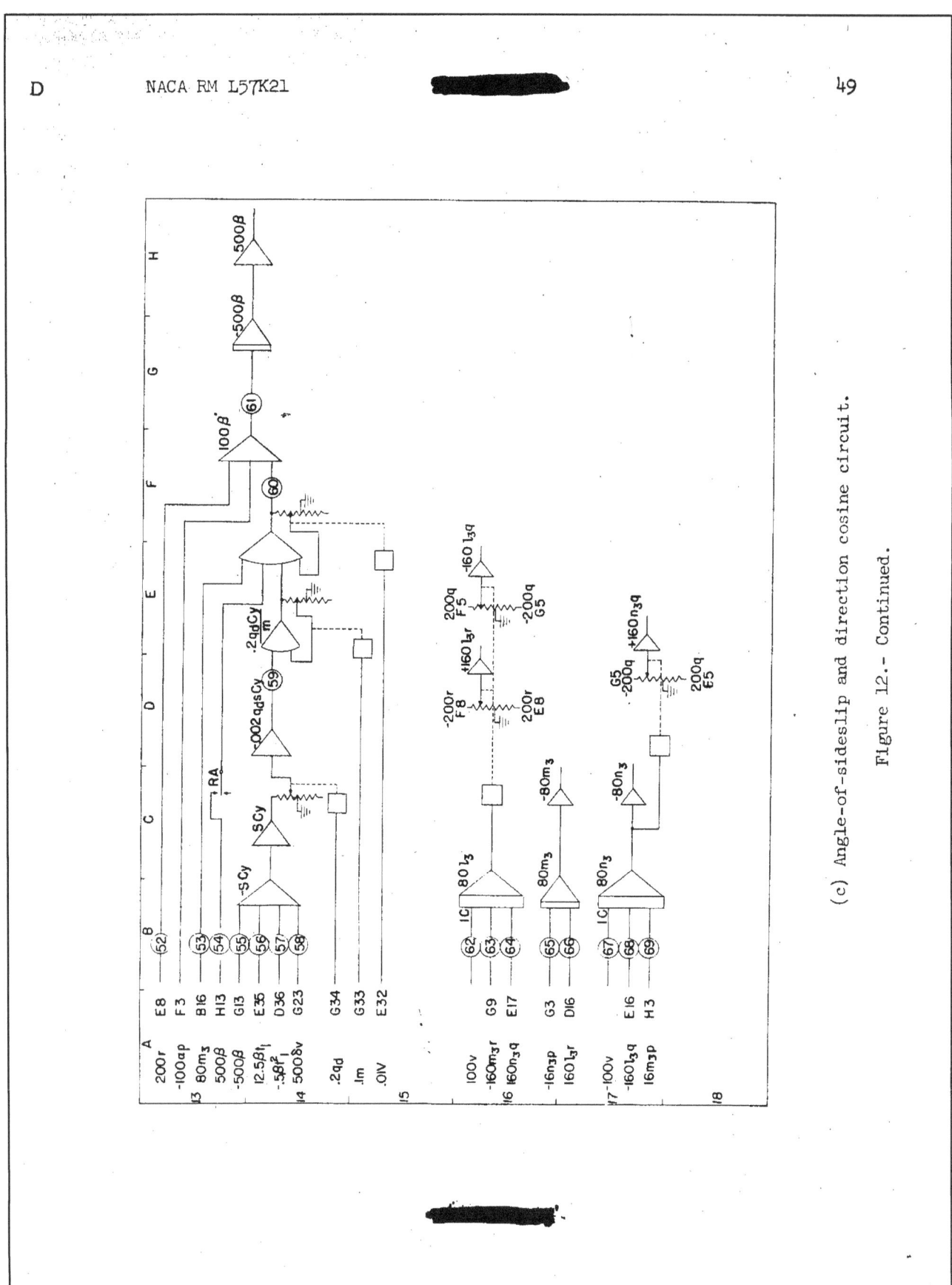

(c) Angle-of-sideslip and direction cosine circuit.

Figure 12.- Continued.

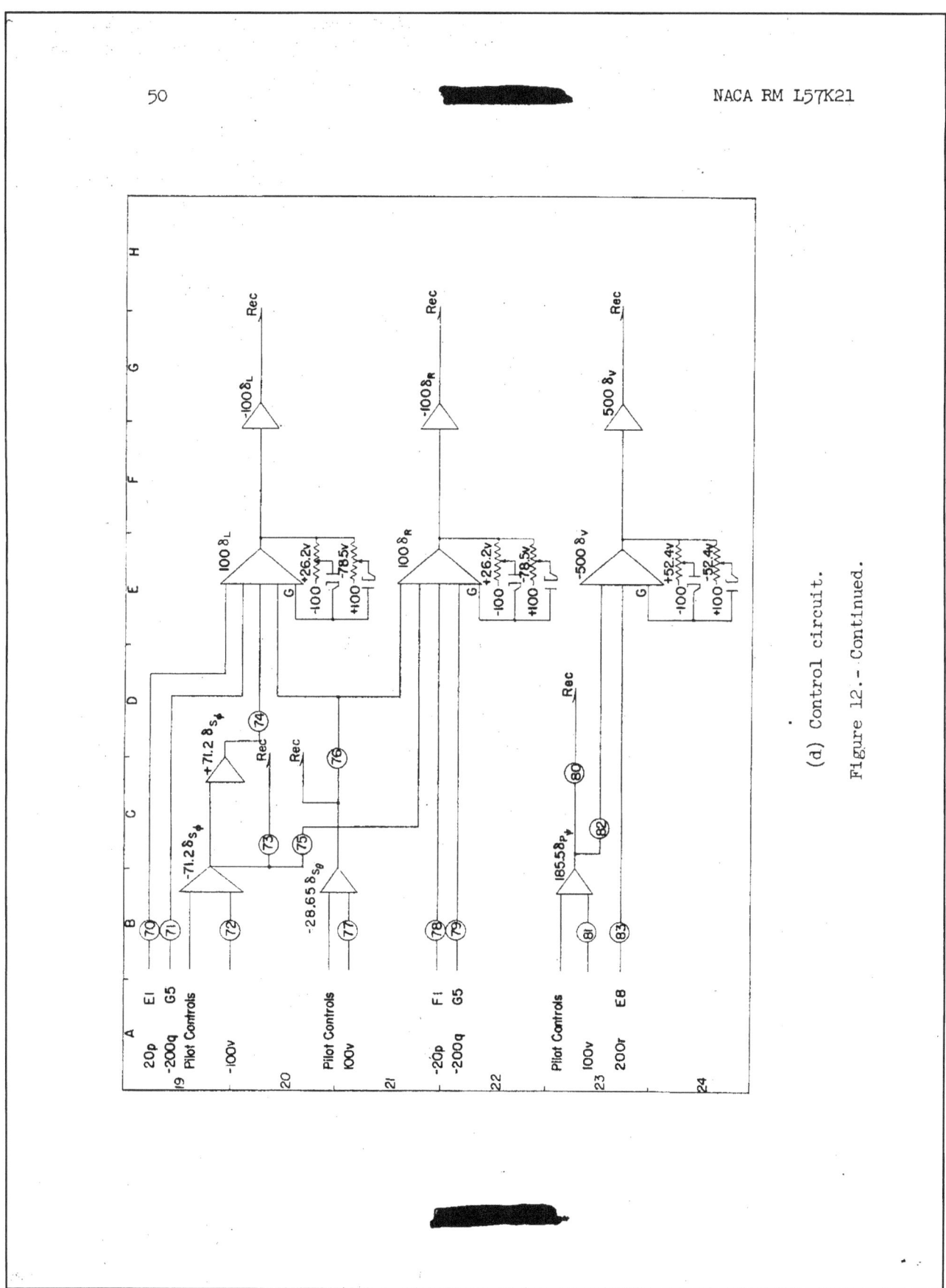

(d) Control circuit.

Figure 12.- Continued.

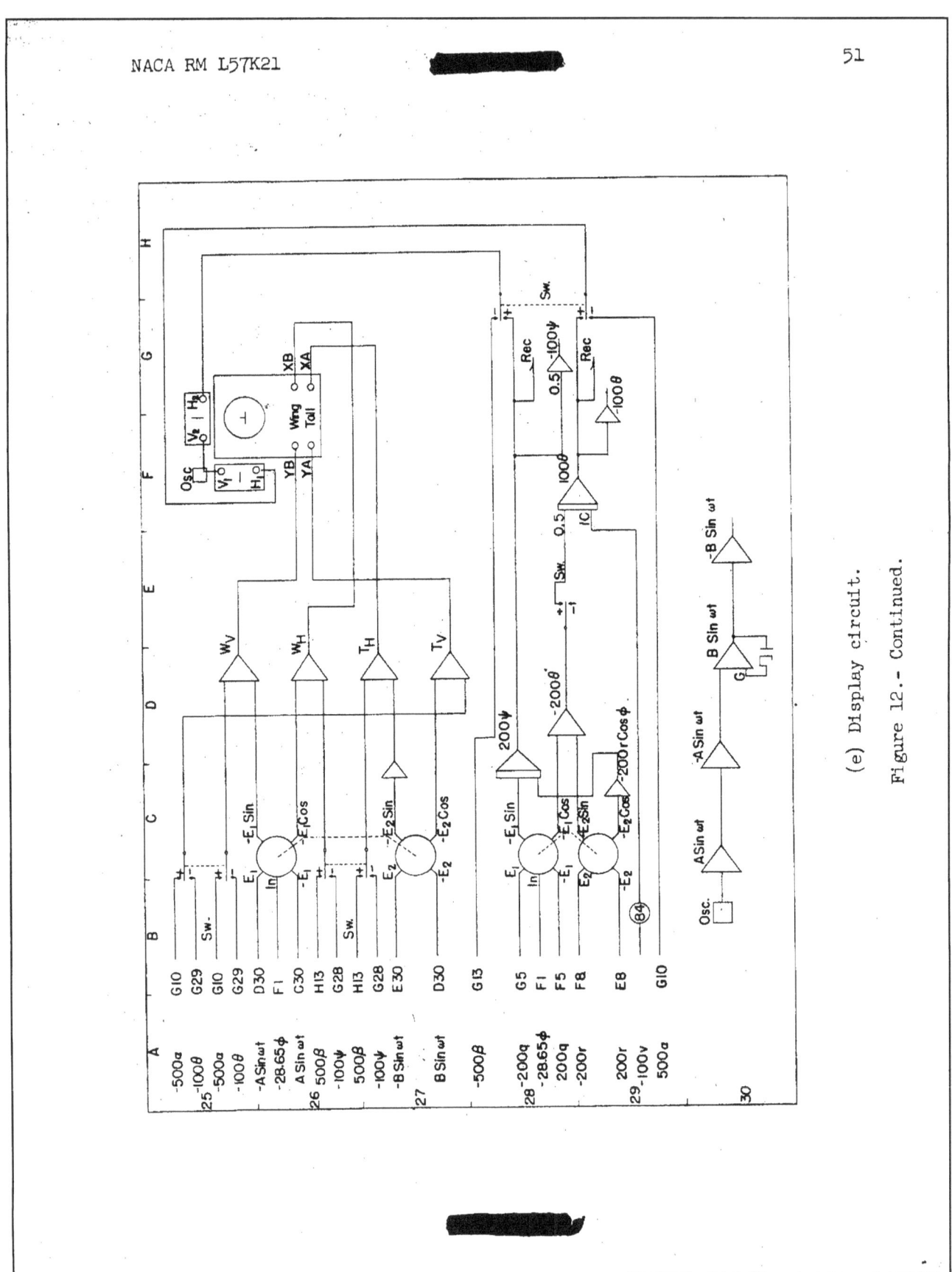

(e) Display circuit.

Figure 12.- Continued.

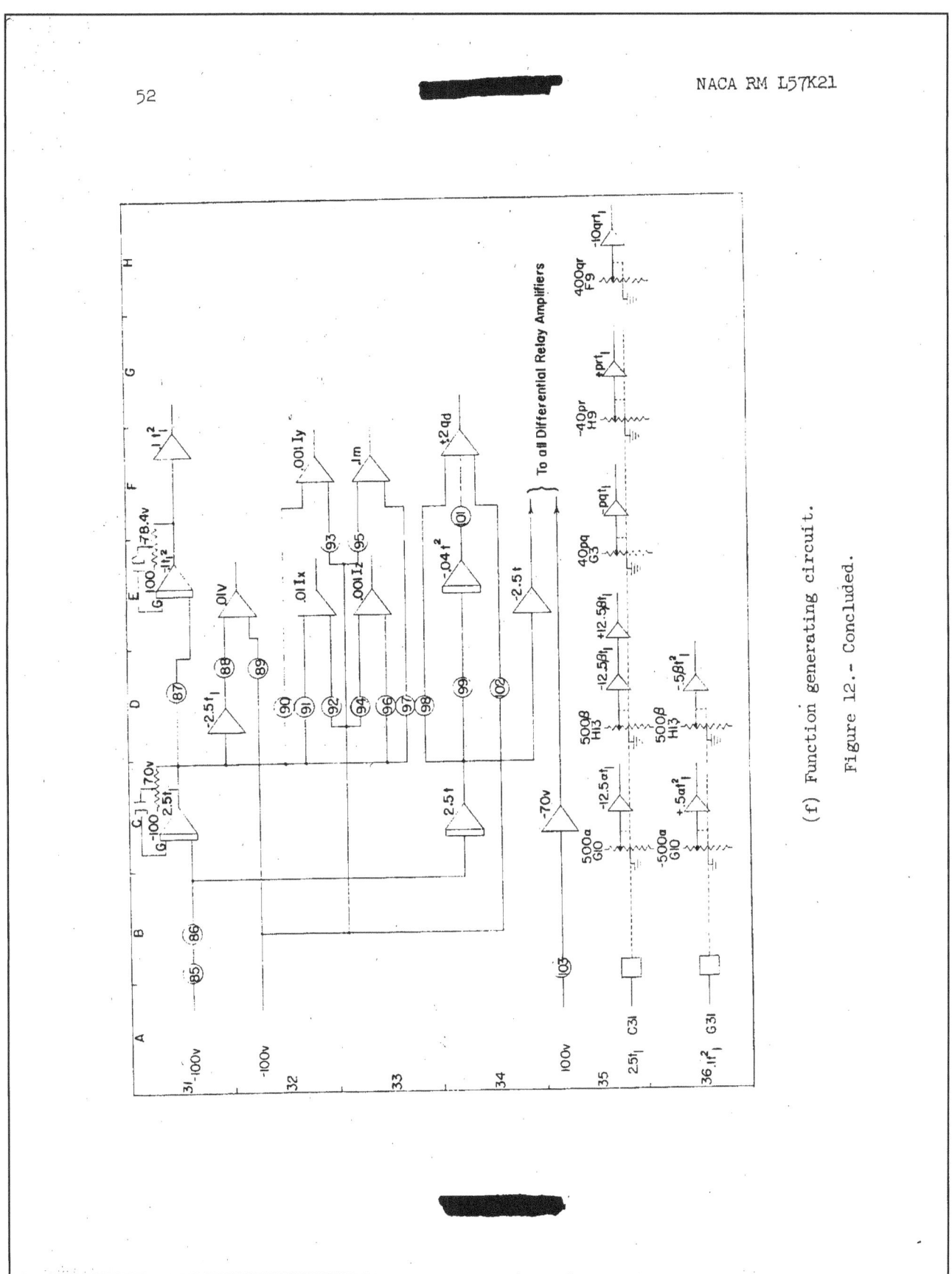

(f) Function generating circuit.

Figure 12.- Concluded.

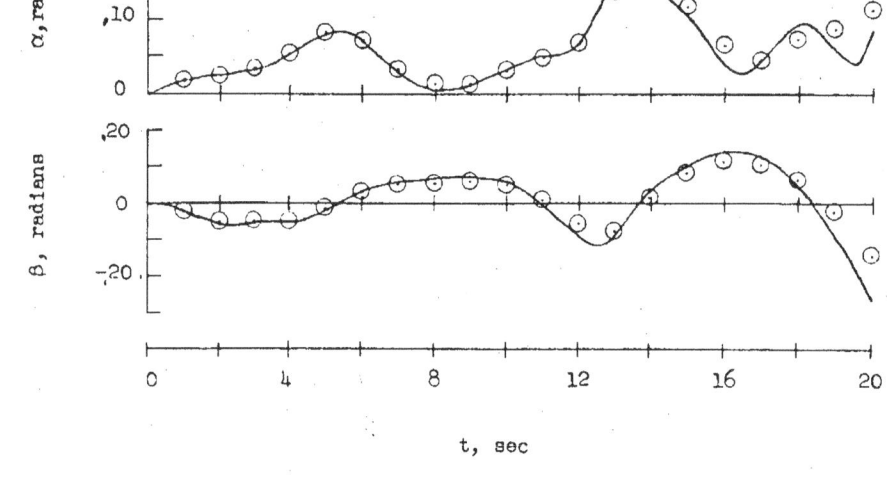

Figure 13.- Comparison of analog computer results with digital check case.

Glossary

A/C	Aircraft
A to D (and A/D)	Analog to Digital
ADI	Applied Dynamics Inc
ADP	Automatic Data Processing
AE	American Express
AFFTC	Air Force Flight Test Center
Alpha	See AOA
AOA (alpha)	Angle of Attack
AOS (beta)	Angle of Sideslip
ARC	Ames Research Center
Beta	Angle of sideslip
Bootstrap	A small program of only a few instructions that loaded itself into memory and then followed this by loading a larger more comprehensive loader routine
Breadboard	To build preliminary logic circuitry
CAL (also CALSPAN)	Cornell Aeronautical Laboratory
CD	Compact Disc
CDC	Control Data Corporation
Chopper	A device to keep an amplifier stabilized. The early tube-type amplifiers would drift (deviate) because of the heat they generated.
$C\mu$	Coefficient of thrust deflected downwards to provide additional lift
Cn/aileron	Yawing moment coefficient with respect to aileron deflection
C_{n_b}	The yawing moment coefficient with respect to sideslip
CPC	Card Programmed Calculator
CPU	Central Processing Unit
CRT	Cathode Ray Tube
CUC	Computer Usage Company
DAST	Drones for Aerodynamic and Structural Testing
D to A (and D/A)	Digital to Analog
DC	Direct Current

Deadband	A type of delay or lag
Derivative matching	A process of determining the nonlinear derivatives for a particular airplane
DFBW	Digital Fly-By-Wire
DFG	Diode-Function Generator
DFRC	Dryden Flight Research Center
Dirty configuration	A term used to describe an airplane that was not aerodynamically clean, which usually meant that the landing gear was down, or the speed brakes were extended, or the flaps down, or for some other reason something was causing a reduction in the airplane's performance
Discretes	Single-bit, on/off-type functions
DOD	Department of Defense
DOF	Degree of Freedom, a movement either up or down, sideways, front or back, or around the pitch, roll or yaw axis
DUHOS	Dual Hybrid Operating System
Dynamic checks	Checks of an analog computer in which, usually, a known time history solution (with known initial conditions and known inputs) was used to determine if a particular implementation was working correctly
EAI	Electronic Associates Inc.
Eightball (8-ball)	The colloquial term for the attitude indicator used in the airplanes of the 1960s and 1970s
EMC	Energy Management Console
Engineering precision	A level of exactness in which the degree of refinement of the measurement being made or the calculation being performed is both adequate and sufficient to provide the accuracy needed for the task at hand but nothing more
FAA	Federal Aviation Administration
FDL	Flight Dynamics Laboratory
Fortran	Formula Translation software
FRC	Flight Research Center
FSL	FRC Simulation Facility
GE	General Electric
GEDA	Goodyear Electronic Differential Analyzer
GPAS	General Purpose Airborne Simulator
GSA	General Services Administration
Heath Kits	"Build-it-yourself" electronic kits sold by the Heath Company of Benton Harbor, Michigan. The company quit selling these kits in 1992.

HiMAT	Highly Maneuverable Aircraft Technology (RPV)
HP	Hewlett Packard Company
HSF	High-Speed Flight Station
HYDAC	Hybrid Digital and Analog Computer
Hysteresis	A type of delay or lag
ICARUS	Immediate Checkout Analog Research Unity Scaled
I/O	Input and/or Output
IAS	Institute of Aeronautical Sciences, Inc.
IBM	International Business Machines
ILS	Instrument Landing System
KU	University of Kansas
LaRC	Langley Research Center
LLRV	Lunar Landing Research Vehicle
LLTV	Lunar Landing Training Vehicle
MH	Minneapolis Honeywell (now Honeywell, Inc.)
NAA	North American Aviation
NACA	National Advisory Committee for Aeronautics
NADC	Naval Air Development Center
NASA	National Aeronautics and Space Administration
PA	Personal Accounts
Parameter estimation	An automated method for obtaining numerical values for aircraft behavior by manipulating multiple differential equations; this technique allowed researchers to determine precisely the differences between values predicted from wind-tunnel data and those actually encountered in flight.
PIO	Pilot Induced Oscillation
Pot padder	A special type of servo multiplier
Pots	Potentiometers
RAIF	Research Aircraft Integration Facility
REAC	Reeve's Electronic Analog Computer
Rep Op	A feature available on most analog computers that allowed the operator to reduce the problem solution time by a ratio of 100:1 with results displayed on a multi-channel oscilloscope

RFP	Request For Proposal, which is a solicitation for bids on a contract
RTF	Real-Time Fortran
RPV	Remotely Piloted Vehicle
SCI	Simulation Councils, Inc.
SCOPE	CDC Cyber Operating System
SCW	Supercritical Wing
SDS	Scientific Data Systems
SETP	Society of Experimental Test Pilots
SAS	Stability Augmentation System
Static checks	A method of determining if the implementation was correct (i.e., were all the components correctly connected and were all the pots and function generators correctly programmed?)
Stick kicker	A device that vibrated the pilot's control stick to remind him or her that he or she was getting into an undesirable situation.
STOL	Short Take Off and Landing
TDY	Temporary duty
TM	Telemetry
UCLA	University of California at Los Angeles
USC	University of Southern California
WWII	World War II
Y2K	Year 2000

Index

A-5, 159
Adkins, Elmer J., 48
Air Force Flight Test Center (AFFTC), vi, 20, 28, 36, 136, 137, 145
Alford, Bill, 36
Algranti, Joseph, 126
Alpha, see angle of attack
Ames Research Center (Ames Aeronautical Laboratory under NACA), 8, 36, 38, 40-41, 51, 96-97, 108-109, 137, 152, 155
Amplifiers, 11
    Drift, 41
Analog programmers, 30-31
Analog simulations, passim but esp. 1 ill., 5-12, 30-31, 33, 39-40, 74-75, 98 n.
Anderson, Rider, 73-74
Andrews, Robert E., 145
Andrews, William, 43, 44
Angle of attack, defined, 29
Apollo Program, 35
Applied Dynamics Inc., 12, 67, 83
Apt, Milburn G. (Mel), Capt., 138-139, 142-143
Armstrong, Neil A., v, 36, 38 ill., 43, 44, 100, 126, 155, 156
Army Missile Command, 120
Atomic Energy Commission Facility, Oak Ridge, Tn., 83

B-17 side-arm controller, 140, 141
Bacon, Donald C. (Don), 78, 83, 84, 89, 91, 93, 94, 114-124, 127, 135, 147
Ballard, Robert R., 105
Banner, Richard D (Dick), vi, viii, 6, 7, 8, 99, 136-137, 140
Barnicki, Roger, 44
Beeler, De Elroy, 7, 41-42, 136, 156
Bell Aircraft, 141
Berry, Donald T., 28
Bikle, Paul, 46
Black boxes, 22-24, 25 ill.
Black magic, 5, 13
Blue box, 147
Boeing 747, 161
Boost-vehicle simulation, 15 ill., 34-45, 35-38 ill., 108, 153
Bostain, John M., 104
Breadboard, defined, 66
Butchart, Stanley P. (Stan), 36, 43, 60, 64, 113, 128, 148, 153-157

C-47, 42
Calibration Hangar, 127
Callister, Betty J., 148
Caw, Lawrence J. (Larry), 26, 27, 33, 44, 56, 60, 61, 63, 83-84, 91, 93, 112, 123-128, 146-148
Centrifuge, Navy, 13, 23, 36-37 ill., 100, 155, see also Johnsville
Cockpit simulations, 10 ill., 14-18 ill., 49 ill., 91 ill., 92 ill., 95 ill., 96 ill., 105 ill., 105-106, 131, 133-134, 135

Comcor Computer Company, 12
Computer "languages" (software programs)
    Assembler, 55, 71, 109
    Fortran, 55, 75, 109
    Libraries, 55
    Loader, 71
    Real-time Fortran (RTF), 55, 81, 109, 121
    SDS Assembly, 55, 81
    Utilities, 55
Computers (human), v, 9 n.
Computers (analog), see also Goodyear Electronic Differential Analyzer
    AD-4, 67 ill., 83-84, 86, 90, 121
    Comcor 175, 96
    Cyclone, 39
    EAI 31R, 9 ill., 34, 99, 102, 109, 110, 125, 144
    EAI 131R, 9 ill., 34, 99, 102, 110
    EAI 231-RV, 12, 27, 34, 67, 79, 95, 110, 125, 128
    TR-5, 61, 134
    TR-10, 33, 61, 109, 125, 134, 149-151
    TR-20, 33, 125
    TR-48, 28, 33, 91, 112, 134, 149-150
    TR-58, 33, 128
    Typhoon, 39
Computers (digital)
    CDC 73, 89-90
    Cyber 72, 75
    CYBER 73-28, 67-68 ill., 80, 83, 86-87, 92-93, 120-123
    SDS 920, 55, 69-70
    SDS 930, 50, 52-55, 70-71, 74-77, 81-82, 97, 111, 118-121, 127, 146
    SDS 9300, 68, 74, 81-83, 89 n., 91, 94-97, 146
    XDS 9300 (formerly SDS 9300), 89 n., 146
Computers (hybrid), 55-56, 65-90
    AD-4, 67 ill., 83
    HYDAC, 67
Computer Usage Company, 81
Control configured vehicle (CCV), 150
Control Data Corporation (CDC), 68
Control stick, 11, 130-131, 155
Controlled Impact Demonstration (CID), 145
Converter
    Analog-to-digital, 66 n., 67
    Digital-to-analog, 66 n., 67
Cooper, Lonnie, 92, 116
Cornell Aeronautical Laboratory (CAL), 59-60, 128, 149
Coupling dynamics, 118
Credit cards, 41-42

D-558, 156
Daedalus, 122
Dalto visual simulator, 132-133
Dana, William H. (Bill), 3, 22, 50 ill., 117, 128, 157-159
Daniels, Walter, 36
Davis, Billy E., 52, 113

219

Day, Richard E. (Dick), vi-viii, 6, 8, 24, 46, 54, 56, 99, 137-140, 141, 144, 157, 159
Deets, Dwain A., 24, 60, 62, 112, 128, 148-153
Degree of Freedom (DOF), defined, 8; mentioned, passim, esp. 68
Derivative matching, 26, 111 (including definition in n.), 116
Digital data communications, 89
Digital integration, 118-120
Diode-Function Generator (DFG), 22, 33
Discretes, 74-75
   defined, 74 n.
Distributive patching, 135
Drake, Hubert M., 7, 145
Draper Laboratory, 151
Drones for Aerodynamic and Structural Testing, (DAST), 97, 108
Dryden Flight Research Center (DFRC), v, passim
Dual Hybrid Operating System (DUHOS), 80-82

Edwards Air Force Base, 4, 20, 36, 52, 139
Edwards, John, 90
Electric control stick, 130-131, 134, 147
Electronic Associates Inc. (EAI), 12, 55, 92, 99 and see Computers
El Paso, Texas, 45
Enevoldson, Einar, 158
Engineering precision, defined, 119 n.
Engle, Joe H., 111
Error signals, 43-44
Everest, Frank (Pete), Lt. Col., 138, 141, 142

F-8 Digital Fly-By-Wire (DFBW) program, 32, 79, 85-86, 117, 131-132, 150-152, 160
F-8 Supercritical Wing (SCW), 159-161
F-15 Remotely Piloted Vehicle, 85, 146, 158
F-100, 6, 7, 13, 108, 136, 148, 153, 156
F-101, 13
F-102, 13
F-104, 13, 14, 26, 56, 143-145, 160
   Reaction controls, 143-144
   Stick kicker, 130
Faster-than-real-time simulation, 93, 118, 159
Film reader, 102 ill.
Flight Dynamics Laboratory (FDL), 108
Flight Research Center (FRC, later Dryden), v, passim
   Move from South Base, 136 n.
Flight Research Center Simulation Laboratory (FSL), vi, 2 ill., 108, passim
Ford Tri-motor, 97
FRC, see Flight Research Center
FSL, see Flight Research Center Simulation Laboratory
Fulton, Fitzhugh L., Jr., 94, 97, 128
Function generators, 11, 43, 48
Fuses, 22

Gates, Ordway B., Jr., 6, 8, 9, 137
Gatlin, Donald H. (Don), 64, 148

Gemini Program, 35
General Electric (GE), 104
General Purpose Airborne Simulator, 59-64, 60-61 ill., 111, 112-114, 128-129, 146, 148-150, 152-153
G-forces, 43 and see centrifuge
Gibbons, John, 94
Gilyard, Glenn B., 28
Glider simulation, 129-130
Goodyear Electronic Differential Analyzer (GEDA), v, 6-9, 20, 99, 136-137, 138-139, 144
Greenfield, Lowell, 87, 91, 92, 115, 123, 129, 146
Gremlins, Gremlinity, 5, 21, 87,
Grounding, 51

Halasey, Robert L., 87
Hanes, Horace A., Col., 141 n.
Harwell, Rebel, 104
Heat transfer, 109
Heath Company, 3, 8
Hedgley, David R., Jr. (Dave) 123
Highly Maneuverable Aircraft Technology (HiMAT) project, 97, 108, 145
High-Speed Flight Station (HSFS), v, 137, 143, 144
HL-10, 17 ill., 83, 85, 91, 93, 115, 117, 128, 146
Hoey, Bob, 54, 91 ill.
Hold mode, 122
Holleman, Euclid (Ed), 1, 10, 40, 41, 43, 44
Hughes, Donald L., 159
Hybrid Digital and Analog Computer (HYDAC), 67
Hyper III, 91, 115

IBM CPC (Card Programmed Calculator), 4
Icarus, 122
Iliff, Kenneth W., 27 n., 113, 116, 117, 121, 122
Immediate Checkout Analog Research Unity Scaled (ICARUS), 68 n., 78-80, 91-92, 121-124, 146
Initial conditions (IC), 28, 115 n. (defined)
Innis, Bob, 36
Input/Output (I/O) routines, 55, 70, 72-74
Instruments, 103-105
Integrated Test Facility (ITF), 127 and see Research Aircraft Integration Facility
International Business Machines (IBM), 86-87, 101, 124, 137
Iron bird, 32, 46, 117, 151
Iron Cross, 153 ill., 154 ill.

Jackson, Hugh, 128
Jackson, Raymond H., 137
Jarvis, Calvin R., 126
JetStar (Lockheed C-140), 59-64, 60-61 ill., 112, 117, 128, 147-148 see also General Purpose Airborne Simulator
Johnson, Richard G., 131
Johnson, William (Bill), 140
Johnsville, Pa., 13, 23, 34-45, 100, 155, 156
Juarez, Mexico, 45

Kempel, Robert W. (Bob), 20-21, 58 n., 60, 63, 93, 117, 128,

145-148, 159
Kerfott (synchro manufacturer), 104
Kier, David A., 94
Kincheloe, Iven, Capt., 142
Kluever, Jack, 126
Kolf, Jack, 54, 93, 118, 159
Kordes, Eldon, 57, 125
Kostrakopf, Serge, 31
Krier, Gary, 148, 160
Kuhl, Albert E. (Al), vi, 6, 7, 8, 99, 136, 142

Landing simulations, 117-118, see also X-15
Langley Memorial Aeronautical Laboratory, v, 17, 143, 145
Langley Research Center, v, 7, 8, 36, 43, 51, 146
Lewis Aeronautical Laboratory (now Glenn Research Center), 4
Lifting-body program, 85, 145-146, 160
simulations, 15 ill., 17 ill., 91-93, 115, 127-128
Little, Mary, 87, 123
Lock, Wilton P. (Wilt), 126, 159, 160
Lockheed, 115, 155
Loschke, Paul, 25 ill.
Lunar Landing Research Vehicle (LLRV), vi, 33, 44, 92, 93, 112, 117, 125 ill.-127, 126 ill., 128, 162
Lunar Landing Training Vehicle (LLTV), 126
Lyons, Jerry, 104

M2-F1, 15 ill., 93, 117
M2-F2, 91, 93, 115, 130, 145
M2-F3, 85, 91, 115, 145, 146, 158-159
Maine, Richard E., 27 n.
Mallick, Donald L., 64, 126 ill., 128, 148
Manned Space Flight Center (later Johnson Space Center), 126
Manning, Theron, 27
Matheny, Neil W., 27, 28
Matranga, Gene J., 126, 156
McKay, John B. (Jack), 47, 111, 125, 155
McKay, James M., 57, 63, 112, 125
McMurtry, Thomas C. (Tom), 159-161
McTigue, John, 146
Mercury Program, 35
Michigan Technological University, 3, 4
Midnight patcher, 20-21
Milliammeter, defined, 104 n.
Moving-base simulations, 32-33, 96 ill., 161
Musick, Richard O. (Dick), 5, 8, 10, 13, 24, 32, 36, 40, 41, 42, 43, 52, 60, 61 ill., 64, 99, 100, 101-106, 101-102 ill., 107, 109, 128, 129, 130, 133, 134, 135, 137, 141, 143, 144, 148, 157
Myers, Albert F. (Al), 84-86, 89, 121,

NASA, vi, 13-162
National Advisory Committee for Aeronautics (NACA), vi, 1- 13, 84, 101, 139, 143
Navy, U.S., 3, 34-45, 100, 145 n.
    Naval Air Development Center (NADC), 34, 51, 139

Navy Aviation Medical Laboratory, 34
Norden display, 91 ill., 133
North American Aviation, 46, 49, 140
Northrop, 131

Operate mode, 116 n., 122
Orbital rendezvous and docking, 107-108 ill., 109-110
Ozalid copy process, 17-18

PA-30, 117
Painter, Weneth D., 117, 145
Paper tape, 73
Parameter identification, 27 n.
Paresev, 25 ill.
Parish, Owen O., 112
Patch panels and cords, 19-20, 61, 135
Perry, Gerald D., 52, 113, 114, 122, 126, 135, 157
Perry, John J., 27, 51, 52, 60, 64, 108, 109-114, 123, 140
Peterson, Bruce A., 117, 130
Peterson, Forrest (Pete), 36, 41, 56
Pinon Hills, 4
Plotters, 53-54
Pontiac Catalina tow vehicle, 93
Pot-Set, defined, 11 n.
Potentiometers, 9, 11, 16, 17, 99
Powers, Bruce G., 94
Putnam, Terrill, 94

Rampy, John M., 28
Reaction controls, 107, 143
Readiger, Al, 116 n.
Real-Time Simulation (RTSIM), 89
    RTSIMII, 89
    SIMII, 89
Ream, H. E., 126
Reeves Electronic Analog Computer, 137
Rediess, Herman A., 61 ill., 128
Redstone Arsenal, Al., 84
Rediess, Herman A., 112-113, 143
Reisert, Donald (Don) 8, 17, 140-145
Remote Batch Terminal, 89
Remotely Piloted Research Vehicle (RPRV), 85, 131, 146
    and see F-15
    Cockpit simulation, 18 ill.
Repetitive operations (Rep Op), 26-28, 116 n. (defined)
Research Aircraft Integration Facility (RAIF), ix, 3 ill., 10, 31, 127
Reset mode, 116 n., 122
Rio Grande River, 45
Robertson, Robby, 105
Robinson, Glenn H., 143
Rocket Site, 83
Rocket staging, 40
Rogers Dry Lake, 138
RPRV lab, 108
Rushworth, Robert, 36, 111
Ryan, Bertha M., 116

Sadoff, Melvin, 1,
Samuels, J. L. (Jim), 32, 48, 52, 108, 114, 157
Sanderson, Kenneth C., 109
Scaling, 29-30, 120 n.
Schilling, Lawrence J (Larry), 2, 88, 89, 124
Schmidt, Stanley, 99-100
Scientific Data Systems (SDS), 52, 54, 76-78 and see computers
Scott, David, 132
Sebastian, Bill, 52, 157
Servo units, 104, 105 ill.
Shock, Lew, 155
Short Take-Off and Landing (STOL) simulations, 78, 94-97, 94-96 ill., 108
Side-arm controller, 35 ill., 36-39 and see B-17
Silver ink, 140 n.
Simson (instrument maker), 104
Simulation Councils Inc. (SCI), 66, 120
Simulations, see aircraft designations, computers
Sissle, Ralph, 140
Smith, John P., 2, 9, 19, 46, 87, 106-108, 123, 146, 157, 159
Slaton, Deke, 126
Soft wire, 143 n
Space Shuttle, 35, 91, 115
   Approach and Landing Tests, 59
Spectrol (servo manufacturer), 104
S-plane technology, defined, 24 n.
Static checks, 117-118
Stillwell, Wendell, 144, 145
Strip-chart recorders, 53-54
Struts, Larry W., 28
Suppona, Art, 13, 52, 113, 126, 129-132, 134,
Swanson, John, 81
Synchro units, 104, 105 ill.
Systems Analysis Group, 123
Szalai, Kenneth J., 59 ill., 62, 112, 128, 150-151

Taylor, Lawrence W., Jr., 27 n., 48, 139
TDY (temporary duty), 41-42
Telemetry (TM), 69-70, 108
Temperature, 21-22, 53
Templates, 18-19 ill.
Testing, 28-30
   Dynamic, 29
   Static, 28
Thompson, Milton, 25 ill., 26, 57-58, 93, 117, 145
Transport simulation, 16 ill.
Triplett (instrument maker), 104
Trunking, 51, 135

United Airlines, 161
University of California at Los Angeles (UCLA), 55, 82, 119
University of Southern California (USC), 119

VanLeynselle, Frank J., 125 ill.
Videan, Edward N. (Ed), 4, 5, 8, 10, 40, 41, 43, 87, 89, 98-101, 101 ill. 103, 137, 138, 140, 144, 159

Visual displays, 131, 161
von Braun, Wernher, 128

Wagner, Charles A. (Charlie), 2, 13, 24, 25-26, 90, 122, 130, 132-136
Walker, Joseph A., 126 ill., 130, 144, 155
Waltman, Gene L., v, ix, 42, 87, 94-97, 108-109, 115, 120, 123, 124
Washington, Harold, 94
Webb, Leo R. (Dick), 122, 126
Weil, Joseph E., 6-8, 137
Wells, Larry, 52
Weston (instrument maker), 104
Williams, Walter C. (Walt), 3, 137
Willow Grove Naval Air Station, 41
Wilson, Al, 103
Wilson, Warren, 54
Wolowicz, Chester H. (Chet), x, 8, 27-28, 106, 137
Wright-Patterson Air Force Base, 112

X-1, vi, viii, and see X-1B
X-1B, 8, 10, 13, 107, 108, 153
X-2, vi, viii, 8, 9, 137, 138-141, 142, 143
X-3, viii, 7, 136
X-15, vi, viii, 2, 5, 8, 9, 10, 12, 16 ill., 21, 22, 23 ill., 25, 26, 27, 28, 34 ill., 41, 46-58, 65, 66, 69, 71-79, 91, 92, 94, 100, 107, 143, 108, 110-112, 117, 125, 127-129, 132, 136, 138-139, 144-145, 148, 153, 157-159, 162
   Centrifuge program, 139
   Energy management, 52-54, 132
   Landing simulation, 56, 111-112
   Lower vertical stabilizer, 46
   Minneapolis Honeywell adaptive controller, 48, 69
   Stability Augmentation System (SAS), 48
X-24, 85, 115, 160
XLR-11 engines, 157
XLR-99 engines, 157
XS-1, vi

Y2K, vii
Yancey, Roxanah, vi, 27-28
Yawing moment coefficient, 138, 142, 143
Yoshida, John, 41, 114

Bibliography

These references are all taken from the NASA/TP 1999-206568: **Fifty Years of Flight Research: An Annotated Bibliography of Technical Publications of NASA Dryden Flight Research Center, 1946-1996,** by David F. Fisher of the NASA Dryden Flight Research Center. The numbers at the beginning of each reference are taken from that bibliography and are the chronological number of citation. Those numbers are used throughout this paper as an easy way to identify the report being referenced. The documents listed here are all the reports that I have been able to find that were written by Dryden personnel about studies that used any of the FSL's (and other simulation facilities') simulation equipment during the period from 1955 to 1976. They are listed below using the conventions in Fisher's bibliography as explained below.

Key to Citations

Typical Citation

[1]**1993**. [2]Burcham, Frank W., Jr.; Maine, Trindel; and Wolf, Thomas. [3]**Flight Testing and Simulation of an F-15 Airplane Using Throttles for Flight Control**. [4]NASA TM-104255, [5]H-1826, [6]NAS 1.15:104255, [7]AIAA Paper 92-4109. [8]Presented at the AIAA Flight Test Conference, Hilton Head, SC, 24 Aug. 1992. [9]<u>August 1992</u>, [10]92N32864, [11]# [12](see also 2004).

1	Chronological number of citation (not a date)
2	Author(s)
3	Title
4	NASA publication number
5	NASA Dryden production number
6	GPO number
7	Assigned conference publication number
8	Conference name, place, and date
9	Date of publication (underlined)
10	Accession number
11	Available on microfiche (#)
12	Chronological number of cross-reference citation

113. Holleman, Euclid C.; and Triplett, William C.: **Flight Measurements of the Dynamic Longitudinal Stability and Frequency-Response Characteristics of the XF-92A Delta-Wing Airplane**. NACA RM H54J26A, <u>January 1955</u>, 87H24535.

120. *Gates, O. B., Jr.; Weil, J.; and *Woodling, C. H.: **Effect of Automatic Stabilization on the Sideslip and Angle of Attack Disturbances in Rolling Maneuvers**. In *NACA Conf. on Autom. Stability and Control of Aircraft,* <u>March 30, 1955</u>, pp. 25–41, (see N72-73193 12-99), 72N73195.
    * Langley Aeronautical Laboratory, Hampton, Virginia

148. Weil, Joseph; and Day, Richard E.: **An Analog Study of the Relative Importance of Various Factors Affecting Roll Coupling.** NACA RM H56A06, April 1956, 87H24558.

158. Weil, Joseph; and Day, Richard E.: **Correlation of Flight and Analog Investigations of Roll Coupling.** NACA RM H56F08, September 1956, 87H24591, 93R19575.

161. Stillwell, Wendell H.: **Control Studies. Part B: Studies of Reaction Controls.** Research-Airplane-Committee Report on Conference on the Progress of the X-15 Project, Langley Aeronautical Laboratory, Langley Field, Virginia, October 26, 1956, 93R21728. Declassified per NASA ccn 14, dated 25 April 1967.

183. Drake, H. M.: **Flight Research at High Altitude, Part 1.** AGARD *Proceedings of the Seventh AGARD General Assembly*, 1957, pp. 74–75, (see N82-73409 12-01), 82N73414.

190. Holleman, Euclid C.; and Boslaugh, David L.: **A Simulator Investigation of Factors Affecting the Design and Utilization of a Stick Pusher for the Prevention of Airplane Pitch-Up.** NACA RM H57J30, January 1958, 87H26852.

203. Holleman, Euclid C.; and Stillwell, Wendell H.: **Simulator Investigation of Command Reaction Controls.** NACA RM H58D22, July 1958, 87H26855, 87H26220.

204. Holleman, E. C.; and Stillwell, W. H.: **Simulator Investigation of Command Reaction Controls.** In NACA Conference on High-Speed Aerodynamics, 1958, pp. 157–165, (see N71-75285), 71N75297. (See also 203.)

208. Finch, Thomas W.; Matranga, Gene J.; Walker, Joseph A.; and Armstrong, Neil A.: **Flight and Analog Studies of Landing Techniques.** This paper is from the Research-Airplane-Committee Report on Conference on the Progress of the X-15 Project held at the IAS Building, Los Angeles, California on July 28–30, 1958, NACA-CONF-30- Jul-58, July 30, 1958, pp. 83–93, 93R21698. Declassified per NASA ccn 14, 29 Nov. 1966.

214. Stillwell, Wendell H.; and Drake, Hubert M.: **Simulator Studies of Jet Reaction Controls for Use at High Altitude.** NACA RM H58G18A, September 1958, 87H26229, 87H24697, 93R19525.

227. Finch, Thomas W.: **Flight and Analog Studies of Approach and Landing Characteristics of Low L/D Configurations.** NASA Conference on Review of NASA Research Related to Control Guidance and Navigation of Space Vehicles, NASA Ames Research Center, February 25–27, 1959.

229. Holleman, Euclid C.: **Utilization of Pilot During the Boost Stage of Multistaged Vehicles.** NASA Conference on Review of NASA Research Related to Control Guidance and Navigation of Space Vehicles, NASA Ames Research Center, February 25–27, 1959.

230. Boslaugh, David L.: **Investigation of Precise Attitude Control—Simulator Program.** NASA Conference on Review of NASA Research Related to Control Guidance and Navigation of Space Vehicles, NASA Ames Research Center, February 25–27, 1959.

238. Williams, Walter C.: **Pilot Considerations in the X-15 Research Airplane Program.** Presented at the Annual Meeting of the American Psychiatric Association, Philadelphia, Pennsylvania, April 29, 1959.

246. Day, Richard E.; and Reisert, Donald: **Flight Behavior of the X-2 Research Airplane to a Mach Number of 3.20 and a Geometric Altitude of 126,200 Feet.** NASA TM X-137, September 1959, 87H25418.

247. Finch, Thomas W.; and Matranga, Gene J.: **Launch, Low-Speed, and Landing Characteristics Determined from the First Flight of the North American X-15 Research Airplane.** NASA TM X-195, September 1959, 62N72019, 87H25292.

256. Day, Richard E.: **Training Considerations During the X-15 Development.** Presented to the National Security Industrial Association Training Advisory Committee Meeting, Los Angeles, California, November 17, 1959, NASA CC-H-157 OTP-1959, 1959.

259. Beeler, De Elroy: **The Supersonic Transport. A Technical Summary.** OTP-1959, 1959.

269. Holleman, E. C.; and Sadoff, M.: **Simulation Requirements for the Development of Advanced Manned Military Aircraft.** NASA TM X-54672, Presented at the IAS National Meeting, San Diego, California, August 3, 1960, 75N72588.

278. Wolowicz, C. H.; Drake, H. M.; Videan, E. N.; Morris, G. J.; and Stickle, J. W.: **Simulator Investigation of Controls and Display Required for Terminal Phase of Coplanar, Orbital Rendezvous.** NASA TN D-511, October 1960, 62N71085, 87H27353.

280. Beeler, De E.: **The X-15 Research Program.** AGARD Report 289, Tenth Annual General Assembly of AGARD, Istanbul, Turkey, October 3–8, 1960.

284. Andrews, W. H.; and Holleman, E. C.: **Experience With a Three-Axis Side-Located Controller During a Static and Centrifuge Simulation of the Piloted Launch of a Manned Multistage Vehicle.** NASA TN D-546, November 1960, 62N71120, 87H26912.

286. Holleman, E. C.: **Utilization of the Pilot During Boost Phase of the Step 1 Mission.** In its Joint Conference on Lifting Manned Hypervelocity and Reentry Vehicles, Part 2 1960, pp. 261–272, (see N72-71002 06-99), 72N71021.

289. Holleman, Euclid C.; Armstrong, Neil A.; and Andrews, William H.: **Utilization of the Pilot in the Launch and Injection of a Multistage Orbital Vehicle.** Presented at the IAS 28th Annual Meeting, New York, New York, January 25–27, 1960, 87H30992.

295. Day, Richard E.: **X-15 Simulation and the X-15 Flight Program.** Presented to the National Academy of Sciences, Panel on Acceleration Stress, ARC, March 11, 1961.

297. Reisert, Donald; and Adkins, Elmor J.: **Flight and Operational Experiences With Pilot-Operated Reaction Controls.** ARS Paper-1674-61. Presented at the ARS Missile and Space Vehicle Testing Conference, Los Angeles, California, March 13–16, 1961.

302. Weil, Joseph; and Adkins, E. J.: **Review of Selected X-15 Development and Operating Experiences.** Presented at the ISA Aero-Space Instrumentation Symposium, Dallas, Texas, April 30–May 4, 1961.

304. Taylor, Lawrence W., Jr.; and Day, Richard E.: **Flight Controllability Limits and Related Human Transfer Functions as Determined From Simulator and Flight Tests.** NASA TN D-746, May 1961, 87H27401.

305. Matranga, Gene J.: **Analysis of X-15 Landing Approach and Flare Characteristics Determined From the First 30 Flights.** NASA TN D-1057, July 1961, 62N71631, 87H27661.

309. Taylor, Lawrence W., Jr.: **Analysis of a Pilot-Airplane Lateral Instability Experienced With the X-15 Airplane.** NASA TN D-1059, November 1961, 62N71633, 87H27667.

322. Hoey, R. G.; and Day, R. E.: **X-15 Mission Planning and Operational Procedures.** Research-Airplane-Committee Report on Conference on the Progress of the X-15 Project, 1961, pp. 155–169, (see N71-75443), 71N75454.

338. Hoey, Robert G.; and Day, Richard E.: **Mission Planning and Operational Procedures for the X-15 Airplane.** NASA TN D-1159, March 1962, 62N10585, 87H27608.

342. McKay, James M.; and Kordes, Eldon E.: **Landing Loads and Dynamics of the X-15 Airplane.** NASA TM X-639, March 1962, 63N12564, 87H26336, #.

348. Taylor, Lawrence W., Jr.; Samuels, James L.; and Smith, John W.: **Simulator Investigation of the Control Requirements of a Typical Hypersonic Glider.** NASA TM X-635, H-226, March 1962, 72N71506, 87H26322.

356. Armstrong, Neil A.; and Holleman, Euclid C.: **A Review of In-Flight Simulation Pertinent to Piloted Space Vehicles.** AGARD Report 403, 21st Flight Mechanics Panel Meeting, Paris, France, July 9–11, 1962.

357. Holleman, Euclid C.; and Armstrong, Neil A.: **Pilot Utilization During Boost.** Presented at the Inter-Center Technical Conference on Control Guidance and Navigation Research for Manned Lunar Missions, Ames Research Center, Moffett Field, California, July 24–25, 1962, 63X14567.

366. Tremant, R. A.: **Operational Experiences and Characteristics of the X-15 Flight Control System.** NASA TN D-1402, December 1962, 63N11123.

369. Holleman, Euclid C.; and Wilson, Warren, S.: **Flight-Simulator Requirements for High-Performance Aircraft Based on X-15 Experience.** ASME Paper 63-AHGT-81, ASME Aviation and Space, Hydraulics, and Gas Turbine Conference and Products Show, Los Angeles, California, March 3–7, 1963, 63A17579.

370. Row, Perry V.; and Fischel, Jack: **Operational Flight-Test Experience With the X-15 Airplane.** AIAA Paper 63-075, AIAA Space Flight Testing Conference, Cocoa Beach, Florida, March 18–20, 1963, 63A15995.

376. Matranga, G. J.; Washington, H. P.; Chenoweth, P. L.; and Young, W. R.: **Handling Qualities and Trajectory Requirements for Terminal Lunar Landing, as Determined From Analog Simulation.** NASA TN D-1921, August 1963, 63N19606.

378. Videan, Edward N.; Banner, Richard D.; and Smith, John P.: **The Application of Analog and Digital Computer Techniques in the X-15 Flight Research Program.** Presented at the International Symposium on Analog and Digital Techniques Applied to Aeronautics, Liege, Belgium, September 9–12, 1963.

381. Weil, Joseph: **Piloted Flight Simulation at the NASA Flight Research Center.** Presented at IEEE 10th Annual East Coast Conference on Aerospace and Navigation Electronics, Baltimore, Maryland, October 21–23, 1963.

378. Videan, Edward N.; Banner, Richard D.; and Smith, John P.: **The Application of Analog and Digital Computer Techniques in the X-15 Flight Research Program.** Presented at the International Symposium on Analog and Digital Techniques Applied to Aeronautics, Liege, Belgium, September 9–12, 1963.

385. Rediess, H. A.; and Deets, D. A.: **An Advanced Method for Airborne Simulation.** NASA TM X-51360. Presented at the AIAA, AFFTC, and NASA FRC Testing of Manned Flight Systems Conference, Edwards, California, December 4–6, 1963, pp. 33–39, 64N12880.

406. Rediess, H. A.; and Deets, D. A.: **An Advanced Method for Airborne Simulation.** NASA RP 337. Reprinted from *J. Aircraft*, Vol. 1, No. 4, July–August 1964, pp. 185–190. Presented at the AIAA, AFFTC, and NASA FRC Testing of Manned Flight Systems Conference, Edwards AFB, California, December 4–6, 1963, 64N31214.

412. Thompson, M. O.: **General Review of Piloting Problems Encountered During Simulation and Flights of the X-15.** NASA TM X-56884, Society of Experimental Test Pilots Ninth Annual Report. Presented at the SETP Symposium, Beverly Hills, California, 1964, 66N83857.

415. Windblade, R. L.: **Current Research on Advanced Cockpit Display Systems.** NASA TM X-56010, 1964, 65N20814.

443. Andrews, W. H.; Butchart, S. P.; Sisk, T. R.; and Hughes, D. L.: **Flight Tests Related to Jet-Transport Upset and Turbulent-Air Penetration.** NASA SP-83, NASA Conference on Aircraft Operating Problems, May 10–12, 1965, 1965, 65N31114.

450. Smith, Harriet J.: **Human Describing Functions Measured in Flight and on Simulators.** NASA SP-128, Second Annual NASA-University Conference on Manual Control, M.I.T., Cambridge, Massachusetts, February 28– March 2, 1966.

457. Taylor, L. W., Jr.; and Iliff, K. W.: **Recent Research Directed Toward the Prediction of Lateral-Directional Handling Qualities.** NASA TM X-59621, AGARD paper R-531 presented at AGARD 28th Meeting of the Flight Mechanics Panel, Paris, France, May 10–11, 1966, May 1966, 67N23242.

458. Berry, D. T.; and Deets, D. A.: **Design, Development, and Utilization of a General Purpose Airborne Simulator.** NASA TM X-74543, AGARD Paper 529. Presented at AGARD 28th Flight Mechanics Panel, Paris, France, May 10–11 1966. May 1966, 77N74646.

478. *Rolls, L. S.; *Snyder, C. T.; and Schweikhard, W. G.: **Flight Studies of Ground Effects on Airplanes With Low-Aspect-Ratio Wings.** NASA SP-124, (see N75-71754 05-98), 1966, pp. 285–295, 75N71774.

* Ames Research Center, Moffett Field, California

482. Jarvis, Calvin R.: **Fly-By-Wire Control System Experience With a Free-Flight Lunar-Landing Research Vehicle.** AIAA Paper 67-273, AIAA Flight Test, Simulation, and Support Conference, Cocoa Beach, Florida, February 6–8, 1967.

483. Matranga, Gene J.; Mallick, Donald L.; and Kluever, Emil E.: **An Assessment of Ground and Flight Simulators for the Examination of Manned Lunar Landing.** AIAA Paper 67-238, AIAA Flight Test, Simulation, and Support Conference, Cocoa Beach, Florida, February 6–8, 1967.

488. Jarvis, C. R.: **Flight-Test Evaluation of an On-Off Rate Command Attitude Control System of a Manned Lunar-Landing Research Vehicle.** NASA TN D-3903, April 1967, 67N23293.

492. Lytton, L. E.: **Evaluation of a Vertical-Scale, Fixed-Index Instrument Display Panel for the X-15 Airplane.** NASA TN D 3967, May 1967, 67N25037.

508. Thompson, M. O.; Weil, J.; and Holleman, E. C.: **An Assessment of Lifting Reentry Flight Control Requirements During Abort, Terminal Glide, and Approach and Landing Situations.** NASA TM X-59119. Presented at Specialists meeting on Stability and Control, Cambridge, England, September 20–23, 1966, 1967, 68N27404.

512. Taylor, L. W., Jr.: **Relationships Between Fourier and Spectral Analyses.** *Three-D Annual NASA University Conference on Manual Control*, 1967, pp. 183–186, (see N68-15901 06-05), 68N15913.

521. Van Leynseele, F. J.: **Evaluation of Lateral-Directional Handling Qualities of Piloted Reentry Vehicles Utilizing a Fixed Base Simulation.** NASA TN D-4410, March 1968, 68N19226.

522. Reed, R. D.: **Flight Testing of Advanced Spacecraft Recovery Concepts Using the Aeromodeler's Approach.** AIAA Paper 68-242. Presented at the 2nd AIAA and Flight Test Simulation and Support Conference, Los Angeles, California, March 25–27, 1968, March 1968, 68A23665, #. (See also 510.)

528. Wolowicz, C.H; Strutz, L.W.; Gilyard, G. B.; and Matheny, N.W.: **Preliminary Flight Evaluation of the Stability and Control Derivatives and Dynamic Characteristics of the Unaugmented XB-70-1 Airplane Including Comparisons With Predictions.** NASA TN D-4578, May 1968, 68N24498, #.

556. Kock, B. M.; and Painter, W. D.: **Investigation of the Controllability of the M2-F2 Lifting-Body Launch From the B-52 Carrier Airplane.** NASA TM X-1713, December 1968, 71N15004, #.

560. *Newell, F. D.; and Smith, H. J.: **Human Transfer Characteristics in Flight and Ground Simulation for a Roll Tracking Task.** NASA TN D-5007, February 1969, 69N17814.

   * Cornell Aeronautical Laboratory, Inc., Buffalo, NY

562. Taylor, L. W., Jr.; Iliff, K. W.; and Powers, B. G.: **A Comparison of Newton-Raphson and Other Methods for Determining Stability Derivatives From Flight Data.** AIAA Paper 69-315, 3rd AIAA and FTSS Conference, Houston, Texas, March 10–12, 1969, 69A22379.

564. Wagner, C. A.: **Visual Simulation Image Generation Using a Flying-Spot Scanner.** NASA TN D-5151, April 1969, 69N23194.

567. Painter, W. D.; and Kock, B. M.: **Operational Experiences and Characteristics of the M2-F2 Lifting Body Flight Control System.** NASA TM X-1809, June 1969, 71N14526, #.

574. Taylor, L. W., Jr.; and Iliff, K. W.: **Fixed-Base Simulator Pilot Rating Surveys for Predicting Lateral-Directional Handling Qualities and Pilot Rating Variability.** NASA TN D-5358, August 1969, 69N35762.

590. Deets, Dwain A.: **Optimal Regulator of Conventional Setup Techniques for a Model Following Simulator Control System.** Fourth NASA Inter-Center Control Systems Conference, Boston, Massachusetts, November 4–5, 1969. (See also 969.)

600. Szalai, K. J.; and Deets, D. A.: **An Airborne Simulator Program to Determine if Roll-Mode Simulation Should Be a Moving Experience.** AIAA Paper 70-351. Presented at the AIAA Visual and Motion Simulation Technology Conference, Cape Canaveral, Florida, March 16–18, 1970, 70A24202.

621. Holleman, E. C.: **Flight Investigation of the Roll Requirements for Transport Airplanes in Cruising Flight.** NASA TN D-5957, H-616, September 1970, 70N38625.

626. Wagner, C. A.: **Frequency Responses and Other Characteristics of Six Fast-Decay Phosphors Applicable to Flying-Spot Scanners.** NASA TN D-6036, H-609, October 1970, 70N42118, #.

630. Manke, J. A.; *Retelle, J. P.; and Kempel, R. W.: **Assessment of Lifting Body Vehicle Handling Qualities.** NASA TM X-2101, October 1970, pp. 29–41, 71N10104.

   * Air Force Flight Test Center, Edwards, CA

673. Kempel, R. W.: **Analysis of a Coupled Roll Spiral Mode, Pilot Induced Oscillation Experienced With the M2-F2 Lifting Body.** NASA TN D-6496, H-633, September 1971, 71N33307 fixed center fin lessened the pilot-induced-oscillation tendencies in the critical flight region.

677. Szalai, K. J.: **Validation of a General Purpose Airborne Simulator for Simulation of Large Transport Aircraft Handling Qualities.** NASA TN D-6431, H-591, October 1971, 71N37823.

678. Szalai, K. J.: **Motion Cue and Simulation Fidelity Aspects of the Validation of a General Purpose Airborne Simulator.** NASA TN D-6432, H-648, October 1971, 71N36672.

680. Kempel, R. W.; and Thompson, R. C.: **Flight-Determined Aerodynamic Stability and Control Derivatives of the M2-F2 Lifting Body Vehicle at Subsonic Speeds.** NASA TM X-2413, H-520, December 1971, 72N11900, #.

697. Layton, G. P., Jr.; and Thompson, M. O.: **Lifting Body Flight-Test Techniques.** NASA TM X-68306, AGARD-CP-85, Paper 10. *Flight Test Tech.,* (see N72-20976 12-02), February 1972, 72N20986.

718. Smith, J. P.: **Research Aircraft Simulators.** Western Simulator Council, Los Angeles, California, July 27, 1972.

722. Deets, D. A.; and Szalai, K. J.: **Design and Flight Experience With a Digital Fly-By-Wire Control System Using Apollo Guidance System Hardware on an F-8 Aircraft.** AIAA Paper 72-881, presented at the AIAA Guidance and Control Conference, Stanford, California, August 14–16, 1972, 72A40060.

724. Strutz, L. W.: **Flight-Determined Derivatives and Dynamic Characteristics for the HL-10 Lifting Body Vehicle at Subsonic and Transonic Mach Numbers.** NASA TN D-6934, H-708, September 1972, 72N30903.

738. Kier, D. A.; Powers, B. G.; Grantham, W. D.; and Nguyen, L. T.: **Simulator Evaluation of the Flying Qualities of Externally Blown Flap and Augmentor Wing Transport Configurations.** NASA SP-320, 1972, (see N73-32934 24-02), pp. 157–800, 73N32948.

770. Powers, B. G.; and Kier, D. A.: **Simulator Evaluation of the Low-Speed Flying Qualities of an Experimental STOL Configuration With an Externally Blown Flap Wing on an Augmentor Wing.** NASA TN D-7454, H-780, October 1973, 73N31951.

799. Matheny, N. W.: **Flight Investigation of Approach and Flare From Simulated Breakout Altitude of a Subsonic Jet Transport and Comparison With Analytical Models.** NASA TN D-7645, H-803, April 1974, 74N19672.

812. Gilyard, G. B.; Smith, J. W.; and *Falkner, V. L.: **Flight Evaluation of a Mach 3 Cruise Longitudinal Autopilot.** AIAA Paper 74-910, AIAA Mechanics and Control of Flight Conference, Anaheim, California, August 5–9, 1974, 74A37890.

* Honeywell, Inc., Minneapolis, MN

837. Smith, J. W.; and Berry, D. T.: **Analysis of Longitudinal Pilot-Induced Oscillation Tendencies of YF-12 Aircraft.** NASA TN D-7900, H-805, February 1975, 75N16560.

867. Gee, S. W.; Wolf, T. D.; and Rezek, T. W.: **Passenger Ride Quality Response to an Airborne Simulator Environment.** NASA TM X-3295, DOT-TSC-OST- 75-40. *The 1975 Ride Quality Symposium,* November 1975, pp. 373–385, (see N76-16754 07-53), 76N16770.

869. Manke, J. A.; and *Love, M. V.: **X-24B Flight Test Program.** Presented at the Nineteenth Society of Experimental Test Pilots Symposium, Beverly Hills, California, September 24–27, 1975, *Society of Experimental Test Pilots, Technical Review*, Vol. 12, No. 4, 1975, pp. 129–154, 76A18659.

* USAF, Edwards AFB, CA

875. Holleman, E. C.: **Summary of Flight Tests to Determine the Spin and Controllability Characteristics of a Remotely Piloted, Large-Scale (3/8) Fighter Airplane Model.** NASA TN D-8052, H-889, January 1976, 76N17156.

882. Petersen, K. L.: **Evaluation of an Envelope-Limiting Device Using Simulation and Flight Test of a Remotely Piloted Research Vehicle.** NASA TN D-8216, H-914, April 1976, 76N21218, #.

About the Author

Gene Waltman graduated from the Michigan Technological University in 1957 with a bachelor's degree in mathematics, and started to work at the NACA High-Speed Flight Station in July of 1957. He worked in the Simulation Laboratory as an analog and hybrid computer programmer and engineer until about 1971. The Sim Lab had received its first analog computer earlier that year and as one of the first programmers he had the opportunity to participate in the early development of the lab. He not only programmed several major simulations but also began buying the lab's computer systems very early in his career. After reassignment to the Systems Analysts Branch in 1971, he became involved with the development of several flight-data processing systems used to process the large volume of aircraft data collected during all of the Dryden's aircraft research flights. He continued to buy computer systems for Dryden until his retirement. When the Center was merged with the Ames Research Center, he became the Dryden representative on the Ames ADP Management Board and also was involved with the process of planning and acquiring the Dryden's computer systems. He became involved with the early development of the Dryden's personal computer (PC) evolution by buying the first personal computer and participating in the procurement, training, and support activities for these PCs for several years. Following his retirement from NASA in 1993, Gene returned to Dryden as an employee of the Woodside Summit Group Inc. in 1996, when that company was awarded the Center's computer support service contract. He has been involved with computer software documentation and the Center's Y2K program. He began to collect information and write about the history of the Simulation Laboratory shortly after returning to Dryden.

Monographs in Aerospace History

Launius, Roger D., and Gillette, Aaron K. Compilers. *The Space Shuttle: An Annotated Bibliography*. (Monographs in Aerospace History, No. 1, 1992).

Launius, Roger D., and Hunley, J.D. Compilers. *An Annotated Bibliography of the Apollo Program*. (Monographs in Aerospace History, No. 2, 1994).

Launius, Roger D. *Apollo: A Retrospective Analysis*. (Monographs in Aerospace History, No. 3, 1994).

Hansen, James R. *Enchanted Rendezvous: John C. Houbolt and the Genesis of the Lunar-Orbit Rendezvous Concept*. (Monographs in Aerospace History, No. 4, 1995).

Gorn, Michael H. *Hugh L. Dryden's Career in Aviation and Space*. (Monographs in Aerospace History, No. 5, 1996).

Powers, Sheryll Goecke. *Women in Flight Research at the Dryden Flight Research Center, 1946-1995* (Monographs in Aerospace History, No. 6, 1997).

Portree, David S.F. and Trevino, Robert C. Compilers. *Walking to Olympus: A Chronology of Extravehicular Activity (EVA)*. (Monographs in Aerospace History, No. 7, 1997).

Logsdon, John M. Moderator. *The Legislative Origins of the National Aeronautics and Space Act of 1958: Proceedings of an Oral History Workshop* (Monographs in Aerospace History, No. 8, 1998).

Rumerman, Judy A. Compiler. *U.S. Human Spaceflight: A Record of Achievement, 1961-1998* (Monographs in Aerospace History, No. 9, 1998).

Portree, David S.F. *NASA's Origins and the Dawn of the Space Age* (Monographs in Aerospace History, No. 10, 1998).

Logsdon, John M. *Together in Orbit: The Origins of International Cooperation in the Space Station Program* (Monographs in Aerospace History, No. 11, 1998).

Phillips, W. Hewitt. *Journey in Aeronautical Research: A Career at NASA Langley Research Center* (Monographs in Aerospace History, No. 12, 1998).

Braslow, Albert L. *A History of Suction-Type Laminar-Flow Control with Emphasis on Flight Research* (Monographs in Aerospace History, No. 13, 1999).

Logsdon, John M. Moderator. *Managing the Moon Program: Lessons Learned from Project Apollo* (Monographs in Aerospace History, No. 14, 1999).

Perminov, V.G. *The Difficult Road to Mars: A Brief History of Mars Exploration in the Soviet Union* (Monographs in Aerospace History, No. 15, 1999).

Tucker, Tom. *Touchdown: The Development of Propulsion Controlled Aircraft at NASA Dryden* (Monographs in Aerospace History, No. 16, 1999).

Maisel, Martin D.; Demo J. Giulianetti; and Daniel C. Dugan. *The History of the XV-15 Tilt Rotor Research Aircraft: From Concept to Flight.* (Monographs in Aerospace History #17, NASA SP-2000-4517, 2000).

Jenkins, Dennis R. *Hypersonics Before the Shuttle: A History of the X-15 Research Airplane.* (Monographs in Aerospace History #18, NASA SP-2000-4518, 2000).

Chambers, Joseph R. *Partners in Freedom: Contributions of the Langley Research Center to U.S. Military Aircraft in the 1990s.* (Monographs in Aerospace History #19, NASA SP-2000-4519).

Those monographs still in print are available free of charge from the NASA History Division, Code ZH, NASA Headquarters, Washington, DC 20546. Please enclosed a self-addressed 9x12" envelope stamped for 15 ounces for these items.

www.ingramcontent.com/pod-product-compliance
Lightning Source LLC
Chambersburg PA
CBHW082116230426
43671CB00015B/2713